Silk Stockings and Socialism

SHARON MCCONNELL-SIDORICK

Silk Stockings and Socialism
Philadelphia's Radical Hosiery Workers from the Jazz Age to the New Deal

The University of North Carolina Press *Chapel Hill*

© 2017 The University of North Carolina Press
All rights reserved
Set in Arno Pro by Westchester Publishing Services
Manufactured in the United States of America
The University of North Carolina Press has been a member of the Green Press Initiative since 2003.

Library of Congress Cataloging-in-Publication Data
Names: McConnell-Sidorick, Sharon, author.
Title: Silk stockings and socialism : Philadelphia's radical hosiery workers from the Jazz Age to the New Deal / Sharon McConnell-Sidorick.
Description: Chapel Hill : University of North Carolina Press, [2017] | Includes bibliographical references and index.
Identifiers: LCCN 2016036381 | ISBN 9781469632940 (cloth : alk. paper) | ISBN 9781469632957 (pbk : alk. paper) | ISBN 9781469632964 (ebook)
Subjects: LCSH: American Federation of Full-Fashioned Hosiery Workers. | Hosiery workers—Pennsylvania—Philadelphia—History—20th century. | Strikes and lockouts—Hosiery industry—Pennsylvania—Philadelphia—History—20th century.
Classification: LCC HD8039.H752 U663 2017 | DDC 331.88/1873097481109042—dc23
LC record available at https://lccn.loc.gov/2016036381

Cover illustration: Art Deco hosiery union logo. Wisconsin Historical Society, WHi-125325.

In memory of Howard and Alice, and my parents
and
especially for Dan

Contents

Acknowledgments xi

Introduction 1

CHAPTER ONE
A Community of Labor 11

CHAPTER TWO
The Evolution of a Fighting Union 42

CHAPTER THREE
From Jazz Babies to Youth Militants 69

CHAPTER FOUR
The Firebrands of the Union: Hosiery's Labor Feminists 103

CHAPTER FIVE
Martyrs and Working-Class Heroes in the Great Depression 133

CHAPTER SIX
Storming the Bastille: The Triumph of Social Justice Unionism 176

Epilogue 219

Notes 227

Index 269

Figures, Map, and Tables

FIGURES

1. View of Kensington looking north from the Bromley Carpet Mill 24
2. Kensington and Allegheny Avenues 73
3. Women strikers in jail 100
4. Alice Nelson Kreckman on Apex picket line 107
5. Hosiery union logo 128
6. Funeral procession for slain striker 157
7. Carl Mackley Houses library murals 205
8. Stalled trolley cars, Apex Hosiery Mill 214
9. Picket line, Apex Hosiery Mill 216

MAP

1. Kensington section of Philadelphia 22

TABLES

1. Kensington household annual budget, 1920 19
2. Reductions in pay under the 1931 National Agreement 159

Acknowledgments

It was through my acquaintance with two extraordinary people, former hosiery workers Howard and Alice Kreckman, that I first became inspired to write this history. Their stories and commitment to social justice, spanning over seven decades, inspired both this project and my life. I thank them for showing me the possibilities that lie within us and for giving me back an important part of my heritage. I am also grateful to others who shared stories with me, put up with my endless questions, and encouraged my scholarship: Jeanne Callahan, Robert Gunther, Joseph, Robert, William, and Marilyn McConnell and Mary Ann and Betty Valderrama; and for the trove of interviews with hosiery workers that were collected in the 1930s by University of Pennsylvania researchers. They all gave me invaluable insights into the multiplicities of everyday life in Kensington.

This book could not have been written without the support and comments of other scholars. I owe a great debt to Kenneth Kusmer, who was there for me at a crucial time for the completion of this book. Without him it may not have happened, and for his support I am truly grateful. I also appreciate those who invited me to discuss this project with them at conferences and research seminars, particularly the Pennsylvania Labor History Workshop and the Pennsylvania Historical Association. These include especially James Wolfinger, Marge Murphy, David Witwer, Anthony DeStefanis, Walter Licht, and Rachel Batch. The support and encouragement of Rachel Batch have been especially consistent and important to me. Earlier drafts of this manuscript were read and commented on by two scholars whose own work has had a great influence on me. Janet Irons put extensive time and energy into helping me revise the manuscript into a coherent piece of work, and her unflagging encouragement was crucial to its completion. Rosemary Feurer gave me her full support and pointed me in directions that opened up important avenues of thought. I owe them both a great deal, not only for their insights but for their encouragement and the expenditure of their valuable time. I also owe a debt of gratitude to Herbert Ershkowitz, whose deep scholarship gave me much to think about; to Susan Klepp, who shared her thoughts and comprehensive knowledge of gender history; to Kathy Walker for her theoretical insights; and to Rick Halpern, for his perceptive suggestions, which pushed me in new directions. Scholars in other fields also helped me to put my own thoughts into perspective. Foremost among them, the British scholar and anthropologist Bernard Wailes was a mentor and friend. The countless hours he spent with me discussing critical elements of the development of complex society and, foremost, the importance of culture, shaped my scholarship in more ways than I can express. He helped me to see that "American exceptionalism" is not exceptional. He will always remain my mentor. The work of the business historian Philip Scranton helped me understand some of the perspectives of the manufacturers. None of my work would have been possible without the help of the librarians and archivists from the various institutions that I visited. To these professionals at the Wisconsin Historical Society, the University of Pennsylvania Archives, the Historical Society of Pennsylvania, the Temple University Urban Archives, the Walter Reuther Archives, the National Archives, the Free Library of Philadelphia, and the Pennsylvania State Archives I extend my sincere thanks. Thanks to Kaitlyn Pettingill of the Historical Society of Pennsylvania for being especially helpful. Special thanks to a union that is still carrying the struggle forward, UNITE-HERE, for their permission to print the groundbreaking hosiery union icon. Elin Danien, scholar and founder of the Bread Upon the Waters Scholarship Fund of the University of Pennsylvania, will forever have my deepest gratitude, not only for the scholarship, but also for her own achievements, her profound love for education, and her unflagging support and friendship. May the bread come back to you. When it came time to turn the manuscript into a book, the staff of the UNC Press was amazing. Thanks to Jad Adkins for addressing my questions and concerns, Ian Oakes, Bill Nelson for assistance with my complicated map, and especially my editor, Chuck Grench. Chuck saw value in the book and stuck with it through its twists and turns. I am sincerely grateful. Thanks to the people at Westchester Publishing Services, Stephen Barichko and Barbara Goodhouse, for meticulous editing that has made the book more readable. For my index I thank Michael Taber.

Finally, my deepest gratitude is to my family—my daughter, Brianna, who consistently told me that I was a good writer; her husband, John; my son Michael and his family, Lisa and Dante; and my niece Mary. Foremost among all, I thank my husband and comrade in life, Dan. A fellow historian, he was my strongest supporter and critic. He spent many, many hours discussing my findings and editing my commas, and never let on that he was probably heartily sick of hearing about hosiery workers! His insights were an important catalyst to my own thoughts. His love kept me going.

And to the people of Kensington, thank you for the story. This book is for you.

Silk Stockings and Socialism

Introduction

On Thanksgiving Day, November 25, 1869, a group of seven men gathered in a Philadelphia row house. It is not clear why the small group chose Thanksgiving to meet, but the results of that get-together would have major repercussions for the nation's laboring classes. For it was there that these men founded a new organization, unique to the history of labor, the Noble and Holy Order of the Knights of Labor (Knights of Labor). The row house was that of Uriah S. Stephens and was located in the 2300 block of Coral Street, in the heart of the Kensington section of the city. Although the original group were all garment cutters by trade, membership in the new organization spread rapidly through the city and across a wide variety of industries. From 1869 to 1875 the Knights established eighty-five local assemblies, seventy in the Philadelphia area. The largest segment were organized in assemblies of textile workers, including carpet, hosiery, upholstery, lace curtain, and dyeing. The Knights of Labor created such a sensation that by 1886 the union was well on its way to its goal of organizing all who labored. By that year it reached a national membership of over three-quarters of a million workers, including many African Americans and women, placing it at the forefront of the country's labor movement in the late nineteenth century.[1]

Kensington hosiery knitter John Makin was one of those early members of the Knights of Labor. In 1889 he was also among a group of men who gathered in another Kensington row house to found a union of full-fashioned hosiery knitters. For his efforts Makin was blacklisted for union activity. Over thirty-five years later, in a different historical period, the Jazz Age of the 1920s, an article in the newspaper of the American Federation of Full-Fashioned Hosiery Workers (AFFFHW) would dub him "the first full-fashioned knitter in America to suffer for being a union man."[2]

This book tells the story of the ideological and activist descendants of Philadelphia's Knights of Labor—Kensington's hosiery workers, their union, and their home community of Kensington—in the period between the two world wars. It is an attempt to return them to their rightful place in history, for in that period the hosiery workers were in the forefront of the country's labor movement. Along the way the story will serve to uncover some little-known but important history about the period leading to the founding of the

Congress of Industrial Organizations (CIO), the New Deal, and the development of an early "labor feminist" movement. Though the book comprises a labor history of the AFFFHW in the interwar period, it has much larger objectives. Tapping into insights from labor geography and the broader field of working-class studies, it seeks to reconstruct the hosiery workers' world of work and life in Kensington. Perhaps even more ambitiously, this history examines how "flapper" culture and new conceptions of youth were incorporated and modified by young hosiery workers and merged with community traditions of radical unionism.

In a period of resurgence of interest in socialism in the early twenty-first century, especially among young people, many Americans are unaware of the rich history of socialist movements in the United States. One of the most remarkable examples of a socialist-led crusade for workers' rights took place in Kensington in the 1920s and 1930s. The story of the campaigns its participants built, the obstacles they encountered, and the support they generated in their neighborhoods and beyond may offer important insights about what a socialist movement looked like on the ground in a real American city.[3]

As the story of Kensington unfolds, it will come as no surprise that this neighborhood birthed such forward-thinking organizations as the Knights of Labor and the AFFFHW. What is surprising is that so little of that story is known. The community of Kensington, the AFFFHW, and its members have been the victims of a historical amnesia. There has been a deep-seated "forgetting" of much of the social justice activity in the 1920s and 1930s centered within the hosiery union. David Montgomery's important article "The Shuttle and the Cross" highlights the early era of Kensington, and the infamous Know-Nothing riots have been much explored by historians.[4] The history of the people of the community over the almost 200 years that have followed is largely missing (with rare but important exceptions[5]), replaced in the popular mind and scholarly presumption by shallow stereotypes of Kensington as a place where little history of interest has occurred. The deindustrialization that devastated Kensington in recent decades erased any potential counternarratives, and even earlier, the repression of the McCarthy era and the negative stereotyping of radical ideologies created what the historian Chuck Keeney refers to as "mind guards," in control of the news, the schools, and public memory. The limited media coverage of the area sporadically reinforced an image of a neighborhood where nothing but racial antagonisms and fires in abandoned factories happened, with residents portrayed as ignorant and standing in the way of progress. Today the image of the neighborhood is one of crime and blight in some areas and gentrification in others. As

Keeney says, "If you paint people as ignorant and backward, then it is easier to marginalize them, it's easier to dismiss them. It's also a good way of burying history."[6]

The full story of Kensington has always been more complex, and never more so than in the 1920s and 1930s. In the 1920s, people working in the full-fashioned hosiery industry in Kensington, the community in which the largest sector of the industry was concentrated, built an organization that became the nucleus of a vital movement struggling against the tide throughout those years of labor's reversals. Its participants advanced a form of labor feminism, established and promoted programs to build an educated and articulate constituency, and built networks both within the community and extending out of it, on a regional, national, and international level, that promoted social justice unionism and a working-class cosmopolitanism. Much of this activity drew upon the class-based, transnational, and radical traditions of their community and touched a broader constituency than just the people who worked in the industry. The AFFFHW, the men and women who participated in and led its activities, and the community of Kensington were important parts of a national and international web that provided the continuity and laid the groundwork for the revitalized labor and social movements of the mid- to late 1930s and beyond. They were, in addition, catalysts for those later movements and were recognized as such at the time, although not subsequently in the works of historians.

The exploits and achievements of the hosiery workers were part of a Philadelphia story, although their story took on national dimensions. Perhaps surprisingly in a labor narrative, Philadelphia's young hosiery workers embraced the 1920s Jazz Age as it roared into the city, even as it was greeted by the most "corrupt and contented" urban machine in the nation.[7] The Volstead Act may have established Prohibition as the law of the land, but in Philadelphia its enforcement was, at most, a desultory affair. By the first few years of the decade, Philadelphia's disregard of liquor laws, along with its gangland activity, was providing reading material for a national audience. But while the city's disregard of "inconvenient" laws continued unabated, its labor police were much less reticent about enforcing the will of powerful textile manufacturers against labor strikes and union activity, and this selective reading of citizen's "rights" was not lost on young hosiery workers, becoming a major organizing tool in the hands of union activists.

In the 1920s and 1930s Kensington was a neighborhood inhabited by diverse groups of people. A "mill town" set in the middle of a large city, it contained the largest working-class population in the area. The ways in which its residents expressed ideas and behaved as political actors were part of a cultural process, intricately related to the material conditions of their lives, historical processes and contingencies, and the influences of the broader society and the times of which they were a part. Interactions among the structural and economic forces at work in Philadelphia, the history of Kensington, and the historical-cultural developments of the time drove the class action that grew in the city in the 1920s and 1930s. The vast majority of Kensington's residents were working-class men and women who actively shaped the economic and sociocultural landscape within their community, and who developed an identity that incorporated a construct of the "rights of working people." That identity, in turn, drew upon community traditions and working-class experiences and ideas that had traveled the Atlantic Ocean along with the transatlantic workforce that contributed Kensington's first inhabitants and continuously supplemented its population. And one of the most enduring of these traditions was the organization of workers' institutions and trade unions, a historical process that directly led to the founding of the AFFFHW.

The structural changes and consumer and mass-culture industries that characterized the United States in the 1920s affected Kensington in ways that were similar, though not identical, to what was happening in other parts of the country. Silk full-fashioned hosiery was itself popularized by the Jazz Age. Changes in fashion and popular culture brought a radical shortening in the hemlines of women's dresses associated with the "modern" woman or flapper, and the hosiery, with its provocative seam up the back, was the iconic accessory to the short dresses of the flapper. Stimulated by what appeared to be an insatiable demand for the sheer, form-fitting stockings, the hosiery industry expanded dramatically, bringing with it an influx of new, young workers. Many of them, male and female, were avid participants in the Jazz Age youth culture themselves: living fast, flouting Prohibition, going to dances and "necking" parties, playing in jazz bands, and participating in consumer culture. They, as much as any other group of young people of the decade, appeared to be determined not to waste what time they had on earth, as encouraged by the premier Jazz Age writer, F. Scott Fitzgerald.[8] And in the 1920s, their union—surprisingly—transformed along with them into a thoroughly "modern" organization, offering sports and a social program that included black bottom dances, boat trips, parties, and picnics that often included jazz music and open defiance of Prohibition.

The hosiery union followed the major expansion of the industry in the 1920s out from Kensington into new sections of the country, catapulting the union very visibly onto the national scene and its activists onto a national stage. But Kensington was its center of power, and for that reason much of the story takes place there. It was in Kensington that the union was born and came of age. It was the home of its largest local, Branch 1, and Philadelphia remained the location of the national headquarters through its full flowering in the 1930s and beyond. And it was there that important members of the leadership consolidated their worldviews.

Branch 1's leadership openly espoused a socialist ideology, and the hosiery union became the largest and most powerful labor organization in the city, as well as a state and regional power. But in the 1920s the rapid expansion of the industry created both opportunities and problems. As a skilled industry, though organized by its union on an all-inclusive industrial basis, hosiery manufacture's increasing demand for trained workers, especially the highly skilled knitters, raised wages and enriched the union's coffers. The nonstop expansion also led to the establishment of many new shops and the relocation of some older mills to other sections of the country and Canada, and eventually to overproduction.

Early ideological and strategic differences had led the first hosiery union locals into two separate organizations, but the sections reconsolidated in 1922. Once united and with the support of its member locals, the AFFFHW enacted a system of high member assessments and set up a "fighting treasury" to begin an aggressive "follow-the-shops" organizing drive in the South, the Midwest, and the Northeast, and throughout Kensington. The doldrums that affected organized labor throughout the 1920s saw union membership decline nationally from approximately 5 million in 1920 to under 3 million by 1933.[9] In contrast to the national trend, hosiery's membership numbers grew rapidly, further adding to its fighting treasury. Along the way, union leadership developed conscious strategies to help rebuild the broader labor movement. As a result of its power and leadership within that movement, the AFFFHW had an immense impact for its relatively small size. In the 1930s it negotiated the so-called Reading Formula, the dominant blueprint for labor settlements under the National Industrial Recovery Act, after it led the first strike wave in the nation as soon as the act was signed; it partnered with the federal Public Works Administration to build the first pathbreaking New Deal housing project; it played an important role in the founding of other major CIO unions, including the Textile Workers Union of America (for which it also provided the top leadership) and the United Electrical Workers; and it was responsible for rescuing labor from the purview of the Sherman Anti-Trust Act in the precedent-setting Supreme Court case *Apex v. Leader*.[10]

The achievements of the AFFFHW are all the more remarkable when we consider that it was never a large union in comparison to some others. It achieved its results by building an idealistic youth movement based on labor as a "cause" for human rights and by promoting a form of working-class cosmopolitanism that encouraged a nonsectarian solidarity that strove to bridge differences within the workforce. Fundamentals such as a stable job, a living wage, decent housing, and the right to free association in a union chosen by the workers were not conceived of as abstract privileges, but as hard-won rights that needed to be defended for those who had achieved them, and fought for and extended to those who had not yet done so. Although the largest segment of the union's leadership was affiliated with the left wing of the Socialist Party, the activists of the AFFFHW included Communists and independent radicals as well. But the union also grew out of a radical community tradition dedicated to unifying and representing all workers. As a historical center of the textile industry and the birthplace of the Knights of Labor, Kensington had a long history of such traditions, which underpinned the workers' movement of the 1920s and 1930s. Human rights, women's rights, and industrial unionism had a crucial interrelationship that reinforced each other and, over time, built a robust form of social justice unionism.

One area of solidarity that was less tested in the 1920s, however, was across lines of race. Textile manufacturers, many of them advocates of Social Darwinism, hired few black workers in the mills, nationally and in Kensington. In fact, only a small number of African Americans were hired in Philadelphia's industries in general, and virtually none in skilled jobs. These biases were so deep-seated that advocates for racial minorities believed for decades that the manufacturers needed to be confronted on this issue. One of the major goals of progressive and philanthropic organizations in the 1920s was to convince reluctant employers that "Negroes" were competent to work in industry, and even as recently as the early 1960s, the historian Thomas Sugrue points out, major civil rights groups in Philadelphia "met with individual employers . . . who were skeptical of blacks' native intelligence and ability or who were hostile to equal employment." At least partially as a consequence of their exclusion from the workplaces of Kensington, very few lived in the area.[11]

Hosiery workers nevertheless took a forthright approach to the issue of race in ways that directly impacted the everyday lives of African Americans—in the activities of the Unemployed Citizens Leagues in neighborhoods throughout the city and in the union's advocacy for antilynching and voting rights legislation, for example. The union preached the moral inhumanity of racism through its engagement with human rights, and the platform of the

Socialist Party explicitly called for an end to racial discrimination in hiring practices and for social legislation that crossed racial and gender boundaries. But I have found no evidence that the Socialist union leaders took on the racist hiring practices of their own industry in this period, and textile's racial occupational hierarchy, for the most part, remained in place. African American workers primarily enter the narrative as part of the hosiery workers' engagement with human rights in the union newspaper, radio programs, and study groups, through holding lectures by leaders of the NAACP and other groups, in the unemployed movement and support for antiracist legislation, and in promoting interracial unionization by seizing the opportunity to organize black workers in the few cases where hosiery manufacturers tentatively began to hire them, such as in the establishment of an African American local in Durham, North Carolina, in 1934, a real rarity in this industry in this historical period.

Central to the entire narrative are the women of Kensington and of the industry more generally. Incorporating some of the insights of the historian Carol Morgan, I argue that the significance of gender in the historical and cultural space that I consider "was the product of an ongoing process of collaboration, conflict, negotiation, and subversion involving working women and men, male union leaders," social and labor feminists, and Socialist Party activists. On the shop floors and picket lines, rank-and-file women and men developed relationships of solidarity, and the sacrosanct right to be "union" came to encompass women's rights as well, and was even internalized by many male workers, challenging the traditional gender hierarchy of the union.[12]

Most accounts of the young flapper have constructed her as frivolous—concerned only with apolitical rebellion, drinking and smoking in public, wearing short dresses, using cosmetics. But a more nuanced reading of youth cultures in other times and places has shown that participation in such pastimes and an interest in consumerism did not necessarily preclude the development of social consciousness. There were other aspects to the "modern woman" that influenced the youth of the decade as well. These included a new sense of independence and rights, and an admiration for the female "heroines" who gained prominence in sports, movies, and the media during the 1920s, sparked by the heroism of the martyrs of women's suffrage, the suffragettes.

As the young men and women of the union began to face mounting arrests and violence in union campaigns, they were reconfigured as "youth militants," in defense of labor as a cause for human rights that crossed the boundaries of gender, ethnicity, age, and race. The modern woman, proclaimed as one who had achieved equality and independence in actions and thought, became a *labor* heroine, wearing her short dresses and stockings as she fearlessly faced off against police and hired thugs. By the late 1920s their union, the AFFFHW, chose as its iconic public image a representation of a young, modern woman with union hosiery held in her raised arms against a cityscape background, epitomizing the Art Deco style while contradicting the standard male representations of most unions. As the women of the union gained a new sense of assurance and self-importance, they pushed not only for programs to address their specific needs, as both women and workers, but also for a larger share of power within the union and its top leadership. For the rebellious youth of the union, "not wasting their time on earth" began to take on a whole new meaning as they began to internalize a concept that they were fighting for the entire labor movement.

Among the key reasons for the success of the AFFFHW were its adoption of a rights-centric language and its community-based approach. As the 1920s moved into the Great Depression of the 1930s, militant unionization campaigns were joined by campaigns to stop the evictions of all workers, to provide health care and relief for the unemployed, to demand old-age pensions, and to defend the rights of women to hold a job and even their right to birth control. Much of this activity drew on the resources of the Socialist Party and the Unemployed Citizens Leagues, but also upon a broader solidarity that included Communists, other unions, a broad range of women's organizations, and ethnic and community organizations.

Throughout this story my approach foregrounds class relations as the locus of struggle. In this historically specific period, class was the primary lens through which a majority of the residents of Kensington viewed their world, though mediated through other factors such as gender, ethnicity, and geography. Class is used in two senses. First, in an economic, Marxist sense—people saw themselves as workers, not owners; in relation to the latter, they had less access to economic resources and power structures. But class is also cultural, and for this reason, the community is as important as the workplace for understanding the struggle of Kensington's workers. Thus, what people read, their experiences with popular culture, how they socialized, and their spatial distribution within their neighborhood are all parts of the story.

This project began with an oral history, through an acquaintance with two rather remarkable people, Alice Nelson Kreckman and Howard Kreckman, both now deceased. They grew up in Kensington, spent much of their lives there, and worked in the hosiery mills during the 1920s and 1930s, each having entered the industry and joined the union at the age of fourteen. What initially inspired me to examine this story was their exceptional lifetime of social activism, which continued into their nineties. I also came to realize just how long and how deep their commitment to a more just and equitable society extended. I wanted to understand what kind of environment produced such a commitment. Over the course of the interviews I had with them, I learned about the Kensington they had known, the conflicts, the solidarity, and the extraordinary independence of some of the women. Interviews with other former residents, as well as a substantive group of interviews conducted in the neighborhood in the 1930s by University of Pennsylvania investigators, gave me added insights and directions. Although there are often issues of accuracy that must be taken into consideration with oral histories, the stories and insights of people who actually lived some of this history add a dimension that I could not hope to otherwise achieve. The Kreckmans' accounts then acted as sort of a "finder's guide" for the other, archival, sources.

No history is ever a complete tale of everything that was happening in a given time or place, and neither is this one. It does not address everyone or give a comprehensive overview of the manufacturers' stories—that story has been ably told by others.[13] It is the story of the union and the working people who built it as they fought the struggle to build a better America. It is also an attempt to give a better understanding of the history of the people of Kensington, a people and a community that have received rather short shrift in written history.

The book is organized into six chapters and a short epilogue, generally arranged chronologically but with some focusing more on certain central themes. The first chapter situates the union within the community of Greater Kensington and explains the context of its long transnational labor traditions. It serves to introduce the community and its people. Chapter 2 addresses the strikes of 1919 and 1921 that led to the union's reunification. It also looks at the product and industry expansion, introduces some people who will be important in the later narrative, and examines the fighting treasury, the follow-the-shops campaign, and early efforts to support the wider labor movement. Chapter 3 deals specifically with the Jazz Age, its youth culture, and the union's creation of an idealistic youth movement. The chapter is divided into two sections, the first of which describes the youth culture in the community. The second, longer section discusses how the union transformed its rebellious youth into a movement of socially conscious "youth militants." Chapter 4 then focuses on the women of the union in the 1920s, examining their increasing struggle for equality and a share in the decision making of the organization. These developments are situated within the context of the so-called modern woman of the 1920s and developments in popular culture and the media that promoted women as having achieved equality, often in heroic terms. Chapter 5 describes how hosiery workers went on the offensive against big business and government during the early years of the Great Depression while trying to aid those suffering the most. In the course of a strike in 1930, the union lost its first martyr, and the ensuing memorial, attended by 35,000 angry workers and residents of Kensington, raised the level of conflict for the remainder of the 1930s. The final chapter demonstrates that the hosiery union's important but heretofore forgotten efforts played a key role in the founding of the CIO, major New Deal programs, and later labor feminism, bracketed by two monumental strike waves in 1933 and 1937. Using the hosiery union as a microcosm of national trends, it also suggests reasons some top CIO officials gravitated toward a top-down structure, increasingly in the orbit of the Democratic Party, while another group struggled to maintain a democratic, bottom-up organizational structure—and what this meant for women and social justice unionism. While the book is primarily concerned with the 1920s and 1930s and the road to the New Deal and the CIO, a short epilogue ties up some loose ends about the later years of the union and the community of Kensington.

In the years between the advent of the Jazz Age and the founding of the CIO, many working people experienced a political and social transformation that succeeded in giving the working class a new importance. Hosiery workers were regular people who lived regular lives. They were ordinary individuals who, by rising to face the challenges they were presented with, created an extraordinary and powerful movement. This new power, which, in the words of Selina Todd, came from "fighting for everything you got," fueled the innovations of major social programs like Social Security, the minimum wage, and unemployment insurance, defended the values of equality and democracy, and gave the working class the right to form unions and join together for the betterment of all society. *Silk Stockings and Socialism* relates an important part of that story.[14]

CHAPTER ONE

A Community of Labor

Why was there so much going on in Kensington in the 1920s and 1930s?
That's where the mills were.
—Former hosiery worker Howard Kreckman

Howard Kreckman was fourteen years old in 1917. Although World War I had been raging in Europe for several years, this was the year the United States would officially enter the war, sending young men of its own into the carnage. At fourteen, Howard was too young to be drafted. Instead, as was common in the working-class community of Kensington, he left the public school system and went to work. Securing a job in a steam-operated hosiery mill, he became a "helper" to a knitter who had immigrated to the neighborhood from England. Meanwhile, Philadelphia businesses were raking in hefty profits from supplying the European war machines. Despite the suffering that ensued from the war, it also paradoxically provided new job opportunities for many, including Kreckman's sister, Dorothea, who was able to get work at the Philadelphia Navy Yard. Until then, as he put it, "they didn't take women much," and she was one of the first to be hired.[1]

Such transatlantic associations were an integral part of the founding and development of the city of Philadelphia, expressed not only through its connections to Europe's imperialistic wars, but also through the fact that its ports had played a significant role in the Atlantic economy from the city's earliest days. In his book *Atlantic Crossings*, the historian Daniel Rodgers argued that "outpost" nations like the United States, which began as the imperial projects of other nations, were especially marked by "complicity in world historical forces." "From the earliest European settlements in North America forward, the Atlantic functioned for its newcomers less as a barrier than as a connective lifeline . . . a key outpost for European trade and a magnet for European capital."[2]

No other American city demonstrated this connection to Europe better than Philadelphia and its Kensington neighborhood. As an industrial district in a major port, Kensington was integrated into the Atlantic economy from its inception, drawing upon both transnational capital and its workforce. This traffic in capital, people, and ideas, in turn, influenced the particular ways in which both culture and industry developed within the surrounding community.

The story of Kensington's hosiery workers was an integral part of the swirling transformations sweeping Jazz Age and Depression-Era America, but it is rooted in an earlier transatlantic movement of an industry and its independent and radical workers from England and Europe. Thus, this chapter looks at the many peoples who settled Kensington's neighborhoods, the physical and human geography of the area, the development of industry, and the working-class traditions handed down to its sons and daughters.

First settled as a remote village in 1682, by the time of the American Revolution, Philadelphia was not only one of the nation's most English cities but, after London, one of the largest English-speaking cities in the British Empire. And the opportunities the city offered attracted thousands of immigrants from across Britain, Ireland, and continental Europe. Although a man of many attributes, Philadelphia's founder, William Penn, was a businessman, very conscious of the commercial facets of his endeavor. He sited his town at the narrowest point between the Delaware and Schuylkill Rivers, thereby allowing its ports to handle goods from all over the Atlantic basin. By 1790 Philadelphia was the capital city and banking center of the new nation, as well as a leading center of craft production. Products and capital flowed between Philadelphia and the Atlantic world, and so too did people, customs, cultures, and ideas.[3]

As a result of all this activity, Penn's original city rapidly ran out of space and, when the industrial revolution reached Philadelphia, land for industrial development had to be found outside of the city. Bounded on the east by the Delaware River, expansion took place into Philadelphia County to the north, south, and west of the central district. Across the Delaware River, to the east, lay Camden, New Jersey, whose industrial development would make it an important member of the developing regional economy. By the early nineteenth century the mills of the Manayunk section of the county colonized the Schuylkill River to the northwest of the original city, and a vibrant working-class community sprang up alongside them. And to the city's northeast, Kensington, destined to become the largest and most dynamic working-class community in the region, rapidly took shape.[4]

During the nineteenth century Philadelphia changed from a commercial port to a major center of specialty and commodity production and developed a diverse economy. Philadelphia's industries manufactured a wide range of products, from shoes, hats, steel, and wood products to locomotives, ships, glass, bricks, and fine instruments. But the textile industry was the city's largest. Indeed, Philadelphia had been one of the largest textile centers in the New World ever since the Revolution.[5]

Manufacturers established a mill system in Philadelphia very similar to the highly exploitative model that had been developed in Manchester and England's industrialized North. The first men and women of the textile trades of early nineteenth-century Philadelphia who followed the shops across the Atlantic were, as Friedrich Engels wrote, "the eldest children of the Industrial Revolution." Often arriving with years of experience in the mills of England, they carried with them a historical experience that incorporated the oppositional strategies—and ideologies—derived from English radical economic theory and trade unionism. They were experienced in the organization of trade unions, and Kensington, though home to many of the city's other industries as well, was a center of textile production. In fact, the first job action in one of its textile manufactories was recorded as early as 1828.[6]

Another distinctive characteristic of Philadelphia was that it was especially conducive to the development of "proprietary" capitalism and was slower to adopt the corporate version associated with the textile industry of Lowell, Massachusetts. Master weavers and others, along with some manufacturers newly immigrated to the city from Europe, set up family firms and set in place the development of early textile manufacture. This pattern is also similar to that which developed in England and spread outward, in which entrepreneurs, forging connections through marriage and other strategies, invested their resources in family-owned enterprises over which they jealously maintained control. When some of them migrated to Philadelphia, they brought with them their ideas and customs of work relations.[7]

The employees of these nineteenth-century entrepreneurs were among the most exploited of workers. They put in very long workdays but earned little pay, often laboring up to fourteen hours a day and seven days a week under working conditions similar to those of the mill districts of England. Such circumstances proved fruitful for the growth of resistance and oppositional ideas, some of which the workers had brought with them across the Atlantic. In the face of growing labor unrest, Austrian immigrant mill owner Joseph Ripka testified before the Pennsylvania factory investigation committee in 1837 that "the Anglo-Irish principles of the Trades' union which has been introduced amongst the laboring classes in general" were the "greatest evil" of the factory system and had been "imported to this country by English and Irish men." The first Kensington textile union was a local in a British international federation.[8]

Kensington's reputation as a center for many trades made it a magnet for skilled labor. Within the textile trades, workers flocked to Philadelphia from England, Scotland, Ireland, and Germany. Philadelphia's working-class leaders, like John Ferrell, who had been radicalized by trade unionism before emigrating, joined with others to unite workers across ethnic and religious differences to defend "concepts of independence and social equality." In the mid-1830s, he led the new nation's first citywide union federation, the Philadelphia General Trades Union, which remarkably "marshaled some fifty affiliates and over 10,000 Protestant and Catholic native- and foreign-born workers in a series of successful strikes." In this period, Irish Catholic and Protestant handloom weavers in Kensington joined together to force employers to pay at least a subsistence wage. This unity, however, could not withstand the severe depression of 1837-44, when manufacturers began using newer poor Irish immigrants to undercut the wages and working conditions of more established groups. Fueled also by religious differences between Irish Catholics and the growing nativism of some Protestant groups, the notorious and much-written-about Know-Nothing riots erupted in 1844, events that have greatly influenced popular conceptions and subsequent interpretations of Kensington. During the riots, several houses and religious institutions of the Irish Catholic community were burned down, including Saint Michael's Church, the first Catholic church in Kensington. In this same period of depression and instability, severe race riots also broke out in sections that housed much of Philadelphia's African American population, in the city's center and areas to its south. This collapse of public order spurred a campaign for the consolidation of all the jurisdictions of Philadelphia County into one municipal corporation, which occurred ten years later, in 1854.[9]

By the last quarter of the nineteenth century much of this turmoil had quieted down, however, and Philadelphia had become an established major industrial center. Accompanying the growth in industry, by the late nineteenth century the population of Philadelphia rose to 1,047,000 and the population of Kensington neared 100,000. About a quarter of the population consisted of foreign-born residents, with the majority coming from Ireland, Germany, Scotland, and England.[10]

The need to live close to sources of work meant that neighborhoods were defined more by job opportunity than ethnicity. Irish immigrants lived throughout the city, but their employment in the textile trades drew many of them, along with large groups of German, Scottish, and British workers concentrated in various skilled trades, to the sections of Greater Kensington. By the early twentieth century there was also a small community of African Americans living in Kensington, although the heaviest residential concentration of this group remained in the south-central part of the original city in neighborhoods convenient to the mansions of Philadelphia's upper class, where many more could find employment as domestics and in service jobs.[11]

In the 1880s another migration from England, particularly from the center of the lace industry in Nottinghamshire, brought in many skilled knitters who had a strong tradition of radical unionism (it was there that the Luddite movement began in 1811). And this was also the period in which the first full-fashioned hosiery mill came to Kensington, another direct transplant from England and the district of Nottinghamshire.[12]

Although the hosiery industry is an old one, tracing its roots to the guilds of the Middle Ages, its full-fashioned sector was a more recent innovation. Traditionally, hosiery was a knitted product made in the form of a tube on a rotary knitting machine. The primary material used in the industry was cotton, although some luxury items were made of silk. The stocking took shape after the dyeing process, when it was dried on wooden boards that were made to the configuration of a leg. Since the shape was not knitted into the product itself, the stockings rapidly lost their shape and sagged with wear.

Full-fashioned hosiery, however, was a very different product. William Cotton, of Nottingham, invented the first full-fashioned hosiery machine in 1864. With this innovation (and later improvements), the fabric for the stocking was knitted flat, on complex machinery. It was also made in two parts, the foot and the leg, and the major occupations within the industry required specialized skill. Knitters were skilled male workers, making the fabric of the stocking through a complicated process in which stitches were either added or dropped to shape the material. In this way, when the stocking was joined together with a seam up the back, it was already in the shape of a leg. The knitters' helpers were young male apprentices who would eventually become knitters themselves. But the complicated process of full-fashioned hosiery manufacture also required other skilled positions, and most of these other jobs were, by tradition, held by women. Women were very important in the industry, working closely with the knitters and performing crucial jobs. These included "topping," a procedure by which the product was transferred from the legger machine (which knitted the leg) to the footer machine (which knitted the foot and joined it to the stocking leg). They also performed other jobs in the knitting department, such as "looping," operating a machine on which the heels and toes were knitted together and a flat seam closed the foot, and "seaming," on special sewing machines in which the ends of the fabric were carefully joined together with a seam up the back to make the finished stocking. These jobs were thought to require elements such as "nimbleness and dexterity" that women were traditionally believed to possess. Although women's jobs required considerable skill, all knitter jobs remained the domain of men. An expensive item, full-fashioned hosiery was, for a long time, a luxury product.[13]

Initially, these stockings were imported from England. In 1884, however, a manufacturer from Sutton-in-Ashfield, Nottinghamshire, established the first full-fashioned plant in the United States—in Rhode Island. Following the success of this plant, two Englishmen, using the time-honored method of appropriating money from one of their wives, established the second American mill in 1887: Nicker and Wessons, on Tulip Street in Kensington. The first workers in the plant were also immigrants from England, some coming by way of the original mill in Rhode Island, and others directly from England. The article that carried this "origins" story in the *Hosiery Worker*, the newspaper of the American Federation of Full-Fashioned Hosiery Workers (AFFFHW), cited the English historians Sidney and Beatrice Webb, claiming that "the hosiery workers of Nottingham were practically 100 percent organized by the 1880s and 90s. It was in those years that the exodus to this country began," adding another chapter in capital's global endeavor to maximize profit by lowering costs.[14]

That some of the workers who followed carried their union traditions with them is not surprising, and can be seen in the story of John Makin. A resident of Kensington since 1887, Makin immigrated to the neighborhood from Nottingham, in England's industrial north, after being blacklisted for participating in a strike there. One of the first things he did upon arriving in Kensington was to join the Knights of Labor. In 1890, following his participation in the founding of an early full-fashioned hosiery knitters union, he took part in a strike. Marching through Kensington, down Broad Street to Fourth and Market Streets in the heart of the city, his group must have presented a rather curious sight, each one carrying a "banner" consisting of a pole to which he had tied a stocking. Makin claimed that they were marching to meet Mary Harris "Mother" Jones, who was in the city in support of the strike. After the strike, he was again blacklisted, this time in his adopted country. Makin's activities offer a prime example of the deep-seated differences that existed between the philosophy of the manufacturers and that of their workers, particularly when it came to labor unions.[15]

The difference between the ideologies of the owners and the workers was manifested, above all, in the way they viewed the industry. By the early twentieth century Kensington's textile manufacturers had formed a group with a strong sense of identity and possessiveness toward the industry. Some of the elders' sons had learned the business in their fathers' mills. But by the first quarter of the twentieth century many manufacturers' sons were receiving a college education at schools like the University of Pennsylvania or practical training at places like the Franklin Institute and learning the new skills of "scientific management." By the time they started running the family business, many of them, and their managers, had moved into large houses in suburbs such as Cheltenham and Chestnut Hill and middle-class sections of the city like East Oak Lane. These "proprietary" capitalists kept a sharp eye on the business, but their understanding of Kensington increasingly diverged from that of those who lived, worked, and socialized within the mill districts. By the beginning of the twentieth century Kensington's mill workers toiled for sixty hours a week or more, many still earning scandalously low wages, and the community's reputation for "tumultuous working-class activity" was well known.[16]

Thus, although Philadelphia of the early twentieth century may have been an especially "American" city, with a large number of skilled and native-born workers living within it, its workers did not experience the oppressions of capital significantly less than others. The living conditions of Kensington's residents, native-born and "new" immigrant, although not monolithic, did not differ dramatically from those of other working-class communities, and many of its working people's lives were full of struggle and hardship. The label "Scab City" that some applied to Philadelphia certainly had more to do with the anti-union endeavors of its bosses and politicians than with any lack of militancy and solidarity on the part of its working-class residents, who gave America its largest bout of class warfare in 1910 in the general strike that occurred there.[17]

By the 1920s and early 1930s, in fact, Kensington would prefigure the radical cultural developments that led to the formation of labor's Congress of Industrial Organizations (CIO), with broad implications that extended beyond the local community. The reasons for these developments included the history of the neighborhood's populace and its unions and strikers, but also the hardships of daily life in the community. For while there were, indeed, numerous skilled laborers, not everyone held jobs that were ranked as such, and in the area of wages and working conditions, even those who did hold skilled positions did not always have an easy life. This industrial section of the city offered a variety of jobs, but many of them did not provide a living wage, and most had seasonal fluctuations. Manufacturers had very few scruples about drastically cutting jobs and wages when necessary in order to keep their profits stable. As a result, wives and children of male workers—members of a "secondary" labor market—often accepted poorly paid employment in order to supplement the family income.[18]

In the late nineteenth century as many as 32 percent of the sons of native-born whites, 36 percent of the sons of Irish immigrants, and 60 percent of the sons of German immigrants were gainfully employed by the age of fourteen. By the age of sixteen these proportions had increased significantly, to 71, 72, and 81 percent, respectively. What is more, this work pattern held true for daughters as well, though in smaller numbers. By the age of fourteen, 11 percent of the daughters of native-born whites, 37 percent of those of Irish immigrants, and 28 percent of those of German descent were gainfully employed. By the age of sixteen, the proportions had climbed to 38, 57, and 49 percent, respectively. Further, the wages earned by these young people were a necessity even among the families of most skilled workers if they wanted to maintain a lifestyle considered "adequate." In fact, the wages of the average skilled worker in the city during the 1880s and 1890s were often inadequate in meeting the needs of a family of five. And even if the average skilled worker could support a family at a minimal level, many could not, and unskilled workers did not earn anywhere near the required amount.[19]

These conditions had not changed significantly by the early twentieth century. Although Howard Kreckman entered the mills at the age of fourteen, this was not his first experience with paid labor, for he had been earning wages well before that time—doing everything from being an errand boy to selling soft pretzels on the neighborhood streets. He spoke (with lingering regret) about the necessity to leave school at the age of fourteen to seek full-time employment: "I started in the mills when I was fourteen and worked fifty-four hours a week as a 'helper,' for about six dollars." Alice Nelson Kreckman also left full-time school at the age of fourteen to take a job in a mill, as did Freda Maurer, a hosiery "topper," who left school in 1914 on her fourteenth birthday, "hoping to help with the bread winning." Margaret Connor was also working as a topper in a hosiery mill by the age of fourteen. But it was not only sons and daughters who entered paid employment to supplement the family income. Married women, even those with children, also worked for wages, particularly in the textile industry. A 1925 survey of working women in Kensington found that over 25 percent of women with children earned wages from employment in a factory or mill, often on piecework.[20]

Susan Porter Benson, in her important work on working-class economies in the interwar years, found that even as consumption was becoming increasingly central to the lives of middle-class Americans, working-class Americans

TABLE 1 Kensington household annual budget, 1920

Rent	$180.00
Fuel and light	51.00
Food	380.12
Clothing	157.70
Medical	27.00
Insurance and savings	100.00
Lodge and union dues	26.00
Reading matter	10.00
Church and charity	13.52
Furniture and general supplies	30.00
Recreation pocket money	54.60
Unclassified	40.00
	$1,069.94

Source: Esther Louise Little and William Joseph Henry Cotten, *Budgets of Families and Individuals of Kensington, Philadelphia* (1920) (Lancaster, PA: Press of the New Era Printing Company, 1920), 145.

were still unable to participate fully in the consumer society, with many remaining largely on the outside. Further, working-class strategies of survival were employed in similar, though not identical, ways across ethnic lines. Benson argues that "in matters of getting and spending money, class outweighed ethnicity," and while those with adequate means were certainly active participants in consumer culture, many with more limited means were involved more marginally.[21]

Much data from Kensington supports these findings for the community as a whole. In 1920 Esther Louise Little and William Cotton, two social workers living in Kensington, constructed a budget based on the necessary requirements to adequately maintain a Kensington textile worker's family consisting of two adults and three children. Using criteria considered "fair" by a majority of those workers, they found that the income required to sustain such a budget could not be met by the bulk of male workers on their own. Included in the account were various items that were part of Kensington mill workers' actual disbursements, but it also included consideration for some things that a majority stated they were always trying to obtain. The resulting budget is found in Table 1.[22]

Entries under food included the allowance of meat once a day, three days a week. And while most individual workers had some sick benefits from a lodge or union membership, these generally did not cover children. In addition, almost all families considered insurance against the loss of the family income through either disability or death to be essential.[23]

Other items listed in the budget help to give a more in-depth view of the lives of the textile workers. Membership in a lodge was seen as customary among mill families, and the authors felt that provisions for union dues were an absolute requirement of a mill family in Kensington. These were primarily a provision for strike benefits and "victimized" benefits (for those who were discriminated against or blacklisted), although there were often relief and death benefits, or "mutual insurance," connected with labor unions as well.[24]

Amounts budgeted for reading matter included newspapers, a magazine or a book now and then, and postage and stationery. Of particular interest was an entry that allowed for the custom among Kensington families to allocate to each income producer a certain amount of pocket money or spending money to be spent as that person chose, no questions asked. This could include tobacco and alcohol or other personal items, and can be seen as recognition of a worker's right, on a small, personal level, to the rewards of his or her labor.

Women were usually the ones who controlled the budget and the household income. This is representative of the myriad ways in which women were important to the family economy. Former resident Jeanne Callahan, recalling how her mother divided up the money for her budget, said, "My mother had envelopes for everything, one for the rent, one for utilities, even one for some kind of roast for Sunday dinner." And she also remembered that her father always received back several dollars for his own use. Money was sometimes additionally set aside for recreation for the family, and a budget considered fair by the majority of surveyed mill workers also made provision for occasional carfare (though not for regular travel to work, as they usually lived near their place of employment), for gifts to friends or relatives other than immediate family, and for a small contingency fund.[25]

In most of the families surveyed, the father did not make the amount required to maintain a family budget such as the one shown in Table 1 on his income alone. Income also fluctuated from week to week due to irregularity of work as well as the cutting of wages. While some highly skilled workers, such as Brussels carpet weavers, could make the necessary amount if they worked a 300-day year, most workers could not do so, even though they worked an average of fifty-four to sixty hours a week. Irregularity of employment was characteristic of textile work in Kensington, and, except for times of labor conflict, loss of time for a part of a week was virtually always due to irregularity of employment in the industry, with little or no time lost on account of illness by the workers. People lived paycheck to paycheck; as one respondent put it, "When work is good, we can live adequately, but when one day out of the week is lost, the cream is taken off." Secondary incomes were often a necessity among mill workers, with children entering the workforce as soon as they arrived at the legal working age (and often earlier) and women, married and single, also doing wage labor or taking in boarders as the opportunities arose—strategies that stretched across the spectrum of working-class lives.[26]

By the twentieth century the ethnic mix of Kensington was also becoming more varied, as western Europeans were joined by other groups of immigrants—Poles, Italians, and Jews from southern and eastern Europe. This influx of new immigrants and migrant labor was itself part of a larger restructuring of the Atlantic economy. Kensington was "Philadelphia's workshop . . . a giant mill town set down in the midst of a metropolis," and it had the heaviest concentration of manufacturing plants and the largest skilled labor force in the city. As such it was a magnet for labor, and its residents developed a strong identity both to the place and as members of a working class. As social and economic stratification increased in the metropolitan area, Kensington developed close-knit neighborhoods where ties between neighbors and webs of kinship provided strong support networks. Life centered around the mills, informal street socializing, and distinct forms of female and male cultural activities. By the 1920s culture contact and "modern" society were forces mitigating ethnic differentiation, particularly among the young, and the traditions of newer residents interfaced with the long traditions of class-conscious labor activity originally transplanted across the Atlantic by Kensington's earliest residents. Ethnic backgrounds and cultures were not forgotten; they were a part of community life. However, other subjectivities, based on where and how people worked and lived, mitigated the persistence of insular identities. One of the primary reasons for the patterns that developed in Kensington was the spatial and social organization of the area.[27]

By the 1920s Greater Kensington could be described in terms of a modern, sustainable community. It had walkable streets, easy access to public transportation, and integrated spaces of residency, work, retail, and leisure. It was not just a geographic area but a cultural entity that crossed several political ward boundaries (see Map 1).

The landscape consisted of mills, church spires, housing (constructed almost entirely in straight brick rows near the factories), local shopping areas of small businesses, movie houses, restaurants, taprooms, fraternal clubs, and union halls. A major investment in mass transit by the city from 1916 to 1934 ensured that trolley lines ran on all of the major streets, and the Frankford Elevated line (the "El"), after a break in construction during World War I, was

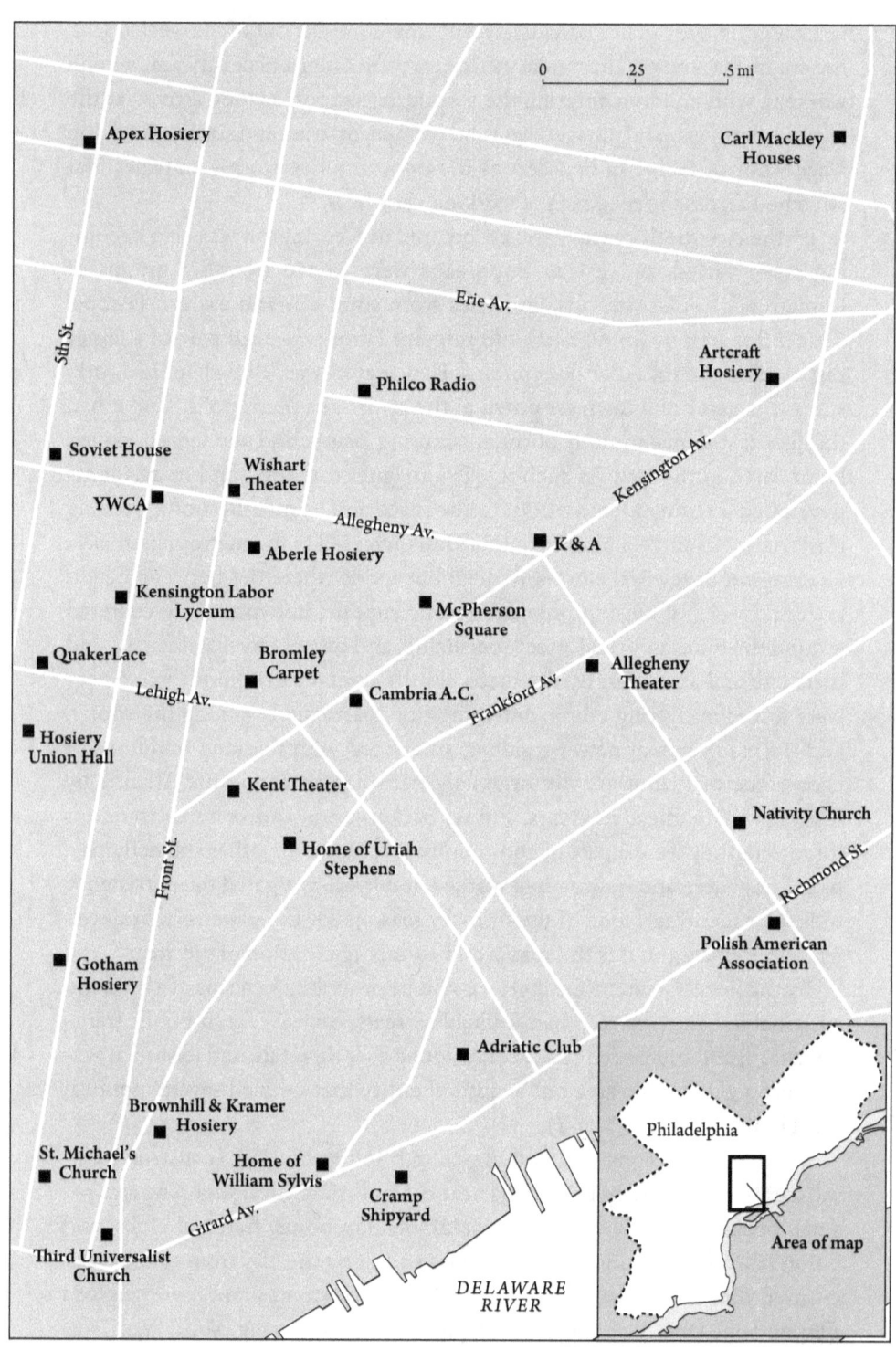

MAP 1 Kensington section of Philadelphia.

completed by 1922. This network connected the neighborhoods not only to the local shopping districts but also to the city's center. Kensington was, in the words of an industrial secretary of the Kensington Young Women's Christian Association (YWCA) in 1925, "one of the greatest industrial communities in the United States," a community of long-term stability.[28]

For the most part, older immigrant groups did not move out as new ones moved in. Although individuals did move on, many long-term residents remained in the neighborhoods, held by jobs, family, and community. This factor created a more dispersed mode of settlement, which in itself contributed to the breakdown of insularity. Thus, new immigrant groups did not move en masse into an area but found housing where they could, often dispersed throughout the neighborhoods. This resulted in the creation of a checkerboard pattern of settlement in which people of various ethnic backgrounds lived in close proximity. Certainly some ethnic clustering did exist. There were some sections where groups of Irish residents clustered together, and others where groups of Italian residents lived, and many Polish immigrants settled particularly in the Richmond section. However, these areas were not ethnically homogeneous, nor were they physically separated from each other, and workplaces and the major shopping districts were easily accessible by walking or a short trolley ride.

Scholarly and journalistic descriptions of Kensington have often painted a rather bleak picture of the area. By the twentieth century Kensington was an area with many factories, often supporting huge smokestacks, many taking up a whole city block. Railroad lines running into the neighborhood brought in raw materials and carried out finished and semifinished products, and rows of "monotonous brick houses" filled countless streets laid out in a grid pattern. Almost all Kensington workers lived in the ubiquitous row houses, another reflection of the district's English heritage. Tens of thousands of textile workers and hundreds of firms inhabited Kensington by the beginning of the twentieth century, and the neighborhood's reputation for turbulence and working-class solidarity was well known. Kensington was all of this, but it was also much more. Through the use of census and archival data and the oral testimonies of former residents, a picture emerges of a rich social life and complex patterns of interaction within the community (see Figure 1).[29]

By the 1920s there was considerable interaction among the various groups that lived within the area, as evidenced by the ethnic variation in the names of those arrested in the labor disputes that erupted during this period. Some of the reasons for this can be found in the active neighborhood life that existed throughout the community. The 1920 census indicates that newer immigrant groups often lived among the long-standing communities of residents,

FIGURE 1 View of Kensington looking north from the Bromley Carpet Mill, B Street and Lehigh Avenue, 1912. Row houses, train tracks, and more mills can be seen in the background. MG-219.2, Philadelphia Commercial Museum Photographs, Image 0785. Courtesy of Pennsylvania Historical and Museum Commission, Pennsylvania State Archives.

sometimes on the same streets and within the same block. Many among the newer groups were second generation by that time, although some were new immigrants, particularly of eastern and southern European descent. Merchants, many Jewish, operated stores in several flourishing retail areas. Most workers lived within two miles of their places of employment and walked to work. Open neighborhood squares, taverns, and the streets of Kensington provided space for socializing and community events. With small houses and no air conditioning in the summers, most residents spent free time on their steps and sidewalks. And, as one observer noted in 1925, "The families ma[d]e up for the lack of a back yard by using the streets as community recreation centers."[30]

Irish, Polish, German, and Italian Catholic churches, Protestant churches, and a Jewish synagogue stood within blocks of each other. The proliferation of churches is indicative of the religious identity of many residents, and scholars have often stressed the importance of church as an organizing principle for community. Oral histories and Kensington residents' labor activities suggest that while religion was certainly important for many people, it was not the overriding or only organizing principle in Kensington in this period. Religion was a given, often part of the way residents thought of themselves and of their cultural backgrounds. Parish, as ethnicity, was a part of their identity, but not all of it. Social identities are always pluralistic in nature, fluid, full of complexity, and continually evolving.[31]

Religious identity has most often been associated with women, and some women were actively involved with a church, attending novenas every Tuesday night or daily masses every morning at 6:30. They were not reflective of the community as a whole, however, and that behavior was especially uncharacteristic of young women in the 1920s. There were many shades of religiosity present in the community, from the devout to the anticlerical and everything in between.

Former resident Jeanne Callahan described her mother, Jane Connor, as a flapper. Jane, born in 1900, was raised Irish Catholic; however, when she came of age she never went to mass, and when she married and had children in the early 1920s, she did not send her children to Catholic schools. Jane learned to say the rosary in Polish from a close girlfriend, but this was more of an interesting cross-cultural experience, not something she identified with religion per se. The rosary provided a common denominator that simplified the translation of the language. Several other residents described their ability to say phrases in other languages as a point of pride.[32]

Jane also loved to dance, and on Sunday mornings she listened to a Polish music program on the radio. Whenever a polka came on the radio she would dance across the floor, her daughter Jeanne in tow. Jeanne, born in 1924, did go to mass as a child in the 1920s and 1930s because her father took her. Although her brother rarely went, and religion was not a big topic at home, this story indicates that her Irish-Italian father had some ideas about the importance of his daughter attending church that may not have been shared by his wife. In fact, because he usually had to rush to get Jeanne to mass on time, her mother would regularly "give him hell," claiming he was going to make his daughter sick.[33]

Robert Gunther, born in Kensington in 1927, said his mother never went to church. She often told him, "It's the way you live your life that matters, not whether or not you go to church." For some residents, ambivalence extended into anticlericalism, as with both Alice Nelson Kreckman and Howard

Kreckman. Howard attempted to join the Young Men's Christian Association (YMCA) as a youth because he wanted to learn to swim, but he resented the fact that the organization pushed religion on members. "This man asked me if I was saved. I told him I didn't know if I was or not." He also described the evangelist Billy Sunday as a "con artist" for setting up a tent on Allegheny Avenue to try to pull in the "poor uneducated masses." Sunday was brought to Philadelphia by the department store magnate John Wanamaker and, as was the case with many such figures, spent a lot of time trying to "reform" working-class people.[34]

Alice Nelson Kreckman also disparaged religion, describing it as a methodology for "brainwashing the young," and she also did not attend any church. Although she went to the YWCA in the 1920s, she claimed it was not religious like the men's association. In the 286 interviews of Kensington hosiery workers conducted in the 1930s by researchers from the University of Pennsylvania, only one mentioned religion, and that was a male claiming that "the company I worked for liked people from my religion because it was against unions." Some of the ambivalence toward religion resulted from such negative attitudes toward unions and the relationships some clergy had with mill owners. Many people, however, just had other things to think about much of the time. But there was also a strand of anticlericalism that was part of the changing views and mores of the "modern woman," an important construct for many young women of the 1920s. This can be noted in some of the material contained in novels, plays, and movies that became popular among the young, and was reflected in the lives of both Jane Connor and Alice Nelson Kreckman, as well as other young hosiery workers, as can be gleaned from articles in the *Pressoff Special*, the newsletter of the employees of the Aberle Hosiery Mill.[35]

Kensington was a thoroughly urban environment, and the structures of the community reflected the landscape of urbanism. Movie theaters were a common feature in the neighborhoods and very popular among the residents. The Allegheny Theatre, in the center of one of Kensington's shopping districts at Frankford and Allegheny Avenues, was a vaudeville theater, and it also showed films. Not only could one see a vaudeville show and a silent film, but the theater also gave a bag of candy to children—all for a nickel. Other places of leisure, such as skating rinks, restaurants, and dancehalls, were popular among residents, particularly young people, as were the abundant taverns. And there were the shopping districts where people could meet each other as participants (on various levels) in the consumer culture of the 1920s.[36]

Ethnic clubs and institutions were prevalent, but many of them opened events and even membership to other residents of the community as well, and some of these clubs were places where men of different ethnicities sometimes met to socialize. Women also attended social events at the various clubs. Joseph Callahan, of Irish and Italian descent, sometimes went with friends to a Polish club, and in the 1920s he and his wife, her sisters, and their husbands attended dances there, as well as events at the Irish Ancient Order of Hibernians club.[37]

Robert Gunther went not only to the Polish club but also to an Italian club and the Irish club. His stories often highlighted the interactions that occurred among different residents in the community. "The Irish club always sponsored a parade on Saint Patrick's Day," and in the course of it the marchers passed by a Polish club. Here they would pause to "serenade" its members with Irish songs. The men there then reciprocated with Polish songs. Later in the evening many of them got together to hold a pig roast and have a party. The next day some of them would meet again at a vacant field to hold a mock funeral, complete with someone playing the role of a priest, to "bury the remains of Paddy's Pig." These stories provide examples of how the rhythms of life—work patterns, fraternal organizations and unions, taverns, institutions like the YMCA and the YWCA, street socializing, and conversations on front steps in densely populated streets—all helped to combat the isolation of residents.[38]

Although Kensington was more ethnically diverse by the 1920s, it was still overwhelmingly white. In fact, most historians of the city do not mention the two small communities of African Americans who were longtime residents of the area. In addition to those two peripheral communities, a small number of mixed-race residents lived in parts of Kensington. This small-scale intermixing is hinted at by a reference to "mulattos" in the *Pressoff Special*, the shop newsletter of the Aberle Hosiery Mill, and confirmed by former residents and census information. Robert Gunther was related to one of the "mulatto" families because his mother's sister married an African American man who was a minister in a Baptist church. In such scenarios—a classic case of what anthropologists call an "insider/outsider" situation—different peoples become part of the dominant social structure on the basis of long-term residency and familiarity or ties of kinship. Gunther's family lived in a part of Kensington that bordered the small African American section known as "Jewtown," and borders are often porous. He and other white men also frequented an illegal after-hours speakeasy run by an African American man in his house in that black section of Kensington.[39]

While a small number of African Americans remained in the area throughout this period, they were the most insulated of the various groups that coexisted in

Kensington, as they were throughout the city. But they were not entirely invisible. Gunther spoke of children in the neighborhood at Halloween. According to tradition, when children went trick-or-treating at Halloween they had to sing a song, or dance, or do something to get a treat. Gunther's mother always liked "the colored kids" because she thought they were the best performers. These stories indicate that some African Americans were marginally present in Kensington and that there was at least a small degree of acceptance among some residents, though it may also indicate the existence of preconceived, stereotypical ideas about them.[40]

By 1920, the city's black residents, though more numerous because of war-induced labor shortages, still accounted for only 7.4 percent of the population. Although their employment in industry grew as migrants found low-skilled jobs in various industries, they were shut out of employment in most of the city's major firms and were not organized by its American Federation of Labor (AFL) unions, which organized skilled workers. Textile manufacturers employed a handful of African Americans, but only in janitorial positions, and this was reflected in the hosiery industry.[41] Few blacks, in fact, worked in any production jobs in manufacturing plants in Philadelphia, with some exceptions such as Midvale Steel. Some did find work on the docks and as laborers, while many others worked as domestics. Black workers, in fact, made up about half the members of the innovative Philadelphia dock workers union affiliated with the Industrial Workers of the World (also known as the Wobblies).[42]

African Americans in the city encountered segregation in residency as well as industry, and these two facts were historically intertwined. They were initially concentrated in areas near the original city boundaries and areas to its south, close to affluent areas where domestic and service jobs were available. As more migrants arrived, they slowly began to expand further north into lower North Philadelphia and other areas of the city. In 1918 there was a well-publicized race riot in South Philadelphia, and again in 1924 racial incidents were reported in that section of the city, which had a relatively large African American population. No racial disturbances, or at least none reaching the level of newsworthiness of the South Philadelphia incidents, were reported in Kensington in this period. The complexity of race relations there can be illustrated by the relatively rare interactions that did occur. For example, in May 1920, Philadelphia's African American newspaper, the *Philadelphia Tribune*, covered a "rematch" baseball game between a black team, the Hilldale Bats, and the Nativity Catholic Club, that took place in Kensington's Nativity Park, adjacent to the traditional "Irish" church in the neighborhood. The paper strongly suggested that the 4–3 win by Nativity was accomplished by cheating. While the story may have implied that racism contributed to the loss, antagonisms remained at the level of insinuation and did not escalate into any kind of altercation. The black community's small size, along with the fact that it formed little source of competition for jobs in segregated industries, and possibly the long tradition of radical ideology which was still viable among some Kensington residents in this period may have been mitigating factors allowing for its ability to coexist on the margins of the larger community.[43]

Whatever race relations may have been on a day-to-day basis, because African Americans were peripheral to the textile industry as a whole, they remained peripheral to its hosiery sector and were not used as scab labor during strikes. As full-fashioned hosiery manufacture required extended specialized training on the job, replacement labor during strikes could not be randomly hired, but was largely limited to other skilled (and white) craftsmen. The fact that African Americans were not used as strikebreakers meant that as a group they did not arouse the ire of the textile workers that was consistently and vigorously shown toward scabs. Such was not the case, however, for the "class enemies" of Kensington's hosiery workers—the manufacturers and their political allies who battled the workers and their union in the mills, streets, and courtrooms of the city.

Jobs, Neighbors, and Networks of Culture

The majority of Kensington's workers had jobs in the mills, many in the textile industry, which was the largest employer. Occupations such as seamer, knitter, weaver, topper, mender, lace maker, mechanic, and welder were common in Kensington. Residents also worked on the docks, in construction, and in other occupations; the census reveals some more unusual jobs as well, such as a "fireman" for a Masonic Lodge who was born in Ireland. Two of Jane Connor's sisters worked in hosiery mills, as did the mother of Robert Gunther. Howard Kreckman and Alice Nelson Kreckman both left school when they were fourteen years old and entered the hosiery mills, Howard in 1917 and Alice in 1921. The mills taught group work and promoted contacts, and the common experiences of working in them created complementary habits among many of the residents that were reflected in neighborhood life. The community became an important base for sociability, underscored by patterns of marriage and networks of work relations that connected the community to the workplace.[44]

These connections manifested themselves in many ways. The primary method of getting a job was through networks of family or neighbors, when someone would "speak" for a job seeker or let him or her know when to show up at the mill. Extended family members often lived near one another, and most people lived within walking distance or a short trolley ride from their jobs. Marriages between people from different ethnic groups were not uncommon. Jeanne Callahan's father was of Irish and Italian descent, and her mother, Jane Connor, was Irish. Robert Gunther's father was German, while his mother was Irish. Howard Kreckman's parents were German and English Canadian, while Alice Nelson Kreckman was Irish and English. In the 1940s Jeanne Callahan married a man of Russian descent, while her brother, Joseph, married a Jewish woman. And, as mentioned previously, there were even a few incidents, though rare, of interracial marriage. The oral testimony of former residents is backed up by census data.[45]

The development of social networks through which people could rely on neighbors for help and support was aided by high residential stability and the proximity of row house living. As Howard Kreckman put it, "When you lived in row houses, you knew if your neighbor was hurting." Interviews with Kensington residents, as well as union records, indicate that neighbors often helped out in times of distress, and people were not only recipients of charity but also frequently donors, helping out family and friends. The construction of such networks of reciprocity was a necessary condition of life, for in a community like Kensington it was not easy to live comfortably without the cooperation of family, friends, and neighbors. Give-and-take was an important part of the community ethos, and coming down too much on either side was looked at askance. Reciprocity is not the same as charity, and it was a central factor in the alternative economy that was necessitated by conditions that often included periods when people were out of work, either when the mills were slow or during the not infrequent times when strikes were in progress. When the Great Depression hit, the hosiery union was to play a particularly strong role in this "alternative economy" of the community.[46]

Distinct forms of male and female cultural networks were evident in the neighborhood. Male activities extended outside of work into such areas as clubs and taverns before, during, and after Prohibition (which was not taken very seriously by most residents, regardless of their ethnic backgrounds). Activities involving physical aggressiveness were also a regular part of masculine culture. Although children were generally raised to be respectful of adults, conditions of everyday life were not conducive to the development of passive behavior; people were expected to stand up for themselves, and such expectations crossed gender lines. These community expectations were an important component of the labor activity that thrived within the community.

If a person felt that some right was being violated or that he or she was not being "respected" (and individuals sometimes defined "respect" rather broadly), altercations could sometimes turn into fistfights, and some men, in particular, used such incidents to demonstrate their physical prowess. According to Robert Gunther, these men developed reputations in the neighborhood as people "you didn't mess with." Men of different ethnicities also spent time in "fight clubs," institutions with a long history in Kensington. Gunther's uncle told him stories about clubs that allowed "bare knuckle" fighting, where the audience could easily come out "spattered with blood." But more legitimate clubs were also important sites of interaction. The Cambria Athletic Club, established in 1917 at Kensington Avenue and Somerset Street, became a popular venue where amateur boxers engaged in "soft-glove" matches in which they were still expected to put on a good show. Gunther described what it was like in the 1930s when his uncle took him there: "If they danced around too much, the crowd would start booing and singing, 'Let me call you sweetheart.'"[47]

Cultural networks also extended from the workplace into the community. Soccer (a reflection of European traditions), pool, and baseball games were popular activities, and hosiery workers from different mills often competed against each other in union-sponsored leagues. Shuffleboard and darts were popular games in the taverns where men sometimes congregated after work. Work itself was central to the lives of Kensington's residents. Members of the community, with few exceptions, embraced a work ethic that saw work as a necessity of life for one simple reason—it was. A job often meant the difference between having a roof over one's head and living on the street. Culture, tradition, and shared connections of kinship and neighborhood also, however, reinforced a concept of justice that embraced this ethic as not only a necessity but a moral right that belonged to them all. People were expected to work, but work was expected to be available and fair. This outlook of the workers of Kensington was described by the contemporary economist George Taylor of the Wharton School of the University of Pennsylvania. Writing in 1931, Taylor claimed that the conflict between Kensington's workers and the manufacturers was "one of a clash of philosophies. Employees, particularly union representatives, retain the concept of a 'just wage,' an ethical concept which is quite evident in union demands that wage rates and earnings should be related to the cost of living. Manufacturers insist that the 'price' of labor is determined in a competitive market where the factors of supply and demand prevail."[48]

There also existed an informal system of redistribution which had a distinctly "us and them" character. Robert Gunther described how younger men jumped onto the coal cars moving slowly along the railroad tracks in the neighborhood and "kick[ed] coal off so that people below could fill up sacks of coal to take home." Howard Kreckman and his brother sometimes drove a truck to the coal country in upstate Pennsylvania, filled it with "bootleg" coal, and then gave it out to neighbors who could not afford to buy it. "This was called 'bootlegging,' not of alcohol, but coal," Kreckman explained. The activity of bootlegging coal was also described in the shop newsletter of the Aberle mill. At no time were any of those involved in such actions considered to be outside of the circle of neighbors. The "us and them" mentality under which these actions were understood was recognized throughout the community. This oppositional ethos included a very important distinction, however, for transgressions against "neighbors" (the term consistently used by all interviewees) were not looked upon as acceptable. The perpetrators of such actions were generally "taken care of within the community," and they might lose the protection of the community.[49]

Female cultural networks also extended from the workplace into the community. By the late 1800s Philadelphia was a center of textile and other light manufacturing industries and, as such, it drew large numbers of women into its shops. In 1880, women made up 26 percent of the city's workforce, almost twice the national average. Most of the city's mills were located in and near Kensington, where three-quarters of the wage-earning women worked in manufacturing, whereas only 13 percent worked as servants. By contrast, in Philadelphia generally, over one-third of all employed women were servants, as were over one-half nationally. The historian Susan Levine found that during this time "Kensington's factory girls provided a crucial link in the area's network of kin relations and family economies," encompassing both home and workplace. "Family ties continued at the workplace, while neighborhood ties reinforced workplace contacts."[50]

These female cultural networks continued into the 1920s. Shared childcare, activities such as shopping, nursing, and midwifery, discussed in oral histories, and work in the mills all reinforced neighborly ties, often across ethnic boundaries. Alice Nelson Kreckman described her mother as being "always up and down the street. It didn't matter who it was, if someone was sick or there was a baby to be born, she was there." There was always a woman in the neighborhood who had "special knowledge" to help women with birth control or an unwanted pregnancy, and although such knowledge was never discussed openly, women knew whom to go to.[51]

Many residents did not embrace the construct that "a woman's place is in the home," though some women did leave paid work when they married if they could afford to. Those with working mothers could see that many women had lives outside of the home, and wage-earning wives and mothers were not uncommon. Often, the second wage made the difference in the battle to have a "decent" life. When Robert Gunther's mother was able to get a job in a yarn factory in the 1930s, the family was able to live a better life. "We thought we were rich," he said. "We were able to move into a house that had inside plumbing!" Howard Kreckman always expressed great respect for his mother, who worked for a shirtwaist manufacturer on the "putting out" system. Shirtwaists were made of cotton, and they always had to be carefully pressed. "She would take the trolley down and pick up the shirts and bring them home to work on, then take them back to get credit. Meanwhile, she still managed to make a home for us."[52]

Women were very visible in the workplaces as well as in the community generally, and streets, where women often congregated, were centers of community life. These women were not uniformly deferential, respectful, or submissive, any more than the men in the community. Robert Gunther said that his mother was "an outspoken lady who always told you exactly what she thought," while Alice Nelson Kreckman's mother, "a little woman who loved animals," did not hesitate to assert herself if the occasion warranted it. Alice remembered one time when a man with a horse-drawn cart stopped outside their house and started to beat the horse. Her mother, incensed, "went out with a broom and started whacking the man." "She beat the hell out of him," Kreckman remembered. "She told him, 'If you touch that horse again I'll knock your head off,' and she would have too. She was like that." Alice and most other women in the hosiery union were not timid either, as demonstrated by their labor activity. When women asserted themselves in the community, physically fought on the picket lines, and spoke up at union meetings, such behavior was continuing a long tradition of "disorderly women" that can be traced back across the Atlantic and was abundantly evident in the textile trades.[53]

Although culturally dominant views of femininity may have been present in everyday life, they varied, were contested, and often contradicted one another. Understandings of gender suggesting that women's place was in the domestic realm, or promoting women as meek and submissive when they did work outside the home, certainly do not describe the patterns of Kensington women's behavior in the workplace or the community. As the historian Eleanor Gordon noted about working women in Scotland, a "subordinate labor market position" should not be conflated with "subordination and submission in the workplace."[54]

While there can be no argument about the legal, political, and employment inequalities women experienced in the public sphere, many of these women were strong and self-reliant individuals. Women suffered oppression on various levels, from the home to the workplace, but the words and actions of Kensington's female workers indicate that they often saw class as the primary site of their exploitation, in common with their male coworkers, family members, and neighbors. This can be seen in Alice Nelson Kreckman's proud reference to herself as a "worker" and in women's militant support of the union, ever more evident as the story progresses. Kensington's female hosiery workers often and increasingly demanded equal treatment from male coworkers and union officials, but they also fought manufacturers for a larger share of the wealth they produced and for better conditions and more respect on the job, and they directed accusations of sexual harassment and exploitation at "bosses."[55]

Kensington women themselves often negotiated what came to be the accepted norm in the community, which frequently differed from prevailing middle-class cultural and ideological views of women's roles. A dialogue centered on middle-class values of domesticity often fell prey to economic necessity and community culture and tradition. The amalgam of these elements helped to provide fertile ground for what can be called the consciousness raising that was to be practiced by union women in the 1920s (discussed in chapter 4). As workers, women received community and family support, and in the hosiery industry their positions were relatively high, giving them some sense of financial independence. By the late 1920s they would incorporate a greater understanding of themselves as women as well as workers, leading some to develop a feminist critique within the union that reflected back on the culture of the community.

Traditions of Resistance

The neighborhood support for the hosiery union and its members that grew throughout the 1920s and 1930s and that we will see throughout the following chapters was not a new or transitory feature of life in Kensington. It was rooted in deep historical traditions, growing out of an internalized conception of what it meant to be from the community. Residents of Kensington formed a strong identity of place. If questioned about their place of residence even by people outside the Philadelphia region, they often responded with simply "Kensington," as if the single word was all that needed to be said. In the early twentieth century, at least in labor circles, it was sufficient, as recognizable as "Paterson" or "Lawrence." Kensington was at the center of Philadelphia's labor activity in the 1920s and 1930s, as it had often been since the early nineteenth century. Its labor activists, in this period centered in the hosiery union, were at least partially able to withstand the coordinated attacks of the manufacturers and their allies because they were sustained in their community by a long history of progressive activity and ideas, connected to regional, national, and international networks. This history had a direct bearing on the activism of the period.[56]

The earliest residents of Kensington, the offspring of the first industrial revolution and the resistance it spawned, sometimes incorporated elements of Enlightenment thought about equality into their compendium of ideas. Some of the same ideas that underlay the American Revolution, the French Revolution, and many of the social movements that developed in the nineteenth century helped, also, to form a critique of industrial capitalism. One strand, rationalism, had a long history among trade union radicals in nineteenth-century Philadelphia. Among the rationalists, Universalism and Free Thought were important currents of thought, and by 1835 there were at least three Universalist churches in Philadelphia, including the Third Universalist Church in Greater Kensington. Also present among the institutions of Kensington was an Ethical Society, housed in a building in the 2400 block of Kensington Avenue. This group supported workers' rights and sponsored regular lectures which residents were encouraged to attend. Aside from more abstract philosophical discussions, they included discussions on suffrage, the employment of women, socialism, and "Can We Do without the Capitalist?" By November 1897 the group had set up a library and classrooms on the first floor of a house occupied by the weavers' union, claiming that the Kensington branch was practically "in the hands" of its working people. New waves of immigrants continued to come into the area in the late nineteenth century and the early twentieth century, bringing their own social and cultural responses. But they came into a community with a long history and tradition of labor-capital discord, which had become a real part of the community's culture.[57]

Robert Gunther, when describing conditions in the mill in which he worked, often talked about techniques of what social historians have termed "everyday resistance" in his workplace: "I would work at a set pace—no slower, no faster. At one point the bosses brought in efficiency experts to set times for everything. These guys watched us and came up with ideas like 'this job takes one and one half men.' But you can't split a man in half, so they would try to get one to do it. If I didn't have a helper, I would just stand there.

When the foreman asked me what I was doing, I would say 'waiting for a helper.' You can't let the bosses get control."[58] This statement could have been something right out of a manuscript by the labor historian David Montgomery. Gunther, however, had never read Montgomery, or any other labor historian, for that matter. He left school when he was sixteen years old to go to work in a factory, and although he was a union member, he was never in the leadership of any organization. He learned these lessons on the streets and in the mills of Kensington. When questioned about his opinion as to why Kensington had such a long history of militancy, Howard Kreckman responded simply, "That's where the mills were." From this statement it is obvious that the construct of labor-capital conflict had become an internalized part of his consciousness. To him, the answer was obvious. He never could quite understand why it wasn't obvious to everyone.[59]

Women, as workers, were part of this class-based conflict. The workers of Kensington often came from families where working in the mills was a long tradition. Men in the family might be full-fashioned hosiery knitters, the mother and daughters toppers or loopers. Or they might be weavers, or menders or examiners working in other types of textile mills. Usually the tradition was older than one generation. The union movement in Kensington was as old as the textile industry itself. As the contemporary economist Gladys Palmer noted, "The sacrifices of the early pioneers and the tradition of historic labor battles fought in the interests of the workers' movement" had given it an emotional as well as an economic significance.[60] Respect for their family's sacrifices was a common denominator among the women and men who worked for, and fought against, the manufacturers. This emotional and romantic memory was a part of community consciousness, and it became an important departure point for activism by the AFFFHW in the 1920s and 1930s.

Labor activism, growing out of these historical roots, often involved individuals and groups with long experience in the fight for labor rights, continuously drawn to the neighborhood. These included British trade unionists, German socialists, Wobblies, communists, and Irish nationalists, carrying with them the legacies of the Enlightenment as well as lessons from individual experience. Hosiery knitter Howard Kreckman remembered that his father often sent him "down Kensington Avenue" to pick up an Irish paper from what he called "the real Irish, the Republicans," who also carried the scars of British imperialism.[61]

Historically, class contradictions in Kensington sometimes demonstrated a struggle between community and private rights, and resulted in spontaneous action by residents. One such case was the 1840 anti-railroad riots. Residents were upset because the railroad was being built on the very streets of Kensington, endangering their children. Protesting to the legislature, they "frame[d] their resistance with appeals to constitutional rights." But their protests were ignored by the legislature, so residents took matters into their own hands, blocking laborers, destroying railroad ties, and diverting shipments of rails. Beyond the site of the "riot," that section of the railroad was never completed, and to this day the tracks stop where their construction was halted by the people of Kensington almost two centuries earlier.[62]

Traditions of resistance spawned by conditions in the mills of England, and transferred to Kensington by trade union veterans, were also common features of the community. William Sylvis, who in 1860 brought several local unions together to form the National Union of Iron Moulders, lived at 1112 Ash Street (now East Fletcher Street) in greater Kensington. After returning from the Civil War in 1866, he founded the National Labor Union, the first national federation of unions in the United States. The story of John Makin, related earlier, is typical of the traditions brought by trade union veterans, as is the story of another textile worker, Edwin Cooke, who came to Kensington in 1887 from Kidderminster, in Worcestershire, England. The son of a carpet weaver whose father was president of his union in England, upon his arrival he went to work at Hardwick and Magee, a Kensington carpet mill, and "became active in the union, as was natural coming from strong union stock." As subsequent influxes of people arrived throughout the nineteenth and early twentieth centuries, a form of "working-class cosmopolitanism" developed within the community, as radical thinkers within it worked to build a broader cosmopolitan movement that forged connections with progressive movements and ideas elsewhere, sometimes with major impact for the labor movement.[63]

The meeting of a group of craftsmen in a Kensington row house to form the Knights of Labor changed the very nature of the American labor movement. The Knights of Labor, arguably the late nineteenth century's most significant labor organization, had important consequences for Kensington's women workers. In 1884–85 an eight-month strike by female carpet weavers in Kensington over pay cuts and working conditions gained the support of male loom fixers, who struck in sympathy, with no demands of their own. The Knights of Labor threw its support behind the strike and collected funds in the neighborhood to sustain the strikers. The Knights generated strong community support, demonstrated through a wave of sympathy strikes, community protests, a "brutal riot" directed at strikebreakers, and a dramatic labor parade that stretched for three miles across the city. When the Knights officially admitted women into the organization in the early 1880s, the female power-loom weavers in Kensington's mills formed one of its first female assemblies. The Knights' ideology included an early form of "labor feminism" which supported not only women's suffrage but also equal pay for women, equal rights within the organization whether women were employed outside or inside the home, and a commitment to female education.[64]

These legacies lived on in Kensington in the continuous support for working-class struggles and "rights." Those struggles included the 1903 silk textile strike and "Children's Crusade," which began in Kensington and grew to include 75,000 workers, 16,000 of them children. That strike prompted another visit to Kensington from Mother Jones when she came to the area to lead it.[65]

In 1910 the Philadelphia general strike, sparked by the arbitrary firing of 173 union men by the Philadelphia Rapid Transit Company, also spun off sympathy strikes in Kensington, generating crowds estimated at 10,000 strong. As violence escalated over the importation of scab labor, the mayor called in "special police" and the state police to subdue the rioting. Confrontations in Kensington led to the wounding of six people, including a fourteen-year-old girl, by armed strikebreakers on one of the trolley cars. When news of the shooting of the girl spread through the neighborhood, a band of men, armed with rifles and shotguns, confronted the strikebreakers. Stopping the progress of the car, the Kensington men "implored [the strikebreakers] to open fire again so that they might have an opportunity to return the fire." The strikebreakers declined, and police arrived in time to disperse the crowd before more violence occurred.[66]

Textile strikes were a recurrent feature of life throughout Kensington's history, and the participation of women, in the workplace and in the community, was often crucial if they were to succeed. These ongoing experiences within its factory-based culture helped to reinforce a form of historical memory that was passed on within the community, laying the groundwork for a class consciousness that celebrated the rights of working people and challenged dominant middle-class gender ideologies. The hosiery union would consciously build on this history to sustain its activities throughout the 1920s and 1930s.

The Full-Fashioned Hosiery Industry and the Union

By the mid-1920s, four out of five of the young workers of Kensington had been born in America, although almost half of them had parents who were foreign born.[67] As the "roaring twenties" hit, the hosiery industry modernized and went through a tremendous expansion, moving from primarily cotton hosiery to a concentration on seamed, full-fashioned hosiery, and shifting to the broad use of sheer silk fibers.

This expansion coincided with the flapper culture and the shorter skirt, which made the stocking an important item for both daytime and evening wear. George Taylor described machines of "increasingly finer gauge, higher speed, and greater capacity," creating an ever-sheerer and fragile product. Stockings also became more affordable, although not inexpensive. The demand for sheer, well-fitting stockings to complement short skirts skyrocketed by the mid-1920s. The hosiery industry became one of the largest in Philadelphia, with shops ranging in size from under 50 employees to over 2,000. In 1929, Philadelphia's hosiery manufacturers valued their products at over $300 million.[68]

Kensington's traditions of solidarity often carried over into the small business community. For example, the Kensington Small Businessman's Association filed a complaint with the mayor in 1930 because police were "spending all their time arresting hosiery strikers." And sometimes neighborhood support could even manifest itself among local officials, as demonstrated during another hosiery strike, during which the *Philadelphia Record* reported: "It has been intimated by the Northeast Chamber of Commerce that magistrates living in the strike area might be prevented through a sense of neighborliness from prosecuting their duties in strike cases as vigorously as possible."[69]

The collective milieu of Kensington provided the base for its history, but the class-conscious, mass united action of the 1920s and 1930s also required the existence of formal organization, and it was the Socialist Party, with local, national, and international connections, that played the largest role in the development of that organization. Ensconced in the left wing of the party, with an ideology that envisioned a broad social and economic democracy, Kensington's Socialists, along with some other radicals, were vital to the efforts to organize hosiery workers during this period.

The prominent role of Socialists in the hosiery union is not surprising, for Philadelphia had a long relationship with socialism. Following the relocation of the Marxist International Workingmen's Association from London to New York in 1872, it was in Philadelphia that the International met in convention two years later. At this convention delegates made the decision to establish "a true working men's party, that is, a socialist party." Socialists were also active among many of the groups that came into the area over the years, and networks extended into and out of the city as activists of different persuasions often joined forces. In 1886 Kensington's German Socialists hosted two members of the German Reichstag on their first stop of a tour of the major cities of the country to help raise money for the election expenses of the Socialist Party of Germany. During the 1910 streetcar strike a female organizer for the Western Federation of Miners who was both "a Socialist and a Suffragist" spoke to Kensington's huge crowds, encouraging them to "show the Rapid Transit Company that we have rights and are powerful." There were also many socialist singing societies in Philadelphia, among them the Karl Marx Singing Society of the German branch of the Socialist Party. German singing societies were a prominent feature of early twentieth-century Philadelphia, and they had a large working-class membership. When Leopold Stokowski, the rising star of the Philadelphia Orchestra, needed a chorus of 180 for a grand performance of Beethoven's Ninth Symphony in March 1914, he turned to Philadelphia's German singers. Listed in the German American clubs' address book for the year 1914 were several societies in Kensington that had large halls in the neighborhood, including the Workers' Men's Chorus, the Women's Chorus of the Socialist School at the Kensington Labor Lyceum, and the Singing Section of the Kensington Labor Lyceum.[70]

Howard Kreckman's father, a textile worker who worked in a dye house, was a Socialist, and Kreckman clearly remembered his own initiation: "My father was a member of the Socialist Party. I was pretty young when he took me to hear Eugene Debs speak. I remember him very well, he was a really great orator. I didn't vote for him because I wasn't old enough. I voted on age, and the first one I voted for was Norman Thomas." Eugene Debs was able to command large crowds when he made public appearances, and his lectures touched the hearts and souls of countless individuals.[71] In Kreckman's recollections, socialism was part of the very fabric of the community: "The Socialists used to hold street meetings all the time. They'd get a soapbox out on the corner, that was common. They would hold concerts also, down at Music Fund Hall, down towards the river. There was a little four-piece ensemble that would entertain and then there would be a speech. They played classical music usually . . . those musicians were from the Philadelphia Orchestra . . . also, Scott Nearing would speak. He'd come every year and lecture at the Friends' Meeting House in Frankford."[72]

Ever since its founding, Philadelphia had been one of the nation's premier commercial cities, with a large, skilled artisan population. During the nineteenth century it transformed into an industrial city that produced a wide variety of goods. Its industries drew many workers who joined unions, which in turn affiliated with the city's Central Labor Union.[73] Many of those unions were in Kensington, and one of them, which started out small but became the most important in the city and one of the most important in the country in the 1920s, was the AFFFHW.

Founded in Kensington at a meeting at B Street and Allegheny Avenue in 1909, the hosiery union had roots that stretched directly back to the Knights of Labor. A member interviewed in 1931, describing the process by which the union was born, said: "Forty-nine men put in their fees that night and formed the union. I was one of them. My father had been a member of the Knights of Labor. A couple of the other men had been members themselves."[74] In 1913 it became a national organization, the AFFFHW, and affiliated with the AFL through the United Textile Workers. The Philadelphia local was Branch 1, and its hall was also the headquarters for the national union. The AFFFHW's union hall, located on Fourth Street near Huntingdon Street in Kensington, was destined to become the central meeting place of the working-class movement in the area.

A multitude of facets of the community of Kensington—its history, traditions, and geography—worked together to counter the doldrums that the general labor movement found itself in throughout the 1920s and early 1930s. The very foundations of the working-class district laid the groundwork for a vibrant labor movement to grow and prosper. But there were other reasons for the success of this crusade for the rights of working men and women. Changing gender ideas, the working-class internationalism of the Socialists and others, and the increasingly militant and sophisticated actions of the hosiery workers' union, as historian Lisa McGirr has said, "built on earlier networks, solidarities, and identities" to turn Kensington's oppositional subculture into a conscious movement that would bridge the gap between earlier high points of labor and women's activism and the reemergence of national movements in the CIO and New Deal eras and beyond.[75]

CHAPTER TWO

The Evolution of a Fighting Union

Since 1918, workers have faced the united onslaught of organized capital. . . . We should not for one moment forget that we are part of the organized workers' movement.

—Gustave Geiges, October 18, 1922

As the country stood on the cusp of the Jazz Age of the 1920s, the American labor movement entered a critical period, and nowhere did this become clearer than in Kensington. In the aftermath of World War I the contradictions between capital and labor were thrown into sharp relief as manufacturers increasingly attempted to control the shop floor, enforce anti-union "open shops," and consolidate power unimpeded by organized workers.[1] As part of the nationwide attempt to destroy the labor movement, in full swing by 1921, hosiery mill owners in Kensington, in association with the National Association of Manufacturers (NAM), initiated an open-shop drive, cut wages, and attempted to increase the workload of their employees. Unlike many working people, who suffered defeats in their attempts to improve working conditions, Kensington's hosiery workers, organized in Local 706 of the United Textile Workers of America (UTWA), decisively won a citywide strike in 1919 that gave them a forty-eight-hour week and control over the industry in Philadelphia. But it was a short-lived victory, for in 1921 battle lines were again drawn when hosiery manufacturers initiated a lockout. Although the result was one of the longest and, for union members, most emotionally wrenching strikes in the neighborhood's history, it was yet again ultimately successful. With strike benefits running low and networks of community and kinship stretched to the limit, the fight by members of Local 706 against a system they compared to slavery gained the support of hosiery workers in locals around the country. Most of those locals were in a different union, the American Federation of Full-Fashioned Hosiery Workers (AFFFHW), which had become an independent union after it had split six years earlier from the American Federation of Labor (AFL) and its own Branch 1, which remained in the AFL as Local 706 of the UTWA.

The strike proved to be decisive for the local union and the AFFFHW, however, for in its aftermath all segments of the union reunited into an organization that would subsequently help change the very direction of the labor movement. By the conclusion of 1922 the AFFFHW was a unified organization, with Local 706 returned to its original designation as Branch 1 of the union and its national headquarters once again back in Kensington. With a mandate from its rank and file, the newly energized organization set out on an ambitious quest to build what it termed a "fighting union," to fully organize its industry in a no-holds-barred follow-the-shops movement. This organizational consolidation would not only change the fate of the hosiery workers but would help rebuild the strength of American labor.

The Strikes for Survival

When Howard Kreckman was hired as a hosiery knitter's helper in 1917, he worked long hours for very little pay. At that time, so-called helpers were paid by the knitters they worked for, and since their wages came out of the knitter's own paycheck, this was reflected in their pay rate. Knitters were also docked for any mistakes found in the product, and they had to pay for extra needles for their machines—expensive items that could significantly affect their compensation. This system kept costs down for the manufacturers, but it did not do much to improve the living standards of the workers. Such conditions had helped to fuel the militancy of Kensington's textile workers throughout their history as these realities of work—combined with life in the community—reinforced resistance among many of Kensington's residents.[2]

The full employment brought about by the mobilization of the economy for World War I brought many gains for American workers in the form of higher wages and greater unionization. But it also brought a dramatic expansion in the repressive machinery of the state. Using the Espionage and Sedition Acts, the Bureau of Investigation infiltrated spies into factories and collaborated with private labor police, and U.S. Military Intelligence ignored the Constitution and spied on civilians.[3]

When the war ended, working-class consumers were hit hard by runaway inflation, which doubled the prices working families had to pay for many necessities compared to those before the war. And as employers attempted to push back gains their workers had made during the war, the country erupted in rebellion, but not always directed against employers. Although Philadelphia escaped the serious racial disorders that affected Chicago, East Saint Louis, and some other cities, it was not immune to the social upheavals that rocked many American communities after the war. Racial disturbances did erupt in communities in South Philadelphia. In 1918 bombs (attributed to an anarchist group) damaged the homes of the president of the Chamber of

Commerce, the acting superintendent of police, and a judge, and during the nationwide strikes of 1919 two bombings occurred in West Philadelphia, and police were, at times, on round-the-clock patrols.[4]

The wave of repression that swept the country in the postwar crackdown on labor began even earlier for Kensington's textile workers, including hosiery workers, as they came under surveillance by Military Intelligence as early as 1917. In September of that year police raided the offices of the IWW Textile Workers Industrial Union, located on East Allegheny Avenue in the heart of the neighborhood, and confiscated all of their records, including many radical pamphlets. In October, while investigating a strike in Kensington, a private agent, along with a member of the American Protective League, sent a report to the Justice Department describing a "visit" that he made to a meeting at the headquarters of the Full-Fashioned Hosiery Knitters of Philadelphia, UTWA Local 706, at which they allegedly overheard discussion planning a general strike.[5]

Although the hosiery union was founded in Kensington in 1909, officially becoming a national union—the AFFFHW—in 1913, divisions within the union, embedded in the politics of a larger debate within the American Left, resulted, by 1915, in a six-year split. Some branches outside of Philadelphia opposed the union's affiliation with the AFL, seeing it as a hindrance to the building of strong unions. These groups, along with one other small branch in Philadelphia (Branch 14, controlling three shops), advocated for independent unionism outside of the AFL-affiliated UTWA. Philadelphia Local 706, which was by far the largest hosiery local in the country, supported the position of working within the mainstream of the labor movement and remained affiliated with the AFL as an autonomous local within the UTWA. In other regions (and in Philadelphia Branch 14) the hosiery federation went off on its own and operated as an independent union. The strength of the two factions was approximately equal, however, and Local 706 contained about as many members as all of the other locals combined as they entered into the Philadelphia general hosiery strike of 1919.[6]

Shortly after his sixteenth birthday, Howard Kreckman, a member of Kensington Local 706, participated in his first strike, the "strike for the forty-eight-hour week." The split in the union meant that Kensington's Local 706 entered the strike with no help from the rest of the hosiery federation, which did not join in. At this time Philadelphia's hosiery workers were working fifty-four hours a week or more, but wages were also an issue, and agitation for wage increases to offset inflation had already begun by the fall of 1918 in Philadelphia. When the Full-Fashioned Hosiery Manufacturers Association (FHMA) refused to agree to a settlement, Local 706 called a strike in January 1919. In February they added the demand for the forty-eight-hour week, as they had agreed to do at the 1918 UTWA convention when a strike vote was taken on that issue.[7]

Over 1,200 union members and several thousand others, many of them women, walked out. Although there were women in the union at this time, most women in the industry were still unorganized, for even though the hosiery union was an industrial organization and had been open to women since 1914, it still functioned essentially as a knitter-led organization with power structures based on a fairly decentralized shop steward system that was male-dominated. Nonetheless, although they were often angry at being ignored in shop meetings, many women workers joined the men on the picket lines. It was during this period that the union uncovered its first known labor spy. Still a knitter's helper at the time, Howard Kreckman clearly remembered when Local 706 uncovered a "fink" from the Railway Audit Company at one of its meetings.[8]

Within three months, however, an upswing in consumer demand for full-fashioned hosiery had begun to develop, and in a move the historian Philip Scranton described as "sacrificing principle to profit," the manufacturers, less organized at the time, agreed to meet with the union. By April 12, 1919, the strike had ended with a clear victory for Local 706. The agreement included the forty-eight-hour week as well as wage increases of from 15 to 20 percent. Management also acceded to the demand that all new machines were to be operated on the basis of one knitter to one machine, and to a stipulation that the wages of the helpers would henceforth be paid by the company and not out of the knitter's pay. This was the first general hosiery strike in the city, and it securely established Local 706 as firmly in control of the Philadelphia industry.[9]

As has been the case throughout the history of labor, it was that very issue of "control" that was the most contentious of the contradictions between the union and the manufacturers. Philadelphia's textile families guarded control of the shops very jealously, never easily accepting challenges to their power. The hosiery workers, on the other hand, as the ones who produced the product, felt that the industry belonged to them as much as it did to the manufacturers. This view was flatly stated by the secretary of the union in 1925, when he said, "I am a firm believer that this industry is just as much ours, if not more so, than it is the employers." Incorporated within the workers' sense of ownership was a strong sense of pride in their work and in their organization. Union representatives emphasized the importance of high-quality work, and it was a matter of principle that workers should be paid fairly, consulted about changes affecting the production of the product, and have a say over their working conditions. Hosiery manufacturers, on the other hand, harbored deep feelings about their "rights" to run shops as they desired, hiring whomever they pleased, demanding long hours, and paying the wages of their choice. In 1921, when the issue of this basic contradiction between the workers and the manufacturers again came to a head, it precipitated an industry lockout that led to another general hosiery strike that sorely tested the resolve of the city's hosiery workers, yet, ultimately, firmly established the heart of the union in Kensington.[10]

These events in Kensington's hosiery sector were part of an intense antiunion drive in Philadelphia led by local industrialists and backed by the city government. Although the city did very little to enforce the federal laws of Prohibition, the mayor and the manufacturers used the power of the police and court injunctions to curtail any organizational momentum within the city's unions. By 1921 the collusion between the two, and the combined violence of city and private police, succeeded in brutally smashing strikes by Kensington's carpet weavers and its shipyard workers at Cramp's Shipyard.

In the case of the shipyard strike, when over 7,000 union and nonunion men struck in protest of management's firing of union members, the company hired professional strikebreakers and armed private police to blatantly attack pickets, resulting in the death of at least one and the wounding of many others. Joining in the carnage, Philadelphia's mayor, J. Hampton Moore, declared martial law and dispatched 1,000 officers and mounted police to the scene. Their brutality gained the strikers much local sympathy and support in Kensington. Local physicians came to their aid; neighbors organized food drives; and shopkeepers refused to sell groceries to strikebreakers. But faltering markets and a recession in many industries made it difficult to maintain funds for the strikers. The lack of funds, police repression, and the craft nature of many of the unions involved in the strike, eventually leading to dissent over jurisdictional boundaries, caused the strike to fall apart by the fall of 1921. During this same period, however, hosiery workers were also out on strike; but for the hosiery union the events of 1921 represented a watershed. Not only did they win, but it was this strike that reunited the hosiery federation and brought about the reestablishment of Kensington as the home of its national headquarters.[11]

The most important issues in the strike were those of shop control, this time as embodied in the fight over the "two-machine system." From the early days of the union, the double-job system, in which one knitter with two helpers operated two machines, was a point of contention. Full-fashioned hosiery knitting machines were complicated pieces of equipment. Very large, with each machine producing many pairs of hosiery at a time, they contained over 10,000 needles that had to be kept in perfect alignment at all times. It was the responsibility of the knitter to make sure that this was always the case. The knitters also worked with expensive and extremely fine threads of silk. As the shops were frequently inadequately lighted, the job often resulted in serious eyestrain for the knitters. In addition to the added stress the two-machine system posed, union workers contended that the system was a "blind alley" for helpers, who would become trained as knitters, only to become part of a "surplus army of labor" for whom there would not be enough skilled knitter jobs. One of the demands agreed to by the manufacturers' association after the 1919 strike was that there would be no doubling of new machines in the Philadelphia area, and that the number of apprentices would be controlled by the observance of a four-year apprenticeship.[12]

In 1921 this issue was once more at the heart of a pitched battle between the union and the manufacturers. By that time the local hosiery manufacturers had assembled a new coalition composed of the FHMA firms and six additional companies, who together employed five out of every six workers in Philadelphia's full-fashioned sector. These sons of the textile trades' elders, along with their local association, affiliated with the NAM and demanded an open shop, in a movement the AFFFHW newspaper described as being "called for the special benefit of scabs and bosses who want to have the workers toil for small wages and long hours, the 'American Plan.'" The owners sought a 15 percent reduction in wages and the two-machine shop—a move designed to increase the pool of knitters and swell the available labor supply. In a secret ballot, UTWA Local 706 refused to accept their terms, and Branch 14 did the same, standing in a spirit of solidarity not seen since the split in the organization. Again, women struck with men, and thus began the general strike of 1921, a strike that would become legendary in the history of the hosiery federation. Almost every full-fashioned mill in the city was closed down or crippled, with only the Gotham and Lehigh mills operating at full force with no change in wage scales and under the single-machine system. By April the manufacturers and the hosiery workers, men and women, were locked in a bitter fight over the principle of a system of labor that the workers defined as equal to slavery. Both union locals refused the manufacturers' offer of minor concessions because the latter were still insisting on doubling the workload of the knitters.[13]

As an autonomous local within the UTWA, Local 706 strikers were receiving little support from that organization (which had very few resources), and funds were running low as injunctions, police intimidation, and attacks by private police escalated dramatically. Philadelphia's notorious labor police charged pickets with drawn clubs, routinely arresting strikers, who were then held on bail as high as $1,500, further exacerbating the situation. The strikers also fought back, physically and by using any other means they could come up with. One strategy was to widely publicize the names of anyone who chose to scab, playing upon the class loyalty of the community. Union literature portrayed "contemptible scabs" and "deserters" as the lowest things on earth, and carried "heroic" stories about strikers. One story described a fight between a sixty-year-old striker and a scab, saying about the striker that "according to all reports, he gave a good account of himself despite his age." Another carried the name of one of Kensington's "soft-glove" fighters who had chosen to be a strikebreaker. This article warned that some of the men in the union were taking boxing lessons "in hopes of getting a crack at the scab."[14]

These stories drew upon traditional community practices of shaming and not only served to ensure that strikebreakers would be subjected to the disdain of the community, but also held them up to ridicule, as they celebrated the "manly" traditions of standing up to the good fight—traditions that had no age limits and were not actually limited by gender either. Drawing on the language of class, union leaders described the strike as "a sort of war between bosses and employees that must be conducted according to laws that workers don't make," and accused the police of assuming autocratic powers, making picketing as difficult as possible, and even interfering with such "innocent pastimes" as strikers playing ball. In fact, the ball playing was an innovative method for circumventing police restrictions in an attempt to access the mill gates. As the stalemate wore on, the situation was becoming desperate on both sides, with some firms offering knitters $60–100 a week, police protection (which, given the disposition of the strikers by this point, it is reasonable to assume they would have needed), and two-year contracts if they would only, as an article in the *Hosiery Worker* put it, "come back as 'instructors' for those skunks that the firm wants to train." Nonetheless, it was not easy for the manufacturers to get many takers, for at this time in Kensington "scabbing it" not only meant that one would be socially ostracized, but also was not particularly healthy for the strikebreaker or anyone associated with him. As one textile worker said in regard to scabbing: "I do care for my hide and I don't like to be called a scab."[15]

Mill owners did not hesitate to hire professional strikebreakers who fired into crowds that often included women, further enraging strikers and sparking sometimes violent retaliation. On one occasion thirteen men and three women were arraigned on charges that they were members of "wrecking crews," or "bodies of men and women who marched around the strike area and battered in doors and smashed windows of houses tenanted by workers who scabbed or refused to go on strike." Often these crews doused the houses with yellow paint as a marker before vandalizing them. Jeanne Callahan remembered that her uncle (a policeman) talked about getting his house on Aramingo Avenue "cheap," because it had been a "scab" house and had yellow paint all over it and lots of broken windows. And if a local "scabbed it," his reputation could follow him to his grave.[16]

As the strike dragged on, the lack of an income was creating an increasingly serious situation for the strikers, and the leadership of Local 706 scrambled to raise funds. Although community networks of kinship, neighbors, and small shopkeepers were helping as much as they could, in a community where subsistence was often a struggle, those resources were stretched to the limit. Local 706 held dances and various other forms of entertainment at the union hall, and officials gave many speeches about "the darkest hour before the dawn" in attempts to keep up morale.[17]

It was at this point that the national AFFFHW executive board entered the fight on behalf of Local 706, although they were not officially affiliated at this time. Sincerely affected by the battle the workers were fighting and fearful that hardship would break the strike, the board sent out a referendum to all of its branches (themselves not involved in the strike) asking for support for Local 706's members "so that the Philadelphia strikers will not have to fight on empty stomachs." As Philadelphia was the center of the hosiery trade, and the membership of Local 706 was by far the largest of any hosiery local in the country, they all realized that the strike had to be won if the association was to survive. But it was also the spirit and sacrifices of the strikers themselves that moved the others, some with close connections to the striking workers, to come to their support. After urgent and intense discussion in meetings in all branches, the AFFFHW membership approved the referendum, and workers in hosiery locals from as far away as Milwaukee, Wisconsin, began to assess themselves to send aid to Kensington's striking men and women so that, as one described it, "workers will not be troubled again by 'war profiteers' who say cut labor first." The AFFFHW's board also approved a donation of $5,000 to be sent for immediate assistance, and personal commitments poured in. A member of Providence, Rhode Island's Branch 15 even offered to support a family of four of a Kensington striker.[18]

By June 1921 the six independent manufacturers settled on the union's terms, without altering pay rates or work rules, but the FHMA still refused to negotiate, even though by this time the loss of production was beginning to intersect with a major growth in demand. Other manufacturers were beginning to enter the industry, and former strikers at the independents also added money to the strike fund. Still, the FHMA group, led by William Meyer of the large Apex mill (an establishment that was to figure prominently in union affairs in years to come), maintained the position that the strikers were "starving," and stubbornly refused to settle for another eighteen weeks. Buoyed by the support they were receiving, however, Kensington strikers were able to continue to hold out, although some had, by this point, been on strike since November 1920.[19]

Finally, by the end of October 1921 all but a very few of the manufacturers fully capitulated, agreeing to maintain recognition of the organization, rescind the cuts, and "single" all jobs. That agreement was a major win for both Branch 1 and the AFFFHW and for the "fighting spirit, endurance, and sacrifice" of the Philadelphia strikers, as the union paper editorialized.[20]

At the end of November 1921 the AFFFHW sent out a referendum ballot to its entire membership. One question was on that ballot: "Should the Federation reunite with Local 706 and affiliate with the UTWA as an autonomous organization?" Under such an affiliation the AFFFHW would retain all jurisdiction over matters not directly affecting UTWA, retain its own central treasury, call its own strikes, and maintain its own constitution and by-laws. When the UTWA agreed "in writing with the signatures and seal of the UTWA attached" to accept the hosiery federation on the same autonomous terms as Local 706, the Philadelphia local reunited with the federation, becoming, once more, Branch 1 of the AFFFHW; the AFFFHW reaffiliated with the UTWA, working within the AFL; and the national headquarters returned, once again, to Kensington. Thus, while labor uprisings were going down to defeat in other areas of Philadelphia, as evidenced by the carpet weavers' and the Cramp's strikes, as well as in large sectors of the national labor movement such as meatpacking and steel, Philadelphia's hosiery workers were moving forward toward the establishment of a strong national organization poised to be among those in the forefront of a movement to rebuild labor and the Congress of Industrial Organizations (CIO) drive for national unity.[21]

The story of the AFFFHW in this difficult period for labor raises the question of why it differed from the national narrative. Certainly market forces played a role. The 1919 strike took place in the midst of a consumer surge for their product. But, more important, the manufacturers were less centralized at that time, and in the face of increasing demand for the product they splintered and settled. But the 1921 strike was long and bitter, with some of the workers on strike for over a year. This time the FHMA was well organized; they had the support and power of the courts and police, both private and public, and they used those powers ruthlessly in their determination to starve out the strikers and break the union. Given those realities, understanding how the union managed to outlast the manufacturers is very important. There were, in fact, several factors that acted together to bring about a victory for the hosiery workers.[22]

The strikers had the support of a community with long traditions of labor solidarity behind them. Kensington was the center of the hosiery trade, and as the industry required a high level of skill, management could not easily replace hosiery workers by randomly bringing in strikebreakers from outside. Some mills recruited experienced workers from other areas, such as Reading, Pennsylvania, and the Midwest, but these scabs met a very cold reception in the community. If fights developed with union workers, they could expect little sympathy from other residents (male or female), who more than likely would end up in the middle of the fray themselves. Within the community the hosiery strikers knew quite well that scabs would be ostracized, and the publication of the names of any who made the attempt assured that these individuals could not do so with impunity.

Most residents also had little sympathy with the strikebreaking activities of the city police, as many had been forced to contend with similar situations themselves, and neighbors often did their best to hinder police activities and attempted arrests. Additionally, as residents of the community themselves, strikers were embedded in multiple networks of kinship and neighborhood that depended upon communal traditions and subsistence strategies to get them through the course of their lives, and they were able to draw upon these networks for financial as well as social support. But in such a long and bitterly fought battle, occurring in the midst of an economic downturn for some industries, community networks were stretched thin and by themselves could not have enabled the hosiery workers to outlast the manufacturers so dramatically. There was another reason that worked in favor of success for the union, one that was to become central in the battles of the 1920s and 1930s: the existence of a coordinated national organization, with a strong progressive leadership, that could provide not only tactical and ideological sustenance, but, through a central treasury, material aid as well.

The historian Lizabeth Cohen, analyzing the failure of the 1919 strikes in Chicago, described the problems encountered by unions with little national organization facing off against employers who were well versed in operating on a national scale. Workers' inexperience with national movements and the existence of union locals in different cities that operated with little coordination weakened the possibility of united action, while employers could utilize their networks, or in the case of very large corporations, direct the national battle against unions from centralized corporate headquarters. In these ways they were able to organize their responses, have a unified strategy to deal with unions, and outlast the resources of their workers.[23]

The hosiery manufacturers in Philadelphia also adopted these strategies, pooling their resources and coordinating their actions in a hard-nosed attempt to force the strikers to accept their terms. While facing the specter of losing business to other areas as the industry picked up, they gambled that the lack of bread and butter would force their workers to capitulate—as it had done in shipbuilding, carpet weaving, and other industries nationally in which unions had been weakened during the period. But as a direct descendant of Philadelphia's Knights of Labor, with strong connections to the left wing of the Socialist Party, and with an open policy of membership that included IWW members and Communists, the AFFFHW, including Branch 1, not only had a democratic form of organization but practiced an ideology of unity, and was experienced with national organization and coordination. What's more, it espoused an expansive industrial form of organization, long encouraged by socialists, that united workers across a spectrum of occupations and ideologies, and also included a central treasury system that could be used to funnel funds where they were needed. Displaying this progressive ideology in national solidarity and promoting an understanding of the economic base of class contradictions, the union leadership closed ranks in a broad-based movement. The money that was forwarded to Philadelphia's strikers provided necessary material aid that helped them to survive long enough to outlast and defeat the manufacturers. The lessons learned by this display of solidarity, including the ability to draw on the central treasury, would be important in the upcoming struggles of the 1920s and 1930s, and in 1921 it helped the newly united AFFFHW move forward into a new era of activism.

Leaders of a New Labor Movement

As the AFFFHW began to take a place in the national labor narrative, a few activists, almost all starting on the shop floor, began to rise from among their contemporaries to play central roles in the history that was unfolding. They can be divided into two categories, the first comprised of older, experienced leaders who had been with the union since its earliest days, and a second group of newer recruits brought into leadership during and after the expansion of the industry in the 1920s. Included in the first group were some from the leadership of branches outside of Philadelphia, like Carl Holderman, who played an important role in implementing national campaigns. Four other "elders" who were of prime importance through the 1920s and 1930s were Philadelphia's Gustave Geiges, Alexander McKeown, and Edward Callaghan, and James Maurer of Reading, the president of the Pennsylvania Federation of Labor. A sixth member of the old guard, Emil Rieve, moved to Philadelphia from his base in Milwaukee as he rose in the reunited union.

Carl Holderman was a member of the AFFFHW from its early period. He was the head of the Passaic, New Jersey, branch and became the president of the New Jersey and New York District Council. In 1929, he was elected vice-chair of the Conference for Progressive Labor Action (CPLA), along with James Maurer.

Gustave Geiges, a knitter in Kensington's Gotham shop, had been in the union since its early days. He was a Socialist and the president of Local 706, Branch 1 in the early and mid-1920s. As president of Branch 1 he commanded a great deal of respect and was extremely important in the decision-making processes of the hosiery federation, serving consistently on the executive board after the consolidation of the AFFFHW. He was elected president of the national federation in 1927 and served for two years, until his retirement in 1929. Through the 1920s he presided over the period of intense expansion within the industry and helped to initiate the important follow-the-shops organizing drives of the union.

Alexander McKeown, the son of an immigrant Scottish steel puddler, was also a knitter, born in Kensington. McKeown first started work in a Kensington mill at the age of thirteen as an apprentice, working sixty hours a week. He was one of the founders of the union, and in its early years he hopped freight trains on weekends to "spread the union gospel" to other areas, most notably Fort Wayne, Indiana, where he helped organize Branch 2. He was vice president of Branch 1, becoming president of the Philadelphia local in 1927 and later of the AFFFHW. McKeown was a prominent Philadelphia Socialist, a member of the CPLA, a founder of the Labor Education Association, and a candidate for mayor of Philadelphia in 1931 on the socialist Labor Party ticket.

Rounding out this Philadelphia group was Edward Callaghan, a radical full-time organizer from Philadelphia. Callaghan had also been with the union from its early days, and his significance increased as the follow-the-shops campaigns gained momentum. Traveling to the South, to Reading, Pennsylvania, to the Midwest, and to any other location where attempts to organize new locals were in progress, he was a stalwart of the organization. Despite numerous threats and arrests, he was always in the thick of the action, usually carrying "a carload of radical literature."

In addition to these union personnel, another person who had a major influence on the development of the union, though he was not actually a member, was James Maurer. Maurer, a machinist from Reading, Pennsylvania, became a socialist after joining the Knights of Labor in 1880. He had been taught to read at the age of sixteen by a fellow worker who was a founder of the Knights. Maurer became a member of the executive board of the Socialist Party of America and president of the Pennsylvania Federation of Labor from 1912 to 1928. He was also elected, as a Socialist, to the Pennsylvania state legislature, from 1911 to 1913 and again from 1915 to 1917, and was a candidate for vice president of the United States on the Socialist ticket with Norman Thomas in both 1928 and 1932. With a deep commitment to eliminating child labor and for workers' education, he was president of the Workers' Education Bureau of America, a board member and founder of Brookwood Labor College, and a founder of the American Birth Control League. Maurer was a regular speaker at Branch 1 events and at national union conventions. An influential ally in the union's legislative initiatives, he was also an important supporter of their campaigns to organize women and build the labor movement more generally.[24]

Toward the end of the 1920s, Emil Rieve, a knitter from the Milwaukee branch, came onto the stage as a leading figure in the union, gaining in importance in the 1930s. Rieve immigrated to the United States from Poland at the age of thirteen and went to work in mills in Reading and Philadelphia, later moving on to Milwaukee. He joined the union and the Socialist Party at an early age. Rieve rose to prominence when he moved back to Philadelphia and was elected president of the AFFFHW in 1929, after Geiges retired and the union established a full-time presidency. There were three nominations for the position, but Alexander McKeown, at the time president of the powerful Branch 1, and Carl Holderman, president of the New Jersey and New York District Council, declined. Rieve would oversee a period of major change within the organization and go on to play a national role in the labor movement.[25]

Although they remained vital to the organization throughout the 1920s and 1930s, these elders of the leadership were also concerned with developing and training leaders from new recruits to the industry. These members of the younger generation were key additions to the union in its campaigns to build cross-generational and cross-gender solidarity.

Alfred "Tiny" Hoffmann started out as a member of the Milwaukee branch of the AFFFHW. He was a knitter, pulled out of the shops at the age of eighteen and sent on a federation scholarship to Brookwood Labor College. Moving to Philadelphia, Hoffmann was elected as a full-time union organizer in 1926. A Socialist and a committed supporter of the union, with an organic understanding of working-class culture, he became one of its most gifted organizers, having particular success in union endeavors to organize in the South.

John Edelman, though not a worker in the mills, was hired by the union in 1926 as its director of research and education. Edelman came to the United States in 1916 from England, during a rather dangerous time for travel, and under fairly obscure circumstances. Although born in the United States, he had been raised in an anarcho-socialist commune in England and educated by an eclectic group of intellectuals. He was a newspaper reporter with the British Labour Party in England, a labor organizer, and a member of the British suffrage movement. He also had connections to the Irish Republican struggle, which may have influenced his sudden 1916 emigration. Part of a broad-based Socialist network, he was originally brought to Pennsylvania, and recommended to the union, by James Maurer. Edelman was a major contributor to the successful Socialist electoral campaign that swept Reading, Pennsylvania, in 1927 (funded primarily by the hosiery union). A brilliant journalist, he turned the union newspaper into a powerful educational and organizing tool and developed extensive media networks that brought the union national attention.

As the union emphasized the organization of women in the 1920s, Anna Geisinger, a topper in the Gotham Hosiery Mill and a Socialist member of Branch 1, emerged as a central figure. A fearless and militant speaker, Geisinger was elected as the union's first full-time female organizer in 1928 and became one of its most effective (along with Hoffmann). She had excellent success organizing men as well as women, in Philadelphia and throughout the "western corridor" into Reading. She was the first female elected to the Philadelphia executive board, in 1927, and continued to be an important figure in the union into the 1930s, when she took charge of Philadelphia's 1933 citywide open-shop strike.

Finally, although the largest group among the union's leadership remained identified with the Socialists, there was a group of Communists in the union in the 1920s as well, and some of them became more prominent in Philadelphia's

Branch 1 by the 1930s. Joseph Burge, a hosiery knitter, was a fiery speaker, a "good orator," and an excellent organizer in the mills, working throughout the 1930s. In 1937 he was elected vice president of Branch 1, playing a role in the campaigns for the CIO in Philadelphia and, later, in other left-led unions.[26]

All of the activists introduced here will appear throughout the story of Kensington's hosiery workers told in this book. But just as most of them emerged from the shop floor to take on a more active role in their union and their community, other men and women continued to rise from the ranks to play irreplaceable roles in the history that unfolded, some in official positions, more in day-to-day organizing and clashes, and a few as martyrs.

A Fighting Union

After the successful strike of 1921 and the reunification of the union, the power of the organization surged, but the problems facing it were just beginning. Although in 1921 the union controlled over 75 percent of full-fashioned hosiery and almost all of the mills in Philadelphia, the industry entered a period of unprecedented growth, and this became a real challenge for the AFFFHW as the decade progressed.

A considerable portion of the investment of full-fashioned hosiery mills was tied up in fixed assets, usable for no purpose other than the knitting of hosiery. Because fixed charges were comparatively large (knitting machines—one for the leg and one for the foot—were expensive equipment) and the cost of silk was also substantial, the direct-labor segment of the cost of producing a pair of full-fashioned stockings was, by 1929, only 20 to 30 percent of the total cost of manufacture. This comparatively moderate percentage of labor cost to total cost existed despite the high level of earnings among hosiery workers in the 1920s. The industry was, therefore, in an intermediate position between capital-intensive industries that tended toward monopoly, such as steel, and cutthroat hypercompetitive labor-intensive industries like garment.

Barriers to entry into the business were still low enough, and the profit margins high enough, for the industry to attract investment from large corporations in the retail business and other textile sectors, and even foreign capital. Over the decade, however, hosiery began to behave much more like the highly competitive labor-intensive industries, attempting to utilize wage adjustments as a means of lowering the selling price of the final product. A steady flow of new companies, or subsidiaries of older ones, cropped up in various regions of the country, training their own help and undercutting union-made products. This development would eventually lead to a three-tier system of wages: one in the unionized sector, one in the sector dominated by Reading, Pennsylvania, and one in the South and parts of the Midwest.[27]

In the first half of the 1920s the expansion of the full-fashioned industry strengthened the hand of the union, as it brought about a situation of increased competition for the skilled labor that the manufacturers needed and the union largely controlled. Wages were high, and skilled union labor was in great demand. But as full-fashioned hosiery expanded, so too did the unorganized workforce, and union leaders became increasingly aware that maintaining control of the industry would require the organization of the workers being trained in the new shops and nonunion sectors. Immediately after the consolidation, union leaders began to work hard to convince members of the need for an aggressive campaign to fully unionize the shops. This would be a two-pronged effort: to bring the union into the new nonunion mills, and to expand union membership in already organized shops from the skilled knitters to include all workers in the mills, in the cases where the full workforce was not already organized into the union's industrial structure.

Branch 1 was the center of both the industry and the union. As the largest local in the union by far, with the right to the most convention delegates, its leadership had an immense influence on the policies of the national organization. When on July 11, 1922, an open letter from Gustave Geiges, president of Local 706, Branch 1 of the reunited AFFFHW, appeared in the *Hosiery Worker*, members throughout the national union would have taken it very seriously. Addressing the hosiery federation and the UTWA, Geiges commended the spirit of unity and cooperation displayed by members throughout the country when, during the strike of 1921, with "remarkable courage, and a desire for liberty, justice, and fair play," they made great sacrifices to ensure a reunited organization. As a result, he continued, the AFFFHW was one of the most progressive labor organizations in the country. But he also reminded the members that the manufacturers were involved in a "war" with the workers, and would do whatever they could to break the ranks of the AFFFHW. "In order to advance the workers' interests," Geiges wrote, "every member in every branch or local has to do his or her part to make their branch a '100%' organization" by being prepared to fight to organize those outside of the union.[28]

In addition to rallying the membership to the cause, union leaders realized they would need other resources. The strike of 1921 had reinforced the centrality of the treasury to successful organizing campaigns, for to engage in a fight with capital would require more than the undisputed courage of the membership. For this reason delegates to the 1922 convention approved a proposal to utilize the period of high wages to make the central treasury a "fighting treasury" for the purpose of building the union and, in the process, help to reinvigorate the labor movement more generally.[29]

To move forward with such plans, however, it was necessary for a steep emergency assessment to be levied on the rank and file, and according to the union's constitution, such a move required a polling of the general membership. A committee of delegates at the 1922 convention drafted a referendum proposal which was then sent to all branches of the AFFFHW for approval: "In the event that the central treasury should fall below $250,000, an assessment should be levied and continued until the treasury reaches $250,000" (the equivalent of $3.5 million in 2015 dollars) in order to "put the Federation in a position to fight Capital." That proposal was accompanied by an appeal for an increase in dues going to the local branches as well. The leadership of all locals were to hold meetings and discussions in their branches and conduct a vote of their membership, with the results to be sent back to national headquarters in Philadelphia.[30]

At meetings and forums and in the union's press, national leaders promoted a vigorous ideological and strategic debate. One article, copied from the financial pages of the *New York Herald*, described a plan by the full-fashioned manufacturers to spend $500,000 a year in a massive advertising campaign. It was accompanied by a pointed editorial in which Geiges, drawing on the labor theory of value, accused the manufacturers of using "stolen wages" to undercut the union: "The manufacturers contemplate this extensive expenditure of unpaid wages while pleading poverty. If they can spend such money to advertise the product, made possible by our labor, we must assume that the sky is the limit in trying to wreck our organization . . . reduce our wages, and further increase profits. While finances are not essential to progressive thought, they are essential to progressive plans of action . . . and we must always be militant, progressive, and if need be radical." When the membership overwhelmingly passed the referendum, the first step in the union's strategic vision was put into action. The treasury was indeed to become an important weapon in the wars with the manufacturers.[31]

Such an involved grassroots decision-making process might seem unusual for an AFL union, but it is reflective of the way in which the organization was structured. The early union membership was composed of individuals from various political persuasions and included Socialists, Wobblies, Communists, and independent radicals; but on the ground these activists often combined forces despite ideological differences that may have existed within the leadership. The union's diverse but democratic left orientation resulted in an activist organizational stance grounded in a socialist worldview but focused on practical advances.[32]

In earlier years many, although not all, of the plants controlled by the union did not sign written contracts, having instead individual verbal agreements with the national union or with its local bodies. These understandings covered wage rates, hours of work, helper regulations, and the acceptance of the policy of one knitter to one machine. The degree of unionization of individual shops varied from organizations controlling all departments to those that included only the knitters. The knitting occupations, legging and footing, as well as topping, looping, seaming, and boarding, were all considered occupations that called for specialized skill. Often, workers in occupations outside of knitting were not organized, although the union had embraced the concept of industrial organization from its inception.[33]

All members of the executive board were elected and had to stand for election every year, and it was required that at least 70 percent of the board consist of members actually working on machines. Those not working in a mill during their period on the board not only did the administrative work of the union but also acted as part-time organizers in various sections of the country. While on the board they received a rate of pay that could not exceed the highest rate paid to a knitter. In addition, there was a constitutional requirement that all major decisions had to be submitted to the membership for a referendum vote, and the constitution further stipulated that all resolutions had to be translated into the language of any member, at his or her request, in order to be valid. While the debates that occurred among delegates to the conventions reflected views within the broader organization, the existence of the referendum vote underscored the union's emphasis on democracy and allows for deeper insight into the extent of support that the rank and file gave to the policies of the leadership.[34]

The union embraced a broad-based policy of organization, and the constitution specifically stated that the organization was open to all individuals in the full-fashioned industry, with no exclusions. Further, another clause in the constitution prohibited discussions on religion, ethnicity, or political affiliation at meetings. However, resolutions and discussions regarding support for particular political positions could be, and were, openly and often heatedly discussed. This antisectarian policy proved to be a real strength in organizing campaigns, for it enabled union organizers to utilize extended networks. In the early period the primary base of power of the locals was located in a decentralized shop-steward system.[35]

While the structure of the organization was democratic in many ways, there were some glaring limitations. Women were admitted into the union in 1914, after it became a national organization and the constitution was drafted, but their power was marginal, and they had voting privileges equal to only one-third of men's—one vote for every 300 paid-up women members as opposed to one vote for every 100 paid-up men. There were no women on the executive board. And as there were no African Americans employed in the industry outside of a few in janitorial, there were none in the union. When they embarked on a campaign of full industrial organizing, union members concentrated their efforts on organizing those who were already employed in hosiery, with increasing attention paid to those who were not part of the highly organized knitting departments.[36]

As the 1920s advanced, however, the union's educational activities increasingly addressed ethnic and racial divisions within the working class, and the union gradually began to make women workers a major focus of organizing campaigns as their visibility increased in the popular culture of the Jazz Age and in the hosiery shops. Some of these advancements developed out of an evolving definition of equal rights that promoted a "solidarity" that crossed differences and a shared sense of common humanity that came out of a class-based understanding of the underlying forces behind inequality. For "class" was the primary lens through which the leadership, and many members, viewed the major contradictions in society. The clause in the original constitution requiring all motions to be translated into the native language of any member was reiterated in the constitution of the reunited organization and reflected the ethnic demographics of both Kensington and the AFFFHW.

As the union's "fighting treasury" began to grow, AFFFHW leadership increasingly encouraged a broad-based solidarity with an undercurrent of socialist internationalism. In the aftermath of labor's defeats, nationally and in Philadelphia, it was not hard to see that the ultimate fate of the hosiery workers could not be separated from that of the labor movement in general, for they had also "felt the hands of the manufacturers in injunctions, police intimidation, and paid thugs." But many also felt a sense of responsibility as members of a working class, as expressed in the union's newspaper: "Since 1918, workers have faced the united onslaught of organized capital . . . having suffered untold misery and privations for principle. Men, women and children have been beaten and leaders framed and sent to prison, even murder has been resorted to in an effort to crush organization. We should not for one moment forget that we are part of the organized workers' movement . . . it is not only necessary to build our organization, but make contributions to others."[37]

Labor solidarity became a hallmark of the hosiery union. It was a "code" incorporated in the union's founding charter, and both the actions and the results of votes by the general membership indicate that this code was disseminated within the rank and file in this period. Over the 1920s the union projected a powerful vision of workers' solidarity both inside and outside of its own organization. It supported community cooperatives and a labor bank in Philadelphia, promoted as an institution to "help prevent the labor hater from using [workers'] own money" against them. And it also projected an identity that incorporated a community sense of "neighborliness" as part of its role. An example of this can be seen in the case of a female member of Branch 1 who became seriously ill and could no longer work. She had three small children dependent on her, and Branch 1 members contributed to a fund to pay her thirty dollars a week until her death, after which they made arrangements to help with the care of her children by relatives. But the union also began to take an ever more aggressive role in promoting an international solidarity based on class.[38]

In 1922 Branch 1 submitted for referendum vote a proposal authorizing a contribution of $1,000 to the Friends of Soviet Russia to be used for relief work, as well as a call demanding recognition of the Soviet Union and the establishment of trade relations. Both passed overwhelmingly. Other votes included a resolution demanding that the governor of California grant pardons to labor leaders Tom Mooney and Warren Billings, and a call to the AFL for a general strike in support of striking railroad workers in 1922, to protest the violence and injunctions used against them.[39]

In late November 1922, following reports that the full-fashioned manufacturers had representatives in Germany for the express purpose of recruiting scabs, the union sent a German-speaking member from Branch 1 on a "secret mission" (kept secret so as not to alert the manufacturers) to meet with the German knitters' association, because leadership believed the Germans did not realize they were being recruited to scab. This trip resulted in a no-scabbing pledge by these workers, underscoring for union members the importance of the leadership's emphasis on internationalism. In January 1924 the membership passed a referendum calling for assistance to the German labor movement because of the "suffering and hardship brought about by the depreciation of the mark on the German people."[40]

By 1924 the organization had set up the outlines of a plan to provide pensions to protect against old age. Following the release of data by the state of Pennsylvania in December 1926 showing that only 6 percent of the dependent aged in America were receiving voluntary aid from firms or corporations,

AFFFHW staff began a legislative campaign for the enactment of government social legislation to protect all workers, making the union "among the first organizations to fight for a nation-wide social insurance program."[41]

As the union's "fighting treasury" grew, so did the union's efforts to help support and revitalize the labor movement and to encourage a broad sympathy for the suffering and struggles of working people as a class. At the 1922 convention delegates authorized a weekly donation of $700 for the New England textile strike, which was being bitterly fought out at the time. Branch 1 collected additional money for the strikers from Philadelphia shops, as well as clothing, including over 5,000 pairs of shoes. All locals were recruited to send aid to miners' strikes in western Pennsylvania, with Branch 1 also sending clothing, blankets, and footwear; and all locals collected aid for the victims of the devastating 1927 "great floods" in Mississippi. In February 1927 the national union provided a loan of $10,000 to the Philadelphia branch of the International Ladies Garment Workers Union to enable the rebuilding of the organization in Philadelphia, and broad-ranging support for a variety of labor organizations continued into the 1930s, solidifying the union's reputation on the national scene.[42] The union even briefly contemplated allying with other unions, though Branch 1 president Geiges, on his return from the General Amalgamated Conference in New York in 1923, recommended against affiliation because it would mean "changing the form of the organization to a less effective one."[43]

It was the union's attempts to build its own organization through full unionization of the hosiery industry, however, that gained national recognition and set a militant example for other unions. The national and international networks that comprised Philadelphia's radical movement provided crucial resources for the union as it embarked on the most extensive organizing campaigns of its existence.

Following the Shops

During the 1920s hosiery industry expansion led to the establishment of many new shops as well as subsidiaries of other mills. By 1926 new shops were springing up in all sections of the country and Canada, training their own help, running double-machine jobs, and ruthlessly underselling the union shops. In Buffalo, New York, companies were paying less than half the union wage; in Reading, Bangor, Lansdale, York, Easton, Nazareth, and several other Pennsylvania towns, lower-wage shops were also growing; southern towns were offering free land and cheap labor to industrialists, and some mills had already relocated to the region; and in New Jersey, rural Massachusetts, and the Midwest, the situation was the same. In Ontario, Canada, the Kayser Company of New York was preparing to open a branch with 200 machines in Sherbrooke; shops were operating in Hamilton with very low pay; and the Holeproof Company of Milwaukee had relocated to London, Ontario, to get away from the union and union rules. While the union had been pursuing a policy of "organizing the unorganized" since the beginning of the decade, the proliferation of new shops, as well as the fact that some existing shops were already beginning the process of relocating, gave an increased urgency to the situation. It was this reality that encouraged union members to agree to the increase in the rate of the per capita tax levied by the union in order to institute the "biggest organization drive in the history of the Federation" as they embarked on a massive campaign to "follow the shops."[44]

After the 1921 strike and the reuniting of the AFFFHW, organizing was immediately increased in Reading, Pennsylvania, an important hosiery center and the home of the largest hosiery mill in the country, the Berkshire Mills. Ruthlessly anti-union, Berkshire was rivaled only by Apex in Philadelphia for its use of private labor police and its connections with conservative political and religious figures. The two also shared ties across the Atlantic to the rising fascist movement in Germany, a factor that would increasingly come to lend an international element to the conflicts. As early as 1923 hosiery strikes began to hit Reading, with a strike at the Rosedale mill quickly followed by strikes at other mills. But the powerful Reading Hosiery Manufacturers' Association, led by the owners of the Berkshire Mills, had an elaborate network of labor spies and many religious leaders and state politicians on its side. The sentiment for unionism may have been there, but the union's capacity to provide adequate protection for these workers was not yet highly developed. The union did establish an active branch in Reading that continued to gain in numbers during the 1920s, but it was an uphill battle. Thus it came as a surprise to most observers when Reading became the only American city to have an all-Socialist city council in the midst of the union campaigns.

The Socialist campaign in 1927 was financed by the hosiery union, and it resulted in the landslide victory of a Socialist city government, sweeping city hall and the city council, and gaining several seats on the school board. This was an especially euphoric moment given that the Berkshire and other non-union plants backed the opposing slate. But secret ballots in a citywide election were quite different from public positions against a powerful adversary that could put a family's very livelihood on the line. With the election victory, including the placement of James Maurer on the council, the union had hoped to gain power in its struggles against the Berkshire group, an expectation that was only partially achieved. The union organizing drives in Reading were but the first stirrings of what would become a major conflict in the 1930s, when the union negotiated the first contract settlement in the nation under the New Deal's National Industrial Recovery Act. Even before the Socialist successes in Reading, Maurer's statewide federation recognized the innovations and achievements of the hosiery union; at the Pennsylvania Federation of Labor's 1923 convention, delegates overwhelmingly passed a resolution calling for all other unions in the state to "organize along the lines of the AFFFHW."[45]

The union also increased organizing in the midwestern section of the country and Canada, with special attention to Fort Wayne and Indianapolis, Indiana, and Milwaukee and Kenosha, Wisconsin, cities in which the full-fashioned industry was growing. The union's foray into Canada met immediate resistance: its organizer was "threatened by the foreman of a shop, forcibly escorted to the border by police and threatened to be beat-up" if he returned. When these acts were brought to the attention of Canadian labor delegates at the AFL convention in Detroit by Thomas McMahon, president of the UTWA, the Canadian delegates promised not only to lend support to the union's next organizing attempt but also to bring the incident to the attention of the Canadian secretary of labour on the grounds of the Canadian law, the Lemieux Act, which guaranteed the rights of Canadian workers to organize and bargain collectively.[46]

A strike in early 1928 at the Allen-A mills in Kenosha (also the home of the anti-union Nash automobile company) brought the union widespread attention through its use of an innovative media campaign, coordinated by John Edelman and largely financed by Philadelphia's Branch 1. Borrowing tactics from Gandhi and the women's suffrage campaign, and using imaginative media stunts, the union propelled the role of women in the labor movement onto the national consciousness. As described in more detail in chapter 4, along with the work in Philadelphia and its surrounding areas, the Kenosha campaign helped to promote labor as an important means of advancement for women's rights.[47]

In the course of the 1920s the southern United States became a region of growing economic importance, as manufacturers increasingly looked for low-wage havens from organized workers. The South offered many incentives for new shops as well as for relocations from the North, not least of which was a history of brutal suppression of unions. The union through which the AFFFHW was affiliated to the AFL, the UTWA, had made several attempts to extend union organization into the region. The authors of *Like a Family* described the UTWA's lack of success in the South as a result of being "too poor, too beleaguered, too parochial, too fainthearted to take on the daunting challenge of cracking the non-union South." An exception was the AFFFHW, and particularly its primary southern organizer, Alfred Hoffmann. "All fire in making speeches, courageous, plain spoken, and sensitive to workers' culture," Hoffmann helped set in motion one of the strongest labor movements in the region.[48]

The first full-fashioned hosiery strike in the South took place in 1925 shortly after a manufacturer opened a mill in Durham, North Carolina, housing 400 full-fashioned machines (earlier textile strikes had not involved hosiery). When the union managed to form a small branch, the shop manager threatened to replace union workers with nonunion men, and Philadelphia's Edward Callaghan sent a wire informing the local leaders that he would personally come down to take charge of the situation. According to Callaghan's colorful recollection of the events, at the end of the telegram he used the word "stop" (as was customary in telegrams). Allegedly misunderstood by the workers as an instruction to "stop work," when Callaghan arrived the entire shop was out on strike. This strike, as Callaghan described it, resulted in "establishing their right to belong to a union" and the solid organization of Branch 31. The story also helped to establish the reputation of the southern workers as "just as committed to the union" as the rest of the membership.[49]

After its 1926 convention, the union adopted a program of expanded full-time organizing and placed additional full-time paid organizers in the field, including Callaghan, Tiny Hoffmann, and Marion Frey, along with the continued use of part-time officers and staff. Hoffmann went south, where he became one of the union's most dynamic organizers. He organized not just hosiery workers but any other industry that showed an interest. Soon after arriving he was visited by a group of black workers interested in starting a union for laborers, and in 1927 he took a leadership role in a brutal strike of 1,000 cotton mill workers in Henderson, North Carolina. Branch 1 organized an extensive campaign to send relief payments to what they called "the lowest wage-slaves of North Carolina," taking up collections from all Philadelphia mills and gaining support from other labor bodies in the North as well. By the end of 1927, Hoffmann was one of the leaders in establishing the Piedmont Organizing Council, "a major step toward the revival of trade unionism in North Carolina." Although there were only 33 delegates at its first meeting, by June 1928 there were over 200, from "thirteen cities, twenty-six trades, and seven central bodies throughout North Carolina, as well as several representatives from international unions, newspaper men, and two ministers."[50]

Among the delegates were women trade unionists and twelve "Negro workers" representing various organizations. The *Hosiery Worker*'s report of the event described a "great show of solidarity in which the colored men were given every consideration, courtesy and encouragement by those at the meeting," indicating, they said, that "the North Carolina labor movement draws no color line." Although simplistic and misrepresentative of the state of race relations in southern labor, the primary purpose behind such articles was propaganda—to establish a *mentalité* that there should not be a color line within the labor movement, and that the organization of workers across race was just as natural and necessary as across gender—a position that was beginning to gain widespread acceptance within the union by this point. By the beginning of July 1928, the Piedmont Organizing Council was organizing workers at the R. J. Reynolds tobacco company in Winston-Salem, North Carolina.[51]

By the later part of the 1920s the AFFFHW was putting a major effort into an educational campaign aimed at building class-conscious workers and "solidarity" crossing differences, and the above account of the council's meeting was part of this campaign. In the near future it was to gain much more momentum and would begin to include stories aimed at promoting an understanding of the special oppression of African American workers, as well as connecting race and imperialism around the globe. This focus was instrumental in the organization of African Americans brought into the southern hosiery industry in 1934.

In 1929 Hoffmann was kidnapped from his hotel room in Elizabethton, Tennessee, by a band of "leading citizens," beaten up, dumped across the state line, and, with a gun held to his head, warned never to come back. The union poured resources into the area, sending Edward Callaghan from his organizing campaign in Clifton Forge, Virginia, and its crack publicity man, John Edelman, into Elizabethton, home of the German-owned Glansdorf and Bemberg plants. When Edelman arrived he found Tiny (who weighed in at well over 250 pounds) recuperating in a private home, guarded by a self-appointed bodyguard of several pistol-carrying women strikers, a delegation from a core group of female textile workers that he had helped to organize in the area. As for Edelman, he spent much of his time trying to contain the escalation of violence, even sleeping with a cache of guns under his bed that he had convinced some of the strikers to entrust to his care.[52]

In addition to the union sending a force of organizers, Branch 1 sent out an appeal for donations to a relief fund, itself contributing over $6,000 by the end of May. One result of the kidnappings and the presence of Edelman was that nationwide attention was focused on the southern battles and the role of the hosiery union. The *Hosiery Worker* consistently carried updates on the southern campaign and placed a picture of Tiny, in overalls, and flanked on both sides by a bodyguard of southern workers carrying shotguns, prominently on the front page—guaranteed to provoke a positive response in Kensington. Deeply committed to the South, Hoffmann urged the union to make organization of the region a paramount concern in its campaigns. Branch 1 subsequently initiated a successful referendum vote requesting that members nationwide agree to another special assessment, this one to set up a fund specifically for the southern campaigns.[53]

Hoffmann had his first experience with being sent to jail on a trumped-up charge of "insurrection" in Marion, North Carolina, during a brutal strike in which workers were gunned down by guards at one of the mills.[54] The support by Kensington workers of southern insurgency, as evidenced by their donations, was likely due in part to the courage and fighting spirit displayed by the southern workers. The brutality of the southern manufacturers and their police allies was something many workers in Kensington could identify with, having had generations of experience with similar conditions, passed on within the lore of the community. As in Philadelphia, Reading, and the Midwest, the South represented a site of intense and often violent conflict between the union and the manufacturers, and the AFFFHW leadership tried to ensure that the courageous fight of the workers did not go unrecognized.

Meanwhile, the "most intense organizing drive in the union's history" was being played out in Kensington on an impressive scale. Always the largest local, Branch 1 was experiencing unprecedented growth, and the revenue raised from the increase in its (relatively) well-paid membership and the emergency assessments they agreed to pay were a major factor in the ability of the union to finance the national campaigns. As the workforce expanded, the new workers in the shops were ever younger "Jazz Babies." To achieve full unionization increasingly required moving beyond traditional methods of organizing to an engagement with the youth culture of the Jazz Age and the "modern woman." The determination of Philadelphia industrialists to smash the union also began to force Branch 1 to adopt a progressively more literal interpretation of its self-identification as a "fighting" union. As the hosiery workers' union attempted to build solidarity locally, nationally, and internationally, its leadership launched imaginative campaigns to reach the young workers in the industry and move the sometimes cynical and rebellious youth of America into an idealistic and militant youth movement focused on "rights." The success of these campaigns would propel the union into a major role in the journey toward the CIO.

CHAPTER THREE

From Jazz Babies to Youth Militants

The older generation had certainly pretty much ruined this world before passing it on to us... and then they are surprised that we don't accept it.
—John F. Carter, *Atlantic Monthly*, September 1920

John F. Carter, who described himself as one of America's post–World War I "wild young people" in an article in *Atlantic Monthly* magazine, fired a salvo in what would become one of the defining narratives of the 1920s: the "problem" of the younger generation.[1] The aftereffects of World War I joined the swirling currents of modernism in convulsing early 1920s American society, particularly its youth. In the harsh reality of the war's aftermath—the horrific casualty figures and the corruption and deception of the war effort—young people began to seriously question the moral codes of the country's elders, leading to reaction, disillusionment, escapism, and youth rebellion.[2]

As the 1920s came roaring in, some strands of that rebellion manifested themselves in changes in popular culture and fashion. As noted earlier, the emergence of the flapper created an insatiable demand for the sheer, form-fitting stocking that became indispensable to the short dresses young women were wearing. And as the industry continued to expand, the new workers who poured into the shops where the stockings were made were overwhelmingly from the younger generation.[3]

Kensington was the nation's leading center of production for the full-fashioned hosiery industry in the 1920s, and Philadelphia's Branch 1 the largest and richest local in the American Federation of Full-Fashioned Hosiery Workers (AFFFHW). After the successful strike of 1921 and the reunification of the union, Branch 1 poured resources into the hosiery federation's central "fighting treasury" in support of the campaigns to "follow the shops," strengthen the labor movement, and, for many of the union's activists, build a socialist alternative to the capitalist system. But the accomplishment of such an ambitious program depended greatly upon the hosiery union activists' ability to fully organize the central production area of Philadelphia. And this goal, in turn, was dependent upon the union's ability to engage with and politicize its youth. For the fledgling labor movement that began to germinate after the strike of 1921, sent out shoots in the follow-the-shops campaign, and grew into a central force in the movement toward the Congress of Industrial Organizations (CIO) in the 1930s was, at its core, a youth movement.

Although the strike of 1921 had given the AFFFHW control of the Philadelphia area, by mid-decade the rapid expansion of the industry sorely tested that control as entrepreneurs and existing manufacturers opened new, nonunion mills. The union leadership faced the challenge of organizing an increasingly young workforce and attempting to instill in it the idealistic and militant spirit that had served the organization so well in the past. The overarching goal of union activists was to create a class-conscious movement that could bring about social change, but to do so would require a balancing act—between engaging the youth culture on its own terms and honoring the historic traditions and labor culture of the organization. As it turned out, skeptics need not have worried. Within the cultural turbulence of the decade there existed the seeds of a new freedom and a spirit of experimentation as discontented youth, and especially and very visibly, young women, openly began to question the legitimacy of the status quo. In fact, it was in this extraordinary period that we see a remarkable flowering of the union, for as young hosiery workers began to experience mounting arrests, injunctions, and violence by private agencies and city police over the course of campaigns for union recognition, they would evolve into what the union came to celebrate as the "youth militant" and become what hosiery knitter Howard Kreckman years later defined as "union by principle." Kensington's youth culture was part of a Philadelphia story, but it also had distinct characteristics associated with the cultural history of the community. This chapter is therefore organized into two sections, the first of which describes the youth culture in the community. The second, longer section discusses how the union, in the context of the struggle for workplace control, engaged and transformed its rebellious youth into a movement of socially conscious youth militants who would have a national impact in the movement for the CIO.[4]

The 1920s Youth Culture of Kensington

"We called ourselves the 'Bachelor Girls.' There were about eight of us and we went around together . . . down the shore, to dances and parties, out with the boys. Oh, we had fun!" said Kensington hosiery worker Alice Nelson Kreckman years later.[5]

By the age of seventeen, Alice had been a looper in a hosiery mill for several years. When she started work in 1921, at the age of fourteen, she chose hosiery because, as she put it, "I wanted to be a worker—and I made good money!"⁶ The seemingly contradictory identities of consciously wanting to be a worker as well as a whole-hearted participant in consumer and leisure activities were not an out-of-the-ordinary occurrence for young hosiery workers in Kensington in the 1920s, as youth became a more visible factor in both the industry and the union, as it was in American society generally.

The 106 million people living in the United States in 1920 were distinctly younger than the nation's population would be later in the century. Over 51 percent of the population were age twenty-four or younger, and only 7.4 percent were over the age of sixty. Another interesting finding of the census that year was that although almost 45 percent of those listed as "white" had either immigrated to the United States or had one or both foreign-born parents, five out of every six white residents and virtually all nonwhite residents had been born in the United States, figures that approximate those for the wards of greater Kensington. These demographics also happened to intersect with seismic changes in the national culture, heralded by the successful campaign for female suffrage and the introduction of Prohibition.⁷

How Kensington's residents and hosiery union members were affected by the decade's changes in social patterns varied within the community's population and Branch 1's membership. For example, while the success of the campaigns for women's right to the vote had complex effects on the community and the union (discussed later), Prohibition was no more accepted by Kensington residents than it was by Philadelphians in general. Although the Eighteenth Amendment has often been seen as a law directed primarily at the lifestyles of immigrant groups, it was resented by a broad section of working-class people; many Kensington residents opposed Prohibition as a violation of their personal rights as well as an intrusion into one of their favorite leisure activities. In Philadelphia, due as much to official corruption as to popular opposition, the enforcement of anti-alcohol laws was very lax. The well-known efforts of U.S. Marine Corps general Smedley Butler, Philadelphia's director of public safety during 1925 and 1926, were largely unsuccessful in stopping the sale of alcohol. There was too much money to be made in illegal alcohol, and violators often bribed police to run protection for them. Besides, liquor violations were just not considered crimes by many people, and certainly not in Kensington, where they tended to be ignored.⁸

During Prohibition, Kensingtonians always knew where they could get an illegal drink, and many people made their own legal wine and illegal beer at home. Some prominent advertisers in the *Hosiery Worker* were businesses selling the necessary ingredients for homemade beer. On certain days when Jeanne Callahan came home from school, she "knew right away" that her parents were making beer because, she complained, "the whole house had that smell." Social drinking was a part of community life and incorporated long-held traditions that provided one of the means for people to interact and form networks. On warm evenings people sat outside to escape the closeness of row house living, and these occasions were often accompanied by a pitcher of beer. Ignoring laws that were regarded as unfair to the community was indicative of the historically ambivalent relationship that residents had with the city police in general. This was also reflected in the popular culture of young people in the 1920s, and that popular culture became an important factor in the union's construction of its "labor culture of unity."[9]

There were various ways in which the community's youth were able to form networks of interaction. Certainly the settlement patterns in Kensington, in which newer ethnic groups often lived interspersed among older residents, were a mitigating factor to the establishment of strictly insular communities. Ethnic shops such as groceries, specialty stores, and bakeries did exist, and people shopped in them for particular staples, but they were not patronized exclusively by one ethnic group. The owners of the shops also often hired local youths of other ethnic backgrounds to help out in their establishments. Alice Nelson Kreckman developed a particular penchant for butter cake, a flat cake topped with a rich concoction of butter and sugar that was a staple of Polish and German bakeries, while Jeanne Callahan made a little money shelling peas and lima beans for a local Jewish grocer.[10]

But residents could not get everything they needed within their local neighborhood and often had to go at least a little further afield. With the completion of the Frankford Elevated Line above the entire extent of Kensington Avenue by 1922, access to the downtown "center-city" area was fast and convenient, and the department stores there always offered the latest fashions, even in their bargain basements. And virtually everyone traveled regularly to local shopping districts, especially "the Avenue," which was the neighborhood shorthand for Kensington Avenue. Here were furniture stores, shoe stores, hardware stores, clothing stores, and a variety of other establishments at which residents of all ethnic backgrounds shopped. There were also restaurants, movie theaters, skating rinks, and places to dance. Young people both worked and encountered each other more informally in these venues, and they became a hub of the youth culture (see Figure 2).[11]

Another important influence on young people was the public education system. Changes in the Pennsylvania Child Labor Law in 1917 required school attendance until the age of sixteen—through the age of fourteen on a full-

FIGURE 2 Kensington and Allegheny Avenues, the hub of the main shopping district, ca.1940. The Frankford Elevated Line dominates the scene. *Philadelphia Record* Photograph Morgue [V07]. Historical Society of Pennsylvania.

time basis and then part-time at a "continuation" school until reaching sixteen. Thus, the young people of Kensington's various ethnicities interacted not only in their neighborhoods and in leisure activities, but also at school and work. And this was very much the case for hosiery workers.

Philadelphia's full-fashioned industry was sufficiently important and interesting that several researchers from the University of Pennsylvania selected it for study in the 1920s and 1930s. In one of these studies, a sociologist found that over 70 percent of the industry's workers, both male and female, were under the age of thirty and that 40 percent were under twenty-one, for the full-fashioned industry experienced the overwhelming majority of its growth in the 1920s, and young people just coming into the labor force were its primary recruits. There were workers over the age of thirty, male and female; but full-fashioned hosiery was, essentially, a young industry.[12]

True to the traditions of the textile industry, there were large groups of workers of English, Scottish, Irish, and German descent in Kensington's hosiery mills, but people of other ethnicities, representative of the newer immigration of the early twentieth century, worked in hosiery mills as well. Specifically, a number of Italian and Slavic names show up in lists of hosiery workers, though the industry's traditional exclusion of black employees was not broken in this period. However, most hosiery workers were born and grew up in the United States. Although some were immigrants, about 80 percent of hosiery workers in Kensington were American-born, though often of foreign parentage. As a high-paying, skilled industry, hosiery was attractive to these youths, who were also a product of the American school system. All of these elements acted to encourage an intermingling of people from different cultures and, together with the long collective traditions of the community, helped to create a form of working-class cosmopolitanism that would come to serve the union well. It would also contribute in a fundamental way to the programs that the hosiery workers developed to combat the problems they came to face as the twenties wore on.[13]

The early decades of the twentieth century witnessed a shift in the types of jobs held by women and the numbers of those employed in gainful labor. But there was also a dramatic change in their appearance and behavior. Although the Progressive-Era women's movement appeared to be foundering in the twenties with the loss of its earlier focus on suffrage, many contemporaries thought that the old established gender arrangements were rapidly falling apart. A new generation seemed to be waging an attack on conventional ideas of femininity and womanhood. Young women shortened their skirts, wore makeup, played sports, went out dancing at night, flirted, and were adamant about leading "modern" lives. Such modern women were not confined to urban areas, and they were present among a broad spectrum of populations and class backgrounds, for during these same years debates about gender were taking place in a wide variety of cultures, including those of Britain, Denmark, Brazil, Japan, and certainly revolutionary Russia. But throughout those cultures, women were remarkably united in their styles, their manners, and their attitudes. Working-class women, as well as those of the middle class, thought of themselves as "modern," and they dressed and behaved in the particular ways embraced by this subculture. Within these groups young people, male and female, related to each other and thought of themselves in generational terms.[14]

In keeping with this trend, Kensington's youth understood and defined themselves in collective terms, often generationally. Whenever Alice or Howard Kreckman described the activities of the period, it was in terms of "we," not "I," as in "we were union," or "we went to the shore," and the women referred to themselves as "girls" and their male compatriots as "boys," just as the men often did. They embraced a distinct way of looking, for modernity was clearly tied to style—women dressed in particular fashions and sported particular haircuts—and these fashions were even to some degree, and in various modifications, picked up by older, married women as well. Howard Kreckman, remembering when his mother came home with her hair shingled, said that at first he "didn't know what to think about it."[15]

The flapper-style dresses were made of light materials and hung straight to the hips with no defined waistline. They required a minimum of undergarments, and flappers entirely rejected the confining corsets of earlier fashion. All of these goods and related services were available in the businesses on the Avenue, where cheap, mass-produced versions of flapper clothing could be purchased, often on layaway, and local hair salons copied the styles from the magazines and women's columns of the newspapers that proliferated in the period. The new clothing could also be seen and purchased in such bastions of working-class life as the Sears, Roebuck catalogue.[16]

In the 1920s, young women and men also displayed more independence and were more open about sexuality than earlier generations, and this was also reflected in Kensington. Although, as Alice Kreckman explained, "back then girls lived at home until they were married," many certainly did not confine their lives to family and domesticity. They went out to work, enjoyed a relatively greater amount of disposable income than earlier generations, and participated in commercial entertainment and consumption. Dances and parties were particularly favored pastimes and routinely included alcohol. Although women and men often traveled in same-sex groups, they lived and worked alongside each other, and they also enjoyed each other's company.[17]

While relationships with men were important parts of their lives, female friends became increasingly important to young women over this period as a source of information, advice, and support, as their experiences began to differ from those of their mothers. The "bachelor girls" that Alice Kreckman referred to are an example of this, as are many of the entries in the Aberle mill newsletter, the *Pressoff Special*. Former resident Jane Connor also regularly went out with several female friends and relatives. Both Alice and Jane had one particular female friend with whom they closely identified. For Jane, it was her Polish girlfriend, and Alice's closest friend was another hosiery worker: "Me and Gertie were best friends ... wherever I went she went."[18]

Many of the ways in which these women represented themselves resulted from commercialized mass culture and mass-produced representations of women, for the mass media was an important factor in the changing attitudes of the decade. Historian Lynn Dumenil found that, by the 1920s, 40 percent of popular magazines carried articles arguing that sex was good for both men and women. Sex adventure magazines like *True Confessions* and *True Story* were widely read. Newspapers directed at working-class readers also serialized stories that carried suggestive titles, such as a 1925 serial entitled "Surrender—The Story of a Girl Who Dared."[19]

Movies also projected a new version of womanhood, and female stars of the twenties were archetypical modern women. Mae West, with her overt and provocative sexuality, was often imitated at young hosiery workers' parties, and similar representations of women were also seen on stage. Somerset Maugham's play *Rain* was the story of a freewheeling woman of questionable morals who was persecuted by an evangelical minister whose zeal eventually gave way to lust. It opened in New York in late 1922 and ran for 174 weeks. According to the theater critic and historian Ward Morehouse, "the opening brought forth an emotional demonstration never exceeded in the theater," and the audience "stood and screamed when the curtain fell on Sadie's denunciation of Davidson at the close of the second act." Before going to New York, *Rain* opened at Philadelphia's Garrick Theater and was reviewed in all of the local newspapers.[20]

Kensington's residents were avid readers of newspapers and magazines of various types, and they regularly attended movies and other performances. There were quite a few theaters located throughout the community, and some of them were elaborate establishments. The Allegheny on Frankford Avenue near Allegheny Avenue, in the heart of Kensington's factory district, was originally built in 1912 as a vaudeville theater. It contained over 2,400 seats and was "lavish and elegantly appointed." The large stage had an orchestra elevator arrangement consisting of eight platform lifts that could be raised or lowered individually or in combination—a Philadelphia first. By the 1920s it was also a movie theater, making it an even more popular destination. The Kent Theatre, located on Kensington Avenue near Cumberland Street, originally built in 1890 as the People's Theatre, was a repertory establishment that also hosted burlesque shows and lectures. It was remodeled and renamed the Kent in the 1920s, adding a large movie screen and a stadium-style seating arrangement for over 1,900 people. By 1922 the then-complete Frankford Elevated Line passed by its front doors. Many other cinema and vaudeville houses, large and small, existed in the community and advertised in the *Hosiery Worker* and other local papers. Kensington's residents had wide-ranging access to the outside world, and they were well aware of broader cultural developments.[21]

It was within this milieu that the full-fashioned hosiery industry and its workers came of age. As the 1920s advanced, the silk full-fashioned hosiery industry was one of the fastest-growing industries in the country, and this fact had an enormous effect on the hosiery workers. From 1919, when about 75 million pairs of full-fashioned hosiery were produced, annual output increased steadily through 1927, when almost 240 million pairs were knitted in the United States. This represented an increase in production of over 200 percent, generated by advertising and consumer demand. As the consumption of the fashioned stockings grew, silk, dyed in various stylish colors after it was knit, displaced cotton as the principal raw material. The rapid expansion of the hosiery industry, and the consequent shortage of skilled labor, resulted in a steady increase in wage rates, both union and nonunion. The economist George Taylor of the University of Pennsylvania's Wharton School, using the index of change in hourly earnings of manufacturing industries for the years before 1930, found that the hourly rates in the full-fashioned industry increased more rapidly than in manufacturing in general. This resulted in a gradual separation upward of hosiery wages relative to other manufacturing wages. By 1927 hosiery workers in Philadelphia earned on average 25 percent more than the average for all industries in the city.[22]

In the 1920s, full-fashioned hosiery workers in Philadelphia lived relatively well and looked prosperous. They displayed particular characteristics peculiar to the industry. The men, who handled slender strands of silk in their jobs, had to have "a sensitive touch," and rough, calloused hands would have been an impediment. They also experienced severe eyestrain, and after a few years most knitters were likely to wear glasses. The need to take care of their hands also applied to the women, who constantly worked on the delicate, unfinished stockings. Shop committees regularly offered hand lotion as well as tools of the trade such as pliers for sale.[23]

At least some of the young workers liked to freely spend the money that they were able to keep for themselves. Alice Kreckman claimed that she was more careful with her money, although she also went to center city department stores and shopped on the Avenue; but her friend Gertie spent "every nickel she had." Many of the men wore white shirts and neckties, and the women wore "modern" hats and dresses. Although their workday began at 7:30 in the morning, they had an active social life. They bowled, played soccer and basketball, performed in orchestras, and often stayed out late at dances and parties. Many of these activities came to be part of union-sponsored programs as the decade progressed. In the summer they went to the New Jersey shore. Alice Kreckman described going with several of her female friends: "We took the ferry across the river and then the train." Because of their relatively high pay, some hosiery workers were also able to purchase consumer items like radios and cars.[24]

One of the richest sources about the youth culture in Kensington is the *Pressoff Special*, the shop newsletter from the H. C. Aberle Hosiery Mill, an establishment that employed over a thousand workers. This series of papers was produced by the workers of the mill and coedited by a male and a female hosiery worker. Along with articles about the union and political commentary, the newsletter also contained extensive information about social activities, events, locations of interest in the neighborhood, and quite a bit of gossip—some of it rather risqué. Articles, comments, and notices were submitted by the employees and give much insight into the social life and work culture of the hosiery workers. Entries in the papers not only back up contentions that the so-called sex magazines were being read by young women, but also make clear that the workers were interested in fashion and parties, and engaged in a variety of social activities. And some of the articles carried rather open sexual references.

The editors of the paper described it as a venue for promoting good relations and sociability among the workers, and the entries were generally uncensored. A column entitled "We Wonder" carried humorous tidbits that included such entries as "What the latest attraction is at Greenwood's for Gertie" and "Why Marge reads love stories." Going on to ask, "What girl doesn't?," this entry continued with "Why Edna chooses love stories such as 'A Man's Kisses,'" "Why men never perform at burlesque shows," and "What topper was being tossed to and from the arms of several knitters at a recent party." Other entries could easily be interpreted in multiple ways: "What was Betty doing out on the porch with Sally? Some fun!" Another column, entitled "Resolutions They Should Have Made," included "Marie—to make my eyes behave; Griggs—to neck only one girl at a time." There were descriptions of events, including a party at which "Lydia did her snake dance, which was indescribable," and a dance at Wagner's dance studio where men and women were "throwing lines at each other as though fishing." Virtually every party had one woman who was the "Mae West" of the party. There were all-female "stag" parties, in which those involved came to work the next morning with obvious hangovers, as well as references to fashion, like Betty's finger wave, Hilda's "blue outfit for Easter," and Jean starting a new style by wearing her beret entirely on one side of her head. And every edition carried jokes—often referencing consumer culture, often sexually suggestive, such as one titled "In High":

FATHER: Your boyfriend talks too much.
He rattles on like a flivver. I'm afraid he is a flat tire.
DAUGHTER: I know, Pa, but his clutch is grand.

This open and unambiguous sexuality was not, of course, limited to hosiery workers, but reflected deeper patterns in the community that had challenged middle-class mores for generations. But it does appear that such topics were explicitly and openly discussed in this period, as indicated by the comments of a middle-class woman from the industrial branch of the Kensington YWCA. She claimed that, in relation to sex, the factory girls who attended the Y meetings "really opened my eyes!" It is difficult to say how these developments in the youth culture were received by older members of the community. A story in one of the editions of the shop newsletter did describe the adventures of one knitter who claimed he "tried to be a gentleman" by walking a girl home after a party, only to be greeted by a "swift kick" from her father. But most young people lived at home, and this fact did not seem to interfere with their social lives.[25]

Entries in the shop newsletter also reflected another side of life in the community—that of working wives and mothers. There were many allusions to married women: entreaties to women to make sure they sent in their name change to union headquarters, and references to women coming back after an absence, with annotations such as "some honeymoon!," as well as to working mothers, as in "Did you know that Nan and Hannah are the mothers of charming daughters?"

The fact that workplaces continued to employ more-mature adults as well as very young workers led to interactions across generations and often made the work site a venue for social education as well. More experienced women could provide younger women with support in their relationships with male peers. Additionally, relationships could evolve between women that provided a rudimentary education in sex and courtship, as when "Celia and Jane" offered to give advice to brides. More-experienced men and women helped younger ones navigate not only the daily frustrations of broken threads and needles, but also the type of behavior they should extend toward bosses. And work culture was, as well, a vehicle for promoting working-class cosmopolitanism and inclusiveness. A submission from the fourth floor of the mill demonstrates the ethnic variety among the workforce: "If we ever need to send a delegation to the League of Nations, the 4th floor would be a good candidate—we have Americans, Germans, Scotch, Irish, Italians, Polish, Jewish, and Czechoslovakians on this floor." But most important, work was a venue for raising consciousness of class, for in Kensington, work culture was strongly shaped by class relations.[26]

Tensions between workers' and employers' interests were an important factor in forging alliances between younger workers and their older counterparts. Responses to the workplace were multifaceted, but were strongly influenced by family and community background as well as by the job. Respect conferred on older workers could also conflict with the formal factory authority structure and support worker solidarity. Work culture embraced specific codes of conduct, and one standard that was referred to constantly and appears to have been of prime importance was the ability to "take it." This code held multiple meanings, from "taking" a joke, to "holding" your alcohol, to staying out late at a party and still being able to make it into work, to holding your own on the picket line. And it was applied equally to both men and women, and across generations.[27]

In Kensington, many parents encouraged self-sufficiency and hard work, and many residents were responsible workers who rarely took time off from their jobs. On the other hand, adults also taught children to stand up for themselves. Alice Kreckman's mother often reminded her that "just because someone has more money than us—they're not better than you."[28] These seemingly contradictory aspects of workers' personalities—responsible hard workers thoroughly integrated into community institutions, but ready to defy any odds to defend themselves or a comrade—were explained by the Italian Marxist theoretician Antonio Gramsci in his description of the "man-in-the-mass": "One might almost say that he has two theoretical consciousnesses . . . : one which is implicit in his activity and which in reality unites him with all his fellow workers in the practical transformation of the real world; and one, superficially explicit or verbal, which he has inherited from the past and uncritically absorbed." The latter consciousness, in the view of the historian Selina Todd, can be based in "the economic imperative of conforming to the status quo," but the more class-conscious one grows "from shared experiences with neighbours, family, and fellow workers of oppression and exploitation, and which shapes dissent."[29]

While the American youth culture of the period had common features everywhere it was found, Kensington's young people lived in a particular community, and the space that surrounded them was comprised not only of places of leisure, but also places of work, union halls, and family and neighbors, many of whom had participated in the battles of the past. The young workers participated not only in the consumer culture, but also in the community culture. They gave parties for pure fun, but also to welcome back a coworker after several months in the hospital or to raise money for someone's loss of a family member. And while some hosiery workers may have had relatively higher wages than others in the neighborhood, this did not separate them from the community, for much of their income was put back into it in contributions to the family economy and services offered to neighbors, as well as in consumer purchases. When Howard Kreckman got his first car, a

Model T, he often used it to help out or entertain family and neighbors. "We would go up to the Poconos, or to a lake in New Jersey... all over the place. I would take a whole carload." Jeanne Callahan also described a similar situation in the 1930s, when her "Uncle Leo," the only one in the family who had a car, took others out for rides, "one group this week, another the next."[30]

While relations between young men and women often revolved around "fun" and had sexual undertones, there was also, as Susan Glenn argued, "a notion of partnership and co-participation with men along class and community lines." This is demonstrated not only by the excerpts from the *Pressoff Special* discussed earlier, but also by the participation of women in strikes, as in 1919 and 1921, when many women walked out in support of men, though they were not in the union themselves at the time. Although most (though not all) jobs held by women and men were separate, they worked closely together, and a knitter's ability to make a good wage often depended on the skill of the women he worked with. Dorothea De Schweinitz, a contemporary sociologist from the University of Pennsylvania, found that toppers in particular were very important to the wage earning of the knitter. The majority "are anxious not to lose their toppers," trying to make sure that the work flowed steadily so that she did not have to wait around. Freda Maurer, a topper in the Brown mill, said, "My knitter offered me two dollars a week extra" to top for him. Men and women learned to rely on each other and to count on solidarity in the shops. Almost forty years earlier men of the Knights of Labor had gone on strike in sympathy with female carpet makers in Kensington even though they had no demands of their own.[31]

Many young hosiery workers carried with them an implicit cultural heritage of "rights," but this did not contradict an involvement in urban consumer society. Rich cultural traditions were embedded in the modern culture. Young workers grew up with a usable past, and union officials would come to consciously promote that past when confronting contemporary problems. The "modern culture" was the foundation for the success of the industry, while the dialectics between the rebellious youth culture and the education and agitation included in union culture were to become the foundation for the success of the union.[32]

Building Unity and the Union in Kensington

In the new world of America's Roaring Twenties, the AFFFHW still had to concern itself with traditional union responsibilities as well as the interests of its young members. Given the high skill factor involved in many knitting occupations and the relative shortage of skilled workers, the union's control of the craft in 1920s Philadelphia allowed it to make real gains in wages and working conditions. But the union's attempts to exercise control over the various features of managerial prerogative went far beyond just concern with the material or economic gains of work. Craft controls in the hosiery industry, similar to what James Hinton found for Britain's engineering industry in the same period, were built and maintained not only in defense of material interests, but also as a means of resistance to the reduction of labor to commodity status. Some leading socialist theoreticians at the time, in fact, argued that skilled craft workers, rather than being bought off by their relatively privileged status, could be the vanguard of a more militant working-class movement, even a revolutionary one. V. I. Lenin, an especially influential authority at the time due to his status as leader of Russia's recent revolution, for example, discussed the likelihood of such a privileged stratum becoming, because of its high level of education and class consciousness, a revolutionary vanguard of the class. In his estimation, high wages and a rich culture were more valuable assets than abject poverty. In January 1917 he argued that metal workers were the "vanguard of the proletariat" there and would likely be so as well in what he saw as "the impending proletarian revolution" in Europe.[33]

Philadelphia's hosiery workers, by and large, saw themselves in the forefront of this movement. This fact is evident in the many discussions held at their conventions as well as the political discourse in their literature. It is also demonstrated by their concrete actions directed not only toward building the hosiery union, but also toward building a broader labor movement that could represent a real challenge to capital. This is the context within which the union's attempts at craft control should be viewed. By insisting on maintaining shop control, but rejecting craft exclusiveness, the union's activist leadership attempted in the 1920s to build a class-conscious constituency and unleash a "revolutionary" potential for change, which they believed to be contained within a united working class.

Although what was known as the great strike of 1921 was undeniably a victory for the union, rapid expansion brought new investment to the industry in Philadelphia as well as other areas of the country. National corporations, such as Marshall Field and Company of Chicago, entered the industry, attracted to Philadelphia by the promise of high profits and skilled workers. As the industry expanded, many new mills operated as nonunion open shops, and shop control became an increasingly contentious issue. Manufacturers began to seriously challenge the Philadelphia union's control, primarily by implementing tactics to increase the supply of labor.[34]

The contest for workplace control manifested itself in various ways, from the fight over the two-machine system, to the training of personnel with shorter terms of apprenticeship, to the attempt to impose longer hours and double shifts. Manufacturers touted the two-machine system as a means of increasing the productivity of an individual worker and cutting the labor component of the cost of production of the final product. But this system made the work of the knitters more stressful and exhausting while it increased the supply of labor by decreasing the number of jobs available. Management drives to increase the number of hours worked were accompanied by attempts to eliminate overtime pay. Longer workdays served to increase production and decrease the costs of manufacture during periods of labor shortage, when starting a second shift was more difficult and costly. These practices also increased the workload of the laborer while decreasing the value of labor. When some shops sought to implement a second shift in order to increase production, the union understood that this policy could result in overcapacity of the market. If the market could absorb all production, increases were not a problem. But if the market became flooded with the product, cutbacks in production would lead to unemployment and a surplus of labor, which, again, would reduce its value. Labor itself became a commodity.[35]

Issues of shop control were not the only means by which the manufacturers were challenging the union. As the demand for labor continued to increase, hosiery manufacturers began recruiting among young people coming out of the schools, reaching into ethnic groups (particularly Italian and eastern European) that did not have the same deep cultural connections to textile work as those of the older workforce and their children. Thus, there developed in Kensington in the 1920s a contest between the union and the mill owners, not only for control of the workshops but also for the hearts and minds of new workers in the industry. These developments, and the challenges they posed, spurred union activists to implement imaginative new techniques of organizing as well as to strengthen those that had been used to build an inclusive union in the past. In the process, hosiery workers embraced a culture of labor that addressed not only the social and recreational life of young Jazz Age members, but also a militant and broad-based unity, built around issues of dignity, justice, and an idealistic construct of labor's "rights."

The importance of working-class institutions and culture independent of capitalism was a recurring theme within radical and socialist circles. In Gramsci's formulation, such institutions were imperative to the creation of social alternatives and should include structures aimed at maintaining the economic well-being of working people. But they also needed to include a new educational system, a "humanistic formative school of general culture." It was through these grassroots schools that workers would learn their "'rights and duties' . . . as basic elements of a new conception of the world." The hosiery union's attempts to build a united labor culture in the 1920s and early 1930s encompassed an investment on several fronts that it hoped would move its membership toward more active participation in efforts to build such a "new conception of the world."[36]

The carnage and destruction of World War I had precipitated an international social crisis that led many on the American Left to predict that the capitalist system would continue to lead the world's people into an abyss from which only an internationally united working class could save it. Part of this belief—that an alternative social organization was indeed possible as well as necessary—was based on what the Marxist historian Bryan Palmer has called "the 1917 moment—the Leninist moment." The successful Bolshevik Revolution of 1917, a result in large part of the war's devastation and demoralization of Russia's people, was widely seen among socialists and communists in the 1920s as a beginning for world socialism, not as an end in itself. At the very least, it showed that radical transformations were possible. The consciousness of many hosiery union leaders, as well as that of many young members of the community, also had been deeply affected by the atrocities of war. In response, in the 1920s, the hosiery union embraced a far-reaching goal that not only saw "labor" as a means to guarantee the rights of working-class people, but as a vehicle through which to build a more just society.[37]

The 1920 article in *Atlantic Monthly* quoted at the start of this chapter was an expression of the cynicism that had taken root in the psyche of many of America's youth:

> Now my generation is disillusioned [sic] and to a certain extent, brutalized. . . . We have been forced to become realists overnight, instead of idealists, as was our birthright. . . . We have seen the inherent beastliness of the human race revealed in an infernal apocalypse. It is the older generation who forced us to see all this. . . . The oldsters stand dramatically with fingers and toes and noses pressed against the bursting dykes. . . . I suppose that it's too bad that we aren't humble, starry-eyed, shy, respectful innocents, standing reverently at their side for instructions . . . but we aren't . . . a determination to face the facts of life characterizes us. . . . We won't shut our eyes to the truths we have learned.[38]

The union leadership faced the problem of convincing young workers that, although their rebellion against society was justified, it was not the "oldsters" who were the problem but the structure of the social order itself. Understanding that, as Judith Butler put it, "no political revolution is possible without a radical shift in one's notion of the possible," they faced the task of convincing young workers that an alternative social organization was, indeed, possible.[39]

As part of efforts to move union membership toward a broader class consciousness, the *Hosiery Worker* often carried highly critical articles on the war, putting the responsibility for its atrocities squarely on the shoulders of capital: "The last great war involved over 50,000,000 able-bodied members of the working class in the brutal task of human slaughter. The wage earners were called to engage in scientific murder because their masters, social, industrial, and political, had quarreled.... War is not an accidental feature of International Capitalism, it is a part of it, and only by the effective use of the political and economic power of the Workers against war can we avoid it."[40] Another issue carried an appeal intended to reach out particularly to young workers, signed by the International Federation of Trade Unions (Amsterdam) and the Socialist Youth International (Berlin). This article, advising young people to think in terms of their "great historical duty," called for the abolition of the capitalist system as a prerequisite for a more just and peaceful society: "The danger of war will endure as long as capitalism itself endures. We must unite internationally ... for there is no other way to uproot the possibility of war than to abolish the capitalist order of society." Armed with a clarion call for a new social order, the union began an organizing drive that, by the end of the decade, would engulf Kensington in a campaign for a new society, one based on "justice" and the "rights" of labor.[41]

The emphasis that union leaders placed on dignity and rights contributed a great deal toward building a broader sense of working-class consciousness among its youth. The constructs promoted under this campaign not only included a view of American history that contested elite constructions of the past, but also built a counternarrative that stressed the ongoing struggle for the achievement of such liberties. This construction of a labor rights discourse was the foundation for union campaigns throughout this period and a major catalyst to their success. Primarily, it was an attempt to create an image of the union as more than just a stepping-stone for material improvements in working-class life and to move members to a more revolutionary sense of themselves as part of a class movement.

Union activists consistently framed organizing campaigns in terms of a binary opposition between the manufacturers and the workers, and in terms of dignity and independence. Articles in the *Hosiery Worker* described the manufacturers' "instinctive desire for mastery" and traditional property rights, arguing that employers would control workers through the anti-union shop and the individual contract. They described injunctions as attempts to prevent workers from organizing or doing anything "to sever or terminate their relation of master/servant." They described the two-machine system in terms of slavery "coming into its own again," and spoke to threats to their young members' self-esteem and independence through the use of terms like "cowed workers" and the requirement to "call the boss mister."[42]

Rank-and-file organizing on the job and within the workshop played a crucial part in the conduct of branch policy, for at no time did the AFFFHW's organized strength rest solely upon the leadership of the union. One of the union's greatest strengths was the participation of the rank and file in the process of organizing new members. Early in the decade articles appeared regularly in the *Hosiery Worker* encouraging the membership to take a personal interest in building the organization through a "call to duty" to attend union meetings. Different strategies for organizing new workers were often at the top of the agenda of these meetings. Determined to have mass participation and get input from young workers, Branch 1 also began a system of fines for any members who did not attend at least one branch meeting a month. Shop stewards collected these fines in the shops, and the money was refunded at the end of the next meeting they attended.[43]

Once they were at the meetings it was not difficult to get members to participate in lively exchanges regarding ways to organize other workers. One means of organizing that socialists had traditionally used was "street meetings." This was a practice that had been a staple of socialist political culture for decades. Howard Kreckman, describing some of the street meetings socialists held in Kensington, said, "The Socialists would stand on a corner and give political speeches. If they had a particularly good orator, a crowd would gather to listen."[44] Beginning in the 1920s, Philadelphia's hosiery union, with input from activists of the younger generation, expanded upon these "meetings" in novel and radical ways.

One contribution of younger members was to increase the union's openness to the use of modern innovations and technology, resulting, for example, in the purchase of a portable amplifier system that enabled organizers to circumvent "no speech" zones set up by injunctions. Branch 1 activists quickly put the system into use, delivering speeches at various shops, often in multiple languages. When picketing at the Apex mill (the largest and most anti-union in the city) was prevented by an injunction, organizers utilized a recently purchased system to reach the employees, many of whom the Apex management had recruited directly from Germany. They mounted the system on the top of a car and broadcast popular music to attract attention. After a crowd had assembled, speakers gave talks about union rights in both English and German, in an appeal that they hoped would stir the Apex employees to join the organization. During the lunch hour they were able to attract sizable crowds, some members of which did join the union clandestinely, and then organized from within the shop.[45]

Branch 1 also held street meetings in districts of Greater Kensington with a larger concentration of Italian residents, especially around the Italian-language Mother of Divine Grace Church in the Port Richmond neighborhood. These meetings sometimes consisted of a concert in which a live band, composed of young hosiery workers, played on a flatbed truck. Rank-and-file organizers parked the truck on a street where they were able to run wires into the house of a sympathizer for electricity to operate the amplifying system. Following the concert, local orators gave speeches, described by the newspaper as "a ringing plea for human liberty," delivered in Italian.[46] In the 1920s the campaign for the freedom of anarchists Nicola Sacco and Bartolomeo Vanzetti became an international cause célèbre. Many Americans believed they were innocent, and this belief resonated in Italian communities. The union's open support for this and other international causes, invoked in their speeches for "human liberty," touched a nerve in the neighborhood. Union members who spoke the language reported that these programs had a "profound" effect on the community.[47]

Union committees distributed printed literature in several languages and gave talks on local radio stations in German, Polish, and Italian as well as English. Not all of the young workers shared the same historical connections to textile traditions, but they lived in Greater Kensington, and many shared in the modern culture of the community and the shop culture. Union-initiated activities also were aimed at reaching the families of the young workers, many of whom were first generation immigrants, for such young workers tended to live at home and were subject to family culture as well. By employing such targeted campaigns, experienced members of the socialist-affiliated leadership, like Alex McKeown and Gustave Geiges, hoped to encourage the disparate groups to respond to calls for justice and rights, incorporated within a framework of class, when delivered in a manner in tune with their own cultures, as part of an attempt to build a broader campaign of unity in the community.[48]

As part their efforts to connect with young members, Branch 1 leadership also brought colorful figures with national reputations to speak at its meetings.

One such person was Jeff Davis, "King of the Hobos." Davis claimed to hold "honorary membership" in almost every union in the AFL. He always managed to solicit laughter as well as admiration from his young audience as he discussed his "scars and wounds suffered in battles with gunmen, thugs, and 'stool pigeons,'" received in dozens of strikes that he had participated in. The union claimed that Davis, with his hobo connections, had played an important role in fighting spy agencies.[49]

Older activists from Kensington's textile industry, some veterans of the Knights of Labor, also became resources for the union and Branch 1. Older workers in the industry had a wealth of work experience, and hosiery management consistently tried to utilize them to train new, preferably nonunion labor. To undermine management's efforts, the union promoted the concept of "passing the torch," utilizing older workers as part of educational programs to consciously teach the history of the industry and the community. The union also drew on conceptions of loyalty and the "neighborliness" that were such a part of its traditions.

Virtually from its beginning, the AFFFHW utilized its newspaper as an educational tool. An article in 1925 reminded the members that "many things are said and done to break a strike," including using age, religion, and nationality to divide the workers. In this article the organization asked older members to remain loyal, and if they could not get another job because of age—a dire consequence in the days before Social Security and unemployment compensation—the hosiery federation would take care of them.[50] This promise had substance because delegates to union conventions, experienced and newly recruited, also discussed this issue in depth, and passed several resolutions on the subject, based on the construct of "loyalty." In one case the union promised to support four members, aged sixty-five, who came out on strike with other members of their branch and could not get another job because of their age. The delegates overwhelmingly voted that they should receive support because they "not only need[ed] it, but absolutely deserve[d] it." One of the striking knitters to whom the union gave support wrote an article for the *Hosiery Worker* thanking the union membership, but also reminding them that the "old soldiers ha[d] gone through many struggles so that the young could enjoy good conditions."[51]

It was this concept of passing the torch that played one of the strongest roles in garnering cross-generational support. The article about John Makin and his struggles during the 1890s, discussed in chapter 1, was part of the campaign to teach the young the historical traditions of textile. But older workers also frequently spoke at meetings and conventions about what they had gone through in the early days. Tobias Hall, a textile carpet weaver, gave a talk at the 1927 hosiery union convention in Philadelphia that received a standing ovation from the assembled delegates, male and female. Like Makin he was an immigrant from England who joined the Knights of Labor upon arriving in Philadelphia. Hall gave a synopsis of this history in a colorful account clearly aimed at winning the approval of the younger members:

> When the boss found out I joined the Knights, he gave me a hard time. I told him "I reserve the right to join anything and everything I please." My father was blacklisted back in England for 15 months before I came to Philadelphia. If he could stand that, I'm ready any minute.... Then I figured "if I am going to get out of here, I will go with flying colors." Inside of 3 weeks, I had every man jack in the Knights of Labor. The next day, the company put up a 10% reduction notice. That was alright, it was rather testing our fighting ability. We stopped the shop and went across the street to a saloon.... After a few hours we came back and gave them an ultimatum "take down that notice, no discrimination!" They agreed. Took 3 hours. We organized Kensington, then went into West Philadelphia ... old original union Local 25 went through all the grilling, and I tell you they were heroic! ... I want to get it into your heads, you have to hammer away at the barriers they put up. Stand up and fight! What's worth having is worth fighting for.[52]

Such programs served to educate young workers about the ongoing struggle for labor rights as well as to promote bonds on a personal level by presenting the older generation as "regular guys" who liked to have fun but were also a proud and militant group of individuals who deserved respect. It was in this field of education that some of the most important innovations of the hosiery workers' "culture of labor" occurred.

Education had been an important focus of workers' organizations since the nineteenth century, and especially among socialist groups. In the 1880s, German groups like the Arbeiter Vereine (Workers' Clubs) in Kensington and elsewhere not only sponsored singing societies but provided for workers' education as well. Kensington's Knights of Labor promoted a program aimed at educating workers, male and female, in the issues of the day. By 1909 New York's Rand School was catering to working students and promoting a program committed to socialist change. At the height of the movement, from the 1920s to the 1940s, there were labor colleges in most industrial cities, including Philadelphia. The movement also included several programs directed specifically at women, such as the Bryn Mawr Summer School for Women

Workers, founded in 1921. An important development for the labor movement in the 1920s, however, was the establishment in 1921 of the Workers' Education Bureau of America, a coordinating body for research, teaching, publication, and extension work in workers' education. It was from this period of the early 1920s that workers' education became a major focus of the hosiery workers' union.[53]

In November 1923, Gustave Geiges published an article in the *Hosiery Worker* entitled "Education, the Hope of the Labor Movement," in which he proposed that the organization offer members educational opportunities as one of the privileges of membership. Such programs, he argued, should develop both "mental and physical powers," and help members to better understand the problems faced by all workers. Otherwise, he said, "our so-called democracy will fail due to lack of interest which leads to lack of vision, ignorance and misunderstanding."[54]

The hosiery workers' labor education movement promoted an expansive vision of class consciousness while also teaching practical skills useful to labor organizers. It included night courses for workers, various labor colleges, and other activities under the auspices of the Workers' Education Bureau. James Maurer, the Socialist president of the Pennsylvania Federation of Labor and a close associate of the hosiery workers, was the first president of the Workers' Education Bureau. The bureau also received the support and funding of the AFL, a fact that would, over time, lead it in a more conservative direction. But in the 1920s it provided an important resource as a service organization, and Geiges encouraged all AFFFHW branches to affiliate with their local chapters. Other important labor schools included the Highlander School in Tennessee and several summer school programs: the labor school at the University of Wisconsin, the Southern Labor School, and the previously mentioned Bryn Mawr Summer School for Women Workers. Although hosiery workers attended all of these, they developed an especially close relationship with Brookwood Labor College in Katonah, New York.[55]

Brookwood was the first full-time, coeducational, residential labor college in the United States. A variety of socialist, pacifist, and labor activists, as well as wealthy liberal philanthropists with connections to the Progressive Era, founded the institution in 1921. Modeled on the British system of labor colleges, it provided a two-year program that not only taught the skills needed to organize and run a union but also provided a broad liberal education to its students. It was open to both single and married men and women, and the AFFFHW's support for the institution went back to the early days of its founding.[56]

One of the primary ways through which the school maintained itself was union-funded scholarships, with tuition set at $500 per year. It was to Brookwood that the hosiery union sent organizer Alfred "Tiny" Hoffmann at the age of eighteen, and it was there that he developed many of the organizing skills that would be crucial in the union's organizing efforts in the South. A review of the courses he took indicates that he received a broad education. The curriculum Tiny pursued included the history of trade unionism in the United States; government; social psychology; trade union administration; finance; organizing; statistics; the materialistic interpretation of history; economics; public speaking; English (written and oral); and the British, French, Italian, Russian, and German political and trade union movements.[57]

The school also accepted students of all races and nationalities. When Hoffmann was there, there were forty-five students in his class, representing nineteen nationalities and twelve trades, including a "Negro teacher from Virginia, a colored dress maker from New York, and three foreign students from Great Britain, Germany and Sweden." Hoffmann thought that this "mingling and close contact" was an education in itself. Students also had the opportunity of unlimited conferences with their teachers and of hearing some of America's most famous economists and lecturers. Several Labour members of Britain's Parliament were lecturers, and Hoffmann claimed to have heard so many of them that "to hear the German President of the German Coal Miners and Woodworkers was a relief." In 1928, because of Brookwood's non-sectarian and radical orientation, the conservative executive council of the AFL voted to withdraw the support of its affiliated unions from the college. The AFFFHW, however, stood by Brookwood, passing a resolution at its 1928 convention to send a strongly worded letter of protest to the AFL leadership and to continue its scholarships. In debate on the resolution, several delegates pushed for the strongest possible language, calling for the convention to either condemn the AFL or, in the words of one female delegate, to "protest in capital letters." During this early period all AFFFHW scholarships went to skilled male knitters, but that would change as the decade wore on.[58]

The creation of an informed and conscious working class out of young workers required education for the masses, but the AFFFHW's scholarships to Brookwood were for training leadership. In order to promote the goal of mass education, the national executive board, headed by Geiges, encouraged all branches to provide educational opportunities for their members on a local level.

Branch 1 provided for members' education through classes held in its headquarters in Knitters' Hall and other venues in the city. Courses offered at the hall included the labor history of the United States, taught by Professor Jesse Holmes of Swarthmore College. Holmes, a prominent Quaker, was also an active member of the Socialist Party and an associate of the Philadelphia Labor Institute. This class was offered at night and ran for two three-month sessions, held on the first and third Fridays of each month. Howard Kreckman, in his early twenties at the time, was quick to take advantage of the educational opportunities and remembered Holmes as "very progressive" and "a nice man with a little goatee." It was during this period that Kreckman developed his lifelong love of learning.[59]

Prominent socialists and progressive individuals were also regulars at hosiery union education programs. They included James Maurer on "Russia as It Is Today" and "The United States and Mexico," the liberal attorney Arthur Garfield Hays on "Labor and the Law" and "Labor and Legislation," and the educational director of the Illinois Miners Federation on "Labor and Education." Branch 1 also sponsored courses in venues outside of Knitters' Hall, and as the decade progressed they joined with other organizations to form the Philadelphia Workers Education Project. This group held courses at the Kensington YWCA, the Upholstery Weavers Hall, the Labor Institute, and the Young Men's Hebrew Association, among other venues. A sampling of courses offered to women at the Kensington YWCA included trade union problems and parliamentary law, current events, history of the labor movement, English, and oratory and public speaking, as well as workshops in social science.[60]

The fight against the use of the yellow-dog contract, in which bosses forced employees to sign a pledge not to join a union, also became a topic of union education forums. James Maurer promised Branch 1 members at a meeting in 1927 that as Pennsylvania Federation of Labor president he would gain the support of unions throughout the state in a "life or death" fight against the practice. Maurer was an excellent orator, and his speeches always received an enthusiastic response. In an address designed to engage young members in the continuing battle over the definition of "American," he baited the manufacturers with insinuations of cowardliness, claiming that "what the manufacturers could not do by fighting in the open they expect to accomplish by legal subterfuges," and telling his audience that everyone who believed in "real" Americanism must join in a militant fight to eradicate "government by judges."[61]

Branch 1 also opened reading rooms and started a book club, and the education committee held numerous programs directed toward opening members' minds to the problems of race. Among these was a symposium, cosponsored by the Labor Institute and held at Knitters' Hall, on the topic "The Race Problem in the US," in which Walter White, the executive secretary of the NAACP, gave impassioned talks on the subjects of lynchings and race riots. It was also during this period that the union's newspaper became a potent weapon in the campaign to construct an educated, informed, and articulate class consciousness.[62]

The addition of John Edelman as director of education and research in 1926 transformed the union newspaper, as he took over as editor-in-chief. Over the course of the next year the paper went through a dramatic change. Although printed in Philadelphia, it carried news and updates from other hosiery locals as well, including not only organizing efforts and strikes that were in progress, but social events, union-sponsored sports leagues, and educational programs. There were articles about labor spies, labor legislation, and the latest consumer and business economic reports, as well as guest columnists writing about the activities of other labor unions. The newspaper regularly listed forums, classes, and meetings from a broad range of progressive and left-wing organizations, socialist and independent. Often incorporating humor and satire to make articles interesting and readable, its broad coverage included issues designed to inform and educate unionists everywhere. Edelman added a special features page that carried news and photos of international events and labor news from around the globe; commentaries on imperialism, fascism, and war profiteers; political and legislative coverage; and a searing analysis of capitalism's incompatibility with the interests of working people.

Articles aimed at awakening the consciousness of readers regarding racial oppression began to take on increasing prominence, including ones comparing the pay differentials for white and African American teachers and condemning the "serfdom" of the "darker races" in the plantation system of Hawaii. News about international anti-imperialist struggles became a regular feature, from the Irish Republican struggle to the campaigns for Indian independence led by Gandhi. The paper ran an editorial series titled "Labor Lives," in which it described the philosophies of "great thinkers" like Karl Marx and Friedrich Engels. In the series on Marx, the union paper claimed that "those who would make a newer, better world have a gospel to guide them" in the writings of Karl Marx, "the first great revolutionary socialist." The *Hosiery Worker* seamlessly blended the popular culture of union members with the most far-reaching and radical analysis and news coverage; a typical front page headlined both "Branch 70 to Stage Big Labor Ball" and "Hosiery Worker Murdered by Richmond Hill Scab!" The paper carried book and movie reviews, poetry, and cultural information as well as articles covering hosiery strikes throughout the industry, and increasingly focused on the actions of the union's "heroic" women.[63]

By 1928 the newspaper had a wide circulation, not only among hosiery workers (it was mailed to every hosiery union member in the country), but also among the leadership of many other major unions, editors of labor journals and trade papers, and liberal colleges and labor circles throughout the country. In addition, the hosiery workers' media campaign sent out articles to "27 local papers, 2 press services, and 140 labor papers in 20 cities." The importance of the union's newspaper lay as much in its readership as in its editorial innovations, for the paper was widely and closely read by most members. Beyond coverage of strikes and organizing activities at the union's own mills and others, the paper was the primary vehicle for dissemination of alternative viewpoints on referenda questions. Workers were keenly interested in learning the pros and cons of issues that they would vote on and that would affect their pay, such as assessments to support other unions and causes, as well as other matters of concern to their working lives. At the first constitutional convention of the CIO in 1938, John L. Lewis called for a labor press that would give attention to national and political issues that were the common concern of all organized labor. The *Hosiery Worker* set a precedent for his call more than ten years before that convention. Through the union's educational programs, young workers were enmeshed in a web of ideas and activities whose primary aim was to instill in them a sense of what a "just" society really meant. Most important, it was an attempt to convince them that it was truly possible to achieve such a society through activism.[64]

The committee on education at the 1927 convention, consisting of three young women and two men, gave a report that contained specific recommendations for educating and organizing within the AFFFHW. These included the continued utilization of Brookwood and other labor colleges; the promotion of labor newspapers; union-controlled sports and their extension throughout the country; labor conferences in the South; and an extensive program of social and recreational activity that would serve to attach the entire family to the union. For social life was, after all, an important element of the youth culture.[65]

The union had always sponsored some social activities for its members, but during the 1920s Branch 1 members pushed for an expanded program of social activity for the hosiery federation, including intershop and interstate sports leagues. These included women's teams as well as men's, and encompassed bowling, softball, baseball, basketball, and soccer. Branch 1 provided funding for equipment for its local shop teams, and competitions often drew large crowds from the neighborhoods. Branch officials sometimes participated in games specifically staged to attract members of the community. As women became more visible in the union in general, some leagues sported mixed-gender teams.[66]

Outings often included excursions to the New Jersey shore, and on one such trip to Atlantic City, Philadelphia's Branch 1 invited locals in New Jersey along. It later ran a fishing trip from Cape May, New Jersey, in which the knitters of the Gotham shop claimed the record for the "fewest fish caught." Sometimes locals experimented with new, often gender-specific ideas, to attract younger people. Examples included a meeting held on the night of the biggest boxing event of the decade: the Jack Dempsey–Gene Tunney rematch to decide the world heavyweight championship. Male members set up a radio in the meeting hall and "sent out the word," which resulted in a packed meeting. The meeting first conducted its business, after which members listened to the fight. Later, two young men staged a boxing match in person, dressed in "gaudy tights." Some of the older men also got into the spirit and "mixed it," showing that they could hold their own with the youth. And, as discussed in the next chapter, women workers also began to introduce specific activities designed to appeal to young women members and to hold their own meetings.[67]

The union's social activities appealed to the families of members, but also engaged directly with the youth culture of the 1920s, even to the point of openly ignoring Prohibition. Some of these activities took the form of excursions that encouraged participation from members of different branches, male and female, promoting camaraderie between these groups. Sometimes locals held picnics to which both organized and unorganized workers were invited along with their families. Among the most frequent social events attended by union members in Kensington were dances, banquets, and parties. In 1923, at the second annual concert and dance in Knitters' Hall, all members and their families were invited to participate. The event was free of charge, and professional talent provided the music for the concert. In addition, for those who wanted to stay out late, Presto and His Melody Monarchs provided dance music until 1 A.M.[68]

As the decade advanced, outings became more elaborate. In 1926, Branch 1's entertainment committee set up a boat trip that took participants up the Hudson River as far as West Point, inviting branches affiliated with the New York and New Jersey District Council to come along. The committee hired one of New York's leading orchestras to furnish music for the entire trip and also made arrangements to ensure space for children and those who wanted to bring a picnic, but participants could also purchase a full-course meal at a nominal price.[69] Branch 1 held another banquet and dance the following year, and the union newspaper reported that it featured "elements described in novels of 'high life,'" including colored lights, confetti, and balloons. Philadelphia radio station WCAU supplied the talent of the Southland Orchestra, and a knitter from a local mill performed selections from a skit, "The Workman," while two attendees gave what the paper dubbed an "especially interesting Black Bottom exhibition."[70]

The black bottom was a popular dance that was considered risqué, even erotic. The dance, like much of the popular culture of the day, originated in the African American community and was adopted by other groups.[71] A dinner dance of over 300 people held by the Brooklyn, New York, local, at which Philadelphia's Federal Hosiery Mill strikers were special guests, also featured the dance in a contest. Brooklyn claimed to win the contest, alleging that "while the branch may not have the best baseball league," they "challenge[d] any local to a 'black bottom' contest." According to the *Hosiery Worker*, the secretary of the Brooklyn local claimed to be the only "sedate" person left by midnight, although the local's president insisted that he remained "dry all evening" due to the weight of his responsibilities.[72]

By holding such events and printing these articles, union representatives made it clear that they were not disposed to be judgmental regarding the youth culture. They even carried tolerance over to amusing stories about strikers, such as one about a young knitter who was prepared to "fight the whole supervisory staff" to get back a yellow-dog contract that he supposedly signed while under the influence of liquor. At no time was there any indication that these social activities were in contradiction to the labor rights–based campaigns of education and organizing. In fact, the camaraderie developed through these activities contributed to the working-class solidarity that became a core element of the *mentalité* of hosiery workers. That solidarity was expressed and strengthened through numerous daily struggles as well as larger organizing campaigns.[73]

The existence of such an all-encompassing labor cultural movement was not unique to the hosiery workers. It was part of a broader socialist culture that stretches back to at least the nineteenth century. Richard Oestreicher used the term "subculture of opposition" to describe the development of such a culture in Detroit during the 1880s which brought together skilled unionists, unskilled workers, independent radicals, German Socialists, and reformers, through the auspices of the Knights of Labor and an Independent

Labor Party. This subculture embraced a network of institutions (from Knights' assemblies, to cooperative stores, to singing societies, to a labor party), as well as "a wide range of informal practices and commonly understood moral precepts," that helped the subculture grow from a minority culture to a mass culture. Daniel Katz, in his study of New York's International Ladies Garment Workers Union (ILGWU) in the 1920s, identified a Yiddish culture of cosmopolitanism brought by the socialist Jewish immigrant founders of the union. Through education, dances, parades, sports programs, and singing groups, the ILGWU sought to create bonds of solidarity across the different groups that came into the industry. David Corbin found a similar situation among union coal miners in rural West Virginia in the early twentieth century. Fighting to establish fundamental economic, political, and legal rights, the miners developed their own political, spiritual, social, and economic institutions. The union became a means through which they strove to obtain social justice. The developments that can be traced among Philadelphia's hosiery workers fit within this historiography. All incorporated characteristics from their specific industries and communities. The common thread that ties them all together was the presence of proponents of radical ideologies, independent and socialist, and the cross-fertilization of ideas and practices that occurred among them, in the context of the lived experience of working-class peoples.[74]

The union's efforts to build a labor culture of solidarity and educate young workers to the possibilities of a new social order began to pay off in the development of militant pro-unionism among its youth. An early example occurred in August 1923, when President Warren Harding died in his third year in office. While his death cannot be said to have significantly affected the country in general, it did have an immediate impact on some of Kensington's hosiery workers. On Friday, August 10, the manager in charge of the Burlington mill, recently purchased by the Marshall Field Company, decided to close the shop in order to observe the national day of mourning that had been declared for the late president. To make up for the time that would be lost, however, he informed the employees that they would have to work two hours per day overtime. The women of the shop—loopers and seamers—refused to work the extra hours, although they did offer to work on the day of mourning. Because of their insubordination they were fired. Although the majority did not belong to the union at the time, union workers took up their cause, warning all potential candidates for those positions to "stay away from the shop." After several weeks of stalemate the entire shop went on strike in support of the women and for union representation. Meanwhile, at union headquarters, shop representatives put plans into effect to support all workers at the mill: knitters, women, and helpers.[75]

Although the male Burlington knitters went on strike out of solidarity with the women of their shop, these actions were also part of the campaign for full industrial organization that had been called for by Geiges and the union leadership. Organizational strikes were on the rise in Kensington in the early 1920s, as Branch 1 members shut down the Mutual and Cambria hosiery mills. Organizing activities were also in progress in the Burlington mill when that strike was provoked.[76]

Shortly thereafter Geiges issued a statement in the *Hosiery Worker* underscoring the seriousness of the situation: "We have reached a point in our industry that if we are to preserve it . . . every individual member must place upon himself or herself the role of organizer." He encouraged the entire membership to never consider a fight lost, and to help to bring about "100% Federation" throughout the industry. Organizing became a point of honor among hosiery workers, and friendly competitions developed among branches. Kensington's Branch 1 started an organization drive that it claimed every one of its members were participating in, "typical of the spirit of the old, reliable organization": "In many of the shops our members carry their lunch and eat before 12 o'clock and during the noon hour visit the un-organized shops, spreading the gospel of trade unionism among those who do not belong to the union."[77]

Branch 1 recruited many new members in these campaigns, not only knitters (still all male at this point) but from every auxiliary department in the shops. It also started a campaign directed at checking the spread of the two-machine system, and a strike over this issue was narrowly avoided at the Aberle mill in 1926. Aberle money also controlled two other mills, the Fidelity and Hancock shops. By the following year the Hancock became a closed union shop, the shop committee declaring that "every worker who does anything with production from the moment yarn enters the mill until it leaves as a finished garment is now a member of the union."[78]

As the campaign gained momentum, Branch 1 members claimed that they were "fighting on all fronts," with a lockout at the Brownhill and Kramer shop in which 95 percent of production was shut down, a strike at the Federal mill, a walkout at the Rodgers Company when management fired union members, and a strike at the Artcraft, a yellow-dog shop. Although in 1920 Branch 1 had fewer than 2,000 members, by 1924 it added three more shops and 500 members, over half of them women, and became recognized by the secretary of the Central Labor Union as "the strongest local in the city and probably the state." It made significant progress in organizing departments outside of knitting as well. This period surpassed any in the history of the branch, as it added 3,000 members in 1925 alone. Geiges claimed that they controlled some of the largest full-fashioned mills in the industry. By 1926 Branch 1 had enrolled 8,000 members. By 1930 it had 9,000, and by 1932 it had 12,000 dues-paying members. Thus, during the same period in which overall union membership in the United States was plummeting, Philadelphia's hosiery workers were experiencing phenomenal growth. By the 1926 convention the union had spent close to $50,000 in strike pay, and delegates to that convention also agreed to an assessment to further increase the AFFFHW's "fighting treasury." The vast majority of these strikes were not over wages, but were for dignity in working conditions, and for representation—the right to unionize. In a speech at the 1928 convention, John Edelman described the campaigns as a "question of freedom." "This appeal," he continued, "has had the most effect. These are the standards that carry the union."[79]

Meanwhile, competition among hosiery manufacturers was becoming intense, and in their drive to lower costs of production, manufacturers began to make unprecedented use of the courts, city police, and private agencies in an attempt to stop the union. As injunctions mounted, Philadelphia judge Harry McDevitt, dubbed the "injunction judge," readily sentenced pickets for contempt of court, often sending them to jail for indefinite periods until the union's lawyer could force their release. City police worked hand in hand with detective agencies; there were six private detective agencies working in the city by this time. Howard Kreckman remembered when the Railway Audit Company actually set up headquarters in a house next to the union hall, "even trying to listen through the walls." During the strike at Brownhill and Kramer, the company brought in strikebreakers, some from Reading, Pennsylvania, and forced them to sign a yellow-dog contract. The mill owners then sent copies to the union and threatened court action if they continued to picket. Union activists responded that the workers had "bartered away their rights as American citizens" and that "pickets would be on duty as usual."[80]

In the Federal strike, where management was demanding a fifty-four-hour week with no overtime pay, strikers' refusal to obey injunctions resulted in escalating arrests. Strike literature heralded the fact that "although led by older and experienced persons," it was "young workers" who had "launched this fight for industrial freedom," and promoted them as an example of the courage and solidarity possible within the younger generation: "There is the same spirit of resistance to injustice, but a newer generation of men and women are carrying it on. . . . . Few have been through strikes before but the

FIGURE 3 Young women strikers in jail shown flaunting their strike banner through the bars. Open-shop strike, March 10, 1931. *Philadelphia Record* Photograph Morgue [V07]. Historical Society of Pennsylvania.

spirit and determination and discipline is equal to anything seen in former battles of the Federation. Workers are out 100% and picket 6 A.M. to 6 P.M. Already 18 arrests have been made, over half of them women. One girl refused strike pay, urging that it be given to a married man with 5 children."[81] The last sentence in this paragraph was an attempt to promote a solidarity that crossed lines of gender and age (see Figure 3).

Through participation in struggles like this, the "youth militant" (in the union's terminology) came into being, a young person who, as John Edelman put it, was "willing to do almost anything for a just principle." What the union's youth were demanding was recognition of their rights to belong to the union. They saw the mounting injunctions and arrests as violations of those rights. As the violence of private agencies and police mounted, the collusion between the manufacturers and state authority became painfully obvious. These facts made real the contradictions between capital and workers—

the discussion of which was a consistent part of education programs—and moved them to a conscious class solidarity. Many not only internalized a construct of "justice," but came to believe that they were "fighting for the entire working class of the country." "Union" came to be not just an affiliation but an identity, and the "right to be union" became a matter of principle, as Howard Kreckman explained years later when he said, "I'm union by principle."[82]

In February 1928, Branch 1 of the AFFFHW sponsored a conference at the Philadelphia Labor College entitled "How to Organize the Unorganized." Primary among the stated goals of the conference was a program of action to make labor a "Crusade for Human Rights." Four policies that were agreed upon to receive priority attention were industrial unionism (the inclusion of all workers within a shop in the same union); the conscious mentoring of young people; the promotion of a wider conception of the labor movement as a "social factor working towards changes in society that would give workers the hope of greater power and control in the context of their own lives"; and the allocation of special attention to the "psychology and problems of women in industry."[83]

The attempts by Philadelphia's workers to exercise control over the various aspects of managerial prerogative, and their insistence on the right to "be union," had precedents in the historical culture of the community. But by the mid-1920s, with capital's intense attacks on labor and so many new workers coming into the shops, the growth of a loyal and militant constituency required more. The emphasis the union placed on "labor's rights" and the struggle to achieve a more just social order became the necessary catalyst for the creation of a militant, idealistic working-class identity among young hosiery workers. Through education and participation in struggle, they internalized an identity that connected labor with the cause of a "just social order"—one for which they were willing to fight. That fight would become so fierce that, by 1931, the Federated Press newspaper *Labor's News* would claim, "It looks like revolution in Kensington." But this "rights" construct became part of a much larger configuration that encompassed not only the workers in the industry, but also the community and a broader labor movement, and included them in a broad-based and inclusive "labor culture" that prefigured that of the CIO well before it came into being.[84]

The fight for rights and justice in the twenties was also a catalyst that helped spark the development of the union's labor feminism. Over the course of the decade the women of the hosiery union came to play an increasingly important role both in promoting organization and on the picket lines, as they became some of the most visible youth militants and, in fact, the "firebrands" of the union. As women became increasingly confident of their importance to the union, they pushed the leadership to promote a program that granted them rights as women as well as workers. They gained increased recognition of their "special" issues and some amount of greater power in the running of the union. But some of them would begin to demand a fully equal share in what they now considered their organization.

CHAPTER FOUR

The Firebrands of the Union
Hosiery's Labor Feminists

In these turbulent times when our city is thrown into an uproar, we cannot conceal from ourselves that women have played the part of firebrands.
—Comité Civil, Paris, 1795

During the strike, it was the girls, right in this room, telling the knitters to get out on the picket line. Throughout the city the girls certainly did do the fighting.
—Hosiery Workers Convention, 1932

It was a cold evening in February 1929 when Anna Geisinger entered the hall of the Dover Eagle Club. Despite the wintry weather in the New Jersey town, the hall was packed to capacity with young women, all of them workers in the full-fashioned hosiery industry. These young workers had braved the cold to hear her speak about labor unions, and women's "special issues" within them. A topper in a full-fashioned mill herself, Geisinger was an organizer for the Kensington, Philadelphia–based American Federation of Full-Fashioned Hosiery Workers (AFFFHW) and a member of the executive board of Philadelphia's Branch 1. She was also one of the union's most popular speakers. Walking to the front of the room, she began her presentation with a discussion of "why women must organize" and join the union: "The union backs up girls in controversies with their employers," she began. "The union is an insurance policy against discrimination and unfair treatment on the job."

By the use of such language she acknowledged that women had issues in the workforce that were related to their gender and, therefore, "special women's reasons" for organization. A self-described married woman and mother, the speaker drew upon her own experiences in the workforce for examples, thus creating a personal bond with her audience: "Girls should not feel that when they get married they are through with the union. Nowadays, no girl gets a permanent and guaranteed divorce from industry with her marriage certificate. . . . Only through organization can she expect to receive good wages and decent working conditions."

But her talk also went beyond local, individual, or shop-based issues to encompass a vision that encouraged identification with a broader, international construct of labor as a cause. Arguing that as well as "special" women's issues, every reason a man had for supporting a union also applied equally to women, she told her audience, "Every woman who works for unionism is working for a better world and more worthwhile life for her children and everyone else's children. The cause of labor is the same everywhere."[1]

The description of this meeting appeared on the front page of the hosiery union's newspaper, the *Hosiery Worker*. By 1929 it was not unusual to see articles on the front page highlighting women. Increasingly over the course of the 1920s, union literature supported, and even foregrounded, the rights and issues of working women, married and single, often as part of their celebration of the "youth militant." The Dover event was part of the broad-ranging organizing campaigns within the industry that had been in full swing for several years throughout Philadelphia and the surrounding region. Appeals to internationalism and the militant and self-conscious participation of women—as women, workers, wives, and mothers—were hallmarks of those campaigns.

Historians of women have begun to challenge a heretofore dominant narrative that constructed the 1920s as a time when a broad struggle for women's social and political rights entered a period of doldrums following the achievement of women's suffrage in 1920. Jacquelyn Dowd Hall, for example, has shown that working women were certainly far from quiescent in that decade. Women in southern textile mills battled for union rights, demonstrating both the independence they brought from their cultural backgrounds and the rebellion and assertiveness gained in part through the influence of popular culture. Yet, the strength of the earlier narrative has been remarkably persistent, even making its way into author Susan Faludi's eulogy to the feminist Shulamith Firestone: "Feminism had been in the doldrums ever since the first wave of the American women's movement won the vote, in 1920, and lost the struggle for greater emancipation. Feminist energy was first co-opted by Jazz Age consumerism, then buried in economic depression and war, until the dissatisfaction of postwar women . . . gave way to a 'second wave' of feminism." Within this narrative, working-class women in particular have not been given the credit they deserve for their contributions to an early "labor feminism," raising demands specifically related to "women's issues," including those of married women and mothers, and pursuing a feminist agenda in the labor movement.[2]

While such accounts of the pre–World War II decline of a female-oriented social agenda among laboring women are unraveling,[3] there still remains a historiographical gap between the early 1920s and the later women's movements that clouds understanding of the evolution of the latter. In particular, we need to recognize the extent to which the attainment of the right to vote and an accompanying discourse of equality brought about a rights-oriented cultural sea change among the broader population of women, not only those of the middle classes, but laboring women as well. Labor feminism has a deep and vital history stretching back well before the twentieth century, but in the 1920s the rank-and-file women of the AFFFHW took it to a new high. They not only demanded the right to unionize, equal pay, and participation in union leadership, but also fought for the rights of married women and mothers to hold jobs and for childcare—allowing women workers to have greater access to the workforce and their union.

The 1920s were critical to the evolution of gender identities in the hosiery union, for it was during this period that women came to play a central role within the hosiery workforce. Over the course of the decade many more women entered both the industry and the union thanks to the expansion of the full-fashioned hosiery industry and the subsequent union campaigns to fully organize all departments in all shops. By 1930, after a period of intense organizing, almost half of the 9,000 members in Philadelphia's Branch 1 were women. As women members became aware of their greater importance, their struggles for a measure of control over their working lives led to demands for full equality of membership, and they began to challenge the top power structures of the organization. Over the course of this period the consciousness of many of them evolved to include ideas of independence and rights that concerned their roles not only as women workers, but also as independent women—single, married, and mothers—merging constructions of "worker" with those of "modern woman."[4]

This process was not one of a direct, linear progression, however, for it developed in the course of a struggle that radicalized and changed the consciousness of the women who participated in it. It was rooted in both the historical values handed down within the union and the community and in elements of a modern consumer culture that incorporated the structural and technological innovations of a rapidly changing world. But it also grew in a world in which the recent movement for suffrage and women's social rights had a broader and deeper impact than has often been realized in historical analyses of this period. All of these influences came together within the AFFFHW, under the auspices of socialist activists in the union leadership, to create a vital—and very colorful—labor feminist movement whose reach grew well beyond the confines of the hosiery union.

Kensington's Working-Class Feminism

Working-class feminism had a complicated history in Kensington, influenced by a number of factors within the culture and history of the community. A form of "labor feminism" had been an important component of the Knights of Labor and was practiced in the Knights' assemblies in Kensington, the birthplace of the organization and a community with a lengthy socialist history. As a center of the textile industry, Kensington had a long history of women engaged in paid labor, including married women, and numerous female textile workers had been members of the Knights.

The Knights' Philadelphia newspaper actively encouraged women to be assertive, making a direct connection between campaigns for labor rights and those for women's rights and arguing that "to organize is justly one of women's rights." Homemakers as well as women employed outside the home were members of "ladies' locals," and all were full members of the organization. The Knights' Philadelphia order supported women's suffrage and acknowledged the full value of all women's work, both inside the home and in the factory. That recognition helped to upgrade women's role and fostered a more expansive conception of "woman's place" in the community. "Committed to broad social reform and the creation of a new social order," as the historian Susan Levine argued, the Knights established precedents especially relevant for Philadelphia's hosiery workers, for the hosiery union had direct roots in the organization. The Knights' vision, though sometimes contested, was carried on within the union and incorporated into its industrial organizing campaigns in the 1920s and 1930s.[5]

Culture, however, is an ever-changing result of a dialectical process, often reflecting the history of a space and the customs and traditions that are reinforced and passed on within it, but also subject to contemporary influences within the broader world as well. On its own, the labor heritage of Kensington's female residents may not have been sufficient to generate the flamboyant women's movement that developed there and spread through the union in the 1920s. But the lessons learned from that history, when combined with contemporary developments in American society, helped the union's women to develop and revitalize working-class feminism within the union.

The hosiery workers of the 1920s frequently came from families with deep traditions in textile, and, as one researcher discovered in the early 1930s, they had "inherited a hard-won philosophy and program" centered on job rights.[6] It was common for females in the community to pass on stories and traditions of resistance just as their male counterparts did. For example, it was from her

FIGURE 4 Alice Nelson Kreckman (first on left) on the picket line of the Apex Hosiery Mill, June 23, 1937. Although hemlines had lengthened by this period, many women still maintained a fashionable appearance. *Philadelphia Record* Photograph Morgue [V07]. Historical Society of Pennsylvania.

mother that hosiery worker Alice Nelson Kreckman said she learned to stand up for herself and for her rights, while former resident Jeanne Callahan always described her mother Jane as a person who "never took anything from anyone."[7]

Alice Nelson Kreckman was one of the ideological descendants of Kensington's early labor feminists. Walking every day to her job as a looper at the Brown hosiery mill near her home, she associated her "worker" status with a sense of entitlement to the rewards of her labor: "I was in the hosiery union. I was a looper. When I was eighteen, I was making good money ... but when you bought full-fashioned hosiery, you paid a dollar twenty-five for them. Some places it was a dollar fifty. Oh my heavens, they were silk! We made them! We felt we were entitled!"[8] Most young people in Kensington—like Alice—left school at a young age in order to earn for themselves and their families. From her remarks, however, it is also clear that the union was important to women like her: "We women went out on the picket lines a lot ... we went on strike ... well, we were union you know!" (see Figure 4).[9] Alice did not refer to being "in the union" or "part of the union." Her statement "we were union" is much stronger, indicative of the formation of an internalized identity. The camaraderie embedded in the "we" that Alice used was an important element in the culture of resistance that developed among these young women and their married sisters and was influenced by intertwining factors within the culture and politics of the community, the time period, and the union. For the rebellious youth culture that followed World War I had particular elements that uniquely affected the development of the social identities of young women, including a sense that they had achieved a new kind of freedom and rights.

It cannot be disputed that women have been discriminated against in the workplace and the public sphere throughout history, but the resistance of women is equally clear in the historical record. At times, resistance has been so strong, and women have been able to achieve such important victories, that some of their contemporaries were led to claim that they had achieved equality. These overstated claims certainly masked the true reality of their lives; nonetheless, women's rebelliousness growing out of an assumption of equality often remained a powerful force. In the 1920s, the outright, victorious battle for women's right to the vote was high on that list of powerful achievements, and the memories of the heroic battles fought for the cause were still fresh in many minds, kept alive by the popular media's fascination with "heroines" of the decade.[10]

The arrests of hundreds of women from the National Woman's Party, and the incarceration of 170 of them during the last few years of the campaign for woman suffrage, made the suffragettes national news and powerful symbols of revolt for many young Americans. In 1920, Doris Stevens, a member of the Woman's Party, published *Jailed for Freedom*, in which she recounted the heroic struggle and near-martyrdom of the militants. Stevens described Alice Paul's role in the campaign in a particularly forceful manner: "She called a halt to further pleading, wheedling, proving, praying.... Those who had a taste of begging under the old regime and who abandoned it for demanding, know how fine and strong a thing it is to realize that you must take what is yours and not waste your energy proving that you are ... worthy of a gift of power from your masters."[11]

Whether rank-and-file hosiery workers actually read Stevens's book is unknown, but many of them certainly saw the coverage of the militants in the newspapers that were widely read in the community and heard discussions at home and in the crowded streets. For Alice Paul was not a stranger to Kensington. In the final decade before victory, after her return from England, she developed and tested some of the militant tactics she would subsequently use in Washington on the streets of the neighborhood. In July 1911 she, Lucy Burns, and several other suffragists attracted large crowds at open-air meetings at Second and Dauphin Streets, Front and Diamond Streets, and Germantown and Lehigh Avenues, all in the heart of the textile district. When she almost became a martyr, it is likely that her presence in the neighborhood and the support she was given were recalled by many residents.[12]

The union's director of education and research and its newspaper editor in the 1920s, John Edelman, was also a longtime supporter of suffrage and had been a member of the English suffrage movement. As the campaigns of the AFFFHW gained momentum, the *Hosiery Worker* frequently incorporated language similar to that of the suffragists, as in articles decrying "slavery" and "subservient" workers that reminded members of the necessity to fight for and to "take" their rights: "Don't ask for your rights, take them. And don't let anyone give them to you, for a right given too easily usually turns out to be a wrong in disguise."[13]

The importance that the struggle of the militants had for a significant group of Americans on the ground in the 1920s has often been underestimated. The fact that the decade of the 1920s has been portrayed as one of relative retreat by the feminist movement has overshadowed its significance in the evolution of gender roles and has led to an underestimation of the broader impact that the suffrage movement made upon American society.[14] For the movement did influence society in various ways, including having the effect of consolidating woman's position as "man's equal," at least as far as the popular press was concerned.

In the decade following the suffrage campaign, "heroic" women became important media subjects. Aside from film stars, the most prominent women in the 1920s were sportswomen, and almost every sport had its female heroes. Tennis star Helen Wills became known throughout the country because of her 1924 match with French star Suzanne Lenglen, which was given national media coverage, while Babe Didrikson, a golfer and all-round athlete, became a celebrated national personality. Some female sporting achievements were so important that they received virtually universal admiration in the press and even challenged the male monopoly on feats of heroism. When American swimmer Gertrude Ederle swam the English Channel in 1926, she broke the world records of three previous male swimmers. Returning to the United States, she was welcomed back to New York City with a ticker-tape parade.[15]

Female pilots also became very visible media figures toward the end of the decade with the successful crossing of the Atlantic Ocean by Amelia Earhart and Englishwoman Amy Johnson's solo flight from England to Australia in early 1930. The popular press broadcast their accomplishments as worthy rivals to those of Charles Lindbergh. Earhart became known popularly as "Lady Lindy." Earhart was also an editor for *Cosmopolitan* magazine and traveled and lectured frequently. Women such as these were unquestionably influenced by the movement for women's rights, and they, in turn, made a huge impact upon popular society. In an interview with the press after her successful flight, Amy Johnson expressed what can be called a feminist sentiment when she claimed that "the greatest achievement of the flight was the vindication of womanhood."[16]

Kensington's young hosiery workers could see these heroic women in newsreels at any of the many movie theaters in the neighborhood and read about them in the popular magazines that proliferated in the period. And many of these famous women, along with film stars like Clara Bow, Joan Crawford, and Mae West, displayed a rebellious, self-willed side that led them to do, say, and, most certainly, wear whatever they chose.

The flapper garb of the 1920s evolved, in fact, from a demand for comfortable clothing stimulated by the growing popularity of sports among women and the growing fame of female athletes. With their low-slung waists and lack of bust lines, these dresses were initially modeled after women's sports attire, designed to allow freedom of movement. The French designer Gabrielle "Coco" Chanel was largely credited with bringing the idea into the early fashion world. And, as often happens in popular culture, the garb was then adopted by a broader audience and became a fashion statement, associated with the flapper.[17]

Whether the flapper was a negative or positive representation of women was a matter of debate in the 1920s, and remains contested among historians. While some historians of women's culture have shown that it was not contradictory for women to be socially conscious as well as fashion conscious, many have portrayed the 1920s women who embraced the flapper as "frivolous" and apolitical. Others, however, have admired the irreverent flapper, and she has even been seen as a revolutionary figure, the "first media depiction of woman as man's sexual and social equal."[18]

The flapper culture rapidly gained popularity among young women in the 1920s, and as hemlines continued to rise, the sheer, full-fashioned silk stockings, formulated in different shades and patterns to accentuate the wearers' exposed legs, became the iconic product of these "modern women." The young women who swarmed into Kensington's hosiery mills during this expansion were influenced by this modern youth culture, absorbing various strains of popular culture and new reconstructions of women in society. But they were also working-class women enmeshed in the long labor culture of the community and subject to the influences of their families and surroundings.

What, then, did working in the silk hosiery industry actually mean for Kensington's hosiery workers? This particular product was not some anonymous industrial commodity, but an important part of the very persona of the modern woman. As a gendered product (and one that carried with it sexual connotations), silk stockings were full of meaning that the workers who made them incorporated into their own lives, both on and off the job. Women in the mills were not only active in the production of the stockings, but they also wore them as part of their self-representation as "modern." Kensington's hosiery workers clearly complicate the stereotypes of the 1920s in important ways.

The manner in which fashion culture shaped the experiences and work culture of hosiery workers was complex and often contradictory. Work culture, as defined by Susan Porter Benson, is "the ideology and practice with which workers stake out a relatively autonomous sphere of action on the job," which may include acceptance of some features of the work environment but also opposition. For female hosiery workers, fashion culture was intricately interwoven with work culture. It moved beyond work, however, to embrace activities that included shopping, parties, dancing, and outings with coworkers, all the while wearing short dresses and showing off their legs in full-fashioned stockings. Such pursuits could have led them in several directions—toward becoming objectified, passive consumers of corporate-dictated culture, or alternatively, toward asserting "modern" independence and challenging older social mores.[19]

For these women the latter option became clearly dominant, as they exhibited increasingly conscious enactments of "modern woman" independence, coupled with resistance to manufacturers and support for their union. Union-made stockings came to represent a sort of "badge of freedom," in the symbolic sense of modernity, but also in the very real sense of providing economic independence for those working in this relatively highly paid industry. However, they were also a symbol of the entitlement, felt by many Kensington workers, to claim the rewards of their labor. Made of silk, they had been items of status for upper-class women, and though they became less expensive through the 1920s, they were never cheap. When Alice Nelson Kreckman said, "We made them, we thought we were entitled!," she was, as Nan Enstad argued, "appropriating a key expression of class privilege for women: fashion and adornment." And such actions fit squarely within the long traditions of the community and the labor theory of value promoted by the union.[20]

For the union leadership itself, its embrace of the "new woman" traversed a rockier path and operated on several different but related levels. First of all, the product was the lifeblood of the union and its members, and modern women (particularly of the middle class) were the major consumers of silk hosiery. Additionally, the overall youth of the workers in the industry necessitated an embrace of youth culture. In order to relate to an increasingly young workforce, the union leadership could not afford to be seen as old-fashioned. But primary among their objectives was to ensure that the workers and the public never saw the consumer product as separated from the labor process that created it. Over the course of the twenties they would develop, and disseminate, a propaganda and iconography that celebrated the modern, independent woman as one who "thinks for herself," with a passion for social justice that placed her squarely within the genre of the heroic women of the decade. By the end of this period, the confluence of all of these factors resulted, with the uneven support of the union, in a situation where women began to come into their own in the organization.

Girl Strikers, Heroes, and the Union

In 1926 John Edelman, soon to become director of research and publicity for the AFFFHW, wrote a review of the German novel *Faber, or The Lost Years*, for the Camden *Post Telegraph*. The book revolves around a plot in which a man returns from World War I to find that his wife has grown, both mentally and spiritually, due to her activities outside the home during his absence. While Edelman's review of the book embodied a complexity of thoughts, he perceived it to be an example of the growing independence of modern women, concluding the review with: "American women, wives as well as their unmarried sisters, certainly have many interests outside the home. They are 'wide awake,' and their fingers are in every pie."[21]

A former member of the British suffrage campaign, Edelman was a Socialist and a supporter of women's rights. He and his wife, a former settlement house worker, had themselves worked out a very far-sighted arrangement to handle domestic responsibilities while allowing both to continue with their public lives. When one or the other was elected to a committee, each got permission to allow the other to act as an alternate. Thus "neither the children nor the committees are neglected, and they take turns at both jobs." Both Edelman's book review and his political and domestic arrangements with his wife are indications of the influence that the movement for women's rights had on the culture of the 1920s, and the AFFFHW was especially attuned to this influence.[22]

The relationship of women and the AFFFHW, stretching back to the early days of the union, was not without problems. Although women were first admitted in 1914, after a hard-fought strike in which they had "proven themselves on the picket line," it was not until 1918 that they were represented at the union's national convention by a member of their own sex (not surprisingly, a delegate from Philadelphia).[23] Although men and women often supported each other in job actions, union affairs continued to be dominated by the highly skilled male knitters through much of the 1920s. As in other unions, early practices of the AFFFHW did not particularly encourage the participation of women on a basis equal with men. Until 1929 women had a vote at the annual convention equal to only one-third of a man's (one delegate per 300 women as opposed to one delegate per 100 men), and there were no national female organizers until 1928.[24]

Women in the mills experienced the same work-related grievances as men (and other grievances related specifically to their gender) and, on numerous occasions, behaved as militantly as their male coworkers. Before the mid-twenties, however, they were often excluded from planning and decision making in the union. Hosiery worker Freda Maurer claimed that this often provoked "angry responses from female hosiery workers because they were ignored when the men stopped the machines to hold a meeting."[25] Yet at the same time, female workers, in a display of the community's traditional solidarity, would sometimes circumvent male power structures by acting on their own initiative. In the 1921 strike, Maurer said, women "had been organizing on their own and so were ready when the strike was called."[26]

After the consolidation of the union in 1922 and the expansion of the industry, the influx of women and the union's goal of full unionization led them to develop a campaign aimed specifically at female workers. This emphasis on organizing women, however, did not result in policies giving them an equal say in the way the organization was run or equal access to the highest-paid knitting jobs, traditionally reserved for men. As late as 1927, when two female knitters were hired in a New England hosiery mill, the *Hosiery Worker* reported triumphantly that they had failed dismally, despite all the "hulabalo by Union enemies," even to the point where one had "her clothes torn off by the machine," a standard trope clearly intended to indicate that women were unqualified to operate the complicated knitting machines.[27]

There was wide recognition in the union that women had rights as workers that included decent working conditions and wages, and the right to work, whether they were single or married, with or without children, a reflection of the broader traditions in the community and the textile industry. But that did not necessarily mean that they were considered to know how to "run the union." This was a battle that still had to be fought, for backward ideas of masculine privilege among some hosiery workers were just as ingrained as they were in more traditional unions. Over the course of this struggle, female hosiery workers not only expanded their consciousness as workers, but also gained a deepened understanding of themselves as women, with rights and special needs that required attention.

One of the most important developments in the campaigns to organize women was their participation in union-sponsored education programs, many developed specifically for them. Just as Philadelphia's Knights of Labor had insisted that women be educated in the issues of the day, so too did the hosiery union's leadership recognize that the ideas, concerns, and consciousness of the growing female membership needed to be addressed. As young women continued to flock into the expanding industry, the leadership of the union was astute enough to recognize both the potential they carried for building the union and the dangers they could pose if they did not develop a strong loyalty to the organization. In addition, the Research and Education Department, headed by John Edelman, had begun efforts to seek the assistance of progressive women's organizations and to gain the support of female consumers in its campaigns to defend union hosiery. The relations the union had with its female members could easily reflect back upon the union and affect the level of public support it was able to acquire. Women's rights were also the subject of an ongoing debate in the Socialist Party that went far beyond suffrage, encompassing issues of equal pay, fashion reform, divorce, and even birth control. Some articles in socialist magazines like *The Masses* even promoted homemaking cooperatives to "socialize the household industry," echoing views expressed by some women in Philadelphia's Knights of Labor. James Maurer, the socialist president of the Pennsylvania Federation of Labor and a close ally of the hosiery union, was an open champion of the right of women to use birth control, helping to found both the American and the Pennsylvania Birth Control Leagues. Under his influence, by early 1926, the AFFFHW also became a catalyst in the launching of a labor-based campaign to "make legal the dissemination of information on birth control." The Pennsylvania state organizer for the American Birth Control League, Elizabeth Grew, an Englishwoman who had begun her career in England as a trade union organizer and suffrage worker, reported a "remarkable growth in public sentiment in Pennsylvania, New Jersey, and New York" due to union support. The union's championing of an issue of such personal importance to young women helped to strengthen the scaffold of female support for the union, as leadership began to implement within overall education campaigns a distinct focus on women.[28]

By the 1926 union convention delegates were submitting, and passing, important resolutions relating to women workers. One established that the national union's office help be paid time and a half for all overtime work and become members of an office workers' union. In another, all union locals were instructed to set up education classes for women and to develop and distribute a series of pamphlets especially for them. As female members began attending these classes, they also began to build cross-class alliances with women in the Workers' Education Bureau, the Women's Trade Union League (WTUL), and the YWCA. By 1927, women were attending hosiery union conventions as delegates and serving on committees more than ever before.[29]

At the 1927 convention Edith Christianson, a guest speaker from the WTUL, complimented the group on the number of women present and praised Branch 1 president Gustave Geiges for his "wonderful" talk at a conference of over one hundred "industrial girls." She then went on to tell them that "far too often labor organizations ... engage in a lot of talk and a lot of smoke, but don't do anything or get anywhere." Then, to the great delight of the women present, she quoted from a Will Rogers movie, saying, "The women did the work and the men went down in history." And in an example of the popular *mentalité* regarding equality that followed the suffrage movement, she informed the convention, "Now that women are equal, you'll forgive me if I use a little swear word—damn it! Women haven't gotten across to men what they have done!" Christianson also reminded the delegates that there were a number of progressive women in Pennsylvania, and in national women's groups, who would be very interested in helping them in their efforts. Included among these was Cornelia Bryce Pinchot, the wife of Pennsylvania's governor, and the industrial secretaries of the YWCA—information that the women of Branch 1 quickly followed up on.[30]

Hosiery women from several branches also contacted the Workers' Education Bureau and started classes that included study in English, citizenship, economics, parliamentary law, public speaking, and social problems. An article in the *Hosiery Worker*, reporting on the women's interest in studying parliamentary procedures, referred to a woman from the Workers' Education Bureau who was teaching the class as "that indefatigable champion of women's rights in industry," and quoted her as saying, "God help the men when we get through!"[31]

The first steps toward building a closer relationship between the Kensington YWCA and Philadelphia's Branch 1 were taken not by YWCA staff but by union members. Women from the mills often joined the industrial clubs at the YWCA as venues for social activities and recreation, having heard about them from friends, fellow workers, or advertisements posted in their factories. Alice Nelson Kreckman first went to the YWCA with a friend and coworker in search of recreation. But strikes and labor issues were frequently part of the conversation in these clubs (along with such topics as sex), and the conditions and grievances discussed were "nearby and everyday occurrences" in Kensington. College educated, the women who sought jobs as YWCA industrial secretaries generally had little previous contact with working-class women, but often did have knowledge of contemporary women's issues, and YWCA records show that on at least one occasion discussions took place regarding the Equal Rights Amendment advocated by the National Woman's Party.[32]

There is evidence that the YWCA industrial secretaries had an influence on the women of the hosiery union. Some of them were outspoken about female independence, both economic and political, and adopted assertive personas in other areas such as dress, including the wearing of pants. Alice Nelson Kreckman and others she knew referred to some of them as "manly women," a description that Alice identified with lesbianism. Whether that was in fact the case is unclear, for fashion itself could be a symbol of revolt, and a segment of the activists for women's rights had included fashion reform and access to more practical and comfortable clothing in their demands. Actresses like Katharine Hepburn who were known for challenging conformity in both character and dress often appeared in pants.[33]

But homosexuality was also a topic of discussion in the 1920s, as part of the general challenge to older sexual mores. Mae West, a favorite in Kensington, was an early supporter of both women's rights and gay rights, though she never called herself a feminist. She was in the news headlines in 1927 when she was arrested on morals charges for her performance in the play *Sex* and then wrote and starred in a play, *The Drag*, which, though banned on Broadway, was one of the first to portray gay men in a sympathetic light. As is true of other historical periods, challenges in one area of sexual mores often led to challenges in others. Whatever the reality of the situation, Kreckman appeared to take in stride the homosexuality that she perceived to be present among some of the women at the YWCA. When questioned, she responded, "They didn't bother me, besides, a lot of what they said about women made sense."[34]

After Branch 1 women reached out to the industrial secretaries of the Kensington YWCA, real relationships of solidarity and support developed between them. The industrial secretaries set up sports classes for women and held social activities, and union women spoke to the YWCA secretaries about the importance of wearing union hosiery. In early 1929, Anna Geisinger made a presentation to the Industrial Committee titled "The Story of Silk Stockings"; it included a "brief picture of conditions in the industry" and an urgent appeal to the women to wear only hosiery produced by "fair firms." Many of the YWCA secretaries began to take a personal interest in the union and provided important resources for them. Women workers were also attending weeklong sessions at Brookwood Labor College and summer schools in several parts of the country, including the Southern Summer School for Women, the Summer School for Workers at the University of Wisconsin, and the Bryn Mawr Summer School for Women Workers. The industrial secretaries of the Kensington YWCA were instrumental in introducing hosiery's female workers to Bryn Mawr, and students included Anna Geisinger, Freda Maurer, and Freda Hoffman.[35]

The interactions female workers had with their "educated" sisters broadened the scope of their experiences and their consciousness about women's rights. The contact those middle-class industrial secretaries had with the union's women had a real influence on their consciousness as well. Some became dedicated allies of the hosiery workers, leading Alice Nelson Kreckman to refer to the YWCA industrial secretaries as "left," a term that became very important to her. Perhaps one of the most important developments of this period, however, and one that flowed from the workers' awakening to a broader sense of women's rights, was the establishment of separate women's meetings within the union.[36]

In early 1927 Branch 1 held a special meeting to which only women were invited, where they discussed problems related specifically to women. The response was so overwhelming (the union paper claimed that Knitters' Hall was packed) that they resolved to hold separate meetings at least once a month in order to "learn more about the union" and to "develop greater ability among female members for leadership," and because they felt that their "special problems in industry" could be handled more efficiently when taken up at gatherings of women members. Union documents show that complaints among women included such items as "forced to work overtime, girls treated rough, boss gets familiar with girls who have nice figures."[37]

The importance of these meetings cannot be overestimated, as they served the purpose of what would, in a later period, be called consciousness-raising. Alice Kreckman remembered: "We would sit around and talk, just us women, about things that were important to women, you know." Branch 1 women also set up an entertainment committee to organize outings just for women, which included parties and dancing, playing cards, attending movies, bowling, and also social visits to women in other union locals. Occasionally they allowed men into their meetings after the business part was over, as when "several knitters were allowed in when it was discovered that they could play music." They also set up sports teams, not only at the YWCA, but also at the Kensington Labor Lyceum, where, in 1928, sports clubs were started for both men and women to participate in gymnasium classes and other indoor athletic groups. All of these activities served the purpose of building social networks and solidarity among different groups of women. It was during this period that Anna Geisinger emerged as an important leader in the organization, becoming, in the words of an article in the *Hosiery Worker*, "an excellent speaker, with excellent judgment and decision-making skills, and a credit to both men and women in the organization." Geisinger also became a member of the WTUL and, subsequently, vice president of its Philadelphia branch.[38]

The separate meetings helped female workers gain more confidence and learn how to formulate their grievances through group support. As a result, women from mills throughout the textile district began bringing up grievances and problems at board meetings of Branch 1, and a delegation began to regularly attend executive board meetings of the AFFFHW. Furthermore, speakers from outside the union helped them to see their place in the movement as broader than their local concerns. The milieu in which union activists operated provided a wide range of contacts that women could draw on, and they utilized these networks, often to invite other women activists to speak at their meetings. These speakers included two young women from Marion, North Carolina, who were on the picket lines during the "Marion massacre" of October 1929 and whom the AFFFHW was sponsoring on a tour of northern unions. Relating their story to a packed meeting of the women of Branch 1, the speakers "brought them to tears" (and gained pledges of increased support) as one woman described how her twenty-three-year-old-husband was "shot in the back by the sheriff's men," saying, "There was no help for the wounded" as "they opened the mill with scab labor while union men bled to death." Such language served to draw the line between union and nonunion labor in terms that underscored the principles of class, "rights," and solidarity. Labor martyrs were not unknown in Kensington and would again become a reality of life over the course of the hosiery organizing drives in Philadelphia.[39]

Speakers also included prominent women like Mary Anderson, the head of the Women's Bureau of the U.S. Department of Labor (who would maintain a long and close relationship with the union), and Clare Annesley, a member of the British Parliament and of the British Labour Party. Anderson, in one of her talks, told them, "No union has been more supportive of women than your union." Cornelia Bryce Pinchot, wife of Pennsylvania's progressive governor, would also become a familiar figure, even supporting union workers on the picket lines. Most of these events were organized by a committee of six female members of Branch 1, headed by Anna Geisinger.[40]

In 1927 the union made an important shift in its approach to women's work when it established a policy that men and women doing the same job, such as boarders, must be paid the same rate of pay, or "the rate for the job." By insisting on "the rate for the job" in its contracts rather than a "family wage" for its skilled male knitters, the union marked a significant advance in the position of women in the organization. Previously very few unions had adopted the "rate for the job" slogan; though there had been scattered support for the notion earlier from groups like the WTUL, it would not become a major focus of labor feminism until decades after the AFFFHW took it up.[41]

Through their educational experiences and increased participation in formal and informal union activity, women also gained the necessary experience and confidence to push for and achieve advances in other areas relating to their "special" issues, such as job security (an issue that would take on added importance during the Great Depression of the 1930s) and childcare. It was during this period that the union began to offer childcare at union events. Following an article in the *Hosiery Worker* in which the paper issued a "special" invitation to women and children to attend a large Christmas party jointly financed by several of the branches, the chair of the women's department of one of the mills, while agreeing that it was certainly "important that families, young girls, and fellows stage joint affairs and make social contact at affairs arranged by and for the union," also advised that "if the union wants to interest wives and mothers, they must take an interest in their children, and provide for their care," and not only at Christmas parties.[42]

Shortly thereafter childcare at union events joined the incentives offered to members. One example was at a family picnic hosted by the union in support of workers in the Cambria and Allen-A strikes. The day started with a caravan of 500 cars leaving from Knitters' Hall, proceeding over the new Delaware River Bridge and through Camden, New Jersey, to end at an amusement park for the outing. The event featured speakers in the evening for adults, along with a thirty-piece band and dancing. Significantly, "arrangements [were] being made to provide child care for families" so that "all c[ould] enjoy" the activities equally. Childcare was to become an increasingly important issue in the union due to its high number of working mothers, and the union's positive response to this issue continued to strengthen the framework on which the support of female members was built. When the union's housing project was built in the early thirties, a nursery school would be a centerpiece of its programs.[43]

The education programs and various experiences with "liberated" women, in everyday and formal settings, dialectically interacted with the history of the union and the historical period, and contributed to the emergence of working-class feminism in the organization in the 1920s. But the union was not just a passive observer of these developments. Some of the leadership, keen observers of modern society, were astute enough to consciously utilize both modern cultural developments and the radical history of the industry to promote the image of the working-class hero, applied to both men and women.

The growth of the industry and the expansion of women's jobs in the mills were making the organization of women an increasing imperative. And the fact remained that the very existence of the product was largely dependent upon the buying power of women. Given this reality, it was important for women, both as workers and as consumers, to be on the union's side. It was within this framework that the union embarked upon a strategy to subvert the meaning of "modern woman" and redefine her in the form of an independent woman who supported social justice. The campaigns directed toward this end utilized the 1920s media fascination with women, but also fit within the portrayal of "heroes" that was so prominent a feature of the popular culture. Following the conference on labor organizing at Philadelphia's Labor College in 1928, the union began a full-out utilization of its resources, newspapers, and connections within the socialist milieu in which it operated to dramatically promote a romantic picture of the labor movement as a "Crusade for Human Rights."[44]

An important change to the union's newspaper in 1926 was the addition of a special features section. These pages not only covered national and international events, but also added an educational focus that sought to promote an understanding of local union struggles as part of a broad working-class movement, better race relations, and, increasingly over the twenties, the concerns of women. The scope of women's activities covered in the paper was extensive, including social events, sports, fund-raisers, and even beauty contests, as well as educational and political activities. A female speaker giving a talk against company unions to the Paterson, New Jersey, branch "proved," according to the newspaper, that a "girl hosiery worker is just as good a speaker as a professor" when she told them that "only a great trade union can and will take care of the workers' interests." Another article described a dance, complete with an orchestra and a dance contest, organized by women members and held at Branch 1's Knitters' Hall for the purpose of building their "special treasury" for organizing women. In another, a topper in Branch 1, insisting that workers should not "feel inferior," encouraged them to attend education classes to gain a clearer and better idea of life and labor. And the paper also began to regularly feature articles promoting the role that women were playing in building socialism in the young Soviet Union.[45]

The *Hosiery Worker* also ran articles about a beauty contest held by Branch 1 at one of its outings to Atlantic City, New Jersey; women workers in short dresses riding on a float in a parade of a local in the Midwest; and a publicity stunt at the Hosiery and Underwear Exposition at the Waldorf Astoria in New York. In the latter article, entitled "Have You Got Em?," readers were told that judges would select "the prettiest pair of legs," and an artist would cast them in bronze to be used for store displays, indicative of the fact that union representatives, and the women themselves, did not contest popular representations of women and dress.[46]

These articles were part of the feminized work culture that was increasingly coming to the fore in the industry in the 1920s. But they often also carried an element of parody and intertwined the identities of union women as producers and consumers. Beauty contests were not a regular feature of hosiery union activities, and, in fact, this one was "arranged at the very last minute" to punctuate the outing of over sixteen hundred members of Branch 1 to Atlantic City, home of the Miss America pageant. Met at the train station by a crowd of union members and their families, the winner, wearing a red bathing suit and full-fashioned stockings, was then escorted by the crowd and a knitter dressed as Father Neptune on a rowdy tour of the town, providing excellent visibility for the union and its organizing campaigns. The article about the parade in the Midwest, captioned "This Is Not a Leg Show," informed readers that the women were participating in a parade sponsored by the Women's Union Label League, and that they were wearing union hosiery that "they helped to make," explicitly making the connection between production and consumption.[47]

Strikes and other militant actions taken by women in support of the organizing activities of the union were increasingly frequent news, and the merging of popular with radical representations became a core feature of the campaigns and strike propaganda. In the coverage of the strikes at the Federal, Cambria, and Brownhill and Kramer shops in Philadelphia, the union's paper increasingly focused on women workers' refusal to abide by injunctions and their willingness to risk arrest in order to exercise their "rights as citizens" to freedom of speech and the right to picket. As time went on, Philadelphia's women workers became increasingly involved in strikes in which violence, both by the state and through private agencies, was used against them. Hundreds were arrested, and many engaged in all-out street battles in support of their comrades, for over the course of the twenties they came to see themselves as the heroic agents of change portrayed in union literature.

The anthropologist Eleanor Burke Leacock, in a classic study of the suppression of women's power and agency in the writing of history, has argued that supposed female "passivity" is but one of many pretexts for explaining away women's oppression: "a characteristic that Western theorists, representatives of nations, classes, and their sex have attributed to their social inferiors, whether they be colonized peoples, people of color, working-class people, or women.... The similarity in the motifs is striking, people who suffer oppression do so because they have neither the ability, the intention, nor the desire to rebel." The actions of women in the hosiery workers' union represented a struggle for autonomy and power over their own lives, as well as within the union hierarchy, that catapulted them to the forefront of the labor movement. The support that they gave to the union's campaigns to "follow the shops" and achieve "100 percent unionism" was not only the impetus for a remarkable public relations campaign by the union, but gained them the respect, admiration, and support of many rank-and-file men. It was during this period that Alice Nelson Kreckman developed her internalized identity as "union" and that the union launched its "labor heroine" campaigns, part of its strategy for building the union and rebuilding the labor movement more generally.[48]

In January 1928 the *Hosiery Worker* carried a front-page article mourning the sudden and tragic death of a woman the paper called "one of the most remarkable figures in the American labor movement." This "heroic" eulogy was written for Sara Agnes Conboy, the secretary-treasurer of the United Textile Workers of America. Mrs. Conboy, who started work in a mill at the age of eleven, was described as "an active organizer, leading many bitter strikes," and the only woman to represent the AFL abroad, as a delegate to the British Trades Union Congress in 1920. She was also a wife and a mother, and had developed an interest in women in penal institutions, serving on a national committee on prison labor. Many women activists had become interested in women prisoners and prison reform after the experiences of the suffragists in prison. Sara Conboy commanded such respect, the article continued, that all officers of the AFFFHW attended the funeral of this "outstanding labor leader," a classic example of the "labor heroine."[49]

As the hosiery workers pushed the campaigns to follow the shops in many sections of the country during the 1920s, women workers became increasingly indispensable to their successes. In early 1928, when a strike shut down the Milfay mill in Buffalo, New York, the *Hosiery Worker* carried pictures of female strikers prominently on the front page, describing them as loyal and determined unionists and also stressing the union narrative that the right to unionize was part of an ongoing struggle for liberty.

The Milfay Company drew its workforce from young people of predominantly Polish parentage, largely female, assumed by the mill owners to be more docile because of their gender and lack of union experience. When, over the course of the strike, the union was nevertheless able to gain their support, company personnel brought in strikebreakers, used red-baiting tactics against union organizers, and tried to gain the sympathy of the surrounding community by challenging the strikers' "Americanism." In response, the union ran articles in its newspaper and printed strike literature constructing a heroic image, portraying these "children of immigrants" as those who showed "real" American spirit by withstanding a tremendous campaign of intimidation, arrests, and company thugs. And it was the "girls" who were the real leaders, deserving of special praise as they maintained the picket line through "rain, snow, and blizzards," standing up to attacks by hired thugs with an unflagging determination so that "nothing but victory could be the outcome of the strike." This heroic contest over the meaning of Americanism became a focal point of strikes in the 1920s and a real strength in organizing campaigns, as the union built an inclusive working-class counternarrative to "100-Percent Americanism" movements, one that stressed the right to organize as a struggle for liberty.[50]

The Kenosha Strike

Kensington was the birthplace and always the strongest center of the hosiery union, but in the 1920s and 1930s its influence spread to other parts of the country. With its low levels of unionization outside of a few large cities, the Midwest was fast becoming a haven for open shops. One of the union's successful campaigns had been the organization of the full-fashioned knitters at the large Allen-A mill in Kenosha, Wisconsin. In early 1928, however, the company expanded, and management attempted to impose the two-machine system, with the dual goals of cutting costs and breaking the union. When women workers walked out in support of the knitters and the company imposed a lockout, the hosiery union unleashed an action and media campaign that took the area by storm.

The concentration on Kenosha was a strategic decision made by the union's Philadelphia-based leadership. The city lay approximately thirty miles south of Milwaukee, a union stronghold with an elected Socialist city government. In addition, it was only fifty miles north of Chicago, the home of a historically strong Central Labor Union (CLU) with which the AFFFHW had many ties. Some of the union knitters in the Allen-A shop had come from Fort Wayne, Indiana, the location in which the AFFFHW had established its second branch (Branch 2) when it became a national organization in 1913, and Kenosha was also the home of the anti-union Nash automobile company, a factor that provided the possibility to reach labor on a larger scale. By this point the union campaigns to win the support of women were in full swing, and the *Hosiery Worker* was explicitly encouraging the historic role that women had to play in the battle for unionization, not only in Philadelphia, but in all other union locations. The strike in Kenosha was to become a catalyst for a nationwide media campaign, initiated in the Philadelphia headquarters and largely paid for by assessments from Kensington's Branch 1. And this very visible crusade, in turn, helped to project laboring women into national visibility.

Although the original point of contention at the Allen-A plant was the company's installation of the two-machine system, when managers told union knitters that they could return on a strictly nonunion basis it became clear that the company really wanted nothing less than to break the union. Over its course the strike became quite violent on both sides, escalating from fistfights and bricks thrown through windows to shotgun blasts and dynamite bombings. The bombings, directed at targets on both sides of the conflict, began in August 1928 and included an Allen-A warehouse, blasts at strikers' homes, and the most notorious, a blast that destroyed the summer home of the president of Allen-A.[51]

Fortunately, no one was killed in these incidents, and it was a testimony to the skill of the union's leadership and its media committee that they were able to create a public relations campaign that enhanced the union's image and built support for the labor movement. Much of this was accomplished through the union's employment of a romantic counternarrative of labor-based "Americanism" and by its focus on women.

After the arrival of union organizers from Philadelphia—Edward Callaghan, John Edelman, and, later, Anna Geisinger—the company filed conspiracy charges against the AFFFHW in Milwaukee's federal court and acquired a sweeping restraining order, called by union attorneys the "most drastic ever in Wisconsin history." Strikers and sympathizers were arrested for violating the order as they marched around the plant, singing songs and protesting what they called "rule by judges," a slogan that had become a signature of the union's campaigns against injunctions. Almost immediately the media campaign coordinated by John Edelman went into full swing. Union personnel, with support from other progressive and labor organizations, began circulating newspapers and literature with headlines crying "Trade unionists fight for Americanism when they uphold the right to organize" and "Trade unionists are translating into concrete terms the intent of the men who wrote the Declaration of Independence."[52]

Before very long the strikers were using theatrical and sensationalist tactics drawn from the history of both labor and women's struggles, including parades and car caravans, to get their message across. Local papers gave widespread and sympathetic coverage to a parade of children whose relatives were involved in the strike. The fact that the company imported armed strikebreakers from outside the city, housed them in the mill, and was receiving support from the large and powerful Nash Auto Company helped the union gain support among the citizenry.

In one incident, 7,000 people marched on city hall to demand that the mayor stop the company from housing the strikebreakers in the mill. In an article titled "Thrilling Moments in the Allen-A Strike," the *Hosiery Worker* described the resolution that "a committee of citizens" presented to the town council, citing the mill for importing "scabs" who were indulging in "midnight orgies," with "booze flowing freely," and women "imported from Chicago for their entertainment," while four machine guns in the basement were "ready for use." It was, after all, the Roaring Twenties, and the union was not opposed to using the sensationalism of the popular press. Two of the young strikers, winners of a dance contest in Chicago, even refused to accept a trophy that was being offered by actress Joan Crawford because she allowed her name to be used for the promotion of Allen-A hosiery. Receiving national attention in the press, Crawford personally wrote to the pair, claiming that she "knew nothing about the strike."[53]

When the strikers continued to defy injunctions, police repeatedly arrested them, and the union members used their notoriety to promote the strike. In one incident, women strikers, leaving the courthouse in Milwaukee where a judge had arraigned them for violating an injunction, dressed in striped prison uniforms and marched into the convention of the Wisconsin Federation of Labor, which had just convened in the city. Marching to the chairman's rostrum, they presented the chair with a miniature ball and chain, a stunt carried on the front page of newspapers throughout the Midwest. The next day they were back on the picket line and arrested once more. When this news was announced at the convention, the entire body of delegates marched to city hall to demand their release. The boldness of the women demanded that the men do something, especially after the news coverage, for to sit by meekly would have been considered an affront to their manhood. Such rebellious behavior was not only a signature of women strikers in Kensington; it was also a trademark of the struggle for suffrage and the "heroic" women who were so visible in the media during the twenties, and such activities by women often had the effect of shaming men into action.[54]

In October, twenty-six strikers, male and female, went to prison for refusing to pay a $100 fine for picketing. The *Hosiery Worker* featured a group picture of them with the caption "Heroic Workers Now Serving Jail Sentences." Channeling the suffrage movement, several female strikers started a hunger strike in prison, claiming that they were political prisoners sent to jail for "exercising their rights as citizens." After a subsequent meeting in Chicago at which such luminaries as Jane Addams and Clarence Darrow spoke for them, the *Chicago Tribune* featured the strikers in articles, and the *Chicago Daily News* carried a front-page article in which they were lauded as "youth militants." The union also sent female strikers on nationwide tours to carry the story to a wide audience, advertising their events in literature with headlines announcing "Heroic is written larger than ever as locked-out workers tour the country, filled with the American ideal of freedom." These women made appearances all over the country, including at large labor rallies, the central labor unions of many states, the AFL convention in Toronto, Canada, socialist events, and huge car caravans. One caravan of hundreds of cars started from Kensington and traveled through New Jersey to a Socialist Party rally in New

York attended by thousands. In September 1929 some of the strikers from Kenosha were featured participants in a "record-breaking" Labor Day celebration held by the Chicago Federation of Labor in Soldier Field. The *Hosiery Worker* reported that a "deafening peal went up to the skies from 100,000 throats" as the float carrying the young strikers came onto the field.[55]

The union also made advances on the political field as a result of its organizing campaigns, including not only the Socialist landslide in Reading, Pennsylvania, in 1926, but a socialist-led Labor Party that captured a majority of the membership of the Kenosha County Board and elected their candidate as municipal judge.[56]

The Feminized Iconography of the AFFFHW

The AFFFHW intensified attempts to influence a broad audience of American women by playing up elements of popular culture while at the same time ensuring that the product was not separated from the workers who made it. It developed a series of illustrated pamphlets and an iconography in support of union campaigns and union-made hosiery that was both directed at, and prominently featured, the "modern" woman. Literature often specifically targeted young women and their self-identity as a group. A flyer advertising union-made brands of hosiery attempted to engage the youth culture by underscoring the "sacrifice of youth" demanded by long hours put into the mills of nonunion manufacturers. Titled "Youth Wages a Long Struggle" and featuring a picture of a stylishly dressed young woman, it stressed that young workers were fighting to protect their health through union standards of hours and wages, saying, "Youth is fed into the machines" along with the raw materials.[57]

Another leaflet clearly attempted to co-opt popular culture at the same time that it underlined the union definition of what it meant to be a "modern" woman:

> To the Well-Dressed Women of America,
> Is the well-dressed woman of today who is so frankly devoted to lovely garments and delicate hosiery to be regarded necessarily as a person insensible to an appeal for social justice? We think not—We believe in the Modern Woman![58]

Some of the material read like movie bills. One, advertising an educational event in New York as "A Story of Heroism—Humor—Thrills—Enterprise and Colorful Incidents," extended a "special" invitation to women workers, informing them that dancing would be held after the talks. And in 1928 the

FIGURE 5 Art Deco representation of hosiery union logo. This image became an iconic representation on union literature in the flapper era. Wisconsin Historical Society, WHI-125325.

union launched what became its iconic image, widely used on union literature advertising union-made hosiery, opposing the yellow-dog contract, and supporting strikes. The very modern imagery featured a geometric graphic of a female, wearing a short skirt, with wind blowing through her short hair, and holding union-made hosiery in her up-stretched arms against a cityscape background, drawn in a distinctly Art Deco style.[59] Labor iconography was clearly not limited to portrayals of muscular male workers (see Figure 5).

Although frequently referred to as girls, these women were emphatically not portrayed as victims. They were independent, stylishly dressed, self-assured, young "modern" women, and this was repeatedly stressed in the literature: "The girls . . . are not merely followers of the men, nor are they simply acting on some blind, emotional impulse, they . . . are keenly aware of the implications of everything they are doing in aligning themselves with the American labor movement."[60]

At the union's 1928 convention in Kensington, John Edelman reported on the scope of union campaigns among labor and women's organizations. "Illustrated circulars were mailed to women's clubs and societies and other sympathetic organizations and the WTULs in many states," he said. "Whole carloads were sent out; one alone contained over 40,000 pieces." They were sent to the "auxiliaries of all international unions, social settlement houses and CLUs throughout the country." Donations were received from machinists as far away as the Panama Canal Zone, and Edelman "wrote at length" to all the more-liberal heads of women's colleges and deans of women in colleges throughout the country. The Women's Union Label Leagues and YWCA industrial secretaries in many states were supplying organizations with names of union-made hosiery, and prominent persons like the head of the federal Women's Bureau, Mary Anderson, were also disseminating the information.[61]

The union's follow-the-shops campaigns strengthened its presence in the general labor movement as it also helped to rebuild labor outside of radical Kensington. The romantic and heroic representations the union used to promote its work in various parts of the country were disseminated on a wide scale throughout both labor and women's organizations, and the evidence of their importance to the union was not lost on its female members.

Pushing the Union for Change

By the 1928 convention at Knitters' Hall in Kensington, Edith Christianson of the WTUL was congratulating the Philadelphia branch on their election of a woman to their executive board, as well as the AFFFHW generally on the increased number of women delegates: "The girls are going to get so good at running meetings that you boys won't have anything to do in the future," she said. This convention was to prove to be a decisive step toward women's rights inside the union.[62]

Of the twenty locals attending the convention, ten included female delegates. As the convention started, women delegates met in caucus to frame recommendations for the adoption of a special policy for organizing women. Following the talk by Christianson, a committee of eight female delegates and one male submitted four important resolutions, introduced by Kensington's Anna Geisinger. Her talk to the delegates just prior to introducing these resolutions gives some insight into the tactics these women used in dealing with male unionists.

Emphasizing that the resolutions were for the purpose of organizing women and making them aware of how important the union was, Geisinger said that the "girls are new to organizing and need the help of the men." However, their conduct indicates the exact opposite. It appears that they may have been "playing the game," by accommodating male delegates' ideas of masculinity, yet the resolutions they proceeded to introduce were specifically intended to forward a female agenda. The resolutions submitted by the female delegates clearly indicate that their experiences over the previous few years had brought them to a tipping point regarding their place in the union.[63]

Resolution 14 required the AFFFHW to secure the services of a woman organizer "to take charge of the organization of women in the industry and the women's problems." Discussion on this matter focused on the argument that a woman was much more likely to be aware of and understand the problems encountered by women in industry. Resolution 15 required that efforts be made to get women to take a more active role in solving their own problems and that leaflets and circulars on women's specific problems be circulated among them. In discussion on this resolution, Anna Geisinger urged all branch members to cooperate with women members, so that they would learn to take part in the governance of the union and not wait for men to do things for them. Resolution 16 then required the officers of all branches as well as all national officers and organizers to "put particular emphasis" on the organization of women in all departments. In discussion on this resolution, the women emphasized that the need to educate married men on the importance of supporting their wives' attendance at meetings should be given priority, with Geisinger insisting that "the knitters are not the most important group anymore, all are important." Referring to herself as a married woman and mother, she described her work with other mothers in the mills where she argued that they needed to take a more active role, because "work for the union was the work of the future."

Resolution 17 was perhaps the most interesting because of the language used to support it, as it unequivocally expressed the degree to which the political consciousness of a core group of women hosiery workers had evolved. This resolution stated: "Whereas lack of leadership among girls has been a big obstacle in their organization and Whereas, leaders no matter how much practical experience they have, need theoretical training in order to get as much knowledge and information as possible if they want to be successful, therefore be it Resolved that the Federation provide a yearly scholarship to attend Brookwood Labor College for the most promising girl," and further, that a woman should be immediately nominated for the award. Up to that point, although women had attended sessions at Brookwood for as long as a week, all two-year scholarships had gone to men.

Convention delegates passed all of the resolutions overwhelmingly, and a statement was entered into the records condemning the "superstition that young people and women could not be organized," indicating how important the organization of women was perceived to be. A female organizer was elected—Anna Geisinger of Branch 1—and the union delegates also elected the first female scholarship recipient, Fannia Sher, a topper from Milwaukee (after Geisinger turned the offer down), and presented her with a copy of George Bernard Shaw's "An Intelligent Woman's Guide to Socialism."[64]

By January 1929, Branch 1's women's meetings had evolved into a women's division complete with its own elected officers, and the union newspaper was backpedaling hard on its earlier stance regarding the inability of women to be knitters. In response to reports that women knitters were being trained in a Philadelphia plant, a newspaper article claimed: "The AFFFHW has never had any objection to women as knitters if they join the union and demand the same rate. Without organization they will be used for cheap labor.... Certainly there should be no divisions between workers." Most important, it was also in 1929 that women finally achieved full equality in voting privileges, when the union's branches passed a referendum for a constitutional change establishing one vote for every 150 members, regardless of sex.[65]

Female workers' independence and conceptions of themselves as women, aside from their position as workers, grew substantially over this period, and this can be seen not only in the achievements they made within the union itself, but also by the types of entries that were submitted to the *Pressoff Special*, the worker-run newsletter of the employees of Philadelphia's large Aberle Hosiery Mill. One entry, in the form of a poem titled "A Woman's Answer to a Man's Questions" (reprinted from an 1876 women's publication), after briefly covering a list of domestic "requirements" a man had for a wife, responded with "Now stand at the bar of a woman's soul, while I question thee." The author then proceeded to list her requirements, ending with "a laundress and cook you can hire with little to pay, but a woman's heart and a woman's *life*, are not to be won that way."[66] Another entry, titled "For an Inquisitive Suitor," stated unambiguously that "the truth about my past must be a secret known only to me," while an entry titled "Poor Eddy" described a wedding shower "Selma's" coworkers gave her in which she was presented with a rolling pin inscribed with that phrase. She proceeded to send it up to Eddy on the fourth floor, as a reminder of what would happen to him if he did not come home immediately after work on Fridays "with his pay envelope unopened."

In other entries the paper reported that "Ethel thinks the saddest thing a girl does is change her name when she gets married," and several women were admonished for being "henpecked" for not going out with the "girls." One of the most interesting entries was in the form of a poetic passage titled "For a Happy Married Life." This entry not only celebrates the "independent woman" but also indicates the high level of literacy that existed among some of the hosiery workers. The poem was, in fact, an excerpt from Kahlil Gibran's *The Prophet* titled "On Marriage," and it gives a clear indication of the degree to which at least some women were internalizing the idea of independence:

> Let there be spaces in your togetherness . . .
> For the oak tree and the Cypress grow not in each other's shadow.[67]

It is significant that this poem, which would become a cult classic during the late 1960s and 1970s, particularly among young women, was submitted, in 1933, by a woman.

The young members of the hosiery workers' union, and in particular its female members, reinvented themselves as modern "youth militants" in the 1920s. The focus of the union on community-based organizing opened the space for labor feminism to flourish as hosiery's women internalized a passion for social justice. Their militant and often selfless and creative actions in Philadelphia, Kenosha, and elsewhere garnered such publicity and became so well known in the labor movement and beyond that they unequivocally influenced the development of a later feminist agenda in labor. And through the course of their struggles they also helped to inspire the revival of the era's stagnant labor movement, including the founding of active labor parties in Philadelphia, Kenosha, and Reading.[68]

But for the union, the end of the decade was to bring many more challenges as it struggled to maintain a "fighting" organization in a city and a nation that were descending into the depths of the Great Depression. As 1929 turned into 1930, the crusade to organize the unorganized would add to its list of heroes its first martyrs, as the union's youth militants continued to play a central role in its campaign for full unionization.

CHAPTER FIVE

Martyrs and Working-Class Heroes in the Great Depression

At a time when most unions say "lay low" because times are bad, the Hosiery Workers reply "Oh Yeah? Let's Organize."
—*The New Leader*, March 1931

On Sunday afternoon, March 9, 1930, Kensington witnessed what the *Philadelphia Public Ledger* called "one of the most amazing demonstrations of all trade union history," when twenty-two-year-old Carl Mackley was eulogized as a martyr for labor's cause. The memorial for Mackley, covered prominently by all the major newspapers of the city, was attended by an estimated 35,000 union supporters and neighborhood residents, jammed into and overflowing McPherson Square, on Kensington Avenue in the heart of Kensington. It was described in detail on the front page of the *Ledger*: "Public services were held over the body of Carl Mackley, strike sympathizer, who was killed Thursday by employees of the H. C. Aberle Company's hosiery mill in a battle growing out of labor troubles at the plant. Thousands, so dense was the throng, never obtained a view of the coffin containing the body of the 22-year-old knitter ... but saw the flight aloft of six white pigeons, released at the bier as a symbol of peace.... Six hundred policemen were assigned to the district." At the ceremony's climax, Edward McGrady, sent as "personal representative of William Green, president of the American Federation of Labor," asked the assembled throng to take an oath that they would continue labor's struggle. Men and women solemnly raised their right hands and men removed their hats as they repeated the oath one phrase at a time: "'I hereby solemnly promise, that I will continue the struggle against low wages, poverty and oppression, and that I will not falter nor be intimidated by hired assassins nor discouraged by subservient and oft-times tyrannical judiciary; That if necessary I too, will lay down my life in order that all those who toil may be delivered from industrial enslavement by the un-American and avaricious industrial despots. To all of which, I, at the bier of our martyred brother, Carl Mackley, do pledge my most sacred word of honor,' Mr. McGrady said in solemn recitative. The repeated words came back to the speakers' stand in waves of sound."[1]

What is particularly compelling about this event is that it occurred during a period that many historians have described as a time of apathy, pessimism, and despair for the working people of the country. By 1930 the nation was mired in the grips of the Great Depression, a devastating and demoralizing experience for many Americans, with a labor movement debilitated by the defeats of the 1920s. But in certain places the organized working-class movement took on the Depression very differently, and Kensington and its hosiery workers represent an example of an alternative story to the defeatism described in many of the histories of the early Great Depression.

Flying in the face of the repressive policies directed at labor in the 1920s, the American Federation of Full Fashioned Hosiery Workers (AFFFHW) put tremendous effort into expanding its organization and supporting the broader labor movement. Building on the history, culture, and resources of Kensington's textile workers and socialists, it constructed a vigorous social democratic movement that drew on regional, national, and international connections to promote labor solidarity and an idealism that responded to a broad range of social issues.

In the 1920s the union had developed a community-based organizational structure that kept it firmly anchored in working-class culture but embraced a modern, cosmopolitan, multiethnic and intergenerational approach to labor organizing. Previous barriers to the advancement of women within the leadership of the organization had begun to crack.

By the end of the decade, however, the union was faced with many more challenges as it struggled to maintain a "fighting" organization. Despite the flowering of women's leadership and the remarkable militancy of the long strike in Kenosha, Wisconsin, the outcome of the Allen-A strike was not a clear victory. The battles there took on such proportions that both sides were required to pour in a huge amount of resources. The AFFFHW was fighting almost single-handedly within a weak regional labor movement, having to maintain strike pay for the workers who did not immediately get other positions, pay fines, and finance the media campaigns. During the 1930s Allen-A went out of business and the union declared victory, but it was clearly a Pyrrhic victory for the workers who had lost their jobs. In 1938 the mill reopened as a cooperative enterprise with a closed union shop, so in the end it was a delayed victory for the union, but the toll was heavy.[2]

It was under conditions such as these that the union embarked on a course that was a radical and controversial departure for many of its members: the negotiation of the first national labor agreement with uniform wages covering an industry in the nation. By 1929 the full-fashioned hosiery industry was approximately 30 percent overexpanded, with unrestrained competition among manufacturers the rule. Price cuts, followed by wage cuts, became common practice in the open-shop areas as the union failed to keep up with the rapid growth of the industry. In 1929 the AFFFHW controlled less than 50 percent of total production nationally. In addition to generally higher wages and, in Philadelphia, often older and less efficient machinery, some union manufacturers were also getting hit by the Depression.[3] While the hosiery workers helped to revive local labor movements during their organizing campaigns, their own immediate status was threatened. The economist George Taylor claimed that the two basic problems facing the industry were the need to correlate production with consumer demand and to eliminate differentials in wage rates among different areas.[4]

In Philadelphia, nonunion manufacturers were able to obtain at least seven draconian injunctions against the union that put sharp limits on picketing and in several cases prevented it entirely. Faced with extensive arrests and heavy fines, the union lost some strikes in the late 1920s. In addition, with the intense competition in the industry, nonunion shops were consistently undercutting the prices of the product of union establishments. In a strategic move, the national union leadership called a meeting with the union manufacturers in 1929 to try to find a joint solution.[5]

The contract of 1929 was an agreement between the union and fifty-two shops nationwide. It set uniform trade policies and called for uniform wage rates in union shops throughout the country and for an impartial arbitrator to settle disputes during the one-year term of the agreement. It also outlawed strikes and lockouts for the term of the contract and specifically stated that the union had the right to initiate organizing campaigns in all departments in the mills and obtain a closed shop. Another important addition to the contract stipulated that union manufacturers had to set aside 1 percent of their payroll in an unemployment fund and open their books to the union, with any profit over 6 percent going into pay raises.

But the agreement also made some concessions to union manufacturers on work rules, particularly in agreeing to the "two-machine shop" in 25 percent of union establishments. In addition, the 1929 contract allowed rate reductions on "extras" for knitters that equated to cuts of up to 20 percent. There were no reductions on women's occupations, which were paid less to begin with. Union officials argued that the contract was part of a two-pronged strategy, offering job security to union workers while they organized all open shops.

Not unexpectedly, given the union's militant rank-and-file traditions, this agreement generated heated controversy. While it did pass the membership by a very small margin on a referendum vote, new leadership led to more centralization of authority in the national executive board and growing rumblings of dissent within the ranks in Philadelphia and other locals.[6]

An example of the tension over centralization was the debate over the ratification process at the 1929 union convention. By the 1929 convention Gustave Geiges had resigned as president of the AFFFHW for stated reasons of health, though his adamant opposition to the two-machine shop may have been a factor. It was then that the union changed its policy of having only part-time officers and established a full-time presidency. Three men received nominations for the office. Carl Holderman, current vice president of the federation, decided not to run. Alexander McKeown, then president of Philadelphia's powerful Branch 1, also declined the nomination. It is quite probable that taking on a job that would entail enforcing the new contract was a factor in their decisions. By default, the third nominee, Emil Rieve, a knitter and executive board member from Milwaukee, Wisconsin, was elected as the new president. Thus, Rieve was the official who oversaw the ratification of the contract. At the convention Rieve introduced a resolution that had passed by a one-vote majority of the executive committee, recommending that the ratification process consist of a vote by the delegates to the convention instead of by a referendum vote of the entire membership. Intense discussion ensued, and a delegate from Brooklyn argued that some members were already complaining that the leadership was "putting things over on the rank and file," and that the ratification process required a referendum vote. A referendum was subsequently voted necessary for the ratification of the contract.[7]

The contract had mixed consequences for the union. The implementation of uniform rates would certainly be a step forward in preventing the rise of low-wage areas if it could be extended throughout the industry. If coordinated bargaining could be achieved, as some members of the leadership stressed, the union would possess the potential to close the industry so that shops in different areas could not be used against each other. On the other hand, the cuts allowed by the contract devalued the labor of the workers and lowered their standard of living. Just as important, the contract signified that manufacturers and workers had something in common—therefore undermining the revolutionary ideology of the union. As long as a "free-market" system with unrestrained cutthroat competition existed, advocates of the compromise argued, manufacturers and workers did have some common interests. But for a segment of the leadership and for a growing number of the rank and file, the union represented more than a simple economic institution—it was a conduit for the ultimate development of a program of social reorganization that saw the future in terms of a social democracy. It was for this reason that union members had agreed to maintain high dues assessments to keep the "fighting treasury" alive. In the years ahead factionalism in the union would become more intense. Meanwhile, however, as the 1930s began, the appalling suffering of working people would push Branch 1 and the AFFFHW to shoulder an even greater role in the community. And the campaigns to organize the unorganized in Kensington would add to its list of heroes its first martyrs, beginning with Carl Mackley.

The Great Depression

In 1929 the capitalist world was hit by the onset of a depression so deep that the very foundations of the system were threatened. During the mid-1920s the AFFFHW's leadership had attempted to take a scientific approach to understanding both the economy and their industry. By 1928 they were predicting that the freewheeling and uncontrolled production that characterized the twenties would lead to oversaturated markets and, in turn, result in economic catastrophe unless a more rational system of planned production was implemented. On October 29, 1929, "Black Tuesday," the stock market crashed, signaling the economic devastation that the Great Depression would bring. The Great Crash of 1929 caught most Americans unprepared, but hosiery workers attempted to develop immediate measures to alleviate suffering while also building a program aimed at fundamental economic transformation. Many of the strategies employed by union members drew upon and built on long traditions of community solidarity, emphasizing the power that came from being part of an organized working class. But radical activists in the organization also strove to link union and community concerns to a broad and far-reaching critique of the capitalist system of corporate power, and this vision animated the organizing and strategic planning of Branch 1, and the federation as a whole, during the early 1930s.[8]

As the Depression deepened and unemployment and even hunger and homelessness spread throughout Philadelphia and the country, Branch 1 strengthened its community roots, becoming in every sense a community organization striving to help residents maintain a sense of dignity and militancy in the face of desperation. Efforts to organize unemployed workers into a class-based movement of self-help, to prevent the evictions of families unable to pay rent, to help people feed and clothe themselves, and to secure planning and control of industry through unionization highlight the activities of this period. But the work it was doing was in no way parochial, and it strived to spread its efforts throughout the organization, the city, and the nation—to increase demands on government to provide relief for the unemployed; to gain fair labor laws; and to build strong labor-based political movements in every section of the country. Over the course of this period, by continuing to connect labor with something ideologically larger than the organization, the term "union" took on an even deeper meaning for its rank and file. To be "union" meant something, an internalized identity that went beyond wages and *standard* of living, to incorporate a *way* of living that represented fairness and social justice and that was worthy of being defended.

There was not, however, consensus on how to accomplish these goals, and this period also saw the beginning of a split, which would grow wider over the years, between those who began to move into the mainstream political processes with a limited, "responsible" trade unionism, and a large section of hosiery workers who continued to support a greater transformation of society. All of these developments were catapulted forward by the onset of the Great Depression.

The years of the Depression were a devastating experience for millions of Americans. Although there appeared to be great economic growth in the 1920s, and there was a tremendous increase in consumer goods, it was based on a market stimulated by advertising, greater access to consumer credit, and consumer debt. With the decline in unions and the gradual widening of the gap between the rich and the working class, consumption was not able to keep up with the vast amounts of consumer goods emerging from ever more productive factories. As businesses overexpanded and then began to shrink, unemployment increased dramatically. By 1932 there were an estimated 28 percent of households nationally that had no wage earner, and by 1933 between 25 and 30 percent of the workforce was officially out of work.[9]

As people lost their source of income, homelessness grew in Kensington and the city at large. In the face of a weakened labor movement, a conservative national administration, and no real system of relief for the unemployed, the suffering of many Americans grew unrelentingly. Hosiery workers Howard and Alice Kreckman experienced the Depression in Kensington first hand, and when recounting their experiences they often spoke of the trials of their neighbors. Alice described conditions as "pretty bad" in Kensington. "The Depression hurt so many people—we saw a lot of suffering. Yeah, things were really tough." Because they both worked in union plants they had some advantages over other residents, and when Howard Kreckman talked about the Depression he was careful to emphasize that conditions were not nearly as bad for him and Alice as they were for some others. "I can't complain about my personal life. We were lucky. But a lot of people weren't. I made out good when I worked. We never had luxuries—if you had a bottle of beer on a Saturday night you were doing good. But we always had enough to eat. A lot of people didn't. A lot of people suffered during the Depression."[10]

Between 1929 and April 1930 unemployment in Philadelphia rose 44 percent; by 1932 almost 300,000 people in the city were looking for work, often traveling great distances on foot. The historian John Bauman tells the story of one man's daily journey in his hunt for a job: "First I go over to Jersey to the soup factory, a furniture factory, and a printing place. Every place the same. 'We're slack. We don't want anybody.' Then I cross the river again and go up Delaware Avenue ... and stop at all the factories and printing places. Then I try the fruit and produce places along the dock." The shelters the city set up for the homeless, such as one at a Baldwin Locomotive Works building, were hopelessly inadequate. Jobless families lost insurance policies, and "less and less money was available for food, housing and clothing."[11]

Kensington had the second largest percentage of unemployed workers in the city. Bauman reports that only the "largely first-generation Italian population in the sparsely settled third district of South Philadelphia had a higher level of unemployment." Because Kensington was almost entirely industrial, the Depression hit it full on. Employment conditions also deteriorated in the hosiery industry because of shop closings, the cutting of hours and wages, and relocations out of the city. By 1932 full-fashioned work dropped 24 percent from its peak in 1929. Often, those who had jobs could get only a few days of work a week, and the hosiery union implemented a policy of job sharing to keep as many people employed as possible.[12]

There were many heartbreaking stories in Kensington during the Great Depression, but even in the face of such hardship many people tried hard to hold together neighborhood life. Community and social networks continued to operate, often participating in a complex of self-help activities among neighbors, as evidenced by the many activities of residents and organizations like the AFFFHW.

Working-Class Cosmopolitanism in Depression-Era Kensington

For those who had lost their jobs, the lack of money and resources was reflected in many ways beyond housing and food; there was often simply no money for clothing and other necessities. The hosiery union collected clothing and shoes for distribution in the community and offered such services as free eye clinics that provided examinations and glasses to its members. (Working on fine strands of silk for many hours at a time, often with inadequate lighting, resulted in eyestrain and serious eye problems for many workers in the industry, making these clinics an important resource for union members.) Branch 1 also contracted with local physicians to set up a general health clinic, located in Knitters' Hall, to provide dental and medical services to the broader community. And in a sign of the increasing significance and recognition of women in the union, the AFFFHW continued its support, financial and moral, of the American Birth Control League, which James Maurer, Pennsylvania Federation of Labor president and longtime hosiery union supporter, had helped to found. The union newspaper carried articles advertising the expansion of birth control clinics and listed their locations. By the beginning of 1932 there were 102 clinics in eighteen states, and supporters were actively engaged in opening more. With relief consisting only of food orders and no cash, access to birth control was a major burden and the risks of an unwanted pregnancy great. The AFFFHW viewed the availability of clinics that distributed birth control as one of the rights workers deserved.[13]

Union members also recognized the importance of seemingly small things in maintaining some semblance of normalcy for families with children, and they always made a point of including candy as part of the food baskets distributed in the community. Children themselves did whatever odd jobs they could find to get such extras. Although Jeanne Callahan's father continued to work for the public transit system during the Depression, his wages were meager, so Jeanne and her brother shelled peas for a local grocer "for a few pennies." Robert Gunther would often "hang around outside a local drugstore" in hopes of being called on to take a delivery to someone or "get a neighbor for a telephone call." Many people did not have telephones, and so the drugstore often received calls for nearby residents, and Robert too got a few pennies for his services. There was also a place in the neighborhood that rented bicycles, and Gunther sometimes cleaned them up for the owner, who would then allow him to ride one for free for an hour or two. Initiatives such as these reinforced the self-reliance that was a part of the general education of young people in the neighborhood.[14]

As the Depression wore on, the need for activities and recreation for youth became a matter of increasing concern. The AFFFHW increased its subsidies to the Pioneer Youth Club to help it expand its recreation programs and summer camps for the children of unemployed workers. Providing for the community's youth was also a growing concern for organizations like the YWCA and the YMCA in Kensington, as well as the Young Men's Hebrew Association (YMHA) in Philadelphia. The *Hosiery Worker* ran a column listing the programs and recreational activities that the YWCA and the YMHA made available (although, interestingly, they carried very little from the YMCA, perhaps due to its greater orientation toward "exporting religion," as Howard Kreckman put it).[15] The industrial secretaries of the Kensington YWCA continued to have strong ties with Branch 1, working closely with them in support of educational forums and programs for young women. The union women's association with the YWCA, in turn, helped to shape the political agenda of these young labor feminists.[16]

One of the YWCA's directors, Alice Hanson, was a particularly close confidante and supporter of the union in the early 1930s. Hanson had joined the German Socialist Party while doing graduate work in Germany in 1930, after having observed firsthand the growing power of the Nazi Party. On her return to the United States she obtained employment at the Kensington YWCA and became active with Philadelphia's Socialist Party and the union. During her stay in Kensington she and her husband lived in a communal house near the YWCA where several other members of the Socialist Party resided, including an African American woman. Called the Soviet House, it was often a place where disparate radicals and intellectuals stayed on visits to the area, and meetings and discussion groups were regular occurrences on the premises. Hanson wrote a series of articles for the *Hosiery Worker* in 1932 describing the rise of the Nazi Party and the escalating confrontations between it and Communists and Socialists in the working-class districts of Berlin and other cities. Her articles were part of a campaign by the Socialists to educate Americans about the dangers of fascism, which they did not see as confined to Germany. She also spoke at numerous events for the union, including a 1932 May Day rally in Kensington for Socialist Party chair and presidential candidate Norman Thomas.[17]

These close ties with the YWCA, which extended to several areas of the country, served important purposes for the union. The YWCA provided a venue for sports and social and educational activities for young women members, and the progressive outlook of many of the industrial secretaries (in tandem with the union's generally receptive attitude toward women's issues) led them to give wide-ranging support to union campaigns. YWCA secretaries disseminated information about union hosiery, and some even walked the picket lines during hosiery strikes.[18]

The effects of the Depression on young women in Kensington were multiple. For those who had jobs, it appears from the Aberle Hosiery Mill newsletter, the *Pressoff Special*, that fashion remained a part of life. But for many it was increasingly difficult to maintain a fashionable appearance, and the women at the Kensington YWCA recognized a "crying need for recreation" among them. But the YWCA secretaries were concerned that young women would not attend programs, fearing that "as clothes become shabby, they do not wish to mingle." To help alleviate these effects, the Y secretaries set up a "fund for girls," which Branch 1's women's division supported and to which they contributed. This fund provided money for such items as "toothpaste, haircuts, lipstick, and powder" to help unemployed women retain their pride and continue to maintain some facet of fashionable life. The union newspaper advertised the fund in recognition of the fact that the maintenance of a degree of fashionable appearance was an important part of the identity of its young women workers. Socializing had always been a vital part of community life, and residents attempted to maintain social networks and a semblance of social life even in the midst of the Depression. The strong community life of the neighborhoods, though under great stress, certainly did not die.[19]

Local cafes, restaurants, and taprooms continued to be places where residents gathered, and these establishments offered specials and reduced prices to help entice patronage. Often, members of the community provided entertainment free of charge. Jane Connor liked to sing, and she and two of her sisters sometimes performed in some of these establishments, accompanied by one of their husbands on the banjo. The *Pressoff Special* also described many occasions where local residents entertained each other. In one, several women "put on their dance" at the Oyster House, while in another, a male and a female customer sang a "melodious duet, to the delight of the happy throng." Sports leagues continued to be popular pastimes as well. The results of the soccer, baseball, and basketball games (male and female) were covered in the union paper, as well as bowling and darts. Often, after an important game, teammates would get together at gatherings hosted by the parents of one or another member. Movies and skating parties enjoyed continued popularity, and clubs, fraternal organizations, and associations such as the Jewish synagogue on Allegheny Avenue helped residents maintain social contact with each other by sponsoring dances and social gatherings. Articles in the *Pressoff Special* also indicate that strong ties continued to exist among the workers in the shops, male and female, employed or unemployed, and those continuing to have jobs were sympathetic to the plight of their less lucky compatriots. Entries in the newsletter often refer to members treating unemployed coworkers, such as when several women, after a union meeting, "celebrated getting their back pay by treating the 'out of work' Aberle knitters at the Log Cabin," a popular gathering place in the neighborhood.[20]

The union-sponsored social and educational activities that had helped unify the hosiery workers in the 1920s also continued in the 1930s. Although many social events were on a smaller scale, Branch 1 continued its educational activities in order to help maintain the morale of the workers. One important feature of the program was the reading rooms established in Knitters' Hall and other venues for the use of unemployed workers. The rooms were furnished with tables and comfortable chairs and provided a variety of periodicals and books, and officials hoped they would function as one means for the workers to keep in touch during "these trying times when all anti-union influences are working overtime to create a sense of defeat and hopelessness among the ranks of the workers." The union also started a library to help establish the organization as a cultural and intellectual locus for workers. Joseph Burge, a Communist member of Branch 1, took on the duties of librarian and wrote book reviews for the *Hosiery Worker*. In one issue he wrote a review of *Georgia Nigger*, a novel by John L. Spivak that exposed the horrors of the system of chain gang labor. Burge used his review to educate readers about what he described as the "new peonage system" in the South and the "new slavery" of the modern world. Formal classes also continued to be a focus of the union's educational offerings, and through them it attempted to develop the critical thinking skills that it saw as imperative to the founding of a new order.[21]

During the 1930s the union sponsored a study group, the Hosiery Workers' Group, at Knitters' Hall that drew male and female students from diverse segments of the community. The stated objectives of the program were to involve the students in "the broader cause of labor and provide a critique of capitalism," but it also attempted to provide examples of alternatives to the capitalist organization of society. It covered various forms of political and economic ideas, from producers' and consumers' cooperatives to both utopian and scientific Socialist movements. One class, titled Creative Reading of the Newspaper, taught students to critique mass media by analyzing the methods it used to increase circulation, such as "coloring news ... stressing the sensational ... displaying that which arouses passions, race hatred, war-scares, and the cowing of a class into acceptance of a hierarchy of wealth and social position." Benjamin Barkas, the instructor, was a teacher at South Philadelphia High School for Boys and later the American Federation of Teachers' representative at the Central Labor Union (CLU). Barkas stressed that "one may not be interested in politics, but when a political killing attracts national attention in a country where many labor massacres went by unnoticed, such news has significance." He emphasized that the media was not an independent entity and that "one must view the news as a player in the drama of life—not as a detached observer from another planet."[22]

This emphasis on developing independent thinking skills had been an important element of the union's educational programs since the 1920s and a critical feature of the oppositional culture in Philadelphia. It helped hosiery workers to put the events of the day in a larger context and to better analyze the underlying causes of their problems. A sample from several essays that the students in the workshop wrote gives the impression that the programs had some success. One student wrote that "assimilation of too much propaganda turns one into an 'insect' as one loses the ability to think freely," while another wrote that a person seeking a liberal education needed to be cautious, and "investigate every sermon, lecture, book, pamphlet, etc. that crosses his path." Similar classes also continued in other union locals in ongoing attempts to expose workers to labor history, discuss current events from a labor viewpoint, and energize the membership, fight dejection, and build class consciousness.[23]

Entertainment also remained a prominent aspect of the union's programs, and shop parties, as well as branch socials and picnics, continued to be important means of bringing workers together. In the early 1930s the AFFFHW was receiving less income due to layoffs and reduced hours, and funding strikes was an ongoing necessity. It was also putting resources into building the unemployed movement, but still trying to maintain some level of social life, which it recognized as essential to maintaining the spirit of the organization. Gone were the days of cruises up the Hudson and large dinner dances with "elements of high life." But union shop committees continued to sponsor skating parties, shop parties, and sports events, and the Philadelphia local sponsored branch-wide picnics. These events were subsidized for families and unemployed members by funds raised within the shops by the entertainment committees. There was a wide range of cultural experiences available to people in Kensington, all offered by fellow workers, including dance lessons of various types, opportunities to play in a band or orchestra, and even opera lessons. The proposal to teach opera to workers in a mill may seem at first glance to be rather unusual, but opera was certainly a "mass" form of music for many Italian Americans, and these activities, along with some of the names of strikers and participants in the Unemployed Citizens League (UCL), demonstrate the not insignificant proportion of workers of Italian descent in the mills. Other hosiery workers even wrote music. William Leader, a member of Branch 1 who would rise in importance as the decade progressed, wrote a ballad titled "Happiness Lane," which he sang regularly on a local radio show.[24]

Internationalist influences in popular culture were also becoming an observable feature in this early period of the 1930s, as the "laboring" of culture expanded into a broader population beyond the organized labor movement. Labor unions were not the only ones contributing to the enlightenment of the working class in Philadelphia, and Branch 1 wanted to make sure that workers knew about all the city's offerings.[25] In January 1931, the *Hosiery Worker* began a new column that was specifically intended to promote progressive cultural offerings available in the city. This column included reviews of movies and plays, and also commentaries on art, literature, and music. The scope of the offerings was quite broad, from a "Negro Revue" at the Schubert Theater to quite an assortment of foreign films, including films from the Soviet Union. The Europa, a movie theater in center city Philadelphia, regularly showed Russian films. In December 1931 the theater was showing *A Jew at War*, a 1930 Russian film directed by Grigori Roshal, whose aim was combating anti-Semitism. Other films included *Golden Mountain*, which the *Hosiery Worker* described as "the new talkie sensation" about the "revolt of the workers against Capitalism." Written by Maxim Gorky about a strike during World War I, the script gave "the actual accounts of the average working man and the events that befell him during the hectic days of the upheaval," and, as an added bonus, the sound track of the movie was composed by Dmitri Shostakovich. When the Europa showed Sergei Eisenstein's *Ten Days That Shook the World* (about Russia's 1917 October Revolution), the film proved so popular that it had to be held over for two additional weeks.[26]

But workers did not always have to travel to center city in order to see such cosmopolitan offerings, for some were also offered at the World, a theater at Third Street and Girard Avenue in Greater Kensington. This venue also showed international films such as *Schubert's Dream of Spring*, about the life and music of Franz Schubert, in its Philadelphia premiere; *Schrecken der Garnison*, a "musical farce about military life" direct from Berlin; and a French film, *Danton*, the "world famous story of the man who shook a world" during the French Revolution.[27]

This period also saw the expansion of another entertainment genre, labor plays, which the union tied in with its educational programs and aimed at the community at large. Although most associated with the artistic programs of the New Deal, dramatic performances were very much a part of workers' education in the 1920s and early 1930s. In March 1932, the *Hosiery Worker* advertised the performance of two one-act plays by Sholom Asch and David Pinski, *Cripples* and *The Street*, presented by the New Theater Group of Philadelphia's Labor Institute. These plays explored the issue of class conflict. In May of that year the Plays and Players Theater, an independent, liberal organization in Philadelphia, brought the play *Precedent*, about labor prisoner and icon Tom Mooney, to the city. As reported in the *Hosiery Worker*, the play had seen a "sensational run on Broadway," and the proceeds of this event were to help support the UCL. But the production that had the greatest intellectual and emotional impact on the textile workers of Kensington was *Mill Shadows*.[28]

In April 1932 the Brookwood Labor Players came to Kensington. A traveling troupe based at the labor college, this group traveled to industrial cities all over the United States to perform plays, songs, and skits before labor unions, organizations of the unemployed, and other groups. In Kensington they brought down the house with *Mill Shadows*, written by Tom Tippett, a former coal miner and union organizer. The play told the story of the 1929 Marion, North Carolina, textile mill strike—of which Kensington's hosiery workers had firsthand knowledge. Sponsored by Branch 1, the troupe put on two performances in Philadelphia. The first performance took place on a Friday night at the Plays and Players Theater in center city Philadelphia, but on Saturday night the troupe played to a packed house at the Kensington Labor Lyceum. The response in Kensington was so enthusiastic that when the curtain fell, the performers, caught up in the spirit of the audience, spontaneously broke out into a rendition of the "Internationale." The *Hosiery Worker* enthusiastically reported that the song was "taken up by all with such feeling that the house rang out with 'arise ye prisoners of starvation.'"[29]

Plays such as *Precedent* and *Mill Shadows* had very real and immediate significance for Kensington's workers, and it is easy to understand why the union supported such offerings. But it supported the arts more generally as well. The union paper carried another article, in April 1932, about Philadelphia city leaders' refusal to allow unemployed musicians to hold a concert in the city because they "feared that [the concert] might provoke a march by the unemployed." However, when Leopold Stokowski, the world-famous conductor of the Philadelphia Orchestra, informed the city that he personally was going to lead the musicians, "the city be damned," they backed down rapidly. Two days later Stokowski conducted a 200-piece orchestra of jobless musicians in an open-air concert in Reyburn Plaza, near City Hall, and raised $25,000 for their support. Stokowski alarmed officials sufficiently to cause Military Intelligence to monitor his activities. An informant claimed, in 1934, that Stokowski had "strong Communistic leanings," even scheduling the playing of the socialist anthem, the "'Internationale,' in one of his concerts for youth in order that they might learn it." In August, the *Hosiery Worker* ran an editorial titled "Labor and the Arts," in which it condemned "snobs and false aristocrats [who] deny the proletariat any authentic link with the arts," going on to say that "the musicians' union is proud of its position in the cultural world and proud of its union." It then ran a list of summer concerts in Fairmount Park offered by the unemployed musicians. The paper also informed readers about the protest by the Theatrical Stage Employees and Moving Picture Machine Operators against theaters unfair to their organization, listing the theaters and encouraging workers not to patronize them.[30]

Defending the Community:
Neighborly Networks and the Union

Networks of kinship and neighborhood were more important than ever for the survival of the community during the Depression. Entries in the *Pressoff Special* described many occasions on which people tried to help their less fortunate neighbors. Committees within the shops regularly visited laid-off workers, and baskets of food, clothing, and other necessities were common accompaniments to the visits. Often workers in the shops took up collections to handle particularly pressing problems. One such occasion concerned a seventy-seven-year-old disabled handyman from the neighborhood, who had no close relatives and lived in a room for which friends "who could hardly spare the money" were paying. Several neighbors, workers at the Aberle mill, found an opening at an "old men's home" for which an amount of $250 would enable the man to gain residence for life. With the agreement of the members, the shop committee offered to borrow the money, and the man moved to the home. When the loan came due, an article in the paper asked for contributions to pay it off. After the receipt of the money, the committee congratulated the members who, through their generosity, had "brought happiness to an old man who having passed his three score and ten years in life, suddenly found himself without a home and without money—but not without friends."[31]

Another time men in the shop held a "party" for one of the knitters whose wife was pregnant with their first child. An article in the paper, written in an amusing manner, listed "gifts" such as "a book on raising babies," supposedly authored by another knitter, "soundproof earmuffs," and "a lesson in how to walk around a chair to put the baby to sleep." However, intermingled among these humorous items were such gifts as a baby carriage, a high chair, and a baby bathtub—along with a statement emphasizing that "all other donations will be kindly accepted." The tone of the article was intended to offset any possible blow to the pride of this male worker, while at the same time attempting to help him out with his new family.[32]

Residents tried in many ways to defend their community and often came up with innovative methods to do so. In addition to "bootlegging" coal and giving it out to neighbors, Howard Kreckman described other tactics residents used to keep people supplied with necessities: "Another thing we did: all the gas supply was by quarters. You put quarters in the meter and you got a quarter's worth of gas. So someone got a bright idea to make a mold out of ice. They would freeze quarters and make copies. Then we would use these copies to get gas for people. There were a lot of tricks like that. We [he and Alice] had work, lots of people didn't. We helped my family, helped her family. Everything we made went for the family."[33]

These individual, shop-based, and neighborly acts reflected the broader historical patterns within the community. But this construct of "helping neighbors" underwent an expansion in meaning and scope during the Depression, as it became a centerpiece of the union's community-based efforts to go beyond "help" and build a movement of resistance to challenge the system that many of its members saw as the cause of such suffering.

At the 1930 national union convention at Knitters' Hall in Kensington, Emil Rieve, president of the national federation, argued, "We cannot as a union live for ourselves alone. We must be part of the community in every respect."[34] Branch 1 had always been immersed in the life of the community, but it broadened its community initiatives as the Depression deepened. In early 1930 local members set up a relief committee that began to quietly make disbursements to members in need. By October the committee had disbursed over $15,000 and was also giving out coal, groceries, and medicine, as well as making arrangements to help out in homes where childcare needs or health problems had arisen. Trying to help members maintain as normal a life as possible, Branch 1 also set up a fund of $10,000 to help families during the holidays.[35] Alexander McKeown, the president of Branch 1, attempted to ensure that no stigma was attached to such aid in a statement placed prominently in the *Hosiery Worker*: "Our organization is happy that it is in a position where it can still aid its members and proposes to continue this effort for just as long as resources permit. Mutual aid is the basis of trade unionism and we can assist our fellow workers without any suggestion of 'charity' entering into the matter."[36]

A questionnaire sent out by Branch 1 officials in an attempt to determine the extent of need among its membership found over 350 families in desperate circumstances. Although in the past families had usually managed to get through periods of hardship with the aid of relatives and friends, the investigators for the union found that current circumstances were so bad that outside help was imperative for many. Numerous cases were reported in the *Hosiery Worker*. One article described the plight of a young topper, the sole support for her grandmother and several younger brothers and sisters, who had fallen on hard times when the mill she worked in closed down. The article explained the problem in a manner intended to place no fault on the worker involved, but to place the blame squarely on the system: "When work was steady no assistance was asked and the family was well cared for," but "loss of employment for the breadwinner reduced this household to actual starvation and privation." The stories of suffering printed in the paper and, significantly, the designation "breadwinner," as well as the assistance given by the union, crossed gender boundaries. In many cases, people had no fuel, or their gas and lights had been turned off. Some families' homes had gone into foreclosure, and they were forced to live with relatives, sometimes faced with having the same situation arise for the people who gave them refuge. The relief committee found homes for a number of these families and paid many gas and light bills.[37]

As the Depression continued, the union's activities continued to be a vital and growing part of community life, expanding in both scope and scale. They included a fund-raiser held by the "girls' division" of Branch 1 that drew 600 persons to a dance at which a hosiery knitter, a regular performer on a radio program, contributed the services of his orchestra for dancing; benefits at local movie theaters such as the Kent Theatre at Kensington Avenue and Cumberland Street; and a benefit performance at Knitters' Hall by the "wonder child dancers," the Kensingtonians, in which they performed "tap dancing, acrobatics, classic and toe dancing," followed by a dance for adults.[38]

But as unemployment, hunger, and evictions continued to grow in their community, union members began to feel that a more dramatic and organized response was needed. It was then that articles in the *Hosiery Worker* began to encourage the fundamental American tactic of "direct action," in an attempt to instill a sense of both power and agency in community members. In early 1932 the union leadership issued a statement: "The time has come when the workers must take what their bankrupt leaders have denied them." With this manifesto it plunged head on into organizing a movement of the unemployed in Philadelphia, and particularly the union's most militant and ambitious community project, the UCL.[39]

By the early 1930s activity around unemployment was becoming more radical. The Communist Party set up the Unemployed Councils, and the Conference for Progressive Labor Action (CPLA), including the left-wing of the Socialist Party, developed the UCLs and the Unemployed Unions. In Philadelphia, the Socialist-led UCL was a strong mass organization, and included radicals of many persuasions and unaffiliated members of the community, as well as some local businesses and various other charities and associations within the city. The AFFFHW and the Textile Workers District Council were the most active in the organization of the UCL, which was headquartered in a building in Kensington donated by the Carpet Workers Union. However, the Philadelphia CLU also gave its endorsement, urging member unions to set up branches throughout the city. One of the most important features of the UCL is that it served not only to help people with utilities and food, and above all to stop evictions, but also to build a movement— united across race, gender, and ethnicity—to empower the unemployed as full citizens of society. Organized first in Greater Kensington, the UCL was extended into South Philadelphia and other parts of the city with the participation of unions and support from students of the Young Socialists' League at the University of Pennsylvania, Bryn Mawr College, Swarthmore College, and Temple University.[40]

The housing situation in Philadelphia was becoming desperate. By 1932 over 1,300 homes and apartment buildings were being sold at sheriff sales every month. The AFFFHW attempted to remedy the situation through a two-pronged approach. The first involved stopping evictions and providing people with food and other necessities through the UCL. The second consisted of building a strong, independent political movement that included the goal of the control of industry, while pressuring the state to pass legislation to provide relief payments and end antilabor injunctions. Howard and Alice Kreckman participated in both segments of the activities of the unemployed movement in Kensington. Howard talked about stopping evictions of neighbors as a point of pride: "We'd open up houses and move people in. It was a group of us, people from the union, the neighborhood. And if they tried to put them out, well, we'd picket the place and move them back in again!" The fact that many residents of Kensington had a history of union affiliation facilitated the founding of a strong movement. Articles in the *Hosiery Worker* and the *Union Labor Record* underscored the importance of solidarity to the success of the group's efforts, emphasizing the role that neighbors had to play.

One article described how the "solidarity and support of Kensington residents and the unions they [were] affiliated with" enabled the UCL to find housing for a woman with three children who, after losing her job, was discovered living over a stable with no heat or facilities. Another described the fate of a constable trying to evict a jobless man. He "narrowly escaped punishment at the hands of the victims' neighbors," and the UCL issued a warning that "any constable attempting to enter a worker's home [would] be treated as a trespasser."[41]

By the middle of 1932 the UCL in Kensington claimed a core membership of 500 steadfast activists, and growing. Over 140 families received relief daily, consisting of produce, coal, and other necessities, often donated by supporters of the organization. Members volunteered their services to collect food from local businesses such as the American Stores and Freihofer's Bakery, which they then distributed—fruit and vegetables on a daily basis, bread on Tuesdays and Saturdays. They also utilized the resources of charities such as the Red Cross, negotiating to obtain flour, which members of a Bakers' Union local then baked into bread. The UCL charged no dues and described itself as a nonpolitical, nonsectarian organization. And UCL members consistently reiterated that they would not discriminate because of "color, creed, race, or nationality." The *Hosiery Worker*'s pages often carried pictures of white and black residents of "Hoovervilles," with captions such as "Distress has killed race prejudice" or "They are victims of the same system," to amplify the need for unity.[42]

The activists did more than just talk about unity. The city's African American newspaper, the *Philadelphia Tribune*, carried numerous articles describing the activities of the unemployed movement, Socialist and Communist, in the black community. In June 1933 a near-riot ensued when the UCL called an "eviction meeting" outside of the home of a black family. Police had to rescue a constable who tried to break into the house to evict the family after he was set upon by white and black workers protecting the home. Police arrested four members of the UCL, including an "un-naturalized Mexican who had been in the country for 21 years." In another case, more than forty white and black men and women, associated with the Unemployed Councils, fought a battle with police who were trying to evict a black woman from her home.[43]

The UCL also distributed the *Union Labor Record*, which carried informative articles not only about the UCL's work, but also national and local news regarding labor, politics, the battle to obtain government-funded relief programs, and the imperative of building a strong, independent movement. Various unions contributed to the paper, and it was sold throughout the city, with all proceeds going to the work of the UCL. Its associate editor was John Edelman of the AFFFHW. Meanwhile, UCL members became increasingly involved in the fight to stop evictions, beginning a "no evictions" campaign in which they boldly informed the sheriff's office that "evictions of unemployed workers will not be allowed."[44]

The *Hosiery Worker* and the *Union Labor Record* began keeping score, chalking up each time the UCL came into conflict with a constable and informing readers, in a tongue-in-cheek manner, that they were just "helping officials to be 'good boys.'" Whenever the UCL received notification of an impending eviction, the call would go out to activists to assemble at the "neighbor's" house in order to confront the constable. People came regularly to the UCL office to inform staff of impending cases in all parts of the community, and confrontations took place on a regular basis. In one case, the *Union Labor Record* alleged that an official "decided to be an honest, self-respecting constable" after notification by the UCL that they were calling a "mass meeting" outside a worker's house and that the eviction would be "protested." The "meeting" consisted of 400 people.[45]

The "no evictions" campaign was predicated upon the "rights of citizens," and the use of the word "citizens" in the name of the UCL reflected this. Union members felt that people should work for a living, but they also believed that having a decent job was their right. If there was no work available it was the fault of the system, not the worker. Human rights were more important than property rights, which in itself was a contested term within the framework of the union and socialism. Unemployed workers were still "citizens," with a moral right to a decent life, and the union used the term to promote an all-inclusive definition of the working class, which it disseminated as broadly as possible. It encouraged all branches to participate in campaigns to stop evictions and challenge local authorities. In addition, union delegates to both the United Textile Workers of America (UTWA) and American Federation of Labor (AFL) conventions submitted resolutions encouraging all members to become involved in campaigns to fight against conditions that robbed workers of their rights. By the end of 1932 there were several hundred thousand members in a national federation of UCLs, connected through the networks of the CPLA, including the left-wing Socialists and, in many cases, the hosiery workers.[46]

All of this activity was defined as defense of community and not regarded as "illegal" activity by the residents. Howard Kreckman openly expressed this attitude in regard to such actions as bootlegging coal: "We didn't consider it stealing ... we never stole from each other." Robert McElvaine, describing the escalation of similar kinds of activities in communities during the Depression, compared them to those of some of the slaves in the Old South: "Some Depression victims developed a distinction between *stealing* (from a fellow sufferer) and what the slaves had called *taking* (what you need)" from those who had exploited you or those like you. This is the outlook that operated in Kensington, and it was reinforced on every possible occasion by the union and other organizations involved in the UCL. The UCLs represented both the growing tide of spontaneous resistance and conscious campaigns, organized to fight against a callous state apparatus that appeared to have no shred of compassion or concern for the rights of its own citizens.[47]

This "champion of human rights" ideology had been a centerpiece of the union's community-based approach since the early 1920s, and the challenges faced by Branch 1 and Kensington during the Depression had the effect of reinforcing the emphasis on community and neighborhood agitation that textile workers had long practiced. The Depression only served to strengthen the hosiery union's radical, class-based strategies, as it moved toward trying to become what G. D. H. Cole described as the "watch dog of those rights which a democracy should guarantee to its citizens." And the activities of the union strengthened the support that it received from the community in ways that would be very important to the campaigns it embarked on in the years ahead.[48]

The Rising Tide of Resistance: The Aberle Strike

Perhaps coincidentally, the date that Carl Mackley was killed, March 6, 1930, was also "Red Thursday," designated by the Communist Party as an "international unemployment day," with demonstrations in many cities in the United States and Europe. The largest U.S. demonstration took place in New York City, resulting in nearly a hundred injuries and arrests. William Z. Foster, the leader of the Communist Party, was arrested when "a crowd of about 40,000 persons were met by a police emergency truck with mounted machine guns and a tear-gas bomb squad" followed by policemen and detectives carrying clubs. In Washington, what a newspaper described as a "mob containing many Negroes" was dispersed with tear-gas bombs, and six marchers and two policemen sustained injuries in demonstrations in which women were reported as being "particularly vicious." In Philadelphia, however, although there was a small demonstration at City Hall, the real action was taking place at the H. C. Aberle Hosiery Mill, located at A and Clearfield Streets, in the heart of Kensington.[49]

The Aberle mill had been running as an open shop since the early 1920s. On December 31, 1929, the company, claiming financial distress because of "Southern competition," announced a wage cut averaging from 8 to 33 percent, with the largest cuts to go to women's departments. Aberle was already paying below the union rate, and the union claimed that "a number of highly skilled girl workers" were earning half the amount on their operations as that usually paid in average mills of the city. When union members refused the cuts (although it was an open shop, the union had signed up a significant number of the workers), management instituted a layoff, and night-shift knitters were refused access to their machines. In response to this lockout on January 7, 1930, the union formally declared a strike, and virtually the entire workforce, 1,400 employees, walked out.[50]

When the H. C. Aberle Company recruited enough strikebreakers (most from outside the community and out of state) to begin operating partially, picket lines were thrown up around the mill. Fights began to break out when someone, as one striker put it, "took a punch at a 'scab' who was walking out with his chest a little higher than it should have been." By January 20, the company had an injunction, police surrounded the mill, and the company hired the services of private police from the Bell Detective Agency. The injunction initially allowed eight pickets at the mill, but soon even they were forbidden, and strikers were not permitted to go near the mill or to "call a 'scab' a 'scab.'" By the end of January there was no settlement in sight.[51]

Shortly after the strike was called, over 7,000 workers crammed into a meeting at the Allegheny Theatre in support of both the Aberle workers and the Northeast Progressive League, a Socialist organization headed by Branch 1 president Alexander McKeown. The crowd was so large that at least 3,000 had to remain outside, listening to speeches through loudspeakers set up around the building. Speakers included representatives from the Brotherhood of Locomotive Firemen and Engineers, the CLU, the United Mine Workers, and the Textile Workers' District Council, as well as the AFFFHW. Meanwhile, the union hall became a locus of strike activity, holding morale-boosting events, dances, parties, and poetry readings. With access to the mill removed by the injunction, the strikers taunted police by parading on nearby streets and loudly singing what the *Hosiery Worker* referred to as "the strike song."[52]

Although the union offered to arbitrate the dispute, the mill owners refused to negotiate. After the injunction removed the pickets, crowds of sympathizers began congregating every evening near the mill. Union workers employed in other mills came to "help out" at Aberle whenever they were not at work, and neighbors joined in the activity as well, allowing strikers onto their porches and bringing them into their homes when police threatened them. Many people had a sense of ownership regarding their jobs, and taking a job that "rightly" belonged to another and accepting the protection of police and private detectives in the process were, in this period, still considered cowardly acts.[53]

Meanwhile, mounted police surged through the crowds, accused by the union, in a sarcastic reference to Teddy Roosevelt, of "'rough-riding,' not over hills but bodies." By the beginning of March many arrests had been made and a tense situation existed, with rumors circulating that Aberle had hired gunmen, "among whom were several Sicilians," in a reference to Philadelphia's notorious gangster activity, which was receiving sensationalist coverage in the press. On March 6, the crisis exploded with the death of Carl Mackley.[54]

The full story of what happened on March 6 is naturally disputed, but the major details are generally agreed upon. The incident started near the mill when strikebreakers, escorted by police, got into their cars to leave. The crowds at the mill were larger than usual on this day, "Red Thursday," and as the "scab" cars pulled away several others containing strikers and sympathizers followed them. According to Howard Kreckman, who was present at the mill that day, since the scabs were not local, strikers often followed the cars to "see where they came from." One of the cars of strikebreakers stopped for a traffic light, and a car following it pulled in front. In this car were riding four union men, including Carl Mackley, a rank-and-file union member employed at another mill. It is at this point that the stories differ. What is clear is that the strikebreakers opened fire on the car, firing so many bullets that the *Philadelphia Record* claimed that the back of the rumble seat was "literally torn apart by the hail of lead." Mackley was killed instantly and two others were wounded, one shot in the back.[55]

The strikebreakers later claimed that they had been attacked by the union men and acted in self-defense. This allegation was disputed, however, by a city park guard who arrested the strikebreakers and put in a call for police. He denied that the union men had attacked the others in any way other than verbally. The strikebreakers were heavily armed; holsters were found strapped to the steering wheel and upholstery of the car, and an automatic pistol had been emptied of shells. None of the four men arrested for the murder resided in Kensington; two of them lived together in a house in the Far Northeast section of the city near the county line. There were no weapons found in the car in which Mackley and the others were riding.[56]

As word of the killing spread through the community, the area surrounding the Aberle mill began to resemble a war zone, and police poured in. The next day, thousands of people began congregating in the area near the mill, filling the porches of houses all along Allegheny Avenue. As strikebreakers began to appear, over 3,000 people rushed into the streets, battling scabs and police who were trying to control the situation with horses and clubs. Flags were flown at half-mast throughout the district, and many houses were draped in black. But it was the memorial that the union held for the young worker that touched the conscience of the city and firmly ensconced Carl Mackley as a "working-class hero" in the annals of the community.[57]

On that Sunday afternoon in March, just three days after his murder, Carl Mackley, a heretofore "almost unknown youth," became the stuff of legend. The entire community was invited to view his body as it lay in state at the union hall and to attend the public funeral. For six hours thousands of people filed past the body. The next day the memorial was held at McPherson Square, in a park that was, ironically, the site of a public library established by a fund set up by that archenemy of labor, Andrew Carnegie. Hundreds of police lined the surrounding streets as the overflow crowd of 35,000 people filled the square (see Figure 6).

William Smith, secretary of the AFFFHW, officiated at the emotional ceremony in which union leadership eulogized the young man as a martyr in the "fight against slavery." Connecting the battle against "wage slavery" and for the right to organize with the historic battle against race slavery was to become an increasingly frequent theme of the union as the 1930s progressed. Following speeches by Branch 1 leadership, Edward McGrady, of the AFL, led the crowd as they raised their right hands and took the pledge. At least 600 cars, preceded by a band playing the "Dead March" from Handel's *Saul*, escorted the dead striker and his family to the cemetery. All arrangements were made by hosiery union representative Edward Callaghan and paid for by the AFFFHW.[58]

Howard Kreckman was present both at the mill that Thursday and at the Sunday memorial. Describing the events and referring, with a smile, to the theatrical staging of the memorial as "propaganda," he nonetheless emphasized how inspiring it was—and how effective. In the March 15 issue of the *Hosiery Worker*, an article entitled "Carl Mackley—The Man" described the young knitter as a "clean-living boy" who "5 years before his death woke to his responsibilities as a worker and joined the union." Giving his life to win the strike, the editor wrote, "a victory for human-rights, for workers' rights is the only monument he would have desired."[59]

The staging of the memorial, the response by the community, the wording of the oath, and the eulogy all drew on the construct of the rights of working-

FIGURE 6 Funeral procession for slain striker entering McPherson Square. Thousands of Kensington residents line the streets and peer from windows. *Philadelphia Record* Photograph Morgue [V07]. Historical Society of Pennsylvania.

class citizens, and served to unite the workers in a deeply emotional bond. And it also tapped a deep-seated sense of betrayal, felt by Kensington's residents toward a system that allowed manufacturers to hire paid thugs to murder "honest working men" defending their rights to strike and unionize. Even the press recognized the significance of the event for the community. An editorial in the March 11 edition of the *Philadelphia Record* claimed that it had "never printed such a picture" as that depicting the massed thousands in the square as they recited the pledge inspired by the tragedy of Mackley's passing: "It was not a mob ... but a great body ... stirred to the Depths of its Community Consciousness by a sense of conditions which it felt to be *unendurable by freeborn Americans*.... When thousands of Philadelphians vow to give their lives, if necessary, to save the toiling multitudes from Industrial Enslavement, the nation may know it confronts an *actual crisis in democracy*."[60]

After Mackley's death the turmoil in the area continued to increase, and union officials claimed that the near-riots and fights in the streets occurred despite their best efforts. Any local residents who dared to be strikebreakers were, at best, socially ostracized and their families treated as social outcasts. Any merchants who were unsupportive of the strike found themselves without customers. Finally, after much pressure from the city and the merchants' association, the Aberle mill owners agreed to arbitrate. The board of arbitrators handed down a decision supporting most of the strikers' demands, and the union felt it was a victory, as all cuts in women workers' wages were restored, rates approximately at union scale were set for most male workers, and none were blacklisted. Although the company did not sign an agreement with the union at the time, it indicated that it would do so by agreeing to put 1 percent of the weekly payroll into an unemployment fund, a clause contained in the national agreement. However, in September, despite a wage concession on the part of the union, the Aberle management formally refused to sign with the federation, prompting AFFFHW president Emil Rieve to issue a statement that management "seriously handicapped the union in efforts to maintain orderly and peaceful relations."[61]

The killers of Carl Mackley were found not guilty by a jury on which no one with any connection to labor or to a union was allowed to sit. It would, in fact, take the open-shop strike of 1931 before the union achieved a closed-shop agreement with the Aberle mills, for the Aberle strike was just the opening salvo of a campaign that spurred the president of the Northeast Chamber of Commerce to claim that in Kensington "we have today a condition of anarchy and terrorism which resembles conditions during the French Revolution."[62]

Revolution in Kensington—1931

"However calm the remainder of America may seem to be, Philadelphia has been giving the impression of being on the brink of revolution," declared the first line of a front-page article in the February 21, 1931, edition of *Labor's News*. The story referred to the hosiery strike in Philadelphia in which thirty out of forty nonunion hosiery mills in the city were affected, less than a year after Mackley's death. Over a dozen mills were completely closed down in the first hours, and police violence, massive arrests, and workers' retaliation were the order of the day. While the Aberle strike was certainly one of the most memorable of the period, it did not end the struggle for the right to organize a union that was at its heart. Nor, unfortunately, did the murder of Carl Mackley end the list of fallen martyrs for the cause.

Following the concessions the union made to the union-shop manufacturers in the national agreement, the nonunion manufacturers introduced

TABLE 2 Reductions in pay under the 1931 National Agreement

Job	1931 Pay Reduction
Legger (male)	35%
Footer (male)	45%
Helper (male)	25%
Topper (female)	30%
Looper (female)	33%
Seamer (female)	30%
Boarder (male and female)	30%*

Source: Gladys L. Palmer, *Union Tactics and Economic Change: A Case Study of Three Philadelphia Textile Unions* (Philadelphia: University of Pennsylvania Press, 1932), 209–13.

*By this point boarders in union mills were receiving the "rate for the job."

another harsh wage cut, and some began twelve-to-fourteen-hour shifts, in a ruthless attempt to drive down their costs and undercut the prices of union hosiery. The Aberle strike and the death of Carl Mackley had roused the community to fever pitch, but the Depression was beginning to exact a serious toll, as the cutthroat practices of the nonunion manufacturers threatened the existence of union shops and the union itself. Competition from outside put tremendous pressure on the organization. The unionized part of the industry had agreed to a national wage scale in 1929, and this was followed by the negotiation of a series of wage reductions to lower their labor costs. But these developments were also accompanied by changes in union governance to give greater power to the national leadership, including vesting the authorization of national referenda in the national executive board. The 1931 agreement allowed even greater rate reductions in return for the policy of a one-machine shop in all union establishments and the closed shop. Cuts ranged from 25 to 45 percent, with the largest cuts going to the more highly paid male knitters, who had already taken cuts in the previous contract (see Table 2).

Even with the cuts, union hosiery wage rates were still higher than in much of the rest of industry. But the agreement meant a serious decline in the workers' standard of living, especially given that many worked only a few days a week. The 1931 contract met serious resistance from the membership. This proposal had not been submitted for a referendum vote, and consequently there was an "insurgent" strike in branches in Pennsylvania, New Jersey, New York, and New England. National federation officials were thrown on the defensive and promised that they were not sacrificing militancy or democracy. This backlash from the rank and file also forced the board to submit another referendum vote in which an overwhelming majority voted that all new agreements had to be submitted to the full membership for vote. Subsequently, the union newspaper ran an editorial telling the workers to prepare for a new organizing drive, and Branch 1 speakers at the YWCA warned their industrial secretaries to expect more strikes. Rank-and-file members of Branch 1 even ran a competitive "radical slate" (composed of Socialists, Communists, and independents) against the incumbents in 1931. The slate was defeated this time, but it was during this election that Joe Burge, a Communist whom Howard Kreckman described as a "great orator," became an influential voice in Branch 1.[63]

In return for wage concessions, the manufacturers agreed to the check-off system of dues payment and to prohibit the contracting out of work to nonunion mills. They agreed to guarantee a minimum weekly rate, to submit a certified statement of earnings for each six-month period, and to revise rates upward if average profits in the industry exceeded 6 percent during the life of the agreement. Union leadership hoped that the reductions would be an incentive for the nonunion manufacturers to join with them in a program for stabilization of the industry. They also hoped that it would mean more work for union members.[64]

But the response by nonunion manufacturers was to institute wage cuts so severe that they brought real unrest to the open shops in Philadelphia. In the latter part of 1930 and early 1931 workers at eight nonunion shops walked off the job even before the union called the general open-shop strike on February 16, 1931. Union representatives issued that call with a blunt statement: "The union cannot do everything for you." If the nonunion workers wanted any help, they would have to help themselves, for rights were not given; they had to be won. The strike call emphasized the conditions that underscored the need for control of the industry, and declared the issue "squarely before the workers themselves." The response was dramatic, as thousands of workers in thirty-eight open shops throughout the city and its suburbs walked out. Once more, women workers were among the strongest supporters of the union, and their fight on the picket lines encouraged them to demand even more rights and power within the organization.[65]

The 1931 strike was marked by police harassment and violence due primarily to the director of public safety, Lemuel B. Schofield. Arguing that "this is no time to strike," Schofield issued a "flat edict against all strike pickets, assemblages, demonstrations, parades, and protest meetings," further announcing, at a meeting with union leaders, that he was going to keep the streets of Kensington "as clean as the floor." Announcing that they would defy the bans, Branch 1 leaders prepared to make a fight to the finish on the question of the right to picket. And in a response that the *Trade Union News* called one that would "probably become a historical document," union leaders further informed the director, whom they dubbed "Mussolini" Schofield, "We'll strike, and we'll picket, and you don't have the power to stop us."[66]

Police arrested hundreds of strikers in daily battles and held them on high bail. As soon as the union posted bail, however, strikers went right back on the picket lines. Headlines in city newspapers were full of strike violence, mostly by police, but strikers, including women, were not opposed to responding in kind, though there is no indication that union members ever responded with weapons in Philadelphia. Nor did the union try to restrain female strikers' actions in an attempt to portray them as victims. Instead, the union representatives continued to emphasize the role women had to play in the unionization of the industry, and "fighting" for labor rights was by no means discouraged. To emphasize their support of women's fighting ability, one edition of the *Hosiery Worker* even carried a speech by the author Sherwood Anderson, given before a group of striking textile workers in the South, in which he claimed that society was entering into a "matriarchy" in which "women will have to take the responsibility of [their] position" and "fight for men." This article, titled "Warriors for a Better World," is one more indication of the popular mind-set among some that women had achieved equality, and perhaps even dominance.[67]

Philadelphia's female hosiery strikers accepted the challenge. Women hosiery workers ignored injunctions, went to jail, physically battled police, and sustained injuries alongside their male compatriots. In one incident, reported in the *Philadelphia Record*, more than 200 strikers and sympathizers, "many of them women," battled police at the Walburton mill. Hundreds of neighbors joined in, "as fists and stones vied with swinging clubs and blackjacks"; over fifty people suffered cuts and bruises, while two were injured so severely that they had to be hospitalized. When it was over, seventy-eight strikers, of whom quite a few were women, were in jail for inciting a riot.[68]

The *Philadelphia Record* article was accompanied by a front-page picture of some of these women, dressed in modern garb, crammed into a cell and displaying a "hosiery striker" banner through the bars (see Figure 3 in chapter 3). In other cases, twenty women were arrested for singing "America" on the picket lines and refusing to move to the other side of the street when ordered to do so by police; eleven were arrested for "shouting at 'scabs'" (and threatening to beat them up), and one was arrested by a policeman, her own father, for disorderly conduct. At her arraignment she had to agree that she would "not wear her union button at home," an indication of just how much some young women had internalized their identity as "union." And there were many other cases in which female workers flatly refused to budge in their support of the union.[69]

The manufacturers imported strikebreakers from as far away as Kentucky and Illinois, and charged that union "terrorism" prevented them from getting enough local people. Although the use of the charged term "terrorism" was part of an effort to turn Philadelphia's citizens against the strikers, it is reasonable to assume that local strikebreakers would have had some concerns about retaliation, and not just from those in the union. Many residents often got involved in the conflicts, some in defense of friends, family, and other neighbors, some because they just did not like scabs. On one occasion, a crowd of more than 500 neighbors and sympathizers congregated outside of the Twenty-Fifth Police District headquarters at Front and Westmoreland Streets in Kensington as pickets were being brought in. When a member of the crowd threw a brick and smashed the glass of the door, "police immediately poured out, but since they could not discover the culprit, and the crowd was so large, they were forced to do nothing about it." And it was not unusual for a bucket of yellow paint to be thrown on the house of a strikebreaker.[70]

But the use of the term "terrorism" is interesting. For one thing, it was applied only to the union side, yet police violence extended to severe beatings and even charging crowds with guns drawn and bullets flying. Mill owners also used private police and hired thugs as strikebreakers, essentially mercenaries, who did not place many limits on their actions, as demonstrated by the death of Carl Mackley. There were multiple other cases that probably could have qualified for the term, such as when forty women having a meeting at the union hall were "menaced" when a bomb exploded outside the building, and two pickets were threatened by several strikebreakers carrying lead-filled hoses and a revolver. And yet strikers, male and female, consistently returned to the picket lines. Their actions are a testimony to just how deeply these young workers had internalized an idealistic construct of "justice" and "rights," which they connected with the union.[71]

Even the mighty Apex mill, a bastion of anti-union management, was hit by the strike. When over a hundred strikers from this mill entered the Kensington Labor Lyceum, they were given a tremendous ovation from the 2,000 other strikers assembled there, and they spontaneously broke into a spirited rendition of the "strike song." Apex mill officials posted private guards and city police at entrances, and their attorney, Arno Mowitz (who also happened to be the counsel for the German government in the region), obtained an injunction to remove pickets, and even to have an office shut down that the union had opened across the street from the mill.[72] Although the injunction was granted, the judge did acknowledge that there was a strike in effect and allowed the union to post ten pickets at the plant, two for each entrance.[73]

In April, Alex McKeown claimed that the nonunion manufacturers' desperate invitation to workers to "return to work" resulted in even fewer workers in the mills than there were before the call.[74] The 1931 strike was notable in that the union employed tactics that bore a striking resemblance to actions from international resistance movements that were being covered in the union newspaper. As evidenced by articles in the *Hosiery Worker*, it used Gandhian tactics of massive passive resistance, it "filled the jails" with strikers determined to make the police tired of arresting them. Over the course of two months police arrested over 1,200 strikers and sympathizers, including virtually all union officials. Anna Geisinger was arrested, along with fifty others at a single plant, and held on charges of disorderly conduct.[75]

Protests against the police began to pour in from residents of the textile area who demanded that Schofield be replaced, and also from the Philadelphia CLU, the Pennsylvania Civil Liberties Committee, and the Pennsylvania Federation of Labor. Even William Green, president of the AFL, issued a statement denouncing Schofield as "an enemy of society, opposed to the principles of freedom, democracy and justice." When a delegation of 110 striking women, all of whom had been arrested and were awaiting hearings, visited Pennsylvania governor Gifford Pinchot, he denounced the violation of civil liberties, in both Philadelphia and other nearby areas to which the strike had spread. He also promised to use his influence to have the strikers' rights restored. But their rights were not restored, and it was during the 1931 strike that another hero, this time a woman, was added to the list of martyrs—with dire consequences for organizer Alfred Hoffmann.[76]

Alberta Bachman, a striker at the Mammoth Hosiery Mill in Stroudsburg, Pennsylvania (a "runaway" Philadelphia shop), was killed when strikebreakers opened fire on a carload of strikers in which she was a passenger. As they had with Carl Mackley, the AFFFHW organized a memorial and funeral services which were attended by thousands of townspeople and a delegation of 900 workers from Philadelphia. All Branch 1 officers were present, and A. J. Muste, the clergyman and labor leader who had been a close associate of the union since the early 1920s, delivered her eulogy. "Her name and sacrifice are known all over the land," Muste said, and then placed the twenty-year-old woman within the canon of revered labor struggles and martyrs: "Someday . . . workingmen and women will bring their children to this shrine and tell them of the sacrifice this girl has made for the things they enjoy . . . her name is now lifted to those who died at Marion, Ludlow, and Philadelphia." Then, in a further example of the power of a great orator, he issued a warning to those in power: "To you in power and authority, I say if we do not grant in this land the elementary rights to all the masses with which to build a new order of life, then will come to pass the condition described by the ancient Psalmists: There shall be left not one stone upon another that shall not be torn down."[77]

While Muste's eulogy helped to swing public opinion to the union and helped them to win the strike, events were not so rosy for Alfred Hoffmann. Mill owners and township officials, in a move to "get" the union, filed charges of conspiracy against him in both the strike and Bachman's death because of his role as the organizer in charge of the strikes in eastern Pennsylvania. Although he was not even present in the town at the time of the incident, Hoffmann was found guilty and sentenced to a two-year prison term, while the strikebreakers who killed the woman went free. Hoffmann's case became a cause célèbre throughout Pennsylvania and garnered nationwide labor support. His case was taken up by the Pennsylvania Civil Liberties Union and many labor unions, and the AFL executive board also gave the hosiery workers their full support. While in prison, Hoffmann corresponded regularly with famed labor prisoner Tom Mooney and wrote a column for the *Hosiery Worker*, "From the Inside," in which he talked about some of his fellow inmates, in prison for the "crime of being poor." Finally, in June 1932, responding to increasing demands from labor and other organizations throughout the state, Governor Gifford Pinchot pardoned "Tiny" Hoffmann, and he immediately resumed his duties with the union. The union had negotiated agreements in twenty mills by September 1931, including the large Aberle mill, but the strikes in the remaining mills were called off.[78]

Political and Social Equality Is All We Ask For

The importance of women to the success of this series of strikes, underscored by Alberta Bachman's death, was recognized not only by the women themselves but by many of their male coworkers. Bachman's ultimate sacrifice ensured that no one in the union could ever again deny that women were in the thick of battle. The union's promotion of its female members, and their overwhelming positive response to the organization, strengthened the bonds between male and female workers that had been forged in the shops and the community. Anna Geisinger was one of the union's most admired speakers and often headlined large rallies. Following her election as the union's first female organizer, Geisinger became a staunch and very successful advocate of the union, traveling up and down the East Coast and to the Midwest, and working especially in Reading, Pennsylvania. Using language that was often "feminized," she drew a tremendous response from both men and women workers. As one of the speakers at a rally in McPherson Square that drew over 10,000 people during the 1931 open-shop strike, she accused the police of battering the children of mill workers: "With blows and speech the police abuse us," she charged. "We must do some housecleaning in this city." She had been arrested several times for refusing to obey injunctions against picketing, and her defiance was an example for others as she called on them to "rededicate" themselves to the "cause of labor." Many of these women and men had formed an internalized identity of "union" by this point, and they took seriously the mandate that people must fight for their rights.[79]

After their efforts in the 1931 strike, women in the union felt that the fight they had put up earned them the right to more representation within the national leadership of the organization. Though they had achieved equal voting rights with men within the union in 1929, there were still no women on national leadership bodies. At the 1931 convention they were able to get a resolution passed that guaranteed them a position on the national negotiating committee. By 1932 they were demanding quotas on the national executive board, with the introduction of a resolution requiring that four members from the mostly female auxiliary departments, one from each of the districts—Philadelphia, New York/New Jersey, New England, and the Midwest—should be placed on the national board.[80]

But the introduction of this resolution was very controversial. Some of the male delegates opposed the resolution on the basis that it would constitute "class legislation" and would not be "democratic" because, as one said, "currently there [was] no law saying who should be on the board." The auxiliary departments now had equal voting rights, the argument continued, and, since executive board members were elected, women should send a delegation "large enough to get them elected to the board." The supporters of the resolution (and they included men as well as women) in turn argued that it was a question of rights. A male delegate from Philadelphia's Branch 1, speaking in support of the resolution, proceeded to tell the convention that "in every case, the girls were the hero in the strike. During the strike, it was the girls, right in this room, telling the knitters to get out on the picket line. I heard it in the Labor Lyceum. Throughout the city the girls certainly did do the fighting, and I'm telling you, you'd better give them their rights soon."[81]

Another male delegate from Philadelphia, a Communist member of Branch 1, argued that if the organization expected to have an industrial union, certainly "departments that make up 50 or more percent of the membership should have a say in how things are run." National federation president Emil Rieve, however, vehemently opposed the resolution, as he had the one the previous year giving women a place on the negotiating committee. He accused "so-called progressives" of "trying to set up a class distinction," and he claimed that "women fought for equal rights, now they demand special rights." After some extremely contentious debate the resolution was finally voted down, but delegates from Philadelphia demanded a standing vote so that all could see who voted against it. Still not ready to let the matter rest, another male delegate, reading aloud from *Webster's* dictionary, argued that its definition of democracy—"political and social equality"—was all that was being asked. At this point a motion was introduced to end the discussion. Although the female delegates concurred in the resolution, one nevertheless exclaimed, to the cheers of both male and female supporters, "Every girl is going to go back and get their girls out and we are going to get our representation." By the 1933 convention, although they did not get their quotas, two women were on the national executive board.[82]

The women were demanding what would in later years be defined as affirmative action, but they did not use the language of "correcting past wrongs." There had been growing recognition of the special problems that many women faced when attempting to increase their activism (as at the 1928 convention when they won a series of resolutions aimed at breaking down male domination of the union), and clearly the institution of separate women's meetings indicates that they recognized the need for support groups. But while such meetings facilitated consciousness-raising and solidarity among women, the ideology that leadership should be vested in male knitters was slow to change within the top hierarchy of the union.

Some within the leadership, however, were open to the position women were articulating: women had served on the Branch 1 (Philadelphia) executive board since 1928. Complete equality was also a plank in the Socialist platform, but at the 1932 convention Anna Geisinger essentially accused Rieve of being a hypocrite regarding his commitment to socialism. As there are no records from the women's meetings, it is not possible to determine exactly what was discussed at them. Although women members had become well aware of past discrimination, the language of "correcting past wrongs" does not appear in union literature or debates at the conventions—but "equality" and "rights" do. Most of the networks that women had forged with men had been formed in the shops and on the picket lines. The women were basing their demands on the fact that they had fought for their rights, had spilled their blood, and therefore deserved such representation, using the same narrative that the union used to describe its history. Male coworkers with whom they had fought side by side, and who had also internalized that narrative, supported them in their demands using the same language.

The position of the national leadership regarding class legislation incorporated a legalistic understanding of the term that appeared only after the negotiations on the 1929 national contract; any reference to class earlier manifestly alluded to the great divide between workers and bosses. Before the contract, in 1928 and 1929, resolutions had been passed that granted concessions on a gendered basis, in education, organizing, scholarships, and meetings. However, arguments opposing class legislation could be—and later were—used in some cases to women's benefit as well, when dealing with employers. Thus, in 1935, class legislation was used to oppose the "marriage bar" that sought to remove married women from the workforce during the Great Depression, protecting their right to work at a time when that right was coming under widespread assault. But the dispute over representation on the national executive board in 1932 was also an indication of the rift that was growing between the top leadership and many of the local leaders and rank and file. Though by 1933 the differences would reach a level that, for a time, would threaten the very unity of the organization, the intensity of the conflict with the nonunion manufacturers and the government in 1931 overshadowed the developing internal discord.

The 1931 strike wave in Philadelphia, along with the hosiery strikes that hit eastern Pennsylvania, Reading, the South (there were 6,000 hosiery workers striking in North Carolina), and the Midwest, were clearly making waves in the labor movement in its period of "doldrums." The campaign to free Tiny Hoffmann grew to the point that he began to be likened to famed labor prisoner Tom Mooney. The Socialist periodical the *New Leader* summed up the importance of all this activity in an article in March 1931 titled "Philadelphia Strike Inspires Other Trade Unions": "At a time when most unions say 'lay low' because times are bad, the Hosiery Workers reply 'Oh Yeah? Let's

Organize.'... Daily the atmosphere is clearing. Workers are beginning to line up, without fear of labels, with those who are constantly pointing to new paths. The tide is turning."[83]

The years of painstaking work to build their union and support a revival of labor were, indeed, beginning to show some results as the economic situation became more desperate by the day. Increasingly the union newspaper's pages aimed to inform members about the growing wave of dissent, and to encourage both the membership and the general citizenry to take things into their own hands: "The workers must help themselves. If the masses were aroused, the industrialists, the financiers and political leaders of the United States would soon enough discover ways and means of getting industry turning once more.... Instead of turning back vast millions to the over-wealthy classes, the government would appropriate all the money that is necessary to alleviate starvation and suffering. This union has always made it very plain that the workers must be militant and have power.... Let loud enough protests be heard from the unemployed, we guarantee that action will soon be taken."[84]

Articles in the paper were constructed to speak to the pride of the workers, but also to their anger, so that any possible sense of despondency would be overcome. They argued that workers themselves were sacrificing and trying to help the victims of the capitalist Depression, while city councils and the rich claimed they could do nothing. Calling such inaction "a death sentence pronounced upon tens of thousands of our helpless fellow citizens by the owners of vast wealth," and vowing "we won't starve," the AFFFHW issued a dire warning to political and industrial leaders that "labor will fight against all... guilty of this appalling and brutal display of class action." It was not difficult to convince working people of the callousness of the country's leaders when the labor press printed comments like one made by an attorney for the Widener estate who, they claimed, "shocked a group of businessmen by telling the trustees they should give $100,000 'to protect their assets,' because 'unless the very rich contribute to help the very poor, we are due for a social and industrial revolution in this country that will destroy property values.'" This statement indicated not only the insensitivity of the capitalist elite, but also their rising fear of the "masses."[85]

By 1931 confrontational sentiment was indeed growing. In February the Socialists held a jobless demonstration at Philadelphia's City Hall which the police violently broke up. The *Hosiery Worker* accused the city of refusing the unemployed the right to hold mass meetings, charging that unless something was done to help families it would become "impossible for police to contend with the condition" that would be created. Meanwhile, the paper began to encourage radical action from both organized labor and the masses of unorganized workers, with articles such as one describing an armed march for relief by farmers in the Midwest, and threats made by Pennsylvania miners to raid local warehouses in order to get the essentials they needed. "Haven't city workers as much gumption as the farmers in Arkansas?" they asked. In one column, "It's a Great System," the paper quoted an advertisement from La Salle Extension University—"Do you know what to do if your home is threatened by foreclosure?"—and answered for them, "Well if you ask us, we'd refer you to certain farmers out in the Midwest who are oiling the old shotguns."[86] Union members often used the language of community pride and class as well as Kensington's labor heritage to encourage confrontational actions: "Let us revive the militant spirit of the textile workers of the Northeast. The mill workers of this section are class-conscious by heritage and training and in times of crisis their fighting blood rises and things happen. It is high time we got our fighting blood up now."[87]

Articles told the stories of people facing starvation and living in boxes, as the publication called upon the unemployed to revolt and "take over the factories, buildings, and food... produce for USE, not profit, and order the world and its wealth to that end." The newspaper also expanded its coverage of national and international events that portrayed the rising tide of resistance to injustice. Under the headline "Freedom Is Bleeding" it covered the World War I veterans' Bonus March on Washington in 1932. It covered miners' strikes in Pennsylvania and clashes in Detroit. The paper covered the Communist-led drive to "free the Scottsboro Boys," and many hosiery workers actively supported that campaign. The newspaper printed pictures of followers of Gandhi lying in the streets of Bombay captioned "Reds and Pacifists alike receive rough treatment from bosses' police all over." It covered a march in which the Irish Republican Army came out from underground after the election in which Eamon de Valera and Labor forces had won control of Ireland and marched through the streets of Dublin, hailed by thousands. Similar events in Nicaragua, France, Spain, and China were described in the newspaper. The author of another article described how he had bummed his way across twenty-four states, seeing people in bread lines everywhere filled with discontent. All of them, he said, "felt moments when they were impelled to violence. Only the threat of having their 'spontaneous' violence met with the bullets, clubs and gas of the 'scientific' violence of police restrained them—but for how long?" And the *Hosiery Worker* began to print, in banner headlines in every issue of the paper, the simple statement from the Declaration of

Independence: "Whenever any form of government becomes destructive of these ends... Life, Liberty and the pursuit of Happiness... it is the Right of the People to alter or abolish it."[88]

Some historians have seen the use of such appeals to "American" ideals by labor and left-led organizations as an essentially conservative representation of the conservative goals of workers. When the union used appeals to American ideals, however, it was instead subverting conservative aims in the process of creating a working class–based Americanism that transcended gender, race, and ethnicity, and incorporated international class solidarity. The union's program claimed for the working classes the values of democracy and rights, but went well beyond abstract political rights to include broad economic rights and control of industry, as part of a Socialist program of social reorganization. And it was this broad vision that the rank-and-file workers responded to.[89]

The union's open policies of membership brought together radicals from a diverse constituency. In the shops and on the streets Socialists struggled alongside Communists and independent radicals and, as indicated by discussions at union conventions and in the union's printed material, members of these groups were open regarding their sympathies. Most were members of the community who worked in the industry and the union. The experience of the hosiery union underscores the fact that the Left in the United States included a broad range of activists, many of whom came from working-class backgrounds and were openly integrated in mass organizations. One thing all of these activists shared, along with many others in the community, was a desire for meaningful social change.

By 1932 even the AFL executive council was shaken by the awakening masses, to the point that, in the words of a *Hosiery Worker* article, it issued at its convention "clear cut demands for unemployment relief, better apportionment of jobs and wealth, aid to farmers, and a special session of Congress to prevent the riots and bloodshed the AFL sees as inevitable unless immediate relief to the masses is administered."[90]

Thinking Globally, Acting Locally

It was becoming ever clearer that small or piecemeal responses to the devastation the Great Depression was wreaking upon working people would not be enough. In June 1930 a large rally held at Shibe Park (later Connie Mack Stadium, home of Philadelphia's National League baseball team) headlined William Green, the president of the AFL, in support of the anti-injunction campaign that the hosiery workers were conducting in the state legislature with the help and support of James Maurer. But the terrible suffering of so many working people was rapidly becoming a central focus of the union and its allies. Describing the so-called commissary system of food handouts as "degrading," the AFFFHW, including Communists within it (though the Communist Party leadership did not participate), along with Philadelphia's Socialist Party and the CLU, formed a joint commission on unemployment at a mass meeting at Knitters' Hall in January 1932 to build support for direct relief to the unemployed. At the beginning of March this group hosted a rally at Philadelphia's Convention Hall that drew over 10,000 people, and in which representatives from practically every union in the city participated. The event featured a brass band provided by the musicians' union, a 100-piece orchestra, an organ recital, and a list of speakers that included Governor Gifford Pinchot.[91]

Street meetings to organize the unemployed into a mass movement for unemployment relief were also becoming a daily feature throughout Greater Kensington. These meetings were often accompanied by a band on a flatbed truck, or music of various types broadcast over an amplifying system. As the UCL's activities expanded, workers in other industries outside of textile became involved, such as Budd Manufacturing, a manufacturer of passenger rail cars, Philco electronics, Nabisco, and even truck drivers in the dairy industry. A large open-air meeting in McPherson Square featuring Anna Geisinger, along with Callaghan, Edelman, a speaker from the UTWA, and another from the Amalgamated Clothing Workers (ACWA), drew thousands of people to hear plans for a mass march on the state capitol in Harrisburg in what the union newspaper called "a legislative onslaught unequaled in the history of the state." The demands included unemployment insurance, old-age pensions, a minimum wage, the outlawing of the yellow-dog contract, and repeal of the eviction law.[92] Alice Kreckman took part in this march, calling it a "women's march" in reference to the large number of women among the participants: "We women were up in the balcony and we were yelling at the politicians. We slept on the floor and everything. For relief. I didn't need it, but I always felt it wasn't just those who need help that should be out there, those that don't need it should be doing something!"[93]

These demands were part of a growing movement throughout the country, and they helped to strengthen third-party initiatives that also contested racism and sexism and provided a larger vision for social change. Alexander McKeown was a founder of Philadelphia's Northeast Progressive League, laying the groundwork for the establishment of a socialist-led Labor Party in

Philadelphia. By the beginning of 1930 the league had developed a strong following in the northeast sections of the city (which included Kensington). By 1931 the league had become the Labor Party with headquarters in Knitters' Hall. The party adopted an impressive platform, similar to that of the Socialist Party, in preparation for a run in the fall 1931 primaries. Labor called not only for the socialization of utilities and transportation, but for unemployment insurance; an end to evictions and for the building of municipal housing; an income tax on the rich; and an end to discrimination on the basis of sex and race. McKeown was the candidate for mayor, and candidates for city council were nominated from every district and included Edelman, as well as Geisinger and a considerable number of other women. It is impossible to guess what kind of support the ticket would have garnered citywide, for the party was knocked off the ballot on a technicality, but its political message was heard by thousands, in meetings and open-air speeches throughout the city.[94]

In 1932 Branch 1 threw its full weight behind the Socialist Party in the national elections. At that year's union convention delegates from Philadelphia introduced a resolution calling on all branches to "cooperate with the Socialist Party in the Fall elections," to give them both "moral and financial support," to form Socialist or Labor Party locals where none already existed, and to "endorse only candidates favorable to labor." But this resolution also caused controversy.

Rieve opposed the resolution, claiming that although he was a member of the Socialist Party himself, it would be divisive because "hosiery workers, as workers, support a variety of views, including Socialist, Communist, Republican and Democrat." In a heated response indicative of the growing tensions between herself and the union president, Anna Geisinger, after informing him that "all I've ever been is a worker," argued in favor of the resolution. She essentially accused Rieve, a full-time union official, of being a bureaucrat and a hypocrite, for he, along with close associates like Sidney Hillman of the ACWA, were already moving away from the Socialist Party's left wing and into the sphere of the Democrats.

The resolution was subsequently defeated, but two members of Branch 1 then introduced another, calling for the formation and support of an Independent Labor Party (ILP) along with a demand that the AFL endorse such a party. Again, very contentious debate ensued, and a delegate from Branch 1, decrying the "threat of fascism in the country" argued that "anyone calling himself a Socialist or Communist, if he doesn't work for the unity of labor, he is committing an act of treason on the working class." McKeown argued that if the AFL united with the Socialists and the Communists, they could reach the goal of the "betterment of mankind." But a Communist member of Branch 1, Ernest Kornfeld, opposed the resolution on the grounds that such a party would be "reformist" and not solve problems that needed to be "fought out before the working class," an indication of some of the differences that existed between the Communist and Socialist leadership. Rieve did support the ILP resolution, saying that "it would allow for labor activity on an independent basis." After much debate, the convention passed the resolution in favor of the ILP with the support of Philadelphia. These heated exchanges indicate the presence of very strong, often contentious, but open debate within the union. Such debate was one of the primary factors underscoring the democratic nature of the organization. Although they went along with the ILP resolution for the national organization, Branch 1 nevertheless continued to stand behind the Socialist Party in the upcoming elections.[95]

Branch 1's connections to the Socialist Party were deep. James Maurer, the party's candidate for vice president, was a longtime friend and staunch ally and a fierce fighter in support of legislation against the use of injunctions and the state police in labor disputes. The platform of the Socialists embraced many of the ideals for which the union had long fought (some of which would be adopted by the Roosevelt administration in the "Second New Deal" as his administration was pushed further to the left). The Socialist Party called for immediate relief for the unemployed, a program of public works, old-age pensions, government health and maternity insurance, the enforcement of constitutional guarantees of economic, political, and legal equality for "Negroes" and women, the enforcement of drastic antilynching laws, and U.S. entrance into the World Court.[96]

Following the death of Carl Mackley in March 1930, Socialist speakers became an increasingly regular feature in Philadelphia. Soon after Mackley's death, Clare Annesley, a socialist MP from the British Labour Party, spoke to the women of Branch 1, telling them, "It's times like these that put the steel into your soul," underscoring the importance of women in the fight to change society. In August of that year Arthur Shaw, the Socialist leader of the British Textile Unions, received a standing ovation at Knitters' Hall when he spoke about the militant traditions of textile workers that extended from Britain to Kensington and back again. In fact, in the early 1930s socialism was very much in the air in Kensington. During the 1932 campaign the Socialist Party of Philadelphia sponsored a May Day event that packed Kensington's Wishart Theatre. Norman Thomas was the keynote speaker, but speakers also included Alice Hanson from the YWCA and Frank Keeney, president of the West Virginia Miners Federation and one of the leaders of the famous "armed march" of 1920. This event was followed by a huge auto parade throughout Greater Kensington and a reception at Knitters' Hall.[97]

When the 1932 elections did occur, the results were encouraging, with the Thomas-Maurer ticket winning close to a million votes nationwide, an increase of over 400 percent from 1928. In Wisconsin, the Socialists doubled their voting strength; in Pennsylvania, two Socialists were elected to the state assembly. Pennsylvanians cast over 91,000 votes for the party, and in Berks County, the home of Reading's powerful Berkshire mills, the Socialists took a full 22 percent of the vote. In Philadelphia, the vote increased from just over 3,000 in 1928 to almost 14,000 in 1932, an almost 350 percent increase. Though not really making a dent in the Republican control of the city, the increase helped to defeat two antilabor associates of the political machine of William S. Vare and his brothers, and election workers also reported an "appreciable gain in Socialist votes among Negro balloters."[98]

By early 1933 the Socialists had opened an office on East Allegheny Avenue in Kensington. In May of that year they sponsored a May Day event, this time at the Schubert Theatre, in which Arturo Giovanitti, a famed Wobbly strike leader and poet, was the featured speaker. In August the Socialists sponsored a picnic and rally that drew 15,000 people to South Philadelphia's Airport Park. This was the first major event held by the citywide Socialist Party in quite a few years and was an attempt to build broader support in other parts of the city outside of the stronghold of radical Kensington. Emil Rieve (still a party member at that point) and Alexander McKeown were speakers at the rally, along with Norman Thomas and Frank Crosswaith, a "prominent Negro Socialist" associated with the Brotherhood of Pullman Porters, who had himself been a Socialist candidate in New York.[99]

In May 1932 Edward McGrady, vice president of the AFL, spoke before a U.S. Senate committee on unemployment relief. In his address he warned that the "sporadic uprisings" that were taking place in industrial centers over the past months represented a mass movement of unemployed men and women who wanted food and shelter. AFL leaders had, he said, "preached patience and obedience to the law," but they would no longer do so. Then McGrady gave the senators an ultimatum: "Unless you furnish relief quickly, the doors of revolt in this country are going to be thrown open.... In every labor meeting there is a good representation of soldiers of the World War, and they are the most angry... if Congress adjourns without providing food for the millions of hungry people, labor will not close the doors on revolt.... I am not going to come before you again to beg for relief... unless you do provide relief, something is going to happen in this country."[100] At the end of the article in the *Hosiery Worker* describing McGrady's speech, the editors inserted a paragraph of their own: "So the spokesman for the AFL invited the hungry workers to be patient no longer, to worry about 'Red perils' no longer, but to feed their families."[101]

The tide was, in truth, beginning to turn, as the fear that the "doors of revolt" might indeed be thrown open began to sink in to the captains of industry. The anger and accompanying actions slowly beginning to gain impetus in the country would, in fact, result in the election of a new president, Franklin Delano Roosevelt, and push him to take notice of the masses of suffering and increasingly desperate people, as the country slipped into the darkest days of the Depression. But as the historian Melvyn Dubofsky said, "American business *never* willingly conceded any of its prerogatives to workers and unions." It would take the coordinated efforts of a united movement of working people, men and women, challenging capital's prerogatives on a national scale, to achieve any real gains from the New Deal. The hosiery workers were to play a strategic role in this movement as the country moved into the era of the Congress of Industrial Organizations.[102]

CHAPTER SIX

Storming the Bastille
The Triumph of Social Justice Unionism

The National Recovery Act speckled the U.S. with strikes [in the month after it was signed into law on June 16, 1933].... Of the 25,000 workers on strike throughout the U.S., 18,000 were in Pennsylvania ... mostly in the hosiery industry as the result of attempts by the American Federation of Full-Fashioned Hosiery Workers to complete unionization of the mills.
—*Time* magazine, July 31, 1933

When I recall the events that took place at Fifth and Luzerne streets on May 6, 1937, they intermingle with the recollections of what I have read over the years about the storming of the Bastille and the Winter Palace. The Apex strike was a thing apart, it was hardly a strike; it was an invasion.
—Hosiery worker Joseph Burge

Philadelphia's hosiery workers entered the mid-1930s with anticipation of a real transformation of their lives, their community, and their country. With growing support for the Socialists, radicalization of leftist-influenced popular movements, and the rumblings of an awakening lion of labor at last beginning to be heard, there was a genuine sense of the possibility of a new society. By the final years of the decade the palpable revolt that was in the air would sweep the city with the fevered cry of "CIO!" For Kensington's hosiery workers it would lead to the seizing of the Apex mill, the most infamous bastion of anti-unionism in the city's hosiery industry, in a sit-down strike they would label the "storming of the Bastille." More significant than the conflict at this single mill, no matter how important it was, Kensington's workers believed they were storming the Bastille in a larger sense too. Working-class power was changing the world, and there were no predefined limits to the transformation it could bring.

On a national level, the vehicle for the assertion of working-class power and influence was the aforementioned CIO—the Congress of Industrial Organizations. "From its founding event—the famous punch that John L. Lewis delivered to the face of an AFL rival on October 19, 1935—the CIO projected manly strength."[1] This famous creation myth recounting the disruption at the American Federation of Labor (AFL) convention in Atlantic City, New

Jersey, is often seen as the beginning of the CIO. Robert H. Zieger, in his comprehensive history of the CIO, certainly focused on the movement's machismo: "Its picket line confrontations, its . . . logistical innovations, its centralized organizing campaigns, and its enormous public demonstrations" all backed up by the "fiery rhetoric of John L. Lewis" and the "legendary militancy" of the very masculine mine workers, "made the CIO appear as a powerful force to contemporaries." This overwhelming "manliness" is also reflected in descriptions of the iconography associated with the movement as a "powerful white male with muscles."[2] It is this organization that many historians see as providing the unifying philosophy that was capable of bringing about the "politicization of organized labor, the recasting of racial and ethnic dynamics of the labor movement, and the expansion of the collective bargaining agenda."[3]

Following that contentious convention, the Committee for Industrial Organization—the predecessor of the CIO and still within the AFL—was founded in November 1935 by a group of representatives from eight AFL unions who felt that the divisive craft union orientation of the AFL was a major impediment to the unionization of the masses of industrial workers, unskilled and semiskilled, who were crying out for organization. The leadership of this group centered around John L. Lewis of the powerful mine workers' union, but also included Thomas McMahon of the United Textile Workers of America (UTWA), Sidney Hillman of the Amalgamated Clothing Workers of America (ACWA), and David Dubinsky of the International Ladies Garment Workers Union (ILGWU), all with large female memberships. First organized as a pressure group for industrial organizing within the AFL, by 1937 the AFL had suspended all of the group's founding unions. Out on its own, the CIO made great strides in organizing such important industries as auto, steel, and meatpacking, and in November 1938, the CIO held its founding constitutional convention in Pittsburgh, Pennsylvania, a major step in the movement to unify labor.[4]

Most histories look at only a few short years before its official founding for the origins of the CIO. But the organization that came about in the aftermath of the "battle of Atlantic City," and the millions of workers that it came to include, had a far longer history. The CIO consolidated a vision of worker unity, but it did not create it. The complex and massive scaffolding underpinning that vision and that organization was built by rank-and-file workers, young men and young women, unions, and radical activists, whose activities stretched back to at least the early 1920s, and they included the men and women of the American Federation of Full-Fashioned Hosiery Workers (AFFFHW).[5]

But the contributions that the AFFFHW made to the CIO went well beyond early on-the-ground testing of actions and structures of organizing that foreshadowed those of the later organization, for there were concrete and specific links between the AFFFHW of the 1920s and the CIO of the 1930s in terms of people, institutions, and ideology. Activists who were part of the hosiery union in the 1920s and 1930s were present at the CIO's very founding and contributed to its major and often competing approaches toward organizing, structure, and internal democracy. Moreover, the AFFFHW's contributions were not limited to the CIO. The union also pioneered important programs of the New Deal that the new president, Franklin D. Roosevelt, promised the American people. Building on the militant and largely successful organizing campaigns of the 1920s, hosiery workers were "sparkplugs" of the nationwide 1933 strike wave, and their organizing activities in Reading, Pennsylvania, led directly to the legal precedent known as the Reading Formula that became the standard mechanism for resolving labor disputes during the period of the National Industrial Recovery Act (NIRA) of the first New Deal. Their far more successful foray into workers' housing, the Carl Mackley Houses, was project number one of the New Deal's Public Works Administration (PWA) and inspired significant advances in initiatives for low-cost housing. Hosiery unionists were among the founders of the Textile Workers Organizing Committee (TWOC) and its successor CIO union, the Textile Workers Union of America (TWUA), and provided its top leadership. CIO strike tactics, such as the sit-down strike, followed directly on experiments by hosiery workers years earlier; one of their most important sit-down strikes of 1937, the Apex strike, led to the U.S. Supreme Court decision removing labor disputes from the purview of the Sherman Anti-Trust Act. Hosiery workers played important roles as organizers for other CIO unions, and they were instrumental in the founding of the largest of the left CIO unions, the United Electrical Workers, whose organizational structure virtually mirrored that of the hosiery union. The AFFFHW's large female workforce was a model for labor feminism, insistently raising demands for women's rights to their employers and to their union, which responded to their active participation in organizing and strikes by throwing union support behind demands for childcare, equal pay, married women's right to work, and a greater role in leadership. Finally, the AFFFHW became early representatives of two of the different wings that would develop within the CIO—one that led to a top-down organization directly tied to the Democratic Party, and another that advocated for a social democratic movement controlled by the rank and file.

This chapter begins with a discussion of the 1933 strike wave that followed in the wake of the Great Depression and during the jurisdiction of the NIRA. It concludes with the explosive strikes of 1937, including the precedent-setting Berkshire and Apex strikes and the *Apex Hosiery Co. v. Leader* Supreme Court decision. In between, it tells the story of the union and the people of the community during this critical period of American history. Specifically, it describes how the earlier activities of Kensington's hosiery workers directly influenced three progressive movements of the late 1930s and beyond: the CIO, the New Deal, and labor feminism. Over the course of a campaign for the rights of working people, in which the possibility of an alternative social organization was made explicit, many came to see their futures as connected to a broad national and international movement that went beyond "moral capitalism" to encompass full social and economic democracy.

On the Threshold of a New Deal: The Strike Wave of 1933

The tumultuous events around the country in the early 1930s gave a sense of urgency to union campaigns for social change. Actions like the World War I veterans' Bonus March, the militant activities of farmers in the Midwest, and the Ford Hunger March reinforced the call to action that the hosiery workers had been demonstrating in their strike activity. The turbulent events in Philadelphia were more than simply a series of random, if militant, strikes and protests. Indeed, they were the visible public manifestations of a clear and conscious strategy by union activists to raise the level of struggle and push both employers and government to respond to the needs of the masses of working people and to move toward a true social democracy. The hosiery workers were not alone in pushing these strategies, but they were very much in the forefront of activities that brought about advances of real significance in the period from 1935 to 1937.

Union activists used an iterative strategy, campaigning for a series of increasingly ambitious goals. Whenever they achieved a victory (or partial victory), they used that new level as a springboard for increased agitation. They were part of the growing dissent that helped to force the new president to acknowledge the rights of labor by instituting Section 7a of the NIRA. Then, using the limited tools and opportunities of this legislation, hosiery workers initiated a massive strike wave immediately following its signing, driving the negotiation of the precedent-setting Reading Formula that called for union elections through the National Labor Board (NLB) and, for a time, strengthened labor's position through the recognition of majority rule in the establishment of union representation. Hosiery's activists knew that a nationwide movement would be needed to achieve their goals, so they continued efforts to help the broader labor movement as part of their expanded militant activities in their own industry in the Midwest and the South.

With the 1932 election of a new president, hosiery workers sought to unite working people in a growing left-wing effort to put labor in control of the New Deal, for the results of that election were an indisputable call for change by the American people. A poll by *Literary Digest* taken just before the election suggested that the discontent of Americans might even have pushed many to consider voting for Norman Thomas on the Socialist ticket. The results of this poll were reported in the *Hosiery Worker*, where union officials portrayed it as a vindication of all the hard work the union had been putting into developing a movement for substantive change. But although the Socialists did gain significantly over their 1928 vote, in the end many Thomas supporters voted for Democrat Franklin Delano Roosevelt, afraid that incumbent Republican Herbert Hoover might otherwise be reelected. The masses of hungry and jobless people were desperate for change, and to many people, that meant Roosevelt's New Deal.[6]

Few people, however, were willing to surrender all hope to the politicians. Increasingly, farmers, laboring people, and the unemployed were beginning to respond to calls to take matters into their own hands. And so it was in Kensington. The activities of the organizations of the unemployed, union organizing drives accompanied by escalating strike violence, marches on state legislatures, and increasing demands that the government take responsibility and initiate programs to ease the suffering were all contributing to heightened fears of chaos, perhaps even what the political journalist Ernest K. Lindley called "revolution boiling up from the bottom." High unemployment and a shortage of work led to various schemes to deal with the crisis. Many involved ways in which to share what work there was among the population. One that actually had some teeth was passed by the Senate in early April 1933, introduced by Senator Hugo Black of Alabama. The Black bill "ban[ned] from interstate commerce any goods made by workers who labored more than a six-hour day or a five-day week," and a subsequent version allowed the secretary of labor to regulate production and set minimum wages. It was backed up by the threat of criminal prosecution of employers who did not comply.[7]

The bill had the support of the AFL, and when its president, William Green, appeared before the Norris subcommittee of the Senate Judiciary Committee, he warned the senators that American wage earners were determined to get the thirty—hour week, either by "the force of the government or ... the force and struggle of the labor movement." In its newspaper and weekly broadcasts over Philadelphia radio station WIP, AFFFHW Branch 1 leadership discussed the bill and called for a nationwide twenty-four-hour strike in order to force its passage. Support for a strong bill was growing so rapidly that many of the country's capitalists began to fear that the Black bill might actually pass the House as well as the Senate. Yet others hoped that "Roosevelt would have the last opportunity to save capitalism and stave off revolution."[8]

After his inauguration in March 1933, Roosevelt, faced with finding ways to deal with the enormity of the crisis, initiated his famous "first one hundred days" to set himself off from the "do-nothing" Hoover. His initial response was aimed at stabilizing the banks and getting business to restart, but that did little to alleviate the widespread suffering of the populace—or the rising tide of discontent that was its accompaniment. In order to head off the Black legislation, the administration gave the go-ahead for a recovery bill that aimed to win the support of labor, but especially of business. Subsequently, the NIRA came to be the centerpiece of the First New Deal legislation. The newly created National Recovery Administration (NRA) set up boards to establish industry codes governing wages, working conditions, and hours of work for each industry. In a small concession to labor, Section 7a of the NIRA provided for employees' rights to establish unions and engage in collective bargaining by representatives of their choice.[9]

Many labor union officials endorsed the promise of economic planning that they thought the NRA represented. They included Emil Rieve, national president of the AFFFHW, who requested "emergency powers" from his union giving him more control over strikes until the legislation was "clarified." The support for the NIRA given by the hosiery workers as a whole, especially Philadelphia's Branch 1, was more critical. On the one hand, a *Hosiery Worker* editorial in early June 1933 argued that the government was forced to adopt rules for industry that would enable labor to organize in order to save the whole economic system. On the other hand, the left wing of the union mistrusted the bill: "With control of wages and hours in the hands of the government, it could turn into Mussolini." Further, "there is no real possibility of anything worthwhile ... unless Labor wields a good, solid, and hefty bludgeon."[10]

This did not stop the union from appropriating Section 7a to use as a mandate to reenergize the labor movement; in fact, among all unions in the country, the hosiery workers were the first out of the gate after the bill's signing in initiating a massive wave of organizing strikes. Building on the experiences of the previous decade, the union launched a campaign to fight for labor control of the New Deal. In the process, the AFFFHW played a central role in developments in the labor movement in 1933 that would come into full flower in the later 1930s. The hosiery workers' experiences also foreshadowed later developments in the CIO with the widening of a split between different ideological factions in its leadership.[11]

A July 1933 article in *Time* magazine reported that the NIRA had indeed increased the number of strikes within the United States as workers sought to unionize, but the strikes that erupted throughout the rest of the country "paled beside the strikes" which were being conducted in eastern Pennsylvania. Even before the president signed the legislation into law on June 16, 1933, the union was engaging in strategies to take advantage of the act's proposed support for labor organizing. In May, the hosiery union was one of a group of unions that joined forces to organize an "apparel trades bloc," aimed at cooperative efforts to take advantage of the opportunities for organizing promised by the NIRA. Along with the AFFFHW, this bloc included the ILGWU, the Cloth, Hat, Cap, and Millinery Workers, the ACWA, the United Hatters of North America, and the International Pocketbook Makers Union. Most of these trades had high concentrations of female employees, although their leadership remained concentrated in the hands of men. The hosiery union, seeing itself in the vanguard of a "new rebirth of labor," shared organizers with members of the bloc, particularly the ACWA, in anti-sweatshop campaigns in Pennsylvania and southern New Jersey.[12]

The ink was barely dry on the president's signature when hosiery unionists launched an organizing drive in every section of the country producing full-fashioned hosiery. At this time the union also changed its name to the American Federation of Hosiery Workers (AFHW) after gaining jurisdiction over workers in seamless hosiery as well as full-fashioned hosiery manufacture. There were approximately 65,000 workers in the seamless industry, adding to the burden of organizing but also to the treasury from those who were organized. Organizing was intensified in Reading, while in Philadelphia, Branch 1 issued a call for all workers in nonunion shops to strike on June 22. Knitters' Hall became the bustling headquarters for an organizing drive that reached into mills both inside and outside of the city. A U. S. Army Military Intelligence agent estimated that 40,000 hosiery workers were on strike, including 10,000 in Philadelphia, signifying the "possibility of grave local disorder."[13] The strikes were directed by a "Committee of 80," and Anna Geisinger, backed up by the broad support of the women's division, was elected to head the committee. The fact that Geisinger was given oversight of the organizing committees in Philadelphia and its surrounding regions was indicative not only of her unquestionable skills and the arrival of women at the top levels of leadership in Branch 1, but also of the developing tensions between Branch 1 and the president of the national union. For in May, Emil Rieve had fired Geisinger as a federation organizer.[14]

The background to the rift between Rieve and Geisinger is not entirely clear, but it is likely that Rieve's opposition to a resolution granting women a position on the national negotiating committee (passed over his opposition at the 1931 national convention) and his opposition to the 1932 resolution guaranteeing a position for women on the national executive board (which, subsequently, did not pass) contributed to the breach. By this point the consciousness of Geisinger and a core group of other women in the union had evolved to include an understanding not only of their rights as women workers, but also of the past discrimination that they had experienced as women within the union. Some members of the union, male and female, were also becoming increasingly dissatisfied with the "take backs" and restrictions on workers' activities dictated by the national contract. Clearly, Geisinger saw Rieve as condescending and hypocritical, as indicated by discussions at the 1932 and 1933 conventions. But Rieve's move toward a bureaucratic, top-down approach that would become more prevalent in the coming years was also becoming apparent, and it was not well received among the members of some of the branches.[15]

The actual catalyst for Geisinger's firing occurred after Rieve removed her from organizing in Reading and assigned her to work for the ACWA in the sweatshops of Allentown. She refused the assignment. In her rebuttal to the decision, Geisinger claimed that she had been told that she was being transferred from her successful position in Reading as an economy measure, but such an "economy" would not be effective if she was assigned to Allentown. She may also have had some differences with the ACWA president, Sidney Hillman (a close associate of Rieve's), and his avowed anticommunism. Although Geisinger was a Socialist (as was Hillman), there were communists in Branch 1 with whom she closely associated, and who supported her in turn. But divisions within the Socialist Party were also becoming evident, divisions which would eventually split the party and virtually destroy it in Reading. There really was little that Branch 1 could do about her firing from her national assignment. Nevertheless, four members of the executive board did vote against the decision. Whatever the actions of the national body, Geisinger was still a member of Branch 1, and the local made its own decisions regarding its organizing campaigns and personnel. Putting Geisinger in charge of the strike committee was clearly a direct slap at Rieve.[16]

The general organizing drive, of which Geisinger's Branch 1 activities were a part, drew a wide-scale response, and hosiery strikes hit the South, the Midwest, and the Northeast and erupted in southern New Jersey and all over Pennsylvania, in labor's first hopeful response to NIRA. The union's focus on empowering workers on the local level also yielded its first important results in interracial organizing, and by mid-1934 it had chartered an African American local in Durham, North Carolina. Those workers were employed in Seamless Mill 6 of the Marvin-Carr Company, a plant that employed only blacks. Although the workers were organized in a separate local, they were part of the Durham branch, and were welcomed into the union at a crowded meeting attended by both black and white workers. William Smith of the national union and southern organizer Henry Adams chaired the meeting, promising the new members that "there never will be discrimination because of color in the AFHW." In his welcoming speech, Smith argued that "no group of workers in the world needs strong labor unions more than the colored workers do," and promised that "the white wage earner will learn more quickly to respect the black wage earner when the colored man gets into an organization and demands the same wages and working conditions that other laboring people are accorded." This statement, though ignoring the past discrimination practiced by some unions, was essentially a restatement of the AFHW's philosophy of "fighting for your rights" and "self-organization," and it was the rubric that underlay the advances that women had been able to achieve in the union, as well as the anger that some of them felt when they ran into the limitations that some of the leadership attempted to impose. Though AFHW leaders did not directly take on the racist hiring practices of the textile manufacturers at this time, they took any opportunity that presented itself to promote their antiracist and inclusive ideology. The meeting in Durham, in which both black and white members publicly stood together, was a harbinger of the inclusive industrial organizing that would become an important element of the Left-led unions of the CIO.[17]

As part of the union's efforts to expand organization of the mills, hosiery strikes also hit the Midwest. Don Harris (a hosiery worker interviewed in the late 1970s and early 1980s for the Iowa Labor History Oral Project) described some of the union's activities in that state. Harris worked as a topper at the Rollins Hosiery Mill in Des Moines, Iowa. The plant employed over 800 people, of whom approximately 80 percent were female. After a two-year campaign the AFHW organized a closed shop in 1934, Branch 50 of the union. Its actions there leapfrogged past just hosiery, however, to spread its radical industrial unionism to other industries. Branch 50 helped workers in many other industries, "anybody [who] needed any help," according to Harris, including laundry workers, cement workers, teamsters, and the employees of the Iowa Power and Light Authority (who were "inspired by the organization of the hosiery mill"). Harris said that the hosiery workers regularly supported other organizing drives and "could turn out two to three hundred pickets when nobody else could turn out more than a handful."[18]

This ability to turn out pickets had always been a strength of the union. Another was its employment of creative tactics such as street theater, which activists had utilized since the 1920s. These included not only band concerts on the back of flatbed trucks and the actions of the Kenosha strikers, but also such stunts as holding "funerals" for scab shops. In the latter events, workers dressed as undertakers paraded with a coffin proclaiming the "death of scab shops." Hosiery union literature widely promoted these attention-grabbing activities, and such mock funerals were held by various locals, from Paterson, New Jersey, in 1929 to as far west as Minneapolis in 1935. During the NIRA-period organizing drives in Philadelphia and Reading, the union was also noted for the use of new, imaginative tactics that would have echoes in the national labor movement in the near future. Geisinger claimed that the union was "using every type of method that we know how to use," starting with tried-and-true tactics in which groups of union workers circulated literature, held mill-gate meetings using amplifiers, and conducted home visits to reach workers in the mills. At the Blue Moon mill in Croydon, just outside of Philadelphia, the union set up a "tent colony" in order to keep twenty-four-hour pickets around the mill. In nearby Lansdale, union pickets and sympathizers shut down the Dexdale mill. When mill owners attempted to reopen that mill with the help of mounted police, "a curly haired girl stepped defiantly over the deadline," and police charged the crowd. "Women and children were trampled, rocks, bricks and bottles flew," and pickets, some of them veterans of World War I, used gas masks to withstand attacks of tear gas. The local police chief "pumped away with a rifle" from the roof. Many were hurt and many more arrested in another violent confrontation in which young women played a central role in the fight for the right to unionize.[19]

The union's vision took hold in cities and small towns alike as hosiery workers continued to spread the union gospel. "Active veterans" of Branch 1 entered drives in New Jersey. In Maple Shade, in the southern part of the state, the town's Unemployed Union exposed the "sweated" working conditions at the Maple Shade Hosiery Company. Alfred Hoffmann spoke to a packed meeting of unemployed trade unionists and other citizens at a town council meeting, protesting the tax concessions given to the mill owners, who were demanding twelve-hour shifts and very low wages. In Washington, in the northern part of the state, the firing of three employees of the Consumers' Research Company for forming a union resulted in a strike. Guards armed with shotguns and rifles patrolled brightly illuminated grounds, often firing at assembled pickets—that is, until "the lamps were put out one by one with pellets fired by a methodical young hosiery worker, who hid in an adjoining cornfield and set a local record for bull's eyes with an air rifle."[20]

In July 1933, workers struck the yellow-dog Cambria shop. Again Philadelphia's courts and police came to the aid of the manufacturers, and violence escalated. Injunctions limited pickets to twelve people, and police began escorting strikebreakers, some of whom were armed, into the plant. On July 24 police arrested Alexander McKeown, president of Branch 1, William Leader, vice president, and seventy-five other pickets, male and female, when McKeown refused to honor the order to limit the pickets. In a theatrical episode staged for the benefit of the press, McKeown and Leader "serenaded the turnkey with a rendition of Sweet Adeline" while in jail, and when released, went back on the picket line. But such bravado was, again, not limited to men, as the women strikers continued to show their defiance at least as often. When police arrested thirty-five women and they were arraigned for refusing to disperse, the judge lectured them about having "no place among the strikers." Informing them that their "place" was at home, he said he was releasing them with the hope that they would not appear before him again. The "strikers left singing," and the next day they also were back on the picket line.[21]

Such carnivalesque activity by both men and women was a means for expressing disdain for a system that they increasingly felt to be illegitimate and unworthy of respect, and it was encouraged by the union and practiced by hosiery workers throughout the organization. It also continued to spread hosiery workers' ideas to a broader public, showing other workers by example that they did not need to accept the restrictions that the system handed them. But for these women, the judge's allusion to their "place" would have been enough of a catalyst in itself to send them back onto the picket lines. Over the course of the previous decade they had become empowered by their union activities, and many of these "modern" women were not going to easily relinquish control over their lives. Their strike activities incorporated a romantic vision of themselves as "heroic agents of change," but they were also very much based in the concrete reality of working-class women's lives. Social independence had a symbiotic relationship with economic independence, and the union provided a vehicle through which they could fight to protect both. Through educational programs of the union, and those of other organizations like the YWCA, Brookwood, and the Bryn Mawr Summer School, the union's women had become aware of how crucial unity and organization were to the achievement of their goals as both workers and women. This awareness was one of the factors that continued to gird their support for Anna Geisinger, and it underpinned the backing that they received from their middle-class sisters in the YWCA, the Women's Trade Union League (WTUL), the League of Women Shoppers, the Women's Bureau, and individuals like Cornelia Bryce Pinchot, the modern, feminist wife of Pennsylvania's governor. For these women also recognized the role that organization and paid work played in the fight of women to achieve independence. At the YWCA's 1934 biennial convention, held in Philadelphia, the industrial division delegates adopted a sweeping statement of policy supporting the movement to organize women workers into general trade unions.[22]

The next stage in the Cambria strike would take a tragic turn, however. The NRA called for the manufacturers to negotiate "in good faith" with their employees, but the actions of the Cambria management in response to the overwhelming sentiment expressed by their workers indicated to the latter that the company had no respect for the rights of working people. This infuriated both the strikers and the nearby neighbors of the mill, who were also fed up with the suffering that the Depression was causing and who felt a sense of solidarity with the people on strike. Although Emil Rieve called for a truce in the hosiery strikes in August in order to "go along with the president's program" and send all disputes to the government's Mediation Board, Cambria management refused to cooperate, and the strike continued. On August 31 someone in the mill placed an NRA "fair labor" Blue Eagle in a window as a taunt to the strikers, and the conflict came to another violent conclusion when strikers and neighbors charged a police-escorted truck of strikebreakers. Gunshots erupted from inside the truck. "Scores" were injured. A twenty-four-year-old woman picket was shot, a twenty-three-year-old woman picket suffered a fractured skull, and two more workers, Clement Norwood, a fifty-one-year-old hosiery worker who had been blacklisted in his hometown of Durham, North Carolina, and Frank Milnor, age nineteen, were shot to death. They joined twenty-two-year-old Carl Mackley and twenty-year-old Alberta

Bachman in hosiery's list of "labor martyrs." In the words of a reporter from the *Philadelphia Record*, "as police rushed in with clubs," strikers and neighborhood sympathizers, in a display of community solidarity, salvaged the bullet-pierced rear curtain of the truck "for use as a war banner." As news of the killings spread throughout the textile district, 10,000 hosiery workers stormed out of their workplaces onto the streets of Kensington.[23]

Thousands of people from the neighborhood and every major union in the city swelled yet another McPherson Square memorial that the union held for the workers killed at the mill. Included among the other unions was the American Federation of Radio Workers (AFRW), representing the newly organized workers of the nearby Philco radio plant. The body of Clement Norwood was then shipped back to his home in Durham for burial. An honor guard of hosiery workers, including a delegation from the union's branch in High Point, North Carolina, accompanied the body of the martyr to his grave. Following the violence and the public backlash that accompanied it, the Cambria mill finally signed an agreement with the union. Through voluntary assessments, Branch 1 members raised $10,000 to create a trust fund for the families of the slain strikers and sent an appeal to all other branches to do the same.[24]

Such union-sponsored memorials, sadly, were becoming a more common feature as hosiery's drive demanding the right of workers to representation spread. In 1935 the union lost another martyr, this time in Rossville, Georgia. Columbus P. Walker, a father of six and a war hero, was gunned down by a scab at the Richmond Hosiery Mill. Thousands filled the Rossville Arena for the memorial sponsored by the union. The Reverend A. L. De Jarnette delivered a stirring eulogy, telling the assembled crowd that "when Moses led his people out of bondage the first union was started." Such memorials, and the eulogies that accompanied them, created a deep emotional bond in both the people present and those who read about them in the *Hosiery Worker*.[25]

In Reading, the union hit the industry with a massive strike wave that brought it to its knees. Even the mighty Berkshire mill was shut down. By July over 14,000 workers were on strike. It was in this strike that the hosiery workers forced a government concession that would become the mechanism nationwide for dispute resolution under Section 7a of the Roosevelt administration's NIRA and its newly created NLB. The 1933 hosiery strike in Reading was the first test of the NLB, which, on August 10, agreed to mediate the dispute. The settlement was predicated on both sides having stepped back from industrial conflict: the union sent strikers back to work, and the company accepted them, allegedly without retaliation. During this period of truce the NLB conducted secret-ballot elections to determine the employees' will regarding union representation. Subsequently, both sides were supposed to hammer out a collective bargaining agreement, with arbitration the final resort for issues that could not be resolved. This settlement, the Reading Formula, established the precedent for future settlements under the NLB nationwide.[26]

In accordance with the formula, Rieve sent the Reading strikers back to work, and the NLB conducted a secret-ballot election; 80 percent of Reading's hosiery workers voted for representation by the union. This included Berkshire employees, who voted for the union by an almost three-to-one margin.[27] The Reading Formula was a real step forward for labor in that it mandated that workers would be allowed to vote for union representation under the supervision of the NLB. The NLB, under pressure from the AFHW, also agreed that the union that received the majority of votes would have the right to represent all of the workers, using the very American principle of majority rule.[28] There was a major weakness with the NLB, however, in that it had no powers to enforce its directives. Since Reading was the first strike settled under the new act, it also revealed the weaknesses of the NRA. Although the union won the representation decision in Reading, the fact that there was no enforcement mechanism available to the NLB allowed wholesale violations by the manufacturers, including the recognition of "company" unions that were essentially management puppets, the continued use of private police, and discrimination against union workers. The National Association of Manufacturers, adamantly opposed to "majority rule," spent a considerable amount of time and energy to ensure that NLB-brokered agreements were not enforced. The fact that most of the labor movement did not have the organizational strength of the hosiery workers meant that the high standards set by the Reading Formula could not be backed up by strong union action. By February 1934 the board had become almost impotent, and a decision in March to allow proportional representation rather than majority rule in the auto industry virtually destroyed it. The hosiery workers' Reading Formula created an important precedent, nonetheless, in that it set up the trajectory that would culminate in the Wagner Act in 1935. The government's reluctance to enforce legislation favorable to labor over business led to even more dissent in the union, however, as many members increasingly began to criticize top union officials, particularly Emil Rieve, and his insistence upon "going along with the president" no matter what it meant to the success of union drives.[29]

Despite its mixed experience with the Reading Formula, the union's campaign in Reading also helped to revive the area's labor movement beyond the hosiery industry. In July 1933, a labor event in support of a "living wage" and union recognition brought out over 20,000 unionists, strikers, Socialists, and "unemployed citizens" in a parade that drew upon historical elements of both the labor and women's movements. It was led by thousands of young women wearing white dresses, reminiscent of the suffrage movement, followed by some 10,000 hosiery workers, and then by other groups of workers in industries as diverse as shoe, hat, garment, laundry, bakery, building trades, and printing. Those in the older skilled trades carried their historical banners, and several bands marched under the simple placard "Band," provided by the American Federation of Musicians. This parade was a manifestation of a new level of the "culture of unity" that had been growing since the 1920s, increasingly uniting working-class people through incorporating an inclusive, idealistic vision well before it became the underlying theme of the CIO.[30]

It was also in the course of the Reading struggle that the union tested an important new tactic, when workers at the Busy Bee plant "pulled a Gandhi" by "striking on the job" in October 1933. The union had used Gandhi-inspired tactics of passive resistance before, but this action took things to a new level, with important consequences for labor. The impetus for the strike was the arbitrary firing of a hosiery knitter. Other workers in the mill "struck while they were on the job," standing quietly before their motionless machines. During the night shifts when management turned off the power, they "remain[ed] in darkness near their machines," therefore virtually occupying the building and preventing management from bringing in strikebreakers to replace them. Hosiery workers in Reading, Lansdale, Philadelphia, and even Durham, North Carolina, subsequently struck on the job as well, using the Gandhi tactic. The resemblance to the famous sit-downs the CIO would use a few years later is remarkable. By the following year workers in other industries in Philadelphia were using the new tactic as well.[31]

One such occasion occurred in the summer of 1934. By that time, the mostly black workers of Local 697 of the Lead, Oil, Varnish and Paint Makers Union had won, with the help of the Regional Labor Board (RLB), an agreement with the Girard Smelting and Refining Company on the northern edge of Kensington. On July 10, in order to force their employer to honor the agreement and rehire a worker they felt was unjustly fired, they employed the new tactic. They stopped work and stood at their machines for a couple of hours until the owner capitulated. They repeated their actions again on two separate occasions when other grievances surfaced. The workers called these actions "Gandhi strikes," and the historian Howell John Harris has described them as "pioneering examples of the kind of non-violent direct action usually associated with the Civil Rights Movement of two to three decades later." The hosiery workers had been practicing the tactic since the early fall of 1933, and it is likely that the workers of Local 697 were aware of their actions, for members of both unions were part of the same labor milieu and attended the same labor events during that period.[32]

In February 1934, over 20,000 Philadelphia workers staged a one-hour general strike, and thousands attended an overflow mass meeting in Kensington in honor of fellow workers who had been victimized by the fascist repression in Austria. Organized labor joined with Socialists to hear Norman Thomas of the Socialist Party and William Green of the AFL "condemn the inhuman persecution of Socialists and labor in Austria." Leaders and members of both the AFHW and the Lead, Oil, Varnish and Paint Makers Union were in attendance. "Pulling a Gandhi" was an important advance that the AFHW made every effort to publicize and that predated the sit-downs of the CIO by over three years.[33]

The troubles within the union leadership really began to take on serious proportions toward the end of 1933 over a conflict regarding the NRA's hosiery code authority. Rieve had sent his name and that of William Smith, national AFHW secretary, to the administration as designated labor representatives to the hosiery board. Members of Branch 1 opposed this move because, as the largest branch, they felt that their president, Alexander McKeown, should be a representative. They demanded that all interpretations of the code authority be printed and distributed to branch secretaries or shop chairs. Branch 1 representatives also lodged a protest claiming that the requirements of the constitution were not being carried out, as a large number of board members were not actually working on machines. When Rieve responded that he would "take it under advisement," it did not go over well. Branch 1 then sent a protest directly to the NLB, generating a reply from them that they felt there was "friction in the union." And of course there was. At the 1933 union convention Rieve's closing address virtually acknowledged this, though he tried to play it down: "There is no difference of opinion as far as the goal we wish to achieve ... but there may be many opinions and many avenues as to how the purpose can be achieved."[34]

Although the national code authority did agree to the policy of "one knitter to one machine," and hosiery wage codes were set higher than those in textile generally, the codes were below the union rate, continued to allow a lower differential for the South, and did not incorporate the thirty-hour week. In addition, manufacturers continued to violate even those codes and resist efforts to unionize the mills. Branch 1 members felt that these results were due to Rieve's suspension of the 1933 general strike during the height of the conflict at the Cambria mill, and they criticized the administration's labor policy board for giving labor only "one member out of five" on the hosiery code authority, fixing "labor's mathematical share of the 'New Deal' at 1/5."[35]

Frustration with the NRA and Rieve exploded for many hosiery workers in September 1934, when he pulled them out of another strike, this time the great nationwide General Textile Strike.[36] Hosiery workers would be ardent supporters of that strike, not only out of solidarity with southern textile workers, but also to redress grievances of their own. The industrial codes of the NRA had been intended to introduce some control over the cutthroat competition that existed in the textile industry. But nonunion shops, not only in the South but also ones like the large Apex mill in Philadelphia and the Berkshire in Reading, ignored the codes and slashed wages even more, laid off workers, and intensified the workload of those they kept. Many nonunion mills had also introduced the exploitative Bedaux system of "scientific management" as part of the intensification of labor that led to the overproduction that union members felt had caused the economic problems in the country to begin with. Hosiery workers in Philadelphia and other sections of the North had taken pay cuts as part of what was intended to be a two-part strategy—keeping the unionized section alive while organizing the nonunion mills. When the 1934 textile strike was called, they pushed for full participation in the walkout by the hosiery division.[37]

The strike started in the late summer of 1934 in the South, and on September 1, 1934, textile workers throughout the country began to walk out. Textile workers in the North joined in large numbers, and soon over 400,000 were on strike nationwide. The strike quickly turned deadly. A headline in the *Hosiery Worker* reported, "Many martyrs were made early," as "heroic boys and girls laid down their lives in the cause for liberty." Mill owners and their state supporters called out thousands of soldiers and private guards. As in the earlier uprisings of the 1920s, union organizers were beaten and sent to jail. Over a dozen strikers were killed and hundreds wounded.[38]

At a meeting of the AFHW national executive board in late August, representatives Leader and Leo O'Driscoll of Branch 1 had submitted a motion that their union declare a general strike in sympathy with the UTWA, calling out all shops. Rieve opposed this motion, and subsequently the board passed a substitute that would call out only the shops that had not signed the general agreement. This would still mean, however, virtually a general strike in Reading, where manufacturers were continuing to violate the NRA settlement. It would also shut down large plants in the Midwest, Philadelphia, and elsewhere. When the strike call came, however, Rieve, claiming that the large response in the South required all resources to be directed to that area, rescinded the call, promising that hosiery workers in the North might be called out later. Meanwhile, southern hosiery workers were fighting valiantly. As the strike took off, 11,000 workers in full-fashioned and seamless mills in Georgia, Tennessee, and North Carolina walked out. Violence was the rule of the day; the *Hosiery Worker* reported that strikers were clubbed and even bayonetted.[39]

Early in the strike the AFHW sponsored a Labor Day memorial service on September 3 at the Durham gravesite of Clem Norwood, one of the strikers killed in Philadelphia's 1933 Cambria strike. The service was both a one-year memorial of Norwood's death and a key event in initiating the strike as a profound and fundamental battle to democratize the textile industry. Led into the cemetery by the Raleigh High School band, the procession of more than 5,000 members of the local labor movement included an element that the *Hosiery Worker* claimed was "unique in the history of the labor movement in the South," being "the first labor gathering of its kind held in a public place in which white and black workers met together and jointly participated in the devotions for a dead brother in the ranks of labor." The workers' voices "rolled like thunder" as "black arms were raised with white" in a pledge to "carry on this great fight ... against oppression" and for "peace in industry based on justice."[40]

In the face of such an inspiring event, reported prominently in an article on the front page of the *Hosiery Worker*, at another special meeting of the national executive board on September 8, Branch 1 representatives reiterated the demand that the AFHW call a general strike in sympathy with the General Textile Strike. Branch representatives also proposed that any new hosiery agreements must expire on September 1, 1935, a year from the beginning of the textile strike; this was a very early attempt to achieve a coordinated bargaining strategy that would have given the union the power to negotiate from a stronger position. It would have required that the terms of some of the agreements be changed and would have been a contentious issue with most employers. Emil Rieve would not endorse this far-reaching proposal, and it was not implemented.[41]

Rieve was one of five members of the executive council of the UTWA conducting the general strike, and as such he was spending much of his time at strike headquarters in Washington. When President Roosevelt set up a mediation board, Rieve assured the members that the president would not have done so if he did not have assurances from the manufacturers that they would engage in negotiations with the union. After three weeks, the UTWA called off the walkout in return for the government guarantees. Instead of negotiations, however, thousands of former strikers were blacklisted throughout their industry. Government "guarantees" proved nonexistent, and there was no recompense for the deaths and injuries that manufacturers had inflicted on the striking workers.[42]

The UTWA leadership, including Rieve of the AFHW, was now committed to following the dictates of the New Deal formula. An "insurgent" strike by hosiery workers in forty-three mills in Philadelphia and Reading resulted in a mass march on Reading, where manufacturers were still violating the government mediated "settlements." At the UTWA convention in New York, a resolution calling upon all officers of the union serving as members of the NRA boards to resign was very narrowly defeated after a stormy debate in a heavily attended session. Rieve, himself a member of both the code authority and the Philadelphia Regional Labor Board, argued that "rather than withdraw from the NRA, the union need[ed] to secure control."[43] But many of the young delegates were new to the labor movement and maintained an idealistic commitment to the "unity of labor," and they vocally insisted that the "AFL accept honest criticism or face the growth of a dual labor movement." In another session, Anna Geisinger introduced two female textile workers from England, members of the British Labour Party, who spoke in support of third-party politics. Convention delegates then proceeded to pass a resolution, to which the newly organized southern delegates gave particularly strong support, calling for the UTWA to establish a Labor Party because of the perceived failure of their Democratic Party "allies" and instructing its delegates to the AFL to support both a new party and the industrial form of unionism. To many of the young workers the message was clear—labor must rely on its own power.[44]

In Kensington, hosiery workers took personally what they considered to be the betrayal of the southern strikers by the top union leadership. Ever since the 1920s they had been contributing to a special fund to help these workers organize and had hosted mass meetings where they listened to the dramatic stories of veterans of those struggles. Southern workers had begun to rebel against their exploitation well before the New Deal, in places like Gastonia, Marion, and Elizabethton—and these names resonated with personal meaning for Philadelphia's hosiery workers, for they had been part of those struggles in a very real sense. The decisions of the leadership threatened the integrity of the long-held traditions and culture of Kensington's textile workers and contradicted the values that the union had been teaching its young workers. Organizers in Reading also reported unrest and resentment from union members there over the fact that they were not being called out in support of the strike.[45]

Philadelphia's hosiery workers had always seen themselves as part of something larger, and they tried hard to spread that philosophy through participating in the General Textile Strike. When Rieve refused to call them out and capitulated to the entreaties of the Roosevelt administration to call off the strike, it reinforced the perception by the rank and file in the hosiery union that Rieve was more interested in gaining favor in Washington than he was in justice for the workers. The primary obstacle to the successful conclusion of the strike, critics such as Janet Irons contend, was not a lack of solidarity between the workers in the North and South, but instead "issues that divided the members of the UTW—North and South—from their leaders."[46] The selling out of the heroic workers involved in the strike, not only by Washington but by their own leadership, underscored the conundrum hosiery workers grappled with. Greater centralization within the organization could create a stronger movement, but at the same time it could undermine the rank and file's ability to hold leadership accountable and maintain working-class power. Many members of Branch 1 felt it was only through working-class power that any real progress toward a more just society could be made.

After the General Textile Strike the dispute between Branch 1 and Rieve became so intense that, for a period of time, the union newspaper even ceased publication while the factions tried to work out a solution. The losses of the 1934 strike increased the pressure on Philadelphia as more and more shops looked to the nonunion areas to cut their costs. Branch 1 leadership was aware that they would have a difficult time out on their own, and they still strongly identified as part of a broader movement. For his part, Rieve was also fully cognizant of the fact that the loss of Branch 1 would essentially destroy the union and greatly diminish his prestige. In the face of such realities, national and Branch 1 representatives worked out an uneasy compromise. In this deal, Branch 1 president Alexander McKeown became first vice president of the AFHW and "special assistant" to Emil Rieve, putting him in line to be the next president of the national union. Branch 1 members elected William Leader as president of the Philadelphia local, and a Communist, Joseph Burge, as vice president. Although this compromise remained uncomfortable for the remainder of the union's association with Rieve, it was enough to carry it through into the era of the CIO. The hosiery workers would continue to contribute to that larger movement, and they would continue to organize in the South, but the losses sustained in the textile strike made their work much more difficult. The 1934 strike can be seen as a turning point, as it also thoroughly undermined the credibility of the AFL-affiliated UTWA. Hosiery workers looked to a new organization that they believed would have the power to unify working people in a more effective challenge to the existing political and economic order than had heretofore been mounted—a new organization in which they hoped it might be possible to reverse the losses of 1934 and create a true, labor-based movement for social change.

Hosiery Workers and the Creation of the CIO

By 1933 labor activity was increasing in Philadelphia, as it was throughout the nation, as workers attempted to take advantage of NIRA's Section 7a to establish unions in various industries. One such place was the large Philco radio and electrical plant in Kensington, where, in early July, virtually the entire workforce walked out shortly after 350 mostly skilled workers called a strike in protest against an increase in working hours. The young workers who moved into leadership of the strike included Socialists and a Catholic trade union activist named James Carey. The company surrendered quickly, and one reason was because "the strikers had the mass support of the Kensington neighborhood's powerful, Socialist-led Hosiery Workers Union."[47] Philco signed a contract with the AFRW that granted significant improvements in wages and working conditions. As an industrial union in an industry nominally covered by an electrical craft union, the best the AFRW could get from the AFL was a charter as a federal local.

In addition to the AFRW locals, workers at other electrical plants around the country were forming their own new industrial unions. Unhappy with the lack of support from the AFL, they came together in 1936 to form the United Electrical and Radio Workers (UE) and chose the twenty-four-year-old Carey as their president. In November the UE became the first union to be directly chartered by the newly founded CIO. While the union's leadership was somewhat diverse in its political orientation, overall the union retained a decided left-wing tilt with an inclusive approach to organizing that came to include demands of equal pay for men and women.

The Philco union's original name, AFRW, was quite similar to that of the AFHW, and the new union incorporated an organizational structure virtually identical to that of the hosiery union. National union officers were elected on a yearly basis, a majority of executive committee members were required to be employed in the shops, and union executives could be paid no more than the top rate paid to a worker in the industry. Such synchronicity is not actually all that remarkable, however, for Philco's AFRW not only received support from the AFHW, but activists from both unions were members of the Socialist Party. In addition, former hosiery workers, many of them women, were now employed at Philco and in the forefront of the organizing campaigns there. As unemployment rose in the hosiery industry, workers often sought jobs in other industries. Some had been blacklisted in hosiery for their union activities, but when they entered other industries, that did not stop them from union organizing. John Edelman claimed that it was a well-known fact: "Everyone knows that Philco was organized by hosiery workers." At the 1946 hosiery workers' convention, Harry Block of the UE (also the chair of the Philadelphia CIO Council) said the same thing: "There has yet to be a labor dispute in this city that the Hosiery Workers did not do their part and perhaps a little bit more.... When we attempted to organize the Philadelphia Philco plants they gave us all of their facilities and placed all of their resources at our command." The UE was to become one of the key Left-led affiliates of the new CIO.[48]

Hosiery workers also provided support and leadership for the CIO in other areas of the country. Don Harris described the contributions made by hosiery workers to the organizing of the CIO in the Midwest. After the hosiery workers were able to win a closed shop at the Rollins mill, they were the largest local of any union in the state of Iowa. This fact made them a powerful force in the labor movement and put them in a position to help other unions to organize. The hosiery workers, along with the miners, *were* the CIO in Iowa, he claimed. "We were young, young gals and young guys, and we was in everything. There never was a picket line, there never was another organizing campaign went on that we weren't involved in and there never was a strike that we didn't put on a dollar assessment and give them money." In 1937 Harris used his experience in the AFHW to become the regional director for the CIO in Iowa (as Carl Holderman did in New Jersey and John Edelman did in Pennsylvania—see below). During the bitter 1938 Maytag strike, led by William Sentner of the UE, Harris brought up checks from his old hosiery local in Des Moines "about once a week ... to keep their soup kitchen going," not surprising given the hosiery workers' long connection to the UE. From 1937 to 1939 he served as the national director for the Packinghouse Workers Organizing Committee, an organization that had its Des Moines headquarters in the AFHW hall, and later as the president of District 8 of the UE. Hosiery workers went to work for other CIO unions after leaving hosiery as well. Joseph Burge, for instance, worked for the United Cannery, Agricultural,

Packing, and Allied Workers of America and helped organize workers in many areas, including African American women crab pickers in Maryland. Later he helped organize Sun Ship in Chester, Pennsylvania.[49]

In Philadelphia, labor activism increased even further with the passage of the National Labor Relations Act (the Wagner Act) on July 5, 1935, part of Roosevelt's "second hundred days." Following on the turmoil of the 1934 strikes and the rising influence of radical organizations, the act finally put some teeth into protecting the right of union organizing. Unlike the perceived failure of NIRA (which had been declared unconstitutional anyway), the Wagner Act set up procedures and gave guarantees for union representation elections and protected workers' rights to strike and engage in other union activities.

In the aftermath of the passage of the Wagner Act, strikes erupted all over Philadelphia. In July 1935, bakery drivers went on strike at the General Baking Company, and in March 1936, bakery drivers and inside workers also struck the Freihofer Baking Company in a violent confrontation. By the summer of 1936 the CIO was seriously concentrating on the Pennsylvania region, and John Edelman of the AFHW was hired as the regional director for the organization. Between 1936 and 1939 he ran organizing drives that included Bethlehem Steel in Bethlehem, Pennsylvania, Sun Ship in Chester, Pennsylvania, and Campbell Soup in Camden, New Jersey, and was instrumental in establishing a CIO union at the Hershey Chocolate Company in Hershey, Pennsylvania. These were not his only activities as the region's CIO representative. In 1938 Eleanor Roosevelt came to Philadelphia as the honored guest of the Philadelphia Council of the National Negro Congress during its celebration of the seventy-fifth anniversary of the Emancipation Proclamation. Along with Mrs. Roosevelt, speakers included A. Philip Randolph, president of the National Negro Congress, and John Edelman of the CIO.[50]

The first full-fledged sit-down strike (going beyond "pulling a Gandhi") in the city of Philadelphia occurred on January 4, 1937, at the Electric Storage Battery Company, a few days after the start of the famous autoworkers' sit-down in Flint, Michigan. Ten days later, on January 14, ten unions formed the Philadelphia branch of the CIO. These unions were the AFHW, the UE, the Battery Workers Union, the American Federation of Teachers, the ACWA, the ILGWU, the Upholstery Weavers' Union, the Plush Workers' Union, the Carpet Workers Union, and the American Federation of Iron, Steel, and Tin Workers. By January 21, the local CIO branch had established permanent offices, and five more organizations had joined, bringing the total to fifteen unions and 80,000 members. Members voted William Leader, president of

Branch 1 of the AFHW, as president of the Philadelphia CIO council, ILGWU member Samuel G. Otto as vice president, and Fred McCall of the UE as treasurer, and raised an initial $25,000 for organizing Philadelphia's mass-production workers.[51]

In 1936 Emil Rieve was appointed as the U.S. labor delegate to the International Labor Organization in Geneva, Switzerland. Accompanied by John Edelman and AFHW organizer Wanda Pilot, he also visited France, meeting with French Socialists and observing firsthand the sit-down strikes that were paralyzing the auto industry in that country. Edelman, in what now appears as a poignant letter to Tiny Hoffmann, described the "wonderful progress" and "modern building" projects that were being carried on in the Socialist-controlled areas. It would be only a few short years before Hitler's Nazis would be marching down the boulevards of Paris.[52]

Ironically, it was on this trip, according to Edelman, that Rieve decided he wanted to be the president of the new CIO textile organization. Now a full supporter of the New Deal, on his return to the United States he officially resigned from the Socialist Party. On March 9, 1937, the CIO and the UTWA entered into an agreement to set up the TWOC. TWOC abolished all of the UTWA federations except for the Hosiery Workers and the Dyers, headed by George Baldanzi. This exception was allegedly due to the fact that they were "self-supporting," but the hosiery workers would certainly not have quietly acquiesced to the abolition of their autonomy.[53]

TWOC's national textile drive officially opened in the spring of 1937. The AFHW contributed $183,000, fielded fifty organizers, and conducted a "whirlwind campaign," particularly in Philadelphia and Reading. In Philadelphia, the campaign opened in March, and Branch 1 president Leader set up headquarters in Kensington and Manayunk (another historic Philadelphia textile center). Unlike TWOC generally, the hosiery union relied heavily on the sit-down strike, and hosiery strikes swept the state. While most accounts of sit-down strikes concentrate on powerful takeovers in very masculine industries such as auto and rubber, with limited mention of retail sit-downs in establishments like Woolworth's, the hosiery strikers included a large female contingent, and women were very much in evidence during the campaigns. In fact, in the Brownhill and Kramer strike, which involved 475 workers, women were the first to sit down when they "quit work at eleven A.M. and sat down at their posts." Women were part of regular shifts of workers that maintained the strike for over a month (although they did not participate in the night shift). Women also maintained the picket lines outside many mills, such as the Artcraft Hosiery Mill in Kensington, where, as part of a large crowd, they distracted police protecting the mill. Women were also very much in evidence at the precedent-setting Apex strike.⁵⁴

The CIO unions were, by this time, the largest in the city. At one very contentious meeting of Philadelphia's Central Labor Union (CLU), an AFL representative warned the many young, new members that they did not fully understand the autocratic nature of the new labor organization. If they joined with the CIO, he cautioned, they would "have officers handed down to [them] from the top, and have a dictatorship like the United Mine Workers." But the AFL had maintained its resistance to industrial unionism for too long, and the young Philadelphia workers who joined the CIO were fired by a vision of class unity. On March 23, the twenty-one Philadelphia unions in the CIO received formal notice that they were suspended from the CLU. By late March the CIO in Philadelphia had an estimated 100,000 members, representing an inclusive, industrial form of unionism that its members believed would help them build a strong movement for change.⁵⁵

One of the reasons for the success of the early CIO was its emphasis on direct action, which resonated with the culture of a workforce fed up with the intransigence of the manufacturers and their government supporters. Equally important was its message of class unity, especially promoted by its left wing, that all workers, whatever their craft, ethnicity, race, or sex, could act together to achieve empowerment and social justice. A 1936 article in Philadelphia's African American newspaper, the *Tribune*, described this unity, announcing that at least 60,000 workers would march in the city's annual May Day celebration: "An organized group of Negro and white workers, representing all religions, political doctrines and nationalities will manifest their single purpose and aim, the strength of American labor." The hosiery union's attempt to build a cosmopolitan culture of unity through education, social activities, sports, support of minority and gender issues, and "rights"-based organizing, painstakingly built up over at least a decade and a half, was coming to fruition in the city.⁵⁶

On May 15, 1939, the CIO called an important convention in Philadelphia. At this convention delegates voted to establish the TWUA, CIO. This union consisted of 302 locals affiliated with TWOC and 126 that were affiliated with the UTWA. Emil Rieve of the AFHW was elected president of the new, consolidated union.⁵⁷

The Rieve–Branch 1 divergence in approaches to industrial organizing represented more than a mere difference in personalities or even strategies. It also revealed two fundamentally opposed understandings of the nature of capitalism and the role of working-class activism in challenging that economic and social system. The resultant structural models each created—Rieve's massive top-down CIO national unions and Branch 1's rank-and-file-controlled and community-based social movements with a mission of empowering the entire working class—had results that outlasted their founders' visions. The shortcomings of the former model likely contributed to the sharp decline in union density and power in succeeding decades, and twenty-first-century activists' prescriptions for change often bear strong resemblance to Branch 1's remarkably successful experiment.[58]

The AFHW and the New Deal

While it might be unsurprising that the AFHW played a key role in the founding and development of labor's CIO, its connection to the Roosevelt administration's New Deal might come as more of a surprise. Just as the CIO had roots that can be traced to the day-to-day organizing and struggles of hosiery workers and others like them, so also the New Deal did not just spring from the minds of Roosevelt's advisers. Much of its agenda was based on work on the ground that had been going on for a long time and had a grassroots lineage. Hosiery workers were among those activists who helped to lay the groundwork for programs like Social Security and unemployment insurance. As Howard Kreckman put it, "Roosevelt didn't come up with these ideas on his own, you know. He got a lot of them from the Socialists." Just as with the CIO, hosiery workers also had direct connections to the New Deal through personnel and in the formation of policies and programs.[59]

As the centerpiece of the early New Deal, the NRA was intended to achieve industrial peace through the negotiation process and by allowing "responsible" unionism. The act set up boards for industry to negotiate codes of fair competition that would "benefit industry, labor, and consumers." In October 1933, Emil Rieve was appointed to both the Hosiery Code Authority and the Philadelphia RLB, and in the process became a full participant in the New Deal bureaucracy and a firm supporter of "responsible" unionism. It was this move away from independence and local empowerment that subsequently estranged a portion of the leadership from the rank and file and helped derail the grassroots-led potential for social change.[60]

As the labor representative on the Philadelphia RLB, Emil Rieve presided, along with the representatives from business, over some very contentious strikes in Philadelphia. One of these was the 1934 strike at the Swedish multinational SKF Corporation. Rieve recommended a settlement under the Reading Formula—that workers go back, continue to negotiate, and send anything not resolved to the board. But given the history of manufacturers virtually ignoring board decisions, the SKF employees decided to stay on strike during negotiations. The company brought in replacements and professional thugs, resulting in four months of often-violent confrontations. Hundreds of Philadelphia's notorious labor police on horseback and motorbikes attacked the strikers. The RLB, and Emil Rieve, "just walked away" from the strike. The 1934 strike defeat temporarily broke the second-largest union in the metal trades in the city and undermined Rieve's stature even more among members of Branch 1, contributing more fuel to the breach between them.[61] Despite the mixed legacy of the AFHW-inspired Reading Formula and the development of conciliatory and "responsible" unionism, however, the union would play a defining role in other unequivocally successful New Deal initiatives.

The AFHW's most important contribution to New Deal programs was its collaboration with the PWA to build its workers' housing project, the Carl Mackley Houses. While the Mackley Houses project was not the first attempt at union-sponsored housing in the United States, it was certainly one of the most important. The PWA opened up the social space that allowed the union to push the government to commit to improving the lives of working people in the most fundamental sense—through housing and jobs. During the Depression housing problems took on tremendous proportions, with large numbers of workers and their families facing evictions. While activities such as those of the unemployed movements took an approach of direct action to prevent the growing numbers of evictions, forward-looking progressives within the union also embraced the necessity of creating permanent solutions in the form of low-income workers' housing.

"Public housing began wrapped in utopian hope," writes Daniel Rodgers. Although some of the fundamental ideology can be traced back to utopian communities of the nineteenth century, the primary influences for the Carl Mackley Houses came from the "social modernist" ideas of workers' housing promoted by socialists in Austria and Germany. This younger generation of European socialists made a conscious effort to incorporate a commitment to labor solidarity into community design, and worked to build housing for the masses of working people with, as Rodgers says, "a creativity unmatched in the North Atlantic economy." In the 1920s the European revolution in housing design came to America.[62]

A small group of people with connections stretching back across the Atlantic took up the cause of establishing an American counterpart to the union-based housing so much a part of 1920s Berlin and Vienna. John Edelman, himself raised in a utopian Socialist community in the Cotswolds in England, was a proponent of workers' art and literature, as well as housing. Through extended socialist networks Edelman met Oskar Stonorov, an architect who immigrated to the United States from Germany in 1929. Stonorov "had studied architecture at the University of Florence in Italy and at the École Polytechnique in Zurich, and had been a pupil of the French architect Le Corbusier." He was greatly influenced by Europe's workers' housing projects, particularly the Karl Marx Hof in Vienna. Stonorov's partner, Alfred Kastner, had studied architecture at the Bauhaus school in Germany.[63]

While socialist influences on the origins of public housing in the New Deal era have been widely understood, the way this brought AFHW values to full flower has not. In 1934 the AFHW undertook a project that would be its most ambitious and lasting effort at community outreach when it began the construction of the Carl Mackley Houses. This ambitious plan of low-cost housing for workers was named after the hosiery worker martyred in the 1930 Aberle strike. Before beginning construction, the union studied the housing situation of its members in Philadelphia, hiring a group of graduate students from Bryn Mawr College to examine hosiery workers' needs as well as what these workers felt would be desired components of an ideal housing situation. Then, inspired by the social modernist themes of workers' housing in Europe, Stonorov and Kastner, along with the architect William Pope Barney of Philadelphia, designed the Mackley Houses. Built in response to the systematic survey of the desires of union members, when completed the project became the foremost model of labor housing.[64]

The essential elements of social modernist architecture, "light, air, spaciousness ... sun, grass, color, form," were incorporated into the Mackley Houses. Many of these features are, today, hallmarks of environmentally conscious living. The project consisted of four three-story units stretching over an entire city block. Each building was named for one of the labor martyrs of the hosiery strikes. Between each building, "green areas" provided protected spaces for children to play. Altogether, these units contained 284 apartments, all of which had cross-ventilation and large windows oriented in such a way as to take advantage of the passive solar potential of full sunlight. The kitchens and bathrooms were designed so that they could use a gray-water system to conserve water. All apartments had kitchens fitted with modern appliances, and most had individual porches. Laundries on the top floor of each building were equipped with washers, dryers, and ironing boards. There was an auditorium located between two apartment buildings that was large enough to be used for dances and other forms of entertainment. The complex also contained a thirty-by-seventy-five-foot swimming pool and a small wading pool for children. The architects had originally planned to build tennis courts, but the survey made it clear that workers living in the middle of a city neighborhood were much more likely to utilize a swimming pool where they could cool off in the hot city summers.[65]

The buildings were managed by a professional staff who took care of needed repairs; the cost of their labor was included in the rent, which also covered heat, water, and electricity. The new development was enormously popular, but, as Howard Kreckman said, "hosiery workers had priority." Built in the textile district, across from Juniata Park and four blocks away from several major textile plants, it was made possible by the first public works housing loan under the PWA: project number 1 of the New Deal. The loan was to be paid back over the course of thirty years. The government employed 1,000 building trades workers, most of whom were on the city's relief rolls, to build the houses, and the land for the complex was provided by the union. In the high times of the Jazz Age a decade earlier, on the advice of its attorney, Michael Francis Doyle, the hosiery union had invested money in city property. To secure the land for the Mackley project, members voted to exchange three blocks of union-owned land in South Philadelphia for the site in Juniata.[66]

Tenants began moving in during January 1935, and Alice and Howard Kreckman were among this first group, renting a one-bedroom apartment facing the park. Joseph and Margaret Burge lived just above them. Aside from attempting to deal with one of the most pressing needs of the workers of Kensington, the Carl Mackley Houses represented a conscious effort on the part of union leadership to create, in microcosm, a new human society, based on a vision of social democracy and the very best of the elements of "community" for which Kensington was historically known.[67]

The organization of space can act as a powerful social force. It can forge bonds of solidarity, empower individuals, and offer a place to, as Margaret Kohn puts it, "explore and develop an alternate set of values" that can integrate persons into "shared conceptions of reality and political power." Such concepts of spatial organization can be used to describe the community of Kensington as a whole and help explain some of its core features. The designers of the Carl Mackley Houses consciously constructed the space they were working with to achieve a goal of modern working-class style and self-sufficiency for the project's residents. As part of the configuration of the political space of the Mackley Houses, the union held a contest for an artist to paint murals in the library. The subjects of the Mackley Houses murals were to be events "marking the advance of labor in Philadelphia." The Mackley

FIGURE 7 Murals for the library of the Carl Mackley Houses. Scenes include the pledge taken at McPherson Square, prominent union leaders, depictions of work, and representations of the strike, along with police violence. *Philadelphia Record* Photograph Morgue [V07]. Historical Society of Pennsylvania.

shooting was the subject of one of the murals. Stonorov said that the intention was to "incorporate some of the feeling, evidenced by the turnout at the memorial and the pledge people took, into the buildings themselves." The complex itself was to be a monument to labor (see Figure 7).[68]

Among its amenities the complex offered a cooperative grocery, a credit union, craft shops, a library, and sports programs. There were dances raising funds for the Loyalists in the Spanish Civil War; according to Howard Kreckman, some of the residents lost their lives in the battle against the fascists in Spain. There were lectures on socialized medicine and the Farmer Labor Party, a mock trial of William Randolph Hearst, and labor education plays, such as *Waiting for Lefty* and "two plays produced by a group of Negroes interested in the education of the worker through the drama." Editorials in the *Mackley Messenger*, the tenant newspaper, supported workers' rights and often criticized capitalism.[69]

One of the complex's most important offerings was a fully staffed nursery school. In 1936 a WPA worker wrote that space was provided in the architect's plan for a nursery school because "many of the mothers would be working and therefore, a school would be a necessity in the community life." The only cost to families was for the food given to the children and the salary of the cook.[70]

The school operated on principles of "progressive" education where children were taught to be self-sufficient and cooperative, not competitive. The director, a professional educator, lived in one of the apartments. During the year 1935–36 there were fifty children enrolled in the school. Slots were also made available for the children of women who did not engage in paid work, in order to provide the mothers with time for themselves for "education, physical and political activities, or just for relaxation." Women organized dinners, put on bazaars, and staged entertainment programs to help fund the nursery school, and union leadership regularly requested voluntary assessments from members of the branches for the same purpose.

Mackley House women also started a Woman's Club that pursued political education for women. They sponsored programs on such issues as cooperatives, company unions, tenements, women in other cultures, economics, and protective legislation. They also sponsored protest actions to the state senate to lobby for relief for the unemployed. To Alice Kreckman these protests were an important part of the social life of the community, and, "if you lived at Mackley, you couldn't help but know about them." The women often also exhibited a sense of supportive sisterhood, such as that shown to a single mother who resided at the complex. The report described her as "a recently divorced woman" and quoted her as saying, "Without the Woman's Club, I could never have held my head up."[71]

The Mackley Houses' modern facilities, recreational space, and educational programs made the apartments truly unique among public housing of the era. Many visitors came to view the houses and speak to the residents. These included not only many officials from other unions, but also Secretary of Labor Frances Perkins in April 1936 and an official delegation from the Soviet Union, which included four architects who pronounced the development "one of the outstanding housing achievements of the world." This delegation of architects, one of whom had won first prize in the design competition for the Palace of the Soviets, said that they planned to use many of the ideas they saw at Mackley in planning housing betterment in the Soviet Union.[72]

The AFHW's involvement in public housing also led to significant advances in federal legislation. Out of the Mackley Houses was born the Labor

Housing Conference, whose first meeting was held in its auditorium on September 6, 1935. Founded by Edelman, Stonorov, and Kastner, and under the active direction of Catherine Bauer, whom they hired in 1934, other union groups soon joined and participated in the first National Labor Housing Conference, in October 1935. This led to the founding of the AFL Housing Committee, which established headquarters in Washington and lobbied for government-sponsored low-income housing. In 1937 these activities resulted in the United States Housing Act, also known as the Wagner-Steagall Act. It established the United States Housing Authority and authorized it to loan and grant money to local public housing agencies for the development of low-rent houses.[73]

When interviewed about the hosiery workers' housing, William Jeanes, a Philadelphia Quaker philanthropist and resident manager of the complex, told a story about a local worker who came in to see the apartments. As the man went through the complex he did not say much, but just before he left he looked at Jeanes and asked, "Did you ever read *Looking Backward*?" In Jeanes's mind, this worker saw the hope of a future order in the Mackley Houses, as suggested by his reference to Edward Bellamy's utopian novel.[74]

The AFHW and Working-Class Feminism

Just as rank-and-file workers (along with union officials) of the AFHW and other unions helped to form the CIO and New Deal programs, so also ongoing work by many rank-and-file women in the same organizations helped lay the groundwork for the labor feminism of the post–World War II era. The actions of the AFHW's female members and the activities they were involved in helped to advance their position within the organization, sometimes pushing them onto a national stage, and served to increase their consciousness as women and as workers. The women of the union broadened their understanding of women's rights and equality in part because they were influenced by depictions of women in hosiery union culture as well as in popular culture—actresses and national "heroines" like sportswomen and the suffragettes and "labor heroines." They also participated in educational and recreational activities that brought them into association with other women who were directly concerned with promoting the advancement of women. Many of the women who worked in the Labor Education Bureau, the WTUL, the YWCA, the Women's Bureau, and the various labor colleges and summer programs for women workers were veterans of earlier struggles for women's rights and activists whose concerns included the empowerment of working women.

What it is important to understand is that the socialist culture that spawned the union, the history in which it was embedded, and the class position of hosiery women were all important components of the manner in which they sorted through and internalized the myriad ideas that were circulating in 1920s and 1930s America.[75]

Some of the same trends that spawned a top-down "responsible unionism" and a countervailing "alternative unionism" that sought to find a more transformative solution to social problems also played out among the women in the hosiery union. This can be seen in the confrontations between Rieve and Branch 1 and some others; Rieve, as he moved into the top labor bureaucracy, downplayed the specific issues of women's leadership, while Branch 1 and others attempted to make women's rights a real part of their movement. But the hosiery union's concentrations on rights and self-organization opened up important spaces of action that these modern working-class children of the earlier women's struggles could use to advance their issues in the CIO period and beyond.

Over the course of the 1920s and 1930s and on into the postwar period, the AFHW forged relationships with national women's organizations and prominent women at the same time that it was supporting women's rights legislation and their rights on the job. This continued and even accelerated after Emil Rieve moved on and Alexander McKeown became the national president. The YWCA and its industrial secretaries, in Kensington and other parts of the country, supported many of the union's programs, promoting their "union hosiery" campaign nationally. They provided connections with women's colleges and held women's labor education programs and were sources of activism for legislative initiatives important to women in labor, such as the hours and minimum-wage legislation pushed by the union. They also provided vital resources for the union's national boycott against Berkshire hosiery in 1937. In addition, the AFHW developed especially deep and long-lasting ties with the WTUL, members of whom had been regular speakers at union conventions since the 1920s. Anna Geisinger was vice president of the Philadelphia branch in the late 1920s, and in the 1930s another member of Branch 1, Freda Maurer, became the head of the Pennsylvania branch of the organization.[76]

Both wings of the hosiery union leadership cultivated ties with prominent women and organizations that played a role in labor and government programs that impacted women workers and influenced their consciousness. These included Frances Perkins, the first female cabinet member and Roosevelt's secretary of labor during the New Deal, who was a much-heralded speaker at a dinner that the women's division of Branch 1 held at the Mackley Houses in 1936. Catherine Bauer, who had been a prominent consultant for the Mackley Houses and had helped the union start the Labor Housing Conference on its premises, wrote a regular housing column for the *Hosiery Worker*. During the mid-1930s, while serving as an activist for the Labor Housing Conference, she campaigned around the country for workers' housing programs modeled on the Mackley Houses, and including provisions for childcare, for the Housing Committee of the AFL.

The wife of Pennsylvania's governor, Cornelia Bryce Pinchot, developed a particularly close relationship with the union. Pinchot was a modern and independent woman who had been a member of the suffrage campaign and an adamant supporter of access to birth control and women's education. It was the union's responsiveness to these issues that forged the enduring bonds between them. Pinchot ran for Congress in 1928 promoting labor law reform, with support from the hosiery union. An internationally known figure, she was active with the League of Women Voters and the National Consumers League and was a frequent speaker at the union's national conventions and at the women's meetings of Branch 1, where she encouraged hosiery's women to take an active part in politics and activity outside of the home. An outspoken activist, she even joined the union's picket lines, including those of the 1933 Cambria strike. Alice Nelson Kreckman said "she was right out there with us," calling her "fiery" and "all for the union." She was so close to the union that when it commissioned murals for the Mackley Houses, she was one of the subjects.[77]

When it came to legislative initiatives, the first president of the Women's Bureau of the U.S. Department of Labor, Mary Anderson, was an important ally, maintaining an enduring relationship with the AFHW. Anderson was a frequent consultant and guest speaker for the hosiery union, especially spending time with the women of Branch 1, where she supported their educational efforts as well as initiatives to gain equality in representation and leadership. This relationship carried over into the 1940s and beyond, when she and her successor, Frieda Miller, spearheaded pay equity legislation to which the union, with Alexander McKeown as president, gave its full support.[78]

In fact, legislative battles regarding the protection of women's economic independence were a particular focus of the AFHW. During the campaigns to achieve unemployment relief and old-age pensions, the hosiery workers were among the supporters of the comprehensive Lundeen bill, introduced into Congress in 1934. The historian Alice Kessler Harris summarized the important ways the Lundeen bill differed from the later Social Security Act. It "provided insurance for all workers, including all wage earners, all salaried workers, farmers, professional workers, and the self-employed. It prohibited discrimination because of age, sex, race, or color, and it specifically included those who worked part-time and in agricultural and domestic or professional work." The bill also would have covered loss of wages due to maternity as well as sickness and old age, unlike the legislation that eventually passed. The union's support for women-centered legislation was ongoing, including the Women's Equal Pay Act of 1945 and, in 1953, an amended version of the Equal Rights Amendment (ERA) that would have also protected the previous gains that laboring women had made in legislation.[79]

Through it all, the struggles of rank-and-file women for control of their lives, on the streets and in the union hall, remained the motor that drove the machine of working-class feminism. Some of the women involved in the union have dropped from the historical record. Much of their activity was centered on grassroots organizing to begin with, for well-known women were not the only or even the most important element in the advancement of labor feminism. It was the work of women in local organizing, as well as in national organizational and educational campaigns, that formed the networks and provided the foundations that allowed working-class feminism to flourish. Such had been the case in Kensington since the nineteenth century when women in the Knights of Labor were fighting for women's rights, both in Kensington and in the larger, national organization.

Support for women's rights on the job and in contract negotiations, and for women's very right to work, was a hallmark of the day-to-day work of the union's women. In Branch 1, women had been serving on the executive board since the late 1920s and had won guaranteed positions on that board by the mid-1930s. A 1935 article in the *Hosiery Worker* described a "spirited discussion" in which the "'girls'" division members "vigorously asserted their rights as workers in the industry," at a meeting in which they chose their two representatives. Although branches like Milwaukee, Rieve's home branch, had disbanded the women's division as early as 1931, that did not happen in Philadelphia. The issue of pay equity also surfaced in many of the struggles of the union. When, in 1933, the union won a partial restoration of the pay cuts they had taken over the years, Branch 1 members decided that a larger percentage of the new funds should go to the workers who were receiving lower wages, in order to achieve greater equity.[80]

The union also continued to respond to the demands of married women for protection of their working rights. During the Depression there was increased pressure, from both government and industry, to limit the right of married women to hold a job, the assumption being that their husbands would take care of them. Given the high level of male unemployment, such an assumption was, to say the least, problematic. In one such case, in 1935, the union was asked by a female member in a Philadelphia shop to intercede when she was fired for getting married, a new policy that had been instituted at her plant. Branch 1 swiftly filed a grievance against the company and won on the grounds that the policy constituted a form of "class legislation" because it applied only to married women and was not applied in a way that gave preference to single men over married ones.[81]

The responsiveness of their union to their problems encouraged the loyalty of women workers to the organization, but, as often happened in hosiery union history, it was the actions of the women that drove the support of the union. Although women of the rank and file participated in lobbying trips and legislative initiatives, they had a major impact on the union through their continued embrace of the organization's trademark activity—direct action. For rank-and-file hosiery union women, a core arena of their struggle for respect and rights remained the picket lines. And so it was that at the strike at the largest hosiery mill in the country, the Berkshire mill in Reading, a central battle site of the CIO era, as it had been during the period of the NRA, women were once again in the forefront of the battles. Beginning in the winter of 1936, the strike involved new and innovative tactics and garnered the support of other unions and major women's organizations, as union literature challenged the mill's policies of "forcing down women's wages" as part of a "Hitlerite policy." This charge was not just standard "leftist" propaganda against a big business, for there were real connections between the owners of the Berkshire and the Nazi government. Aside from the fact that the mill owners used the same attorney as the German government, Berkshire owner Gustave Oberlaender, on a trip to Heidelberg in June 1936, attended a banquet where he and his wife were given a "place of honor" at the table of Hitler's notorious minister of propaganda, Joseph Goebbels. The *Reading Eagle* carried a glowing description of the event in its social columns.[82]

From its initial phase, the Berkshire strike turned violent, and pictures of picketing workers, male and female, fighting tear gas and Pennsylvania's notorious state police made headlines around the country. Over the course of the strike the participants evolved another new Gandhi-style, nonviolent resistance tactic, once more presaging those that would be used in both the future civil rights and antiwar movements. They dubbed these new demonstrations "lie-downs," and they consisted of strikers, many of them women, lying down in a solid mass, in bitter cold weather, blocking driveways and entrances to the mills. The union's publicity network generated a nationwide campaign that also included pictures of strikers' parents marching in the place of their children who had been arrested. Playing on the themes of justice and heroic women, one release quoted the mother of two jailed strikers, portraying her as an example for women nationally: "In other years the men did the fighting while women had to sit at home and worry. But now, I intend to do my share against injustice. I'm marching for my children who are in jail." The education department sent out copious amounts of literature to other unions and women's organizations with pictures of young women in clouds of tear gas, captioned: "Every American worker, every red-blooded American, would thrill at the story of how the girls at the Berkshire, when tear gas was coming out in clouds, calmly dipped their handkerchiefs in water, covered their mouth and nose and kept right on picketing." Even magazines like *Look* and *Life* carried pictures of the strikers, again projecting them onto a national stage.[83]

This very visible concentration on women once more paid off in the support generated among female consumers for a nationwide boycott of Berkshire hosiery and a secondary boycott of Woolworth's Department Stores. The union's campaign received national support from the YWCA, the National Consumers League, and the League of Women Shoppers, who picketed Woolworth's in New York City and other locations. Female-owned businesses also weighed in and pledged not to carry Berkshire hosiery.[84]

This strike lasted through the winter of 1936 and into early 1937, paralleling the simultaneous, and more well-known, Flint sit-downs of the United Auto Workers, for the massive CIO challenge to the prerogatives of capital was in full flower. And one of the most significant episodes in that struggle, again, took place in Kensington, between the hosiery workers and its bastion of anti-unionism, the Apex Hosiery Company. This struggle led to a historic Supreme Court decision that had major repercussions for the labor movement.

Storming the Bastille

Ever since the early 1920s, Philadelphia's largest hosiery mill, the Apex, and its proprietor, William Meyer, had been leading the anti-union forces in Philadelphia's hosiery industry. In the past the Apex owner and his attorney had used connections with the city to maintain a permanent injunction against the union, and they consistently used labor spies and intimidation to keep the union out. In the spring of 1937 Branch 1 began a series of sit-down strikes in the Philadelphia mills and quickly scored a string of victories, including one at the large Artcraft mill, which was as virulently anti-union as the Apex and also had a permanent injunction against the union. At the beginning of the strike there, according to a Military Intelligence informant, "a strong column of at least 1000" rushed forward in a main attack and took possession of the mill "in less than five minutes."[85] During this campaign, however, the city's police force behaved very differently than in previous years. Howard Kreckman said, "There was no head cracking." Kreckman claimed that Branch 1 president William Leader had an "in" with the mayor because he had supported his election campaign. The mayor, S. Davis Wilson, elected in 1935, was nominally a Republican, but given the turmoil in the city he became a reformer. He embraced the New Deal and authorized WPA programs in areas such as housing and recreation, creating some jobs for city residents. He also set up a labor board to help resolve labor disputes, and the hosiery union's William Leader was the labor representative on that board. The Artcraft would prove to be a dress rehearsal for the taking of the Apex.[86]

On April 29, 1937, hosiery workers staged a big demonstration outside the 2,600-employee Apex mill. A week later open warfare ensued as a group of workers estimated by the *Philadelphia Bulletin* at 5,000 strong overwhelmed the police force guarding the mill and attacked the plant entrance. A spy working for Military Intelligence described the attack in even more dramatic terms: "On the said date, a mob estimated to contain between eight and ten thousand souls . . . surged down upon the Apex Mill. . . . The attacking forces formed a strong column and made what might be fittingly termed a 'penetrating attack' upon the building . . . a terrific battle raged through the mill."[87]

Although the spy was inclined to lean toward hyperbole in his description of events, the Apex strike was, in fact, a takeover, not initially a sit-down. Within a few hours of the assault 250 sit-downers took control of the plant. One of them was a brother of Carl Mackley, and the great majority of the crowd's members were between the ages of eighteen and thirty. Years later Joseph Burge, vice president of Branch 1 at the time, described the Apex strike as "the storming of the Bastille."[88]

By noon crowds were so large that city trolley cars were unable to get through the street, and a systematic attack began to take shape as part of the crowd poured through the windows of the plant (see Figure 8). Following a rush for the main gate, police were overwhelmed, and the strikers broke open the door, rushed inside, and evicted general manager Harry Strube and owner William Meyer. Both of them were smeared with ink but otherwise appeared to be unharmed. Most members of the huge crowd were not workers at the mill, nor were all of the sit-downers.

FIGURE 8 Strike sympathizers tie up traffic, including several trolley cars, at the Apex Hosiery Mill, May 6, 1937. George D. McDowell *Philadelphia Evening Bulletin* Photograph Collection, Special Collections Research Center, Temple University Libraries, Philadelphia, Pennsylvania.

The sit-downers held the mill for over a month, during which time they established a "strikers' band" to entertain themselves, played games of various sorts, and conducted regular exercise periods to keep people occupied. The union set up a central kitchen and sent in regular meals, sometimes including ice cream donated by a local manufacturer.[89] The military spy again lapsed into hyperbole when describing the union's "commissary system": "Mysterious influences, and a vast sum of money, are among the assets of those who have seized mill properties.... Whole carcasses of steers are brought from abattoirs, great hampers of succulent vegetables are carted in, and soon juicy steaks, ragouts, and pastries, enter into repasts savory enough to make the shades of the ancient disciples of Epicurus turn green with envy."[90]

It is clear from these reports that the Roosevelt administration's War Department was maintaining continuity with the administrations of his predecessors in terms of domestic spying, and that at least some of its officials were concerned with the possible repercussions of the actions of the hosiery strikers. The agent went on to claim "certain sinister aspects of the situation in

Philadelphia," to wit, at the Kensington Labor Lyceum "instruction in shooting marksmanship is being given. What does this mean?"[91] He felt that, in regard to the Apex and other strikes by hosiery workers in Philadelphia, the "spirit of lawlessness is gaining like a prairie fire. . . . The very foundations of the Government are being undermined."[92]

The Apex company took the union to court for violating its six-year-old injunction and sought to have the strikers evicted. It also filed suit in federal court for treble damages under the Sherman Act. In the middle of June the U.S. Court of Appeals declared the Apex strike illegal on the grounds that it was not in reality a strike by Apex employees but a seizure by the union. After a lengthy conference William Leader agreed to vacate the plant while negotiations continued. The sit-downers, led by Leader and the mayor of Philadelphia, "marched from the plant to the cheers of 15,000 workers" who had assembled outside. Although the strikers agreed to leave the plant, the union promised to throw up such a picket line that the company would not be able to open anyway. Consequently, a 3,000-person picket line around the mill kept it closed until the end of July, when a compromise settlement was reached. Alice Kreckman, along with a large group of other women, was a regular participant on that picket line. And as demonstrated by photographs of these women in the city's newspapers, although skirts had lengthened by 1937, many of them still strove to maintain a fashionable appearance even on the picket lines (see Figure 9).[93]

In February 1938 the union won a closed-shop agreement with the mill, but while they were in the plant some of the strikers had damaged the expensive machinery, leaving the union open to a lawsuit. These actions angered many hosiery workers, including Howard Kreckman, who referred to the perpetrators as "Luddites." He said that the damage was done by a minority and was opposed by the union, particularly its "left" wing: "We supported the sit-down, we went in and all, but when it came to doing any damage, well we didn't agree with that. People go to extremes." The damage was a spontaneous action brought about by the many years of antagonism and anti-unionism practiced by the company. Branch 1 eventually reached an agreement with the company that called for the payment of $110,000 in damages.[94] In a statement relating to the settlement, Alexander McKeown, then national president of the AFHW, said that the hosiery union never sought to avoid its responsibility in the matter: "We are too proud of our reputation, built up in thirty years, to destroy it in any attempt to dodge. We know, too, that we have a responsibility to the entire labor movement . . . and we feel, in the settlement,

FIGURE 9 Thousands participate in picket line at Apex Hosiery Mill, June 22, 1937. Many women participated in the picket lines and can be seen to be fashionably dressed. Sign on right reads "CIO Rat Exterminators" with a picture of a gallows with a rat hanging from it. George D. McDowell *Philadelphia Evening Bulletin* Photograph Collection, Special Collections Research Center, Temple University Libraries, Philadelphia, Pennsylvania.

that we have forever answered those critics of trade-unionism who delight in talking about the 'irresponsibility' of labor without having a single fact to back up their theories."[95]

The suit for treble damages under the Sherman Anti-Trust Act ultimately went to the U.S. Supreme Court. In a 1940 landmark decision the court ruled in favor of the union, declaring that a strike was not a combination or conspiracy in restraint of trade but was for the purpose of gaining union representation, thereby removing labor strikes from the purview of the Sherman Act. Apex had been the last large mill operating without a closed-shop contract in the city, but in February 1938 the citadel fell.[96]

Conclusion

The legacy of the AFHW lived on in campaigns for human rights and social and economic democracy that were a part of the CIO and later movements for civil rights and women's rights and the 1944 Philadelphia Declaration of the International Labor Organization.[97] But the question of why these individuals behaved in the manner they did, given the reality of the times in which they lived, remains. Responding to a strike call in the 1920s and early 1930s was not an easy thing. Virtually everything was on the line. If the union lost the strike, the strikers lost their jobs. There would be few or no strike benefits, no unemployment insurance, no relief. There were no "unfair labor practices," and employers were not obliged (before 1935) to bargain with a union just because the majority of their employees wanted them to, nor were they obligated to reinstate strikers after the strike was over. At times even workers' very lives might be on the line, for manufacturers did not hesitate to use violence, both official and private, against strikers. Several hosiery workers paid the ultimate price. Perhaps Joseph Burge provided the best answer:

> In the thirties many people were beginning to suspect that the economic system was not of divine origins. More and more people were convinced that it had been devised By men, to serve SOME men. Why couldn't it be changed to answer Tennyson's question "when shall all men's good/Be each man's rule ... ?" Why must we be bent to suit the system, why couldn't the system be bent to accommodate us?
> The cement that held us together was economic, philosophical, and cultural. Unlike some people of our time we believed we should and could have a large say in how we would work and how we would live: that we could stiffen ourselves into stanchions and hold the sky on our shoulders. And for a while we did.[98]

They did so, however, not by preaching to their fellow workers or advancing pie-in-the-sky fantasies. Rather, as organic parts of their communities, the union activists themselves developed and grew throughout this period. Pushed from the outside by the manufacturers and their allies and from within by their own members, especially women and youth, the leadership crafted strategies that became increasingly inclusive of class and community and correspondingly more sophisticated in their approach to their adversaries. Hosiery's activists grew out of and built on Kensington's long traditions of working-class identity, and they patiently built a radical subculture that included dances, parties, and picnics as well as picket lines and sit-down strikes. But most important, they built a vision for social change that they believed could achieve a better world for all working peoples. Their young members, and especially the women, internalized this vision, and they were willing to fight for it. Undaunted by the strength of their opponents or the magnitude of their goals, they expanded their ambitions from raising wages to building one of the twentieth century's most significant housing experiments. Though their example did not spread widely enough to become a prototype for an alternative America, their contributions to the founding of the CIO, the New Deal, and labor feminism did materially affect the direction of them all.

Epilogue

The struggles of Kensington's hosiery workers and their union in the 1920s and 1930s left a legacy that continued into the 1940s and beyond. Although the cost was steep, the 1937 Apex strike ended in a victory for Branch 1, the American Federation of Hosiery Workers (AFHW), and the entire labor movement. By the end of the 1930s the AFHW had a new president, Alexander McKeown, and under his leadership it strove to uphold the union's democratic traditions and focus on social justice. Although the union honored the "no-strike pledge" during World War II, it continued community-oriented programs with some success. After the war, the AFHW operated in an increasingly hostile environment and in a shrinking industry, and its adamant demands for autonomy and concentration on organizing led it to run afoul of Emil Rieve's rightward-moving Textile Workers Union of America (TWUA). In later years, the fate of the union in decline would once again prefigure that of the general labor movement. That decline paralleled a similar fate for the neighborhood.

Deindustrialization hit Kensington hard in the second half of the twentieth century and created new problems for its residents. Decline and blight in some parts of the neighborhood accompanied the loss of jobs, and social problems accelerated, especially among the often unemployed young. But there remained bright spots of a vision carried on.

After Alexander McKeown, still an adherent of socialism, was elected president of the AFHW, the union struggled to maintain a social vision and a role as a social movement. The leadership encouraged its branches to continue to be involved in community issues and to help other unionists. It maintained an emphasis on labor education, in 1940 investing in a camp north of Reading, Pennsylvania, for building a labor institute, while its national headquarters remained in Philadelphia. Branch 1 and the national leadership continued to push an ambitious social agenda, fighting regressive local legislation like Philadelphia's city wage tax and advocating for a universal health care system and pay equity legislation. It also continued its legislative program focused on civil rights, demanding legislation against lynching and the poll tax and for full voting rights in the southern states. It became a fully industrial organization, including janitors and sweepers in its contracts. In 1944, after

Philadelphia transit employees in a company union lost a representation election to the CIO's Transport Workers Union in a landslide, the disgruntled losers called a strike over the promotion of African American workers on the trolleys. The AFHW opposed the racist strike; as described by Joseph Burge, "hosiery workers had nothing but scorn for those trolleymen who would go on strike when the PRT would assign Negroes as motormen." And the union promoted a platform calling for equal pay for equal work and an end to job categories designated as "women's jobs." Women gained access to all jobs in union shops, and they continued to serve on the national executive board.[1]

Low-income housing remained a focal point of the organization. In 1945 the AFHW hired William Rafsky, a labor economist and urban planner, to head its Education and Research Department and launched another effort in support of low-cost housing. Holding up the Carl Mackley Houses as a shining example, Rafsky testified before the Congressional Joint Committee on Housing in 1948 in support of the Taft-Ellender-Wagner Bill, which would have provided government financing for affordable housing.[2]

The AFHW was not a Communist-led union, and McKeown and other Socialists often had real policy differences with the Communists. But there were Communists active in the union, as there always had been, and the AFHW had a commitment to internal democracy, still allowing all political viewpoints and taking major decisions to the rank and file. As early as 1940, in his opening address to the hosiery convention, McKeown was warning about the need to "defend civil rights and liberties" in the coming period: "In the hysteria which may develop out of the tragedy of war let us build bulwarks against the 'witch hunts of Salem.'" Although the AFHW supported President Franklin Roosevelt and Vice President Henry Wallace, by 1943 McKeown was warning that "no permanent progressive political party which labor can afford to support will ever result" from the Democratic Party "so long as it is supported by . . . political machines of the most corrupt and reactionary type."[3]

The divide between Rieve and the AFHW was made manifest in October 1947 when Rieve, then president of the TWUA-CIO, became the first CIO union president to file the noncommunist affidavit mandated by the Taft-Hartley Act. That legislation marked the resurgence of an anti–New Deal conservative movement and also included a raft of other antilabor provisions as well that rolled back much of the Wagner Act of 1935. In November Rieve suspended the hosiery workers' representatives, Alex McKeown and William Smith, from the TWUA executive board for the union's "nonpayment of dues." In 1948, as the CIO "purges" of the Left-led unions were imminent (purges in which Emil Rieve, also a vice president of the CIO, quickly became one of the most ardent crusaders), the AFHW membership voted overwhelmingly to leave the TWUA, claiming that it was violating the AFHW's right to autonomy as guaranteed by the affiliation agreement. The leadership also claimed that Rieve's call for an increased dues assessment hindered the union's ability to fund an expanded force of desperately needed organizers. Although they received support from organizations as varied as the Kentucky CIO Council, the Iowa State Industrial Union Council (IUC), the Philadelphia IUC, and the Wisconsin State IUC, the AFHW was expelled from the CIO and remained independent until 1951. At that time it applied for and received a charter from the AFL as an autonomous union—over the objections of the UTWA-AFL.[4]

In 1939 there were approximately 45,000 members in the national union, in full-fashioned hosiery, seamless hosiery, and finishing departments. By the time they left the TWUA, their membership had declined to about 29,000. The manufacturers' quest to find ever-cheaper sources of labor and materials had taken a great toll on workers in the hosiery industry. By the end of the 1930s, Kensington's hosiery industry was already in decline, and many Branch 1 members were looking for work. Silk was unavailable during the war and, afterward, the expanded use of new materials like nylon, which was more resilient and could be made to stretch to fit the leg more closely, removed some of the skill from the knitting process. Newer machines also added to the problems by eliminating some job categories, and in some mills entire knitting departments were eliminated, causing even more reductions in the labor force. As advocates of what they called "scientific" socialism, union leadership recognized what a postwar return to "normalcy" would bring. At the 1946 convention McKeown warned: "The influx of investment capital will hurry the day of 'completely normal' competition with all of the problems which 'completely normal' embodies; machine obsolescence, goods surpluses, cut-throat competition, price cutting, wage cutting, bankruptcy, and mills moving are all part of that 'normalcy.'" He called for long-range planning to supplement private employment with public, as layoffs would inevitably hit war-swollen industries.[5]

Once again, the hosiery union prefigured the experiences of the broader labor movement, a cautionary tale of how capital deals with labor when capital is not in a boom period. The newly reunited AFL-CIO's Industrial Union Department selected the AFHW in 1957 for a case study in a scathing report on the effects of ten years of the Taft-Hartley Act. As it described, shops searched ever more aggressively for locations with lower labor costs and fewer controls over working conditions. Many were in small, rural towns where the hosiery union was the only labor organization in the area and was the first seeking to bring the ideals of unionism to the workers. In 1950, the AFHW was still fielding an organizing staff of forty-one permanent and part-time organizers. But the passage of the Taft-Hartley Act in 1947 made it increasingly difficult to organize these workers, as many states became right-to-work bastions of anti-unionism, the closed shop and the right to picket were limited, and important union tactics like secondary boycotts were made illegal. These and other hardball tactics affecting the hosiery industry foreshadowed what was to happen to American industry generally when it encountered a crisis of accumulation and profitability in the 1970s. Industry responded with all the tools that have become associated with neoliberalism: free trade, privatization, deregulation, and anti-unionism. The labor movement, having given up its militant and idealistic vision that called for a more rational system of production controlled by labor, followed the experience of the hosiery workers on a grander scale as industrialists lost their fear of working-class power.[6]

In the 1920s and 1930s the hosiery union had been able to make remarkable gains, while facing another hostile environment, by organizing around an idealistic and unifying vision of justice and rights. As it dropped in numbers, it nevertheless was still able to pass on these beliefs and its experience to a new generation of workers in other growing industries. At the AFHW's 1946 convention, a guest speaker from the United Electrical Workers made that point when he said that "even the misfortunes" of the AFHW had benefited labor when they "caused hosiery workers to go to work elsewhere and so brought organization into the new plants that would not have been touched had not some people been trained in unionism by the Hosiery Workers Union and gone to work there."[7]

After the war the AFHW struggled valiantly to influence the labor movement on the importance of maintaining a focus on community concerns, opposing the ending of price controls and fighting against rent increases. But beginning with the huge postwar strike waves of 1945–46, the leadership of the broader labor movement made a Faustian deal with industry. Several of the largest and most important unions capitulated on issues that affected the community, such as price controls, and agreed to management prerogatives in contracts in exchange for wage increases and narrow "bread and butter" advances that did not incorporate workers' rights to control the labor process. With an ear attuned to the community, McKeown criticized leaders of the postwar strikes with a prescient assessment of one effect of the strike settlements: "More effective leadership would have separated revision of job rates from cost of living demands, [and] the two together made the total wage demand large enough to alienate public sympathy." Although he said that the strikes in the basic industries were "clear cut victories," the "so-called" radical demands were not radical at all, as they concentrated only on pocketbook issues, "easy to sell to the guy in overalls." "While the guys in the shop rested on their laurels," he continued, "business marshaled all its forces and built its strength for political warfare." The result was Taft-Hartley. "Labor won the battle but may lose the campaign."[8]

By 1949 many in the labor movement's upper echelons ratcheted up their deal with management by embracing the anti-Left agenda of Taft-Hartley and the Truman-McCarthy Red Scare and expelling unions with Communist leadership. The labor purges helped to remove the vision that had built labor in the 1920s and 1930s as the national leaders moved increasingly into a "business unionism" with little room for idealism. The hosiery union had been expelled a year before and in addition to the structural and political problems the union faced, hosiery locals were raided by other unions, both CIO and AFL. In 1965, after McKeown had retired, a much-weakened AFHW reaffiliated with the TWUA, then an affiliate of the AFL-CIO. Howard Kreckman, still believing that the corporate capitalist system itself was responsible for much of the suffering of working people, summed up the loss in this way: "If you accept capitalism you accept inequality. There's always going to be someone on the bottom. Capitalism leaves working people little choice but to fight each other over the crumbs."[9]

After hosiery was no longer an option for employment in Philadelphia (the last big bastion, the Apex, left the city in 1954), Howard Kreckman worked at a number of different jobs. He worked as a timer during the building of part of the Lincoln Tunnel and even as a merchant seaman for a short time before becoming a maintenance man at a high school in his later years. He and Alice raised her niece after the death of her sister. Howard and Alice Kreckman remained "union by principle," and activists in a number of peace and justice movements, all of their lives.[10]

Some members of the union were directly affected by the witch hunts of the McCarthy era. Joseph Burge was blacklisted. Although the Kreckmans were socialists, they had great respect for former Communist Party member Burge. "Joe was persecuted because he was one time a member of the Communist Party. But there shouldn't be anything wrong with that. And he never would give the committee any names. Some of the big guys caved, but not Joe. He was a real champion of democracy. He was a hero." Alice Kreckman said that the government used communism as an excuse to eliminate dissent: "If you disagreed with them they really tried to do you in."[11]

The historians Ronald Filipelli and Mark McColloch, discussing the McCarthy era's labor purges, argue that the purges were pure and simple political repression. "To hold unpopular, even patently wrong, political views, is not a crime in the United States. The left wing of the labor movement was purged for its political ideas, not for any failure as trade unionists." The historian Ellen Schrecker stresses that the 1947 Taft-Hartley Act was part of the business community's "well-organized effort to roll back the gains that labor had made since the late 1930s." The decimation of the left-led unions eliminated "organized labor's most persistent advocates of social change." Howard Kreckman also saw a more sinister motive in the repression of labor's Left: "They have to destroy your heroes, leave you with nothing to believe in."[12]

The anti-Left campaigns also affected how labor feminism would develop. Dorothy Sue Cobble has shown how it continued to grow in many unions in the second half of the twentieth century, usually associated with the liberal wing of the Democratic Party. But that is not where it began. The historian Judith Stepan-Norris focused on the role that the Left-led unions played in the gains made by laboring women in this later period, while the historian Kate Weigand convincingly argued that Communist feminists made important contributions to the theoretical developments of second-wave feminism. Alice Kreckman, referring to the identity that she and other women developed in the Kensington of the 1920s and 1930s, conceived of it as "left," and she retained that identity all of her life: "People say we were to the left. I don't care. People ask me now, 'are you to the left or are you to the right?' I'll say, 'Damn it! I'm not to the right, I'm to the left!'"[13]

The community of Greater Kensington has gone through many changes since its heyday in the 1920s and 1930s. Some parts have become a picture of urban blight as the loss of industry devastated neighborhoods. Other parts, those with more convenient access to the center city area, are going through a process of gentrification as new young professionals flock in. Either way, it is a process of culture change. During and after World War II the African American population of the city grew, reaching 33 percent by 1970. The city's Latino population also grew proportionately. But these new residents came into a city that was rapidly deindustrializing, and the doors of most of the once ubiquitous factories were already closed forever. In those job-challenged decades, there were increased instances of racial hostility, when the western border of Kensington became the sharply racially different community of North Philadelphia, an area that had been diverse but majority white in the

1920s and 1930s. Yet even after World War II, interracial housing continued to exist during the process of racial transition of some of Philadelphia's neighborhoods. Many working-class whites in Philadelphia, in fact, continued to reside in their old neighborhoods after blacks moved in, and even continued to buy homes there.[14]

Though little of the memory of Kensington's radical hosiery workers remained by the 1970s, driven out by time, deindustrialization, and McCarthyism, some subconscious elements did remain—many young people there just seemed to know that "you didn't cross a picket line," for example. And, as befits its long history, social justice activism erupted in the Kensington of that decade, led by ideological descendants of the hosiery workers, though they did not know they were their descendants at the time. They formed a radical community movement to organize and educate residents of all ages around health care, housing, jobs, and police harassment, and formed coalitions with African American and Latino groups to oppose racism and the police brutality of the Frank Rizzo administration. A women's group among them took on issues of gender, joining with their sisters of color around issues they had in common—those of being poor and women—and in the process evolving a greater understanding of the special issues of race. That group took its name, October 4th Organization (known to its supporters as O4O), from an event during the American Revolution when Kensington residents "liberated" hoarded food from wealthy merchants. But its members were not aware of the more recent radical history of the neighborhood's hosiery workers. Other groups, like the Kensington Welfare Rights Organization, organized cross-racial coalitions to fight the poverty of many residents. For these activists also had an idealistic vision of the possibility of a better world. How much more might have been achieved if the earlier visions and legacies of the community had not been lost?[15]

Many of the people discussed here went on to other industries and unions, including some that were also expelled from the CIO, such as the UE and the United Cannery, Agricultural, Packing, and Allied Workers of America. Some, like John Edelman, became government officials; yet Edelman too faced some of the poison of McCarthyism when his name was removed from consideration for the post of assistant secretary of labor because of his radical history. He continued to work for social causes, moving on to organizations advocating for expanded Social Security and becoming the president of the National Council of Senior Citizens, where he was one of the architects of the Medicare bill. He claimed that one of his "most satisfying moments" was to be present at its signing. William Rafsky became Philadelphia's housing coordinator and orchestrated Philadelphia's Central Urban Renewal program, attempting to "scatter" smaller low-rise public housing projects (based on the Mackley Houses model) as a way of lessening segregation and propping up sagging neighborhoods. He always insisted that residents be consulted in any plans for their communities. In the 1960s President Lyndon B. Johnson appointed him to the task force that organized the Department of Housing and Urban Development. Emil Rieve retired to Fort Lauderdale, Florida, in 1960. Alex McKeown retired, in 1957, to a row house in Kensington, in the district in which he was born, where he planned to work more with the youth of the community. Both Alice and Howard Kreckman remained active in social movements—marching for civil rights and women's rights and against war, and advocating third-party politics—throughout their lives. Both felt that a "party of labor" was a necessity to reclaim democracy. As long as they lived they remained firm believers in what they called "the rights of the people."[16]

Today the struggles to improve the well-being of working people and society as a whole face many obstacles. But eruptions of protest and a newfound interest in socialism by a generation largely untainted by the effects of McCarthyism suggest that exciting developments may lie in the future. If the experiences of the AFHW can provide any insights for these movements, the union will indeed leave an important legacy. The AFHW and its activists believed that real social change happens only when there are democratic organizations concerned with the masses of working people, across differences, that recognize that the concerns and needs all of them share are rights, not privileges; that the working class must join together to defend those rights; that there is a need to develop "spaces" of community and cosmopolitanism, an "imagined community," if you will, that brings people together both socially and politically; that "everyone must be an organizer." And that, perhaps most of all, there is a need for an educational and political program that helps people understand the role that capital and corporations can play in the destruction of a fully democratic society, and that can provide a template for the achievement of a more just world for all. Kensington's AFHW was able to create individuals who carried such a vision of social justice with them all of their lives. The achievements of this little "fighting" union and those it fought beside, are evidenced in the legacies of the New Deal, and underscore the power that can lie within a transformed labor movement. As the historian Selina Todd put it, "If the past teaches us anything it is this: if the people want a better future, we can, and must, create it ourselves."[17]

Notes

Abbreviations in Notes

AFHWR	American Federation of Hosiery Workers Records, 1922 to 1965. Wisconsin Historical Society, Madison, WI.
BBP	Benjamin Barkas Papers, Series 3, Labor Unions 1934 to 1968. Urban Archives, Special Collections Research Center, Temple University, Philadelphia, PA.
BLCR	Brookwood Labor College Records, 1921–1937, Accession Number 567, Series IV, Student Files, Walter P. Reuther Library, Wayne State University, Detroit, MI.
CIOST	Congress of Industrial Organizations, Secretary-Treasurer Papers. Walter P. Reuther Archives, Wayne State University, Detroit, MI.
FMCS	Federal Mediation and Conciliation Service Records, RG 280. National Archives, College Park, MD.
HDWPA	Housing Division, Works Progress Administration Reports. Urban Archives, Special Collections Research Center, Temple University, Philadelphia, PA.
HWCF	Hosiery Workers Case Files. Urban Archives, Special Collections Research Center, Temple University, Philadelphia, PA.
ILHP	Iowa Labor History Oral Project, Iowa Federation of Labor. State Historical Society of Iowa, Des Moines, IA.
JEP	John Edelman Papers, 1926 to 1963. Walter P. Reuther Library, Wayne State University, Detroit, MI.
KEP	Kate Edelman Papers. Walter P. Reuther Library, Wayne State University, Detroit, MI.
KYWCA	Young Women's Christian Association of Philadelphia, PA, Kensington Branch, Records, 1891 to 1981. Urban Archives, Special Collections Research Center, Temple University, Philadelphia, PA.
MID	Records of the Military Intelligence Division, RG 165. National Archives, College Park, MD.
MIR	United States Military Intelligence Reports: Surveillance of Radicals in the United States, 1917 to 1941. Microfilm, 34 reels, 1984, Frederick, MD.
NCF	Newspaper Clippings and Miscellaneous Files. Urban Archives, Special Collections Research Center, Temple University, Philadelphia, PA.
NLRB	National Labor Relations Board Records, RG 25. National Archives, College Park, MD.

PCLU   Philadelphia Central Labor Union Records. Urban Archives, Special Collections Research Center, Temple University, Philadelphia, PA.
PLMS   Philadelphia Labor Market Studies, 1936, 1937, Works Progress Administration. Urban Archives, Special Collections Research Center, Temple University, Philadelphia, PA.
PMC   Population Manuscript Census, 1920, 1930. U.S. Department of Commerce, Bureau of the Census, Washington, DC.
WIR   Wharton School Industrial Research Unit Records, 1900 to 1996. University of Pennsylvania Archives, Philadelphia, PA.

Introduction

1. The primary source for the location of the meeting comes from Carroll D. Wright, who was the first U.S. commissioner of labor, from 1885 to 1905. He claimed that he got his information from past officers of the Knights and that they had approved his document as "true in all its statements of fact." Uriah Stephens was elected grand master workman of the organization, a post he held for ten years. He remained at his Kensington address until his death in 1882. The story then appears in other accounts of the Knights' origins from the late nineteenth century. Terrence Powderly, Stephens's successor and rival, later gave a slightly different account, playing down the role of Stephens. Carroll D. Wright, "An Historical Sketch of the Knights of Labor," *Quarterly Journal of Economics* 1, no. 2 (January 1887): 137–68; Walter J. Books et al., *Living Leaders of the World: Graphic Biographies of Men and Women of Greatest Eminence, Influence, Wealth, Power or Fame* (Atlanta: H. C. Hudgins and Co., 1889), 397; see also "Knights of Labor," *Philadelphia Encyclopedia*, http://philadelphiaencyclopedia.org/archive/knights-of-labor/, accessed May 5, 2016; Judith L. Goldberg, "Strikes, Organizing and Change: The Knights of Labor in Philadelphia, 1869–1890" (Ph.D. diss., New York University, 1985); Susan Levine, *Labor's True Woman: Carpet Weavers, Industrialization, and Labor Reform in the Gilded Age* (Philadelphia: Temple University Press, 1984), 34, 69, 121.

2. "The Struggles of '90," *Hosiery Worker*, June 1, 1927; *Hosiery Worker*, June 15, 1927.

3. On renewed interest in socialism in the United States, see "'Socialism' the Most Looked-Up Word of 2015 on Merriam-Webster," *Guardian*, December 16, 2015, and "Why Are There Suddenly Millions of Socialists in America?," *Guardian*, February 29, 2016.

4. David Montgomery, "The Shuttle and the Cross: Weavers and Artisans in the Kensington Riots of 1844," *Journal of Social History* 5, no. 4 (Summer 1972): 411–46; see also Sam Bass Warner, *The Private City: Philadelphia in Three Periods of Its Growth* (Philadelphia: University of Pennsylvania Press, 1968).

5. Important exceptions include Susan Levine on the Knights of Labor, Philip Scranton on industry in Kensington, and Amy Sonnie and James Tracy on community organizing in the 1960s and 1970s; Levine, *Labor's True Woman*; Philip Scranton, *Figured Tapestry: Production, Markets, and Power in Philadelphia Textiles, 1885–1941* (Cam-

bridge: Cambridge University Press, 1989); Amy Sonnie and James Tracy, *Hillbilly Nationalists, Urban Race Rebels, and Black Power: Community Organizing in Radical Times* (New York: Melville House, 2011), chap. 4.

6. Chuck Keeney as quoted in Mark Hand, "Rednecks Symbolize Solidarity: W.Va. Mine Wars Museum Reclaims Union Identity," *Counterpunch*, August 10, 2015, http:/ /www.counterpunch.org/2015/08/10/rednecks-symbolize-solidarity-w-va-mine-wars -museum-reclaims-union-identity/, accessed May 5, 2016.

7. Lincoln Steffens, "Philadelphia: Corrupt and Contented," *McClure's Magazine*, July 1903.

8. "But it was too late. He had angered Providence resisting too many temptations. There was left but heaven where he would meet only those who like him had wasted earth." F. Scott Fitzgerald, *Tales of the Jazz Age* (New York: Charles Scribner's Sons, 1922), 272.

9. Leo Troy, "Trade Union Membership, 1897–1962," *Review of Economics and Statistics*, 47, no. 1 (February, 1965): 93.

10. Although there is no comprehensive literature on the AFFFHW, bits and pieces can be found in several works, including Irving Bernstein, *The Turbulent Years: A History of the American Worker, 1933–1941* (Boston: Houghton Mifflin, 1970), and Scranton, *Figured Tapestry*.

11. Mark Hendrickson, *American Labor and Economic Citizenship: New Capitalism from World War I to the Great Depression* (New York: Cambridge University Press, 2013), 234; Thomas Sugrue, *Sweet Land of Liberty: The Forgotten Struggle for Civil Rights in the North* (New York: Random House, 2009), 123.

12. Carol E. Morgan, *Women Workers and Gender Identities, 1835–1913: The Cotton and Metal Industries in England* (London: Routledge, 2001), 15.

13. See Philip Scranton, *Proprietary Capitalism: The Textile Manufacture at Philadelphia, 1800–1885* (Philadelphia: Temple University Press, 1983); Scranton, *Figured Tapestry*; Philip Scranton and Walter Licht, *Work Sights: Industrial Philadelphia, 1890–1950* (Philadelphia: Temple University Press, 1986).

14. Selina Todd, *The People: The Rise and Fall of the Working Class* (London: John Murray, 2014).

Chapter One

1. Howard Kreckman, interview with author, Willingboro, New Jersey, October 7, 8, 1998.

2. Daniel T. Rodgers, *Atlantic Crossings: Social Politics in a Progressive Age* (Cambridge, Mass.: Belknap Press of Harvard University Press, 1998), 1.

3. Roger D. Simon, *Philadelphia: A Brief History* (University Park, Pa.: Pennsylvania Historical Association, 2003), 1.

4. Carolyn Adams et al., *Philadelphia: Neighborhoods, Division, and Conflict in a Postindustrial City* (Philadelphia: Temple University Press, 1991), 6; Cynthia Shelton, *The Mills of Manayunk: Early Industrialization and Social Conflict in the Philadelphia*

Region, 1787–1837 (Baltimore: Johns Hopkins University Press, 1986); Simon, *Philadelphia: A Brief History*.

5. Bruce Laurie and Mark Schmitz, "Manufacture and Productivity: The Making of an Industrial Base, Philadelphia, 1850–1880," in *Philadelphia: Work, Space, Family and Group Experience in the Nineteenth Century: Essays toward an Interdisciplinary History of the City*, ed. Theodore Hershberg (New York: Oxford University Press, 1981), 44–47.

6. Shelton, *The Mills of Manayunk*; Friedrich Engels, *The Condition of the Working Class in England*, trans. and ed. W. O. Henderson and W. H. Chaloner (Oxford: Blackwell, 1958); Gladys L. Palmer, *Union Tactics and Economic Change: A Case Study of Three Philadelphia Textile Unions* (Philadelphia: University of Pennsylvania Press, 1932), 16.

7. Philip Scranton, *Proprietary Capitalism: The Textile Manufacture at Philadelphia, 1800–1885* (New York: Cambridge University Press, 1983). For an excellent description of the development of this system in England, see Leonore Davidoff and Catherine Hall, *Family Fortunes: Men and Women of the English Middle Class, 1780–1850* (Chicago: University of Chicago Press, 1991).

8. Bruce Laurie, *Working People of Philadelphia, 1800–1850* (Philadelphia: Temple University Press, 1980), 18–20; Shelton, *Mills of Manayunk*, 148; Sam Bass Warner, *The Private City: Philadelphia in Three Periods of Its Growth* (Philadelphia: University of Pennsylvania Press, 1968), 180.

9. Kerby A. Miller, *Emigrants and Exiles: Ireland and the Irish Exodus to North America* (New York: Oxford University Press, 1985), 275–76; Theodore Hershberg et al., "A Tale of Three Cities: Blacks, Immigrants, and Opportunity in Philadelphia, 1850–1880, 1930, 1970," in Hershberg, *Philadelphia: Work, Space, Family*, 461–91. Sources on the Know-Nothing riots as well as various street gangs and race riots of the period include Warner, *The Private City*; Laurie, *Working People of Philadelphia*; David Montgomery, "The Shuttle and the Cross: Weavers and Artisans in the Kensington Riots of 1844," *Journal of Social History* 5, no. 4 (Summer 1972): 411–46.

10. Laurie and Schmitz, "Manufacture and Productivity," 45, 49–50. Laurie and Schmitz's data comes from the United States Manuscript Census of Manufacturers for 1880; Irwin Sears, "Growth and Population in Philadelphia, 1860–1910" (Ph.D. diss., New York University, 1960), 11–13.

11. Miller, *Emigrants and Exiles*, 522; Walter Licht, *Getting Work: Philadelphia, 1840–1950* (Philadelphia: University of Pennsylvania Press, 1999); Lloyd M. Abernethy, "Progressivism, 1905–1919," in *Philadelphia: A 300 Year History*, ed. Russell F. Weigley (New York: W. W. Norton, 1982), 531.

12. Warner, *The Private City*, 180. The Luddites were hosiers who protested against new labor-replacing machinery, sometimes destroying the machines and even the factories. "How the Fashioned Knitting Industry Started in the U.S.," *Hosiery Worker*, May 16, 1927.

13. Dorothea De Schweinitz, *How Workers Find Jobs: A Study of Four Thousand Hosiery Workers in Philadelphia* (Philadelphia: University of Pennsylvania Press, 1932), appendix B.

14. "How the Fashioned Knitting Industry Started"; *Hosiery Worker*, June 1, 1927. Sidney and Beatrice Webb were English historians and Fabian socialists; see Sidney and Beatrice Webb, *The History of Trade Unionism* (London: Longmans, Green, 1911).

15. "The Struggles of '90," *Hosiery Worker*, June 1, 1927; *Hosiery Worker*, June 15, 1927.

16. For the outlook of the manufacturers, see Scranton, *Proprietary Capitalism*; Philip Scranton, *Figured Tapestry: Production, Markets, and Power in Philadelphia Textiles, 1885–1941* (Cambridge: Cambridge University Press, 1989); Philip Scranton and Walter Licht, *Work Sights: Industrial Philadelphia, 1890–1950* (Philadelphia: Temple University Press, 1986), 65.

17. For data on the influence of skill in Philadelphia's workforce, see Warner, *The Private City*; Scranton, *Proprietary Capitalism*; Scranton, *Figured Tapestry*. The "Scab City" designation is referenced in Howell John Harris, *Bloodless Victories: The Rise and Fall of the Open Shop in the Philadelphia Metal Trades, 1890–1940* (Cambridge: Cambridge University Press, 2000), 152, and in Licht, *Getting Work*, 181. For other challenges to Philadelphia's reputation of labor conservatism, see Peter Cole, *Wobblies on the Waterfront: Interracial Unionism in Progressive-Era Philadelphia* (Urbana: University of Illinois Press, 2007); James Wolfinger, *Running the Rails: Capital and Labor in the Philadelphia Transit Industry* (Ithaca, N.Y.: Cornell University Press, 2016).

18. For a discussion of the manufacturers, see Scranton, *Figured Tapestry*.

19. Claudia Golden, "Family Strategies and the Family Economy in the Late Nineteenth Century: The Role of the Secondary Workers," in Hershberg, *Philadelphia: Work, Space, Family*; Eudice Glassberg, "Work, Wages and the Cost of Living: Ethnic Differences and the Poverty Line, Philadelphia, 1880," *Pennsylvania History* 66 (January 1979): 17–58.

20. Interview with Howard Kreckman; Alice Nelson Kreckman interview with author, Willingboro, New Jersey, October 7, 8, 1998; interview with Freda Maurer, in Palmer, *Union Tactics*; Jeanne Callahan, interview with author, Philadelphia, Pennsylvania, March 8, 1998; Gwendolyn Salisbury Hughes, *Mothers in Industry: Wage-Earning by Mothers in Philadelphia* (New York: New Republic, 1925).

21. Benson used data from reports on home-visit interviews with woman wage earners conducted by field agents for the Women's Bureau of the U.S. Department of Labor during the 1920s and early 1930s (many from Philadelphia) and studies of families confronting unemployment that were assembled by settlement workers and academic social scientists during the late 1920s and the 1930s. Susan Porter Benson, *Household Accounts: Working-Class Family Economies in the Interwar United States* (Ithaca, N.Y.: Cornell University Press, 2007), 6, 7, 9.

22. The authors, Esther Louise Little and William Joseph Henry Cotton, used surveys they conducted of two dozen mill families as well as a representative sample from the payrolls of two large Kensington textile mills. The families kept daily detailed records for the research, and the authors felt that the figures were accurate. Both authors had a personal connection to the neighborhood and some of the families, Little having lived there for eight years as a worker in a settlement house, and Cotton having worked in the mills himself. The study did not, however, include families of the lowest-paid

and least-educated workers. Esther Louise Little and William Joseph Henry Cotton, *Budgets of Families and Individuals of Kensington, Philadelphia* (Lancaster, Pa.: Press of the New Era Printing Co., 1920).

23. The entry under insurance is of special interest, corresponding to a similar finding observed by Robert and Helen Lynd in their book *Middletown*. In their study, the Lynds found that among the working classes of the community, due to the general precariousness of life, insurance was always one of the last items to be let go in times of hardship. Little and Cotton, *Budgets*, 133; Robert S. Lynd and Helen Merrell Lynd, *Middletown: A Study in American Culture* (New York: Harcourt, Brace and World, 1956).

24. Little and Cotton, *Budgets*, 18.

25. Ibid., 133; Benson, *Household Accounts*, 10; interview with Jeanne Callahan.

26. Little and Cotton, *Budgets*, 70, 147; Benson, *Household Accounts*, 145; interview with Jeanne Callahan. Irregularity of work is also supported by the records of the American Federation of Hosiery Workers (AFHW).

27. Warner, *The Private City*, 179. The authors of the groundbreaking work on southern mill culture, *Like a Family*, described a similar culture in the mill villages of the southern United States. One significant difference between the two, however, was the ethnic diversity of Greater Kensington by the 1920s, as "new" immigrants from eastern and southern Europe were drawn to the manufacturing center in the early twentieth century, before the turmoil leading to World War I. Jacquelyn Dowd Hall et al., *Like a Family: The Making of a Southern Cotton Mill World* (Chapel Hill: University of North Carolina Press, 1987). For discussion of the influence of radical traditions, see James R. Barrett, "Americanization from the Bottom Up: Immigration and the Remaking of the Working Class in the United States, 1880–1930," *Journal of American History* 79 (December 1992): 996–1020.

28. Warner, *The Private City*, 193; interview with Howard Kreckman; Karen Sue Mittelman, "'A Spirit That Touches the Problems of Today': Women and Social Reform in the Philadelphia Young Women's Christian Association, 1920–1945" (PhD diss., University of Pennsylvania, 1987), 25.

29. Warner, *The Private City*, 179; Scranton and Licht, *Work Sights*, 58–65.

30. PMC, 1920; Warner, *Private City*, 177–83; De Schweinitz, *How Workers Find Jobs*, 55–60; Salisbury Hughes, *Mothers in Industry*, 33.

31. Caroline Golab, *Immigrant Destinations* (Philadelphia: Temple University Press, 1977).

32. Interview with Jeanne Callahan.

33. Ibid.

34. Robert Gunther (pseud.), interview with author, Philadelphia, Pennsylvania, March 8, 1998; interviews with Alice Nelson Kreckman, Howard Kreckman; Herbert Ershkowitz, *John Wanamaker: Philadelphia Merchant* (Conshohocken, Pa.: Combined Pub., 1999).

35. Interviews with Jeanne Callahan, Robert Gunther, Alice Nelson Kreckman, Howard Kreckman; Work File, 1923 to 1956, Philadelphia study, Box 9, Folder 33, Em-

ployment and Unemployment Studies, 1912 to 1956, WIR; *Pressoff Special*, passim, Box 1, AFHWR. The changes and influences of the "new woman" and popular culture are discussed further in later chapters.

36. Interviews with Howard Kreckman, Alice Nelson Kreckman.

37. Interview with Jeanne Callahan.

38. Interview with Robert Gunther.

39. Marvin Harris, *Emics and Etics: The Insider/Outsider Debate* (Newbury Park, Calif.: Sage, 1990). "Jewtown" got its name from the settlement of Russian Jews in the area in the early twentieth century. Originally called "Jewery Town," over the years the name was shortened to "Jewtown." Daniel Sidorick, "The 'Girl Army': The Philadelphia Shirtwaist Strike of 1909–1910," *Pennsylvania History* 71 (Summer 2004): 323–69; interviews with Jeanne Callahan, Robert Gunther; *Pressoff Special*, October 10, 1932, Box 1, AFHWR.

40. Interview with Robert Gunther.

41. Golab, *Immigrant Destinations*, 19, 22–23; Licht, *Getting Work*, 45–46; Charles Hardy, "Race and Opportunity: Black Philadelphia during the Era of the Great Migration, 1916–1930" (Ph.D. diss., Temple University, 1989). For a challenge to the paradigm that no unions organized black workers, see Cole, *Wobblies on the Waterfront*. Some of the members of this Industrial Workers of the World union were residents of Greater Kensington.

42. Cole, *Wobblies on the Waterfront*; Hershberg et al., "A Tale of Three Cities," 476. In the nineteenth century the growing industrial middle class in England embraced a number of "justifying ideologies," such as Social Darwinism, to explain their exploitation of poor and working peoples and also as a justification for colonialism and the imperialist exploitation of peoples of color. They assigned less intelligence, based on constructions of skull shape, to people of color and women. These ideas traveled back and forth across the Atlantic just as industrialists did. When the steel magnate Andrew Carnegie traveled to England in the early 1870s, he brought back not only the Bessemer system of steel production but also a strong admiration for Social Darwinism as well as its most ardent proponent, Herbert Spencer. The textile industry would remain highly segregated throughout the United States until the barriers fell under the onslaught of the civil rights movement in the 1960s. Perhaps the best scholarly discourse on such developments in England and their cross-Atlantic connections is Douglass A. Lorimer, *Colour, Class, and the Victorians: English Attitudes to the Negro in the Mid-Nineteenth Century* (Leicester: Leicester University Press, 1978); also see Mike Hawkins, *Social Darwinism in European and American Thought, 1860–1945* (Cambridge: Cambridge University Press, 1997). On Carnegie, see Harold Livesay, *Andrew Carnegie and the Rise of Big Business* (New York: HarperCollins, 1975); for segregation in the textile industry, see Timothy Minchin, *Hiring the Black Worker: The Racial Integration of the Southern Textile Industry, 1960–1980* (Chapel Hill: University of North Carolina Press, 1999). Daniel Sidorick discovered similar policies at the Campbell Soup Company in the twentieth century, as one employee talked about his "job" of informing African Americans that Campbell's did not hire them in its Chicago plant (until 1942); see Daniel

Sidorick, *Condensed Capitalism: Campbell Soup and the Pursuit of Cheap Production in the Twentieth Century* (Ithaca, N.Y.: ILR Press Cornell University Press, 2009).

43. "Race Riot in Philadelphia," *New York Times*, July 29, 1918; *Philadelphia Tribune*, May 8, 1920, January 26, 1924.

44. PMC, 1920; interviews with Jeanne Callahan, Robert Gunther, Howard Kreckman, Alice Nelson Kreckman; interviews, Boxes 6, 7, HWCF.

45. De Schweinitz, *How Workers Find Jobs*; Licht, *Getting Work*; PMC, 1920; interviews with Jeanne Callahan, Robert Gunther, Alice Nelson Kreckman, Howard Kreckman.

46. Interviews with Howard Kreckman, Alice Nelson Kreckman; Correspondence File, Box 1, AFHWR; *Pressoff Special*, Box 1, AFHWR; Little and Cotton, *Budgets*; for the moral economy, see E. P. Thompson, *The Making of the English Working Class* (New York: Pantheon Books, 1964). The Great Depression and the union are discussed further in chapter 5.

47. Interview with Robert Gunther.

48. Interviews, Boxes 6, 7, HWCF; *Hosiery Worker*, 1925–1935; interview with Howard Kreckman; George W. Taylor, *The Full-Fashioned Hosiery Worker: His Changing Economic Status* (Philadelphia: University of Pennsylvania Press, 1931).

49. Interviews with Howard Kreckman, Robert Gunther; *Pressoff Special*, January 4, 1933, Box 1, AFHWR. Jean Seder also recorded similar activity among residents. Jean Seder, *Voices of Kensington: Vanishing Mills, Vanishing Neighborhoods* (Ardmore, Pa.: Whitmore Publishing, 1982).

50. Susan Levine, *Labor's True Woman: Carpet Weavers, Industrialization, and Labor Reform in the Gilded Age* (Philadelphia: Temple University Press, 1984).

51. Interview with Alice Nelson Kreckman.

52. Interviews with Robert Gunther, Howard Kreckman.

53. Interviews with Robert Gunther, Howard Kreckman, Alice Nelson Kreckman. Important discussions about "disorderly women" can be found in Jacquelyn Dowd Hall, "Disorderly Women: Gender and Labor Militancy in the Appalachian South," *Journal of American History* 73, no. 2 (September 1986): 354–82; Carol Morgan, *Women Workers and Gender Identities, 1835–1913: The Cotton and Metal Industries in England* (New York: Routledge, 2001); Elizabeth Roberts, *A Woman's Place: An Oral History of Working-Class Women, 1890–1940* (Oxford: Blackwell, 1984).

54. Eleanor Gordon, *Women and the Labor Movement in Scotland, 1850–1914* (Oxford: New York: Clarendon Press, 1991).

55. Interviews, Boxes 6, 7, HWCF; interview with Alice Nelson Kreckman; Correspondence File, Box 1, AFHWR.

56. William Jeannes, *Housing of Families of the American Federation of Full-Fashioned Hosiery Workers, Local No. 1, Philadelphia, June–July, 1932* (New York: Kastner and Stonorov, 1933). I am referring here to Paterson, New Jersey, and Lawrence, Massachusetts, both famous locales within labor history circles.

57. R. A. Smith, *Philadelphia As It Is in 1852: Being a Correct Guide to All the Public Buildings; Literary; Scientific; and Benevolent Institutions, etc.* (Philadelphia: Lindsey

and Blakiston, 1852), 321; Bruce Laurie, *Working People of Philadelphia*, 69, 70; *The Cause* (Society for Ethical Culture: Church Press Association), June 1896, November 1896, February 1897, March 1897, November 1897; Barrett, "Americanization from the Bottom Up."

58. Interview with Robert Gunther. For a discussion of "everyday resistance," see Thompson, *The Making of the English Working Class*; Herbert Gutman, *Work, Culture, and Society in Industrializing America: Essays in American Working Class and Social History* (New York: Knopf, 1976).

59. David Montgomery, *Workers' Control in America: Studies in the History of Work, Technology, and Labor Struggles* (Cambridge: Cambridge University Press, 1979); interview with Howard Kreckman.

60. Palmer, *Union Tactics*, 15. Palmer was also an economist at the Wharton School of the University of Pennsylvania.

61. Interview with Howard Kreckman.

62. Michael Feldberg, "Urbanization as a Cause of Violence: Philadelphia as a Test Case," in *The Peoples of Philadelphia: A History of Ethnic Groups and Lower-Class Life, 1790–1940*, ed. Allen F. Davis and Mark H. Haller (Philadelphia: Temple University Press, 1973), 58–59.

63. *McElroy's Philadelphia Directory* (Philadelphia: E. C. and J. Biddle & Co., 1860), 973; Edwin Cooke, quoted in Palmer, *Union Tactics*, 143, 144. Hardwick and Magee was a carpet manufacturer located at Sixth Street and Lehigh Avenue in Greater Kensington.

64. Judith L. Goldberg, "Strikes, Organizing and Change: The Knights of Labor in Philadelphia, 1859–1890" (Ph.D. diss., New York University, 1985); Levine, *Labor's True Woman*, 34, 69, 121.

65. Elliott J. Gorn, *Mother Jones: The Most Dangerous Woman in America* (New York: Hill and Wang, 2001), 132; "The Heroic Struggle of the '90s," *Hosiery Worker*, June 1, 1927.

66. Scranton, *Figured Tapestry*, 269; "Six Are Shot Down by Strikebreakers," *New York Times*, March 9, 1910.

67. Fifteenth Census of the United States—1930—Population, vol. 3, part 2: Montana-Wyoming, table 23, p. 750.

68. Taylor, *The Full-Fashioned Hosiery Worker*; De Schweinitz, *How Workers Find Jobs*.

69. *Philadelphia Record*, March 15, 1930, April 10, 1931.

70. Dorothy Gondos Beers, "The Centennial City, 1865–1876," in Weigley, *Philadelphia: A 300 Year History*, 435, 436; "German Socialists Coming," *New York Times*, April 2, 1886; "Strike Leaders Facing Defeat," *New York Times*, March 8, 1910; PCLU; Kevin Ostoyich, "The Sound and Silence of the German American Apollo: The Musical Score of Eugen Klee and the Kaiser Prize," *Pennsylvania History: A Journal of Mid-Atlantic Studies* (Winter 2016): 59–96. The singing societies listed were Karl Marx Ges. Ges. Sekt. Deutsche Br. d. Soz. Partei; Arbeiter Maennerchor; Damen Ch. des Sozialist. Schul. V.; Ges Sekt. d. Kensington Labor Lyceum Ass'n.; all in *Deutsch-Amerikanisches*

Vereins-Addressbuch fuer das Jahr 1914 (Milwaukee, Wis.: German-American Directory Pub. Co., 1914).

71. Interview with Howard Kreckman; Max Ehrmann, "Eugene V. Debs as an Orator," *Appeal to Reason*, August 1907.

72. Interview with Howard Kreckman. Scott Nearing was a professor of economics at the Wharton School of the University of Pennsylvania. In 1915, he was fired from his position of ten years for engaging in "radical activity and uttering intemperate public remarks." He had been lecturing and writing articles against sweatshop labor. In 1919, the Woodrow Wilson administration prosecuted Nearing for writing an antiwar pamphlet, *The Great Madness*. He was acquitted after a thirteen-day trial. *Philadelphia Bulletin*, April 4, 1972.

73. The Philadelphia Central Labor Union was also supportive of women's suffrage, passing a resolution in 1909 calling for woman suffrage and encouraging all member unions to work for its passage; PCLU.

74. Interview with Charles Seifert Sr., in Palmer, *Union Tactics*, 170.

75. Lisa McGirr used this phrase in relation to the international coalition that developed around the cause of Sacco and Vanzetti in the 1920s. Lisa McGirr, "The Passion of Sacco and Vanzetti: A Global History," *Journal of American History* 93, no. 4 (March 2007): 1085–115. I borrow the term "subculture of opposition" from Richard Oestreicher, *Solidarity and Fragmentation: Working People and Class Consciousness in Detroit, 1875–1900* (Urbana: University of Illinois Press, 1986), 5.

Chapter Two

1. For a discussion of the struggle for control of the shops, see David Montgomery, *Workers' Control in America: Studies in the History of Work, Technology, and Labor Struggles* (Cambridge: Cambridge University Press, 1979).

2. Howard Kreckman interview with author, Willingboro, New Jersey, October 7, 8, 1998; George W. Taylor, *The Full-Fashioned Hosiery Worker: His Changing Economic Status* (Philadelphia: University of Pennsylvania Press, 1931).

3. Interview with Howard Kreckman; Alan Dawley, *Struggles for Justice: Social Responsibility and the Liberal State* (Cambridge, Mass.: Belknap Press of Harvard University Press, 1991), 201.

4. Dawley, *Struggles for Justice*, 199; Charles H. McCormick, *Hopeless Cases: The Hunt for the Red Scare Terrorist Bombers* (Lanham, Md.: University Press of America, 2005); Nell Irvin Painter, *Standing at Armageddon: The United States, 1877–1919* (New York: W. W. Norton, 1987), 346; Federal Bureau of Investigation, Philadelphia Division, http://www.fbi.gov/philadelphia/about-us/history/famous-cases/famous-cases-1919-bombings, accessed May 2, 2016.

5. Gladys L. Palmer, *Union Tactics and Economic Change: A Case Study of Three Philadelphia Textile Unions* (Philadelphia: University of Pennsylvania Press, 1932); reel 3, September 9, 1917, and October 23, 1917, MIR.

6. This second position, supported by Local 706, was given added weight by the translation and publication in 1921 of Lenin's *"Left-Wing" Communism: An Infantile Disorder*. In this work, directed to the American Left among others, Lenin issued an unambiguous call for organizing within the mainstream of American labor and opposed the isolation of a "militant minority" within dual unions. V. I. Lenin, *"Left-Wing" Communism: An Infantile Disorder*, in Lenin, *Selected Works*, English ed. (Moscow: Foreign Languages Publishing House, 1952), vol. 2, part 2; Lawrence Rogin, *Making History in Hosiery: The Story of the American Federation of Hosiery Workers* (Philadelphia: AFHW, 1938), 9; Bryan Palmer, *James P. Cannon and the Origins of the American Revolutionary Left, 1890–1928* (Urbana: University of Illinois Press, 2007).

7. Philip Scranton, *Figured Tapestry: Production, Markets, and Power in Philadelphia Textiles, 1885–1941* (Cambridge: Cambridge University Press, 1999); Rogin, *Making History in Hosiery*, 12.

8. Rogin, *Making History in Hosiery*; interview with Freda Maurer, in Palmer, *Union Tactics*, 146; interview with Howard Kreckman.

9. Scranton, *Figured Tapestry*, 399; Eleanor L. Bailenson, "Hosiery Workers in Politics and Social Legislation," Bryn Mawr College, May 1941, pp. 4, 5, Box 22, AFHWR; Palmer, *Union Tactics*, 118; *Philadelphia Public Ledger*, January 12, 1919, March 3, 1919, March 9, 1919, March 12, 1919, March 18, 1919.

10. Scranton, *Figured Tapestry*; Proceedings, Fourteenth Annual Convention, September 1925, p. 24, Box 24, AFHWR. The seminal work on the struggles over control of the workplace is Montgomery, *Workers' Control in America*.

11. Thomas R. Heinrich, *Ships for the Seven Seas: Philadelphia Shipbuilding in the Age of Industrial Capitalism* (Baltimore: Johns Hopkins University Press, 1997), 207, 208, 209.

12. Palmer, *Union Tactics*, 93, 95.

13. *Hosiery Worker*, December 31, 1920, January 7, 1921, March 29, 1921, April 7, 1921; Rogin, *Making History in Hosiery*, 12; Scranton, *Figured Tapestry*, 363; Palmer, *Union Tactics*, 106.

14. *Hosiery Worker*, March 29, 1921, April 7, 1921, April 19, 1921. The reference to "soft glove" was due to the fact that bare-knuckle fights also took place in Kensington in this period.

15. The newspaper, underscoring the solidarity of hosiery workers despite being in different organizations at the time, also remarked that if they had wanted to scab, the Kensington strikers could have done so long before, but they could not be recruited as strikebreakers for a Brooklyn, New York, shop that was being struck by the AFFFHW. *Hosiery Worker*, April 25, 1921, May 3, 1921; quoted in Scranton, *Figured Tapestry*, 273.

16. "Judge Threatens to Bar Strikers' Attorney," *Philadelphia Inquirer*, March 3, 1921; *Philadelphia Inquirer*, March 13, 1921, March 25, 1921; interview with Jeanne Callahan.

17. Rogin, *Making History in Hosiery*, 12; interview with Howard Kreckman.

18. *Hosiery Worker*, April 22, 1921, May 19, 1921, May 26, 1921; Rogin, *Making History in Hosiery*, 12.

19. Scranton, *Figured Tapestry*, 365; *Hosiery Worker*, May 19, 1921.

20. *Hosiery Worker*, November 2, 1921, November 8, 1921.

21. *Hosiery Worker*, December 12, 1921. Though Communists were a small minority in the union, at this time the Socialists in the union were affiliated with the "left wing" of the Socialist Party, and this change in strategy, abandoning "dual unionism," was in accord with Lenin's 1921 pamphlet; see earlier note on Lenin.

22. Scranton, *Figured Tapestry*, 350, 366; Rogin, *Making History in Hosiery*, 9.

23. Lizebeth Cohen, *Making a New Deal: Industrial Workers in Chicago, 1919–1939* (Cambridge: Cambridge University Press, 1990), 40, 41.

24. *Hosiery Worker*, June 2, 1922; Proceedings, Eighteenth Annual Convention, September 1929, p. 29, Box 24, AFHWR; Leilah Danielson, *American Gandhi: A. J. Muste and the History of Radicalism in the Twentieth Century* (Philadelphia: University of Pennsylvania Press, 2014), 124; "Socialist Labor Picks City Ticket," *Philadelphia Record*, July 27, 1931; "McKeown, 67 and Ill, Retiring as Head of Once Great Union He Helped Build," *Sunday Bulletin*, May 5, 1957; James Maurer, *It Can Be Done* (New York: Rand School Press, 1938).

25. "Emil Rieve Elected President of Federation," *Hosiery Worker*, April 30, 1929; Proceedings, Eighteenth Annual Convention, September 1929, p. 143, Box 24, AFHWR; "Emil Rieve, Unionist, Dies; Headed Textile Workers," *New York Times*, January 26, 1975.

26. Proceedings, Fifteenth Annual Convention, September 1926, p. 200, Box 24, AFHWR; John W. Edelman, *Labor Lobbyist: The Autobiography of John W. Edelman*, ed. Joseph Carter (Indianapolis: Bobbs-Merrill, 1974). Edelman came to the United States "in the Spring of 1916," which was also the period of the Easter Rising in Ireland. One of the martyrs in the aftermath of the Rising was Roger Casement, an anti-imperialist who had exposed the plight of the rubber workers in the Congo. When Casement was accused of participation in the Rising, he was defended by the Philadelphia attorney Michael Francis Doyle, to no avail (Casement was hanged by the British as a traitor). Shortly after Edelman was hired by the union, Doyle was hired as its attorney. Gary M. Fink, ed., *Labor Unions* (Westport, Conn.: Greenwood Press, 1977); Proceedings, Fifteenth Annual Convention, September 1926, p. 203, Box 24, AFHWR; Proceedings, Sixteenth through Twenty-Second Annual Conventions, September 1927, 1928, 1929, 1930, 1931, 1932, 1934, Box 24, AFHWR; interview with Howard Kreckman.

27. Taylor, *The Full-Fashioned Hosiery Worker*, 26, 27.

28. *Hosiery Worker*, July 22, 1922.

29. *Hosiery Worker*, July 11, 1922, October, 10, 1922; Proceedings, Eleventh Annual Convention, September 1922, pp. 36, 37, Box 24, AFHWR.

30. Proceedings, Eleventh Annual Convention, September 1922, p. 37, Box 24, AFHWR.

31. Ibid.; *Hosiery Worker*, October, 10, 1922, May 15, 1923, December 3, 1923.

32. During this period there was much cross-fertilization between the different radical groups within the organization. Later in the 1930s, however, factions would become stronger; see chapter 6.

33. Taylor, *The Full-Fashioned Hosiery Worker*, 1; Rogin, *Making History in Hosiery*.

34. "Constitution and By-Laws," 1914, Box 2, AFHWR.

35. Ibid.

36. In the 1930s this campaign would come to include African Americans as they began to be hired in some of the seamless hosiery mills in the South, but this was not the case in the 1920s. Rogin, *Making History in Hosiery*; "Constitution and By-Laws," 1914, Box 2, AFHWR.

37. *Hosiery Worker*, October 18, 1922.

38. "Philadelphia's Coop Bank," *Hosiery Worker*, June 12, 1923; "Laying Plans for a Coop Mill," *Hosiery Worker*, July 11, 1922; Eleventh Annual Convention, September 1922, p. 142, Box 24, AFHWR; *Hosiery Worker*, January 11, 1922, July 11, 1922; Proceedings, Sixteenth Annual Convention, September 1927, p. 213, Box 24, AFHWR.

39. Tom Mooney was an American labor leader convicted along with Warren Billings of a bombing in San Francisco in 1916. Although a commission set up by Woodrow Wilson found little evidence of his guilt, he served twenty-two years in prison before being pardoned in 1939 after a worldwide campaign to free him. He was one of the most famous political prisoners in America. Curt Gentry, *Frame Up* (New York: W. W. Norton, 1967); *Hosiery Worker*, November 2, 1921; Proceedings, Eleventh Annual Convention, September 1922, p. 40, Box 24, AFHWR; *Hosiery Worker*, January 1, 1924.

40. Proceedings, Eleventh Annual Convention, September 1922, p. 32, Box 24, AFHWR; *Hosiery Worker*, January 1, 1924; Proceedings, Twelfth Annual Convention, September 1923, p. 7, Box 24, AFHWR.

41. "Old Men," *Hosiery Worker*, February 12, 1925; Proceedings, Twelfth Annual Convention, September 1923, p. 20, Box 24, AFHWR; *Hosiery Worker*, May 28, 1924; *Hosiery Worker*, April 1, 1927; Proceedings, Thirteenth Annual Convention, September 1924, p. 130, Box 24, AFHWR; Eleanor L. Bailenson, "Hosiery Workers in Politics and Social Legislation," Bryn Mawr College, May 1941, pp. 112, 113, Box 22, AFHWR.

42. *Hosiery Worker*, October 10, 1922, July 15, 1927, December 15, 1927, March 1, 1927; Proceedings, Sixteenth Annual Convention, September 1927, p. 156, Box 24, AFHWR; *Hosiery Worker*, August 17, 1926; Proceedings, Fifteenth Annual Convention, September 1926, p. 213, Box 24, AFHWR.

43. *Hosiery Worker*, May 15, 1923.

44. Proceedings, Fifteenth Annual Convention, September 1926, pp. 78, 79, Box 24, AFHWR; *Hosiery Worker*, October 11, 1926.

45. "Report from State Convention," *Hosiery Worker*, May 15, 1923; "Landslide Sweeps Socialists into Control," *Reading Eagle*, November 9, 1927; "Socialists Appear to Have Made a Clean Sweep," *Reading Times*, November 9, 1927.

46. "Organizing News," *Hosiery Worker*, November 10, 1926.

47. Proceedings, Seventeenth Annual Convention, September 1928, p. 15, Box 24, AFHWR. For labor as a means to promote women's rights, see Dorothy Sue Cobble, *The Other Women's Movement: Workplace Justice and Social Rights in Modern America* (Princeton, N.J.: Princeton University Press, 2004).

48. Jacquelyn Dowd Hall et al., *Like a Family: The Making of a Southern Cotton Mill World* (Chapel Hill: University of North Carolina Press, 1987), 218; Cletus Daniel,

Culture of Misfortune: An Interpretive History of Textile Unionism in the United States (Ithaca, N.Y.: ILR Press, 2001).

49. Proceedings, Twelfth Annual Convention, September 1923, p. 56, Box 24, AFHWR; Proceedings, Fourteenth Annual Convention, September 1925, p. 224, Box 24, AFHWR.

50. Dowd Hall et al., *Like a Family*, 196, 197, 218; *Hosiery Worker*, September 5, 1926, September 1, 1927; "Over 200 Delegates at Newly Formed Piedmont Organizing Council," *Hosiery Worker*, June 1, 1928.

51. The historian Robert Korstad wrote about the R. J. Reynolds workers in a slightly later period in his book *Civil Rights Unionism: Tobacco Workers and the Struggle for Democracy in the Mid-Twentieth-Century South* (Chapel Hill: University of North Carolina Press, 2003). "Over 200 Delegates at Newly Formed Piedmont Organizing Council."

52. "Southern Textile Workers Revolt," *Hosiery Worker*, April 30, 1929; "Armed Mob in South Kidnaps Hoffmann," *Hosiery Worker*, March 30, 1929; memo from John Edelman to William Smith, n.d. [1929], Box 2, JEP; "Help for Elizabethton," *Hosiery Worker*, June 15, 1929; Edelman, *Labor Lobbyist*.

53. "Help for Elizabethton"; Proceedings, Eighteenth Annual Convention, September 1929, p. 1250, Box 25, AFHWR.

54. "Southern Mill Owners Swear to 'Get' Hoffmann," *Hosiery Worker*, November, 15, 1929; Dowd Hall et al., *Like a Family*, 218.

Chapter Three

1. John F. Carter, "These Wild Young People: By One of Them," *Atlantic Monthly*, September 1920, 301.

2. The United States mobilized 4,355,000 men for the war. In the short time in which the nation participated, 116,708 were killed and 204,002 were wounded. Compare this to the Vietnam War, in which, of 8,744,000 mobilized, 58,168 were killed and 153,303 were wounded. Fatalities for other World War I combatants include Russia, 1,700,000; Germany, 1,773,700; and the British Empire, 908,371. "WWI Casualty and Death Tables," http://www.pbs.org/greatwar/resources/casdeath_pop.html, accessed May 3, 2016.

3. For an example of the many references to the decade "roaring in," see Charles Warner, *Media Selling: Broadcast, Cable, Print and Interactive* (Ames, Iowa: Iowa State Press, 2004), 5.

4. Proceedings, Seventeenth Annual Convention, September 1928, p. 286, Box 24, AFHWR; interview with Howard Kreckman, Willingboro, New Jersey, October 7, 8, 1998.

5. Interview with Alice Nelson Kreckman, Willingboro, New Jersey, October 7, 8, 1998.

6. Interview with Alice Nelson Kreckman.

7. U.S. Bureau of the Census, *Historical Statistics of the United States, Colonial Times to 1957* (Washington, D.C.: GPO, 1960); David Kyvig, *Daily Life in the United States,*

1920–1939: Decades of Promise and Pain (Westport, Conn.: Greenwood Press, 2002), 11; *Fifteenth Census of the United States—1930—Population*, vol. 3, part 2, table 23, p. 750 (Washington, D.C.: GPO, 1930).

8. Charles Hardy III, "Talking History," http://www.talkinghistory.org/hardy.html, accessed May 3, 2016; Arthur P. Dudden, "The City Embraces 'Normalcy,' 1919–1929," in *Philadelphia: A 300 Year History*, ed. Russell F. Weigley (New York: W. W. Norton, 1982).

9. Interview with Jeanne Callahan, Philadelphia, Pennsylvania, March 8, 1998. Lizabeth Cohen argued that commercialized mass culture and leisure activities, with some limited exceptions, did not significantly break down barriers among different ethnic groups in Chicago (and, by extension, other American cities) in the 1920s. Nationalities were still insulated, people incorporated mass culture selectively, and, after the defeats of the early 1920s, their class consciousness was low. By the 1930s, when immigration was more distant, people became more Americanized, more susceptible to mass culture, and less isolated by nationality. In this period the activities of the CIO and the Communist Party created a "culture of unity" and raised their level of class consciousness. In Kensington, this process began earlier, in the 1920s. Lizabeth Cohen, *Making a New Deal: Industrial Workers in Chicago, 1919–1939* (Cambridge: Cambridge University Press, 1990).

10. Interview with Alice Nelson Kreckman; interview with Jeanne Callahan.

11. Interview with Alice Nelson Kreckman; interview with Jeanne Callahan. Other scholars have discussed ways in which different peoples formed associations through interacting in both places of work and leisure. Some include Tyler Anbinder, who discussed poor Irish and African American residents in New York and their cross-cultural interactions in basement clubs, with results that included the invention of tap dance. Kevin Mumford wrote about districts in Chicago and New York where black and white residents met each other at places like dance halls. Nan Enstad discussed the contacts among young workers of different ethnicities at work sites, bargain basements, and dance halls. Tyler Anbinder, *Five Points: The 19th-Century New York City Neighborhood That Invented Tap Dance, Stole Elections, and Became the World's Most Notorious Slum* (New York: Free Press, 2001); Kevin J. Mumford, *Interzones: Black/White Sex Districts in Chicago and New York in the Early Twentieth Century* (New York: Columbia University Press, 1997); Nan Enstad, *Ladies of Labor, Girls of Adventure: Working Women, Popular Culture, and Labor Politics at the Turn of the Twentieth Century* (New York: Columbia University Press, 1999).

12. Dorothea De Schweinitz, *How Workers Find Jobs: A Study of Four Thousand Hosiery Workers in Philadelphia* (Philadelphia: University of Pennsylvania Press, 1932), 15–20.

13. According to De Schweinitz, other countries represented in small numbers included Albania, Belgium, Canada, Czechoslovakia, Denmark, France, Holland, Italy, Yugoslavia, Poland, Lithuania, Norway, Romania, Switzerland, and "one or two South American countries." Ibid., 25, 27.

14. Jacquelyn Dowd Hall described similar developments among young women in the mill towns of the South. Jacquelyn Dowd Hall et al., *Like a Family: The Making of a*

Southern Cotton Mill World (Chapel Hill: University of North Carolina Press, 1987). See also Alice Kessler Harris, *Out to Work: A History of Wage-Earning Women in the United States* (New York: Oxford University Press, 1982); Adrian Bingham, *Gender, Modernity and the Popular Press in Inter-war Britain* (Oxford: Oxford University Press, 2004); Billie Melman, *Women and the Popular Imagination in the Twenties* (London: Macmillan, 1988); Birgitte Soland, *Becoming Modern: Young Women and the Reconstruction of Womanhood in the 1920s* (Princeton, N.J.: Princeton University Press, 2000); Sueann Caulfield: "Getting into Trouble: Dishonest Women, Modern Girls, and Women-Men in the Conceptual Language of *Vida Policial*, 1925–1927," *Signs* 19, no. 1 (1993): 146–76; Barbara Hamill Sato, "The Moga Sensation: Perceptions of the *Modan Garu* in Japanese Intellectual Circles during the 1920s," *Gender and History* 5, no. 3 (1993): 363–81; and Miriam Silverberg, "The Modern Girl as Militant," in *Recreating Japanese Women, 1600–1945*, ed. Gail Lee Bernstein (Berkeley: University of California Press, 1991), 239–66.

15. Interview with Alice Nelson Kreckman; interview with Howard Kreckman.

16. Interview with Alice Nelson Kreckman; Stella Blum, *Everyday Fashions of the Twenties as Pictured in Sears and Other Catalogs* (New York: Dover, 1981).

17. Interview with Alice Nelson Kreckman.

18. Interview with Jeanne Callahan; interview with Alice Nelson Kreckman.

19. Lynn Dumenil, *The Modern Temper: American Culture and Society in the 1920s* (New York: Hill and Wang, 1995); "The Story of a Girl Who Dared," *Camden Post Telegraph*, July 6, 1925, Box 90, JEP. This trend is also described in Robert S. Lynd and Helen Merrill Lynd, *Middletown: A Study in American Culture* (New York: Harcourt, Brace and World, 1956).

20. Mary Ryan, "The Projection of a New Womanhood: The Movie Moderns in the 1920s," in *Our American Sisters: Women in American Life and Thought*, ed. Jean E. Friedman and William G. Shade, 3rd ed. (Lexington, Mass.: D. C. Heath, 1982), 500–518; Ward Morehouse, *Matinee Tomorrow: Fifty Years of Our Theater* (New York: McGraw-Hill, 1949), 194–97.

21. Esther Louise Little and William Joseph Henry Cotton, *Budgets of Families and Individuals of Kensington, Philadelphia* (Lancaster, Pa.: Press of the New Era Printing Co., 1920); *Pressoff Special*, October 10, 1932, Box 1, AFHWR; Irvin R. Glazer, *Philadelphia Theaters: A Pictorial Architectural History* (Philadelphia: Athenaeum and Dover Publications, 1994).

22. George W. Taylor, *The Full-Fashioned Hosiery Worker: His Changing Economic Status* (Philadelphia: University of Pennsylvania Press, 1931), 11, 13, 22, 23; De Schweinitz, *How Workers Find Jobs*, 15.

23. De Schweinitz, *How Workers Find Jobs*.

24. *Hosiery Worker*, June 15, 1925; interview with Alice Nelson Kreckman.

25. *Pressoff Special*, March 3, 1929, November 3, 1931, May 10, 1932, October 10, 1932, Box 1, AFHWR; Karen Sue Mittelman, "A Spirit That Touches the Problems of Today: Women and Social Reform in the Philadelphia Young Women's Christian Association, 1920–1945" (Ph.D. diss., University of Pennsylvania, 1987).

26. *Pressoff Special,* July 10, 1931, October 10, 1932, November 6, 1932, April 10, 1933, Box 1, AFHWR.

27. Interview with Alice Nelson Kreckman. References to the ability to "take it" appear throughout the run of the *Pressoff Special.*

28. Interview with Alice Nelson Kreckman.

29. Antonio Gramsci, *Selections from the Prison Notebooks* (London: Lawrence and Wishart, 1971), 641; Selina Todd, *Young Women, Work, and Family in England, 1918–1950* (Oxford: Oxford University Press, 2005), 151. Todd reports a quote from a Lancashire woman remarkably similar to the quote here from Alice Kreckman.

30. Interview with Howard Kreckman; *Pressoff Special,* July 10, 1933, Box 1, AFHWR; interview with Alice Nelson Kreckman; interview with Jeanne Callahan.

31. Susan A. Glenn, *Daughters of the Shtetl: Life and Labor in the Immigrant Generation* (Ithaca, N.Y.: Cornell University Press, 1990), 23; *Pressoff Special,* March 3, 1929, November 3, 1931, May 10, 1932, October 10, 1932, Box 1, AFHWR; De Schweinitz, *How Workers Find Jobs,* 80; interview with Freda Maurer, in Gladys Palmer, *Union Tactics and Economic Change: A Case Study of Three Philadelphia Textile Unions* (Philadelphia: University of Pennsylvania Press, 1932), 148; Judith L. Goldberg, "Strikes, Organizing and Change: The Knights of Labor in Philadelphia, 1859–1890" (Ph.D. diss., New York University, 1985).

32. Among authors who have discussed similar influences of a usable past are Nan Enstad, *Ladies of Labor;* Susan Glenn, *Daughters of the Shtetl;* and Jacquelyn Dowd Hall, *Like a Family.*

33. Hinton discusses the engineering industry in England and the development, during World War I, of a shop stewards' movement led by revolutionary socialists committed to the goal of workers' control. This movement originally concerned skilled workers, but came to embrace less-skilled workers and women. The democratic organization of these groups and their organization into local branches show many similarities to the organization of Kensington's hosiery workers. James Hinton, *The First Shop Stewards' Movement* (London: George Allen and Unwin, 1973); V. I. Lenin, *Selected Works,* vol. 1 (Moscow, 1960), 831–32.

34. "Girls in Burlington Shop in Trouble," *Hosiery Worker,* August 10, 1923; *Hosiery Worker,* September 11, 1923.

35. For the manufacturers' aims, see Taylor, *The Full-Fashioned Hosiery Worker.*

36. Antonio Gramsci, "Marxism and Modern Culture" and "The Organization of Education and Culture," *The Modern Prince and Other Writings* (New York: International Publishers, 1957), 129, 130. Gramsci was active in promoting workers' councils in Turin in 1920 during the factory occupations there, which included four hosiery mills.

37. Eugene Debs went to prison for his opposition to the war, and locally, Scott Nearing, then at the University of Pennsylvania, was blacklisted and narrowly escaped prison. Howard Kreckman often spoke of the Kensington Socialists' opposition to the war. Hinton, *The First Shop Stewards' Movement;* Bryan Palmer, American Historical Association Annual Meeting, Session 175, January 4, 2009; see also Bryan Palmer,

James P. Cannon and the Origins of the American Revolutionary Left, 1890–1928 (Urbana: University of Illinois Press, 2007); interview with Howard Kreckman.

38. Carter, "These Wild Young People," 301. See discussion in Frederick Lewis Allen, *Only Yesterday: An Informal History of the 1920s* (New York: Harper and Row, 1931), 81–85.

39. I borrow this quote from the gender theorist Judith Butler, *Gender Trouble: Feminism and the Subversion of Identity* (New York: Routledge, 1990), xxiv.

40. "War and the Worker," *Hosiery Worker*, July 22, 1924.

41. "Militarism vs. Anti-militarism," *Hosiery Worker*, August 12, 1924.

42. *Hosiery Worker*, May 28, 1924, July 8, 1924, May 28, 1925, June 14, 1927, July 1, 1927.

43. "Call to Duty," *Hosiery Worker*, June 26, 1923; Proceedings, Fourteenth Annual Convention, September 1925, p. 4, Box 24, AFHWR.

44. Interview with Howard Kreckman. Mark Wild discussed the practice of "street speaking" in his book describing Socialist attempts to mobilize the culturally diverse neighborhoods of early twentieth-century Los Angeles. Mark Wild, *Street Meeting: Multiethnic Neighborhoods in Early Twentieth-Century Los Angeles* (Berkeley: University of California Press, 2005).

45. "A Year of Fighting with the Hosiery Workers," 1929, Box 2, AFHWR; *Hosiery Worker*, August 15, 1929, August 31, 1929.

46. *Hosiery Worker*, August 15, 1929.

47. Ibid.

48. While Kensington's settlement patterns were a limiting factor to the development of strictly insular identities, Branch 1's overall goal was to build a socialist sense of unity with the international working class. *Hosiery Worker*, August 15, 1929, August 31, 1929.

49. "King of the Hobos," *Hosiery Worker*, July 2, 1928.

50. "Old Men," *Hosiery Worker*, February 12, 1925.

51. Another appeal affected a hospitalized member of the Paterson, New Jersey, branch. Paterson delegates to the convention told the membership, drawing on traditions of "loyalty," that although the man had had lung trouble for years, he proved himself a "man among men" by refusing one of the best jobs in the mill when the branch called a strike against the company. "Old Men," *Hosiery Worker*, February 12, 1925; Proceedings, Twelfth Annual Convention, September 1923, p. 20, Box 24, AFHWR; *Hosiery Worker*, May 28, 1924.

52. The union often brought in veteran speakers from other areas of textile, as well as from other industries, in an attempt to promote the unity of labor. "Tobias Hall," Proceedings, Sixteenth Annual Convention, September 1927, pp. 198–200, Box 24, AFHWR.

53. Eric Arnesen, *Encyclopedia of U.S. Labor and Working Class History* (London: Routledge, 2006), 394, 395; Ges Sekt. d. Kensington Labor Lyceum Ass'n., in *Deutsch-Amerikanisches Vereins-Addressbuch fuer das Jahr 1914* (Milwaukee, Wis.: German-American Directory Pub. Co., 1914); Susan Levine, "Labor's True Woman: Domesticity and Equal Rights in the Knights of Labor," *Journal of American History* 70, no. 2 (Septem-

ber 1983): 323–39; see also Goldberg, "Strikes, Organizing and Change"; *Philadelphia Tocsin*, August 7, 1886, cited in Levine, "Labor's True Woman," 327; Robert E. Weir, *Workers in America: A Historical Encyclopedia* (Santa Barbara: ABC-CLIO, 2013), 393, 394; Workers' Education Bureau of America, *Report of the Executive Committee to the National Convention* (New York: Workers' Education Bureau of America, 1922, 1925).

54. Geiges was president of both Branch 1 and the AFFFHW at this time. He also argued that education would help protect democracy, as it encouraged workers to "aspire to a higher and fuller life." He was a supporter of the socialist tradition that, through education, workers would gain an understanding of the real meaning of "rights." "Education the Hope of the Labor Movement," *Hosiery Worker*, November 7, 1923.

55. The union also had a close association with the Bryn Mawr school. This is discussed further in the next chapter. Proceedings, Thirteenth Annual Convention, September 1924, p. 152, Box 24, AFHWR.

56. Among these were Josephine and Martin Bennett, who donated their property in Katonah, New York, for the school. Josephine was a suffragist as well as an ardent supporter of union organizing. Evelyn Preston, a wealthy philanthropist and president of the League of Women Shoppers, was another prominent founder, giving money to build a women's dormitory. A board of directors governed the school, including A. J. Muste, founding chairman and head of the faculty; James Maurer, president of the Pennsylvania Federation of Labor; and Rose Schneiderman, president of the Women's Trade Union League. Jonathan Bloom, "Brookwood Labor College," *Contributions in Economics and Economic History: The Re-education of the American Working Class*, ed. Steven H. London (Westport, Conn.: Greenwood Press, 1990).

57. Proceedings, Fifteenth Annual Convention, September 1926, pp. 163, 164, Box 24, AFHWR; Alfred Hoffmann, Series IV, Student Files, Boxes 67, 85, BLCR.

58. Proceedings, Fifteenth Annual Convention, September, 1926, 163-64, Box 24, AFHWR; Leilah Danielson, *American Gandhi: A. J. Muste and the History of Radicalism in the Twentieth Century* (Philadelphia: University of Pennsylvania Press, 2014), 109; Proceedings, Seventeenth Annual Convention, September, 1928, 650–52, Box 25, AFHWR.

59. *Hosiery Worker*, February 8, 1927; Workers' Education Bureau of America, *Report of the Executive Committee to the National Convention* (New York: Workers' Education Bureau of America, 1921–25), https://catalog.hathitrust.org/Record/012100177, accessed May 3, 2016. Howard Kreckman continued to attend these classes and then night classes at Philadelphia's Brown Preparatory School. Remarkably, and quite unusually for a Kensington resident, he also aspired to attend college. Between his work as a knitter and a part-time job, he was able to save the approximately $300 to cover costs at the College of William and Mary, which he attended in 1930 for one year and where he made the honor roll. He had to leave after that year, however, and return to hosiery work in order to help his family and friends weather the Depression. Many years later, after hosiery was no longer a viable industry in the Philadelphia area, he took a job as a maintenance man in a public high school. Part of his job was to destroy

books that were no longer considered useful. He ended up bringing most of them home because, as he put it, "I couldn't bring myself to burn a book." "Proficiency List for Undergraduate Men," *Flat Hat* (College of William and Mary), January 16, 1931, 10; interview, Howard Kreckman.

60. *Hosiery Worker*, February 8, 1927, November 15, 1927; interview with Howard Kreckman; *Union Labor Record*, April 6, 1933; John W. Edelman, *Labor Lobbyist: The Autobiography of John W. Edelman* (Indianapolis: Bobbs-Merrill, 1974). By the late 1920s other unions in the city were participating in labor education programs, including the Philadelphia branch of the Amalgamated Clothing Workers of America (ACWA), which offered programs after 1929. Elizabeth Fones-Wolf, "Industrial Unionism and Labor Movement Culture in Depression-Era Philadelphia," *Pennsylvania Magazine of History and Biography* 109, no. 1 (January 1985): 3–26.

61. *Hosiery Worker*, November 1, 1927.

62. *Hosiery Worker*, May 8, 1928.

63. Proceedings, Fifteenth Annual Convention, September 1926, p. 274, Box 24, AFHWR; *Hosiery Worker*, November 1, 1927, November 15, 1927, May 8, 1928, March 21, 1929, January 8, 1932, January 12, 1931, April 15, 1931; Proceedings, Sixteenth Annual Convention, September 1927, p. 401, Box 24, AFHWR; *Hosiery Worker*, January 25, 1935, February 8, 1935.

64. Proceedings, Seventeenth Annual Convention, September 1928, pp. 121–22, Box 25, AFHWR; Report to First Constitutional Convention of the CIO, Pittsburgh, Pennsylvania, 1938, p. 2, CIOST.

65. Proceedings, Sixteenth Annual Convention, September 1927, p. 401, Box 24, AFHWR.

66. *Hosiery Worker*, February 5, 1926, April 20, 1927, August 6, 1927. The Philadelphia Joint Board of the ACWA, after its founding in 1929, also promoted a sports program and in 1934 operated a gym, handball courts, and organized bowling leagues. The movement spread through Philadelphia's union movement in the 1930s. Fones-Wolf, "Industrial Unionism," 8.

67. *Hosiery Worker*, July 15, 1927, October 13, 1927, February 1, 1928. Chapter 4 provides details on women's gender-specific activities in the union.

68. *Hosiery Worker*, November 13, 1923.

69. *Hosiery Worker*, July 16, 1926.

70. *Hosiery Worker*, November 15, 1927.

71. The black bottom was a solo challenge dance that featured "the slapping of the backside while hopping forward and backward, stamping the feet, and gyrations of the torso and pelvis, while occasionally making arm movements to music." The theatrical show *Dinah* brought the black bottom to New York in 1924, and the George White's Scandals featured it at the Apollo Theater in Harlem from 1926 through 1927. The dance became an overnight sensation and ended up overtaking the popularity of the Charleston, eventually becoming the number-one social dance. Marshall Winslow Stearns, *Jazz Dance: The Story of American Vernacular Dance* (New York: Macmillan, 1968), 110, 111.

72. *Hosiery Worker*, November 15, 1927.

73. *Hosiery Worker*, February 25, 1928.

74. Richard Oestreicher, *Solidarity and Fragmentation: Working People and Class Consciousness in Detroit, 1875–1900* (Urbana: University of Illinois Press, 1986), 62 and passim; Daniel Katz, *All Together Different: Yiddish Socialists, Garment Workers, and the Labor Roots of Multiculturalism* (New York: New York University Press, 2011); David A. Corbin, *Life, Work, and Rebellion in the Coal Fields: Southern West Virginia Coal Miners, 1880–1922* (Urbana: University of Illinois Press, 1981).

75. The Burlington was an open shop. While male knitters were members of the union, the other departments were not. "Girls in Burlington Shop in Trouble"; "Knitters Out," *Hosiery Worker*, September 11, 1923.

76. *Hosiery Worker*, August 21, 1922, September 15, 1922.

77. Organizing, *Hosiery Worker*, November 26, 1924.

78. Ibid.; "How about You?," November 26, 1924; Organizing, *Hosiery Worker*, May 20, 1925, May 14, 1926, August 15, 1927.

79. Strike File, Box 1, Folder 3, AFHWR; Palmer, *Union Tactics*, 107, 124. Palmer claimed that there were approximately 19,000 members nationally in 1929. Proceedings, Fourteenth Annual Convention, September 1925, p. 5, Box 24, AFHWR; Proceedings, Fifteenth Annual Convention, September 1926, p. 11, Box 24, AFHWR; Gary M. Fink, ed., "American Federation of Hosiery Workers," in *Labor Unions* (Westport, Conn.: Greenwood Press, 1977); Proceedings, Seventeenth Annual Convention, September 1928, pp. 132–33, Box 24, AFHWR. Union membership also increased in every other area of the country where mills were relocating.

80. Proceedings, Fifteenth Annual Convention, September 1926, p. 111, Box 24, AFHWR; interview with Howard Kreckman; "Brownhill and Kramer Force 'Yellow Dog' on Scabs," *Hosiery Worker*, January 2, 1927; Strike File, Box 1, Folder 2, AFHWR.

81. Strike File, Box 1, Folder 2, AFHWR; "Old Time Fighting Spirit Still Alive," *Hosiery Worker*, November 15, 1927.

82. Proceedings, Seventeenth Annual Convention, September 1928, p. 378, Box 24, AFHWR; interview with Howard Kreckman.

83. *Hosiery Worker*, February 15, 1928.

84. *Labor's News*, February 21, 1931; Staunton Lynd, ed., *We Are All Leaders: The Alternative Unionism of the Early 1930s* (Urbana: University of Illinois Press, 1996).

Chapter Four

1. "Girl's Best Friend Is the Union," *Hosiery Worker*, February, 15, 1929; Proceedings, Eighteenth Annual Convention, September 1929, p. 653, Box 26, AFHWR.

2. Jacquelyn Dowd Hall, "Disorderly Women: Gender and Labor Militancy in the Appalachian South," *Journal of American History* 73, no. 2 (September 1986): 354–82. Stephen Norwood's study of young telephone operators in Boston, concentrating on a slightly earlier period, has also shown how young, militant telephone operators combined a new culture of consumption with union organizing and feminist self-assertion.

Stephen Norwood, *Labor's Flaming Youth: Telephone Operators and Worker Militancy, 1878–1923* (Urbana: University of Illinois Press, 1990); Susan Faludi, "Death of a Revolutionary," *New Yorker*, April 15, 2013.

3. Dowd Hall, "Disorderly Women." Recent work by the historian Dorothy Sue Cobble identified not only a significant labor women's movement in early post–World War II America, but also the enduring networks formed by the much earlier liberal women's reform internationalism of the International Federation of Working Women, which, though formally disbanded by 1924, helped to sustain labor women's activism in the later period. Julia Mickenberg has also identified a "decidedly internationalist" struggle, closely associated with socialist agitation, that opened space for American feminists to conceive a new model of citizenship that encompassed both political and economic rights. Dorothy Sue Cobble, *The Other Women's Movement: Workplace Justice and Social Rights in Modern America* (Princeton, N.J.: Princeton University Press, 2004); Dorothy Sue Cobble, "A Higher 'Standard of Life' for the World: U.S. Labor Women's Reform Internationalism and the Legacies of 1919," *Journal of American History* 100 (March 2014): 1052–85; Julia L. Mickenberg, "Suffragettes and Soviets: American Feminists and the Specter of Revolutionary Russia," *Journal of American History* 100 (March 2014): 1021–51.

4. Gladys Palmer, *Union Tactics and Economic Change: A Case Study of Three Philadelphia Textile Unions* (Philadelphia: University of Pennsylvania Press, 1932), 124.

5. Susan Levine, "Labor's True Woman: Domesticity and Equal Rights in the Knights of Labor," *Journal of American History* 70, no. 2 (September 1983): 323–39; Judith L. Goldberg, "Strikes, Organizing and Change: The Knights of Labor in Philadelphia, 1869–1890" (Ph.D. diss., New York University, 1985); *Philadelphia Tocsin*, August 7, 1886, cited in Levine, "Labor's True Woman," 327.

6. Palmer, *Union Tactics*, p. 15.

7. Alice Nelson Kreckman, interview with author, Willingboro, New Jersey, October, 7, 8, 1998; Jeanne Callahan, interview with author, Philadelphia, Pennsylvania, March 8, 1998.

8. Interview with Alice Nelson Kreckman.

9. Ibid.

10. Lois W. Banner, *American Beauty* (New York: Knopf, 1983), 275.

11. Doris Stevens, *Jailed for Freedom* (New York: Boni and Liveright, 1920).

12. Susan Poulson, "Philadelphia and the Suffrage Movement: Place, Memory, and Symbol," paper presented at the Pennsylvania Historical Association, Philadelphia, November 2014; Caroline Katzenstein, *Lifting the Curtain: The State and National Woman Suffrage Campaigns in Pennsylvania as I Saw Them* (Philadelphia: Dorrance, n.d).

13. *Hosiery Worker*, September 15, 1929.

14. The historian Eleanor Flexner contends that scholars have underestimated the contributions of the National Woman's Party even to the degree that they have ignored its status as the first victim of the Red Scare; Eleanor Flexner, *Century of Struggle: The Women's Rights Movement in the United States* (Cambridge, Mass.: Belknap Press of

Harvard University Press, 1975). Julia Mickenberg has also made a strong case for the broad impact of the Woman's Party. Mickenberg, "Suffragettes and Soviets."

15. Stephanie L. Twin, ed., *Out of the Bleachers: Writings on Women and Sports* (Old Westbury, N.Y.: Feminist Press, 1979); Banner, *American Beauty*, 276.

16. Susan Butler, *East to the Dawn: The Life of Amelia Earhart* (New York: Da Capo Press, 1999); Elgin Long and Marie K. Long, *Amelia Earhart: The Mystery Solved* (New York: Simon and Schuster, 1999); Adrian Bingham, *Gender, Modernity and the Popular Press in Inter-war Britain* (Oxford: Oxford University Press, 2004), 151.

17. Margaret C. Christman and Claudia B. Kidwell, *Suiting Up: The Democratization of Clothing in America* (Washington, D.C.: Smithsonian Institution, 1974); Edmonde Charles-Roux, *Chanel: Her Life, Her World, and the Woman behind the Legend She Created*, trans. Nancy Amphoux (New York: Knopf, 1975).

18. Many of these arguments are based on the work of Thorstein Veblen, who claimed that women's fashion was part of conspicuous consumption and reflected women's status as property. Carolyn Kitch argued regarding the young flapper of the 1920s: "In the decade that began with the passage of the Nineteenth Amendment, she redefined American women's freedom as sexual rather than political"; she became "a crucial weapon in disempowering women by idealizing the body of a girl." The scholars Rayna Rapp and Ellen Ross argue that, during the 1920s, "themes of female independence" disappeared from the political sphere but "resurface[d] in advertising" and other popular media that contained advertising. Thorstein Veblen, *The Theory of the Leisure Class: An Economic Study of Institutions* (1899; reprint, New York: Macmillan, 1912); Carolyn Kitch, *The Girl on the Magazine Cover: The Origins of Visual Stereotypes in American Mass Media* (Chapel Hill: University of North Carolina Press, 2001), 122; Rayna Rapp and Ellen Ross, "The Twenties Backlash: Compulsory Heterosexuality, the Consumer Family, and the Waning of Feminism," in *Class, Race, and Sex: The Dynamics of Control*, ed. Amy Swerdlow and Hanna Lessinger (Boston: G. K. Hall, 1983), 93–107. Nan Enstad and Jacquelyn Dowd Hall, however, have contested such one-dimensional representations of women's relationship to fashion, as has Elizabeth Wilson, who has seen a revolutionary potential embodied in the flapper. Nan Enstad, *Ladies of Labor, Girls of Adventure: Working Women, Popular Culture, and Labor Politics at the Turn of the Twentieth Century* (New York: Columbia University Press, 1999); Dowd Hall, "Disorderly Women"; Elizabeth Wilson, "All the Rage," in *Fabrications: Costume and the Female Body*, ed. Jane Gaines and Charlotte Herzog (New York: Routledge, 1990), 29.

19. Susan Porter Benson, *Counter Cultures: Saleswomen, Managers, and Customers in American Department Stores, 1890–1940* (Urbana: University of Illinois Press, 1986), 228; Vicki Howard, "'At the Curve Exchange': Postwar Beauty Culture and Working Women at Maidenform," *Enterprise and Society* 1, no. 3 (September 2000): 591–618.

20. Interview with Alice Nelson Kreckman; Enstad, *Ladies of Labor*, 150.

21. Jacob Wasserman, *Faber, or The Lost Years* (New York: Harcourt, Brace, 1925); Camden Post Telegraph, March 16, 1926, Box 90, JEP.

22. Correspondence, Box 88, JEP.

23. Lawrence Rogin, *Making History in Hosiery: The Story of the American Federation of Hosiery Workers* (Philadelphia: American Federation of Hosiery Workers, 1938), 64.

24. Women in the Labor Force, Box 14, Folder 2, Employment and Unemployment Studies, 1912 to 1956, WIR.

25. Interview with Freda Maurer, in Palmer, *Union Tactics*, 146.

26. Ibid.

27. *Hosiery Worker*, October 1, 1927.

28. May Wood Simon, "Co-operation and Housewives," *Masses*, November 1913. In 1916, Emma Goldman claimed that "the question of birth control is above all a workingwoman's question," and *The Masses* praised birth control advocate Margaret Sanger. Emma Goldman, "Emma Goldman's Defense," *Masses*, June 1916, quoted in Levine, "Labor's True Woman," 327; "Labor Forces Aid New Birth Control Drive," *Reading Tribune*, April 26, 1926; James Maurer, *It Can Be Done* (New York: Rand School Press, 1938). As the historian Linda Gordon has argued, "When the birth control movement developed ideologies, these ideologies often arose from aspirations and motives that had already propelled people into political action." Linda Gordon, *The Moral Property of Women: A History of Birth Control Politics in America* (Urbana: University of Illinois Press, 2002), 3. For an overview of connections among socialism, labor, and women's rights, see Bonnie S. Anderson, *Joyous Greetings: The First International Women's Movement, 1830–1860* (Oxford: Oxford University Press, 2000).

29. Proceedings, Fifteenth Annual Convention, September 1926, p. 267, Box 24, AFHWR; Proceedings, Sixteenth Annual Convention, September 1927, pp. 524–27, Box 24, AFHWR.

30. Proceedings, Sixteenth Annual Convention, September 1927, pp. 524–27, Box 24, AFHWR.

31. Ibid.; *Hosiery Worker*, January 1, 1927.

32. Although union leadership maintained that they were in complete agreement with the principle of equal rights for men and women, neither they nor the union's female activists considered the ERA to be the central issue in their struggles; the day-to-day battles in the shops and on the picket lines remained the primary focus of their attention. Karen Sue Mittelman, "A Spirit That Touches the Problems of Today: Women and Social Reform in the Philadelphia Young Women's Christian Association, 1920 1945" (Ph.D. diss., University of Pennsylvania, 1987), 64; "Blue Triangle Boosters" Club Reports, Box 5, Folder 21, KYWCA. The hosiery union leadership was conflicted on the subject of the ERA. As was the position of labor generally, the union did not support the amendment as originally proposed, believing that it would jeopardize protective legislation that women workers had won through struggle. However, they also would not allow the name of the union to be used in opposition, refusing a request by the director of the Women's Bureau, Mary Anderson, to include the union's name on material opposing the amendment. Later in the ERA debate, when an amendment was introduced that read, "The provisions of this article shall not be construed to impair any rights or benefits now or hereafter conferred by law upon persons of the female sex," the union supported it fully. In a letter to the U.S. Senate, Alexander McKeown,

president of both Branch 1 and the national AFHW, wrote that they were "in complete agreement with the principles of equal rights for men and women," and felt that the amendment would "safeguard women against the loss of rights now held." Letter from William L. Rafsky to Mary Anderson, July 26, 1945, Box 8, AFHWR; letter from Alexander McKeown to Senator Carl Hayden, June 8, 1953, Box 8, AFHWR.

33. Wilson, "All the Rage"; Banner, *American Beauty*; interview with Alice Nelson Kreckman.

34. Wilson, "All the Rage"; Banner, *American Beauty*; Marybeth Hamilton, *When I'm Bad, I'm Better: Mae West, Sex, and American Entertainment* (Berkeley: University of California Press, 1997); interview with Alice Nelson Kreckman; interview with Howard Kreckman.

35. *Hosiery Worker*, July 1, 1927, November 30, 1928, January 15, 1929, July 15, 1929; Karyn L. Hollis, *Liberating Voices: Writing at the Bryn Mawr Summer School for Women Workers* (Carbondale: Southern Illinois University Press, 2004); John Edelman, *Labor Lobbyist: The Autobiography of John W. Edelman*, ed. Joseph Carter (Indianapolis: Bobbs-Merrill, 1974).

36. Interview with Alice Nelson Kreckman.

37. Memo from Nora Piori, April 6, 1931, Box 5, WIR.

38. Interview with Alice Nelson Kreckman; *Hosiery Worker*, January 1, 1927, May 2, 1927, October 15, 1927, April 2, 1928, June 1, 1928, September 30, 1928; "Women Honor Anna Geisinger," *Hosiery Worker*, December 4, 1931.

39. "Help to Organize South Is the Plea," *Hosiery Worker*, November 15, 1929. Following the hosiery workers' actions, by 1934 the Philadelphia branch of the ACWA was also starting women's meetings in an effort to attract more women activists. Elizabeth Fones-Wolf, "Industrial Unionism and Labor Movement Culture in Depression-Era Philadelphia," *Pennsylvania Magazine of History and Biography* 109, no. 1 (January 1985): 11.

40. *Hosiery Worker*, March 15, 1929, March 7, 1930, June 1, 1928.

41. Proceedings, Sixteenth Annual Convention, September 1927, pp. 524–27, Box 24, AFHWR.

42. *Hosiery Worker*, December 15, 1927.

43. Ibid.; *Hosiery Worker*, June 30, 1929.

44. *Hosiery Worker*, February 15, 1928.

45. *Hosiery Worker*, July 15, 1927, June 15, 1928, April 30, 1929.

46. *Hosiery Worker*, August 15, 1927, December 1, 1927.

47. *Hosiery Worker*, August 15, 1927, August 1, 1928. Joan Sangster has shown how union beauty contests could be used to publicize unpopular labor practices and could also be a challenge to the notion of decorative beauty, substituting the beauty of courage and militancy. Joan Sangster, "'Queen of the Picket Line': Beauty Contests in the Post–World War II Canadian Labor Movement," *Labor: Studies in Working-Class History of the Americas* 5, no. 4 (Winter 2008): 83–106.

48. Eleanor Burke Leacock, *Myths of Male Dominance: Collected Articles on Women Cross-Culturally* (New York: Monthly Review Press, 1981), 3; Angela J. Latham, *Posing*

a Threat: Flappers, Chorus Girls, and Other Brazen Performers of the American 1920s (Hanover, N.H.: Wesleyan University Press, 2000), 7.

49. *Hosiery Worker*, January 16, 1928.

50. *Hosiery Worker*, March 1, 1928, August 1, 1928. James Barrett discusses such counterdefinitions of "Americanism" in James R. Barrett, "Americanization from the Bottom Up: Immigration and the Remaking of the Working Class in the United States, 1880–1930," *Journal of American History* 79, no. 3 (December 1992): 996–1020.

51. Proceedings, Seventeenth Annual Convention, September 1928, p. 290, Box 25, AFHWR; "13th Kenosha Bomb Injures Woman," *Chicago Tribune*, September 6, 1928.

52. *Hosiery Worker*, March 15, 1928, April 6, 1928.

53. *Hosiery Worker*, May 1, 1928, August 1, 1928; "Strikers Refuse Trophy," flyer, Allen-A, Strike File, Box 1, AFHWR; "The Second Year of the Allen-A Lockout," correspondence, Allen-A, Strike File, Box 1, AFHWR.

54. *Hosiery Worker*, July 15, 1928. Historical studies that have discussed the methods women have used to shame men into action include, among others, Dominque Godineau, *The Women of Paris and Their French Revolution* (Berkeley: University of California Press, 1998); Carol Morgan, *Women Workers and Gender Identities, 1835–1913: The Cotton and Metal Industries in England* (London: Routledge, 2001); Elizabeth Roberts, *Women's Work 1840–1940* (Basingstoke, England: Macmillan, 1988); and Christine Stansell, *City of Women: Sex and Class in New York, 1789–1860* (New York: Knopf, 1986); Dowd Hall, "Disorderly Women."

55. *Hosiery Worker*, October 31, 1928, November 15, 1928; Proceedings, Seventeenth Annual Convention, September 1928, p. 297, Box 25, AFHWR; "Heroic Written Larger Than Ever," flyer, Strike File, 1928, Box 1, AFHWR; *Hosiery Worker*, September 15, 1929, October 15, 1929.

56. Proceedings, Eighteenth Annual Convention, September 1929, p. 297, Box 25, AFHWR.

57. "Youth Wages a Long Struggle," flyer, Strike File, 1929, Box 1, AFHWR.

58. "To the Well Dressed Women of America," flyer, Strike File, 1929, Box 1, AFHWR.

59. "The History Making Lock-Out of the Allen-A Full-Fashioned Hosiery Workers," Strike File, 1928, Box 1, AFHWR; "Would a Lady Decorate Her Limbs with the Symbol of the Yellow Dog?," flyer, Box 1, AFHWR; "Buy Union Made Hosiery," Strike File, 1928, Box 1, AFHWR; Hillier Bevis, *The World of Art Deco* (New York: E. P. Dutton, 1971); *Hosiery Worker*, December 15, 1929.

60. "Beauty Lives with Kindness," flyer, Strike File, 1929, Box 1, AFHWR.

61. Proceedings, Seventeenth Annual Convention, September 1928, pp. 277, 278, Box 25, AFHWR.

62. Ibid., p. 26, Box 25, AFHWR.

63. Ibid., pp. 26, 211, 652, Box 25, AFHWR; *Hosiery Worker*, September 15, 1928. For a discussion of women's manipulation of male agendas, see Carroll Smith-Rosenberg, *Disorderly Conduct: Visions of Gender in Victorian America* (New York: Knopf, 1985), 8.

64. Proceedings, Seventeenth Annual Convention, September 1928, pp. 652–60, Box 25, AFHWR; *Hosiery Worker*, October 15, 1928.

65. "Br 1 Girls Celebrate Their Eighth Anniversary," *Hosiery Worker*, January 15, 1937; *Hosiery Worker*, November 15, 1929; Proceedings, Eighteenth Annual Convention, September 1929, p. 1036, Box 26, AFHWR.

66. *The New Century for Woman*, May 13, 1876, 8.

67. *Pressoff Special*, April 9, 1929, October 10, 1933, April 10, 1934, November 6, 1934, November 9, 1934, Box 1, AFHWR; Kahlil Gibran, *The Prophet* (1923; New York: Knopf, 2008), 15, 16.

68. For a discussion of later labor feminism, see Cobble, *The Other Women's Movement*. The importance of a left-wing analysis to the development of these later movements has, however, been clearly demonstrated. Kate Weigand, *Red Feminism: American Communism and the Making of Women's Liberation* (Baltimore: Johns Hopkins University Press, 2002).

Chapter Five

1. "Thousands in Throng at Rites for Slain Striker," *Philadelphia Public Ledger*, March 10, 1930; *Philadelphia Record*, March 10, 1930; "Hosiery Strikers and Workers Fight," *Philadelphia Evening Bulletin*, March 10, 1930; *Hosiery Worker*, March 15, 1930; "American Federation of Full-Fashioned Hosiery Workers," *Fortune*, January 1932, 49–108.

2. "The Second Year of the Allen-A Lock-Out," Strike File, 1929, Box 1, AFHWR; Carol and Carlisle Shafer, "A Community Creates Real Jobs," *Survey Graphic: Magazine of Social Interpretation* 28 (1938): 532.

3. George W. Taylor, *The Full-Fashioned Hosiery Worker: His Changing Economic Status* (Philadelphia: University of Pennsylvania Press, 1931); Lawrence Rogin, *Making History in Hosiery: The Story of the American Federation of Hosiery Workers* (Philadelphia: AFHW, 1938), 19, 20; Irving Bernstein, *The Lean Years: A History of the American Worker, 1920–1933* (Boston: Houghton Mifflin, 1960).

4. *Hosiery Worker*, March 1, 1929; Taylor, *The Full-Fashioned Hosiery Worker*, 30.

5. Gladys L. Palmer, *Union Tactics and Economic Change: A Case Study of Three Philadelphia Textile Unions* (Philadelphia: University of Pennsylvania Press, 1932), 108, 115; Proceedings, Eighteenth Annual Convention, September 1929, p. 620, Box 26, AFHWR; Bernstein, *The Lean Years*.

6. Taylor, *The Full-Fashioned Hosiery Worker*, 10; Palmer, *Union Tactics*, 97, 120, appendix A; Proceedings, Eighteenth Annual Convention, September 1929, p. 620, Box 26, AFHWR.

7. Proceedings, Eighteenth Annual Convention, September 1929, pp. 621–30, Box 26, AFHWR.

8. Proceedings, Seventeenth Annual Convention, September 1928, Box 24, John Edelman report on research and education, AFHWR.

9. David E. Kyvig, *Daily Life in the United States, 1920–1940: How Americans Lived through the "Roaring Twenties" and the Great Depression* (Chicago: Ivan R. Dee, 2001), 210–12.

10. Alice Nelson Kreckman, interview with author, Willingboro, New Jersey, October 7, 8, 1998; Howard Kreckman, interview with author, Willingboro, New Jersey, October 7, 8, 1998. A clause in the 1929 national agreement required the union shops to pay 1 percent of their payroll into an unemployment fund for the workers. Taylor, *The Full-Fashioned Hosiery Worker*, 191.

11. John F. Bauman, "The City, the Depression, and Relief: The Philadelphia Experience" (Ph.D. diss., Rutgers University, 1969), 32, 34, 36, 37. For an excellent description of homelessness during the Depression, see Kenneth Kusmer, *Down and out, on the Road: The Homeless in American History* (Oxford: Oxford University Press, 2002), chap. 6.

12. Bauman, "The City, the Depression, and Relief," 30, 31; Philip Scranton, *Figured Tapestry: Production, Markets, and Power in Philadelphia Textiles, 1885–1941* (Cambridge: Cambridge University Press, 1989), 411; Works Progress Administration, Schedule No. 2199, PLMS.

13. *Hosiery Worker*, January 22, 1932, January 6, 1933.

14. Jeanne Callahan, interview with author, Philadelphia, March 8, 1998; Robert Gunther (pseudonym), interview with author, Philadelphia, March 8, 1998.

15. Brochure, Pioneer Youth Club, n.d. [1930s], Box 99, JEP; *Hosiery Worker*, March 24, 1932; interview with Howard Kreckman.

16. *Hosiery Worker*, November 20, 1931.

17. Alice Hanson Cook, *A Lifetime of Labor: The Autobiography of Alice H. Cook* (New York: Feminist Press, City University of New York, 1998), 67, 68, 84; *Hosiery Worker*, March 24, 1932, May 12, 1932.

18. *Hosiery Worker*, March 21, 1931.

19. Ibid.; *Hosiery Worker*, January 22, 1932.

20. Interview, Jeanne Callahan; *Pressoff Special*, April 10, 1934, May 10, 1934, September 11, 1934.

21. *Hosiery Worker*, December 4, 1931, October 7, 1932; Joseph Burge, "The Philadelphia Hosiers' Hectic Years," in author's possession.

22. Individual Progress Sheets, Hosiery Workers Group, Box 39, BBP; Creative Reading of Newspapers, Hosiery Workers Group, Box 39, BBP; Peter M. Pizzola, "Union Social Activity and Worker Unity in Depression-Era Philadelphia" (Ph.D. diss., Lehigh University, 2004).

23. Essays on the topic "Liberal Education vs. Propaganda," November 4, 1934, Box 39, BBP; Pizzola, "Union Social Activity"; John W. Edelman, *Labor Lobbyist: The Autobiography of John W. Edelman*, ed. Joseph Carter (Indianapolis: Bobbs-Merrill, 1974).

24. *Pressoff Special*, October 10, 1933; *Hosiery Worker*, September 15, 1933. The great opera tenor Mario Lanza was also growing up in working-class Philadelphia during these years. Derek Mannering, *Mario Lanza: Singing to the Gods* (Jackson: University Press of Mississippi, 2005).

25. I borrow "laboring of culture" from Michael Denning, *The Cultural Front: The Laboring of American Culture in the Twentieth Century* (London: Verso, 1996).

26. *Hosiery Worker*, December 4, 1931, December 11, 1931, April 29, 1932, May 13, 1932.

27. *Hosiery Worker*, February 12, 1932, February 26, 1932, March 4, 1932.

28. *Hosiery Worker*, March 26, 1932, May 20, 1932.

29. *Hosiery Worker*, April 22, 1932; "Brookwood Labor College Traveling Troupe," pamphlet, n.d., JEP.

30. *Hosiery Worker*, April 22, 1932, May 11, 1932, August 12, 1932; "Third Corps Area—Summary of the Intelligence Situation," February 1, 1934, p. 2, MID; *Trade Union News*, May 6, 1932.

31. *Pressoff Special*, April 9, 1933.

32. *Pressoff Special*, May 10, 1934, July 10, 1934, April 11, 1935.

33. Interview with Howard Kreckman.

34. Proceedings, Nineteenth Annual Convention, September 1930, p. 65, Box 24, AFHWR.

35. *Hosiery Worker*, May 15, 1930, May 31, 1930, October 15, 1930.

36. *Hosiery Worker*, October 15, 1930.

37. *Hosiery Worker*, October 30, 1930.

38. Ibid.; *Hosiery Worker*, November 29, 1930, December 15, 1930; *Union Labor Record*, December 2, 1932.

39. *Hosiery Worker*, February 12, 1932.

40. The Conference for Progressive Labor Action was founded in May 1929 by 33 unions, labor educators, members of the League for Industrial Democracy and the Young People's Socialist League, as a challenge to the conservative unionism of the AFL leadership. In June, the members elected A. J. Muste as chair, Carl Holderman of the AFFFHW and hosiery union supporter James Maurer, as vice chairs. Leilah Danielson, *American Gandhi, A. J. Muste and the History of Radicalism in the Twentieth Century* (Philadelphia: University of Pennsylvania Press, 2014), 124; *Hosiery Worker*, January 22, 1932, February 25, 1932.

41. Interview with Howard Kreckman; *Union Labor Record*, December 2, 1932; *Hosiery Worker*, August 6, 1932.

42. *Hosiery Worker*, July 1, 1932, July 29, 1932, August 6, 1932. The shantytowns of homeless people that sprang up in many places throughout the country during the Great Depression were known as "Hoovervilles."

43. "Eviction Causes Near Riot," *Philadelphia Tribune*, June 1, 1933; "Fists, Furniture and China Fly as Communists Battle Police Who Evict Tenant," *Philadelphia Tribune*, February 4, 1932.

44. *Union Labor Record*, December 2, 1932.

45. *Hosiery Worker*, February 3, 1933; *Union Labor Record*, November 13, 1933.

46. Proceedings, Twenty-First Annual Convention, September 1932, Box 25, AFHWR; Danielson, *American Gandhi*, 144.

47. Interview with Howard Kreckman; Robert S. McElvaine, *The Great Depression: America, 1929–1941* (New York: Times Books, 1983), 174.

48. The historian Rosemary Feurer identified a movement by the United Electrical Workers (UE) in St. Louis that she called "civic unionism." Building on the struggles of the unemployed in the 1930s, activists, particularly Communists, in the UE "used the concepts of 'human rights over property rights' and 'civic unionism' to express goals that sought to connect work-place and community concerns; challenge management rights; mitigate social divisions based on skill, gender, and race; and suggest that workers might have a role in planning for a local and national economy." Rosemary Feurer, *Radical Unionism in the Midwest, 1900–1950* (Urbana: University of Illinois Press, 2006), introduction; G. D. H. Cole, *What Marx Really Meant* (New York: Knopf, 1934), 169.

49. "Many Rioters Hurt in Radical Rallies," *Philadelphia Public Ledger*, March 7, 1930. Of particular interest in the article were descriptions of the Washington demonstration, in which the use of such terms as "mob," "vicious," and "sorry spectacle" clearly expressed the racist bias of the paper. For work on William Foster, see Edward P. Johanningsmeier, *Forging American Communism: The Life of William Z. Foster* (Princeton, N.J.: Princeton University Press, 1994).

50. "Why 1400 Aberle Workers Quit 'Good Jobs,'" broadside signed by Local 706, Branch 1, Box 1, AFHWR.

51. Interview with Griggs Pierce, in Palmer, *Union Tactics*, 160.

52. *Hosiery Worker*, January 15, 1930, January 31, 1930; interview with Griggs Pierce, in Palmer, *Union Tactics*, 160.

53. *Hosiery Worker*, February 28, 1930, March 15, 1930; interview with Howard Kreckman.

54. *Hosiery Worker*, February 28, 1930, March 15, 1930.

55. Interview with Howard Kreckman; "Youth Killed and 2 Shot as Strike-Breakers Fire On Car of Union Backers," *Philadelphia Record*, March 7, 1930.

56. *Hosiery Worker*, March 15, 1930; "Thousands in Throng at Rites for Slain Striker," *Philadelphia Public Ledger*, March 10, 1930; "Hosiery Strikers and Workers Fight," *Philadelphia Evening Bulletin*, March 10, 1930.

57. Palmer, *Union Tactics*, 160; "Thousands in Throng at Rites for Slain Striker."

58. "Thousands in Throng at Rites for Slain Striker"; *Philadelphia Record*, March 10, 1930. The union claimed that there were 70,000 present and that a cortege of twelve hundred cars followed the hearse; *Fortune*, January 1932, 49–108.

59. Interview with Howard Kreckman; *Hosiery Worker*, March 15, 1930.

60. Interview with Howard Kreckman; *Philadelphia Record*, March 11, 1930, emphasis in the original.

61. "A Lesson from the Strike," *Hosiery Worker*, March, 28, 1930; "Aberle Mill Owners Agree to Arbitrate," *Pennsylvania Labor Press*, March 15, 1930; "Real Representation for Aberle Employees Stressed in Decision," *Hosiery Worker*, April 15, 1930; "Aberle Company Refuses to Sign Agreement with Federation," *Hosiery Worker*, September 15, 1930.

62. "Mayor Asked to Sit as Magistrate for Hose Strike Cases," *Philadelphia Record*, April 1, 1931.

63. Palmer, *Union Tactics*, 101; *Hosiery Worker*, August 31, 1931, December 4, 1931, December 23, 1932.

64. Palmer, *Union Tactics*, 103.

65. *Hosiery Worker*, March 16, 1931; Palmer, *Union Tactics*, 113; "Mackey Tells Parley Order Must Be Kept," *Philadelphia Record*, April 10, 1931.

66. "130 Are Jailed in Mill Strike as Schofield Bans Picketing," *Philadelphia Record*, February 19, 1931; "98 Held in Strike Kept at Station," *Philadelphia Bulletin*, March 14, 1931; "Non-union Hosiery Workers in Big Philadelphia Strike," *Trade Union News*, February 20, 1931.

67. "Police Shots Rout Pickets: Women Hurt in Wild Melee," *Philadelphia Record*, March 21, 1931; "Captain Hartley Slugs 76 Strikers; Declares He's Too Lenient," *Trade Union News*, March 13, 1931; "Warriors for a Better World," *Hosiery Worker*, May 15, 1931.

68. "Fifty Are Hurt as Clubs Flail Rioters' Heads," *Philadelphia Record*, March 10, 1931.

69. *Philadelphia Record*, March 10, 1931, March 14, 1931; *Trade Union News*, April 24, 1931; *Philadelphia Bulletin*, March 27, 1931.

70. "Union Hosiery Workers Picket I. Miller Store," *Trade Union News*, April 24, 1931; "Mackey Demands Order," *Philadelphia Record*, April 10, 1931; "Crowd Jeers as Cops Seize More Pickets," *Philadelphia Record*, February 21, 1931; *Philadelphia Record*, March 21, 1931.

71. "Women Menaced as Bomb Explodes at Knitters' Hall," *Philadelphia Record*, April 17, 1931; *Philadelphia Record*, April 4, 1931.

72. "Apex Mill Joins in Hosiery Strike," *Philadelphia Record*, March 19, 1931; Scranton, *Figured Tapestry*; "Fifty Are Hurt as Clubs Flail Rioters' Heads."

73. Fred Knightly to Hon. H. L. Kerwin, Director, Bureau of Conciliation, March 9, 1931, Box 210, File 170-6100, FMCS.

74. Fred Knightly to Hon. H. L. Kerwin, Director, Bureau of Conciliation, April 23, 1931, Box 210, File 170-6100, FMCS.

75. "Crowd Jeers as Cops Seize More Pickets" ; "Big Labor Leaders in Court Today on Contempt Charge," *Philadelphia Record*, April 25, 1931.

76. "Green Assails Schofield," *Hosiery Worker*, February 28, 1931; "Crowd Jeers as Cops Seize More Pickets"; "Pinchot and Mackay Assail Schofield as All Labor Protests," *Hosiery Worker*, February 28, 1931; "Pinchot Hits Police Fight on Strikers," *Philadelphia Record*, February 21, 1931; "Slain Girl Striker Buried as Martyr to Labor's Cause," *Philadelphia Record*, February 28, 1931.

77. *Philadelphia Record*, February 2, 1931, February 28, 1931; *Hosiery Worker*, March 5, 1931.

78. *Hosiery Worker*, April 15, 1931; *New Leader*, May 23, 1931; letter to John Edelman from Pennsylvania Civil Liberties Committee, n.d., Box 4, WIR; "The Case of Alfred Hoffmann," correspondence from Allan G. Harper, Executive Secretary, Pennsylvania Civil Liberties Committee, January 12, 1932, Box 99, JEP; "Conspiracy to Organize Workers in PA," Pennsylvania Civil Liberties Committee, February 1932, Box 99, JEP; *Hosiery Worker*, June 10, 1932.

79. *Philadelphia Record*, April 12, 1931.

80. Proceedings, Twentieth National Convention, September 1931, pp. 945–48, Box 25, AFHWR; Proceedings, Twenty-First National Convention, July 1932, pp. 1405–31, Box 25, AFHWR.

81. Proceedings, Twenty-First National Convention, July 1932, pp. 1405–31, Box 25, AFHWR.

82. Proceedings, Twenty-First Annual Convention, July 1932, pp. 1405–31, Box 25, AFHWR; Proceedings, Twenty-Second Annual Convention, September 1933, pp. 124–25, Box 25, AFHWR.

83. "Philadelphia Strike Inspires Other Trade Unions: Hosiery Workers Stand Out for Aggressive Labor Policies in Time of Depression," *New Leader*, March 28, 1931.

84. *Hosiery Worker*, December 15, 1930.

85. *Labor's News*, February 21, 1931.

86. *Hosiery Worker*, November 20, 1931, November 27, 1931, December 4, 1931.

87. *Hosiery Worker*, February 26, 1932.

88. The Scottsboro Boys were nine African American teenagers accused in Alabama of the gang rape of two white women in 1931. The landmark set of legal cases dealt with racism and the right to a fair trial and included a frame-up and all-white juries. It is considered an example of a grave miscarriage of justice in the legal system. Burge, "The Philadelphia Hosiers' Hectic Years"; *Hosiery Worker*, April 1, 1932, April 4, 1932, May 6, 1932, August 5, 1932.

89. For the conservative aims of workers, see Lizabeth Cohen, *Making a New Deal: Industrial Workers in Chicago, 1919–1939* (Cambridge: Cambridge University Press, 1990); for the Left, see Gary Gerstle, *Working-Class Americanism: The Politics of Labor in a Textile City* (Princeton, N.J.: Princeton University Press, 1989); Michael Kazin, "Struggling with Class Struggle: Marxism and the Search for a Synthesis of U.S. Labor History," *Labor History* 28 (Fall 1987): 502.

90. *Hosiery Worker*, July 22, 1932.

91. *Hosiery Worker*, June 30, 1930, January 29, 1932, February 19, 1932, March 11, 1932. The Communist Party was also building a movement of the unemployed separate from the UCL.

92. *Hosiery Worker*, February 19, 1932, May 4, 1932, July 8, 1932, December 30, 1932; "Governor Heckled in Mass Demonstration," *Philadelphia Bulletin*, March 2, 1932.

93. Interview with Alice Kreckman.

94. *Hosiery Worker*, January 31, 1930; "Socialist Labor Picks City Ticket," *Philadelphia Record*, July 27, 1931.

95. Proceedings, Twenty-First Annual Convention, July 6–18, 1932, pp. 1478–1501, Box 25, AFHWR.

96. *Hosiery Worker*, May 27, 1932.

97. *Hosiery Worker*, March 30, 1930, August 15, 1930, May 12, 1932.

98. *Hosiery Worker*, November 11, 1932; *Philadelphia Record*, November 10, 1932; *Philadelphia Tribune*, November 10, 1932.

99. *Hosiery Worker*, May 5, 1933, August 11, 1933.

100. *Hosiery Worker*, May 13, 1932.

101. Ibid.

102. Melvyn Dubofsky, *The State and Labor in Modern America* (Chapel Hill: University of North Carolina Press, 1994), 38.

Chapter Six

1. The "rival" was William Hutcheson of the Carpenters' Union. Robert Zieger, *The CIO, 1935–1955* (Chapel Hill: University of North Carolina Press, 1995), 2.

2. Ibid.; Nelson Lichtenstein, *State of the Union: A Century of American Labor* (Princeton, N.J.: Princeton University Press, 2002), 88, 89.

3. Zieger, *CIO*, 2.

4. Ibid., 15.

5. For information on other unions active in the 1920s, notably those associated with the Communist-led Trade Union Unity League, see Philip S. Foner, *History of the Labor Movement in the United States*, vol. 9 (New York: International Publishers, 1991). Another example, from Chicago's meatpacking industry, is described in Rick Halpern, *Down on the Killing Floor: Black and White Workers in Chicago's Packinghouses, 1904–54* (Urbana: University of Illinois Press, 1997), chap. 3.

6. Robert S. McElvaine, *The Great Depression: America, 1929–1941* (New York: Three Rivers Press, 1993), 133.

7. Ibid., 156.

8. "No Hope in Voluntary Action by Employers," *Hosiery Worker*, January 13, 1933; "Industry Control Looms," *Hosiery Worker*, April 21, 1933; "Nationwide General Strike Urged," *Hosiery Worker*, March 17, 1933; McElvaine, *The Great Depression*, 135.

9. Arthur M. Schlesinger Jr., *The Coming of the New Deal* (Boston: Houghton Mifflin, 1959); Robert F. Himmelberg, *The Origins of the National Recovery Administration: Business, Government, and the Trade Association Issue, 1921–1933* (New York: Fordham University Press, 1976).

10. *Hosiery Worker*, May 26, 1933.

11. Ibid.; "Organize, Organize, Organize," *Hosiery Worker*, June 2, 1933, July 1, 1933, July 14, 1933.

12. "Unionization and Strikes," *Time*, July 31, 1933; *Hosiery Worker*, May 5, 1933, June 9, 1933, July 1, 1933.

13. "Third Corps Area—Summary of the Intelligence Situation," September 1, 1933, p. 1, Box 3643, File 10634-624, MID.

14. *Hosiery Worker*, June 23, 1933, June 30, 1933; Lawrence Rogin, *Making History in Hosiery: The Story of the American Federation of Hosiery Workers* (Philadelphia: AFHW, 1938), 25; National Executive Committee, May 21, 1933, Box 1, AFHWR.

15. Proceedings, Twentieth Annual Convention, September 1931, p. 1041, Box 24, AFHWR; Proceedings, Twenty-First Annual Convention, September 1932, p. 1405, Box 24, AFHWR. See Staunton Lynd, ed., *"We Are All Leaders": The Alternative Unionism of the Early 1930s* (Urbana: University of Illinois Press, 1996), for a discussion on rank-and-file versus top-down unionism.

16. National Executive Committee, May 21, 1933, Box 1, AFHWR; "Dear Comrade" letter to John Edelman from Organizer, Socialist Party Local, Berks County, September 21, 1936, Box 7, Correspondence and Research, JEP.

17. *Hosiery Worker*, August 10, 1934. See Jacquelyn Dowd Hall et al., *Like a Family: The Making of a Southern Cotton Mill World* (Chapel Hill: University of North Carolina Press, 1987), for a discussion of separation of workers by race. For the Left-led unions and race, see Robert Korstad, *Civil Rights Unionism: Tobacco Workers and the Struggle for Democracy in the Mid-Twentieth Century South* (Chapel Hill: University of North Carolina Press, 2003); Halpern, *Down on the Killing Floor*; Daniel Sidorick, *Condensed Capitalism: Campbell Soup and the Pursuit of Cheap Production in the Twentieth Century* (Ithaca, N.Y.: Cornell University Press, 2009); Judith Stepan-Norris and Maurice Zeitlin, *Left Out: Reds and America's Industrial Unions* (Cambridge: Cambridge University Press, 2003).

18. Don Harris, interviewed by Paul Kelso, Waterloo, Iowa, June 8, 1978, ILHP.

19. "Death of Scab Shops," *A Year of Fighting with the Hosiery Workers* (special newspaper circulated to delegates to the Fiftieth Annual Convention of the American Federation of Labor), 1930, Strike File, Box 1, Folder 1, AFHWR. The Minneapolis strike is also discussed in Elizabeth Faue, *Community of Suffering and Struggle: Women, Men, and the Labor Movement in Minneapolis, 1915–1945* (Chapel Hill: University of North Carolina Press, 1991), 119; "Union Campaigns Sweep City," *Hosiery Worker*, June 30, 1933; *Hosiery Worker*, August 18, 1933; "Unionization and Strikes," *Time*, July 31, 1933.

20. *Hosiery Worker*, May 26, 1933; Federal Writers' Project of the Works Progress Administration for the State of New Jersey, *The WPA Guide to 1930s New Jersey* (New Brunswick, N.J.: Rutgers University Press, 1986).

21. "Hosiery Union Grows Fast 'Spite 'Stools' and Threats," *Hosiery Worker*, July 28 1933; "Union Officials and Picketers Arrested," *Philadelphia Evening Bulletin*, July 24, 1933; "McKeown and Leader Released by Magistrate," *Daily News Record*, July 25, 1933; *Philadelphia Evening Bulletin*, July 12, 1933.

22. Pinchot's "modernity" was also partially defined by fashion, and newspapers often made a point of describing her flamboyant dress when she appeared on the picket lines. *Hosiery Worker*, April 10, 1931, May 11, 1934; "Cornelia Pinchot Accuses Police of Violating Rights of Strikers," *Philadelphia Record*, August 9, 1933; "Mrs. Pinchot Raps Harriman, Lauds Workers," *Hosiery Worker*, August 17, 1934; Karen Sue Mittelman, "A Spirit That Touches the Problems of Today: Women and Social Reform in the Philadelphia Young Women's Christian Association, 1920–1945" (Ph.D. diss., University of Pennsylvania, 1987); Dorothea Browder, "From Uplift to Agitation: Race and Coalition in the Young Women's Christian Association" (Ph.D. diss., University of Wisconsin, Madison, 2008), 48.

23. In Reading, "going along with the president" was to result in the first settlement under the NRA, the Reading Formula. "Hosiery Strike Truce Ordered," *Philadelphia Evening Bulletin*, August 7, 1933; "Strikers Shot by Workers at Cambria Plant," *Philadel-

phia Record, August 31, 1933; "2 Pickets Slain, 20 Hurt in Cambria Strike," *Evening Public Ledger*, August 31, 1933; *Philadelphia Evening Bulletin*, August 31, 1933.

24. "10,000 Mourn Youth Slain in Rioting at Silk Hosiery Mill," *Philadelphia Record*, September 4, 1933; interview with John Edelman and "Tiny" Hoffmann by Constance Williams, Box 5, December 17, 1936, WIR; *Hosiery Worker*, September 8, 1933; Leader to National Executive Committee, November 12, 1933, Box 1, AFHWR.

25. "Hosiery Worker Murdered by Richmond Hill Scab," *Hosiery Worker*, February 8, 1935. The interesting juxtaposition of southern evangelism and militant unionism can also be seen in other places such as those documented by Erik Gellman and Jarod Roll in *The Gospel of the Working Class: Labor's Southern Prophets in New Deal America* (Urbana: University of Illinois Press, 2011).

26. Schlesinger, *The Coming of the New Deal*, 147.

27. *Hosiery Worker*, July 14, 1933; "Union Wins Most Mills in Reading in Secret Balloting," *Hosiery Worker*, August 25, 1933; "NLB to Act on Reading," *Hosiery Worker*, September, 15, 1933; Irving Bernstein, *The Lean Years: A History of the American Worker, 1920–1933* (Boston: Houghton Mifflin, 1960).

28. Schlesinger, *The Coming of the New Deal*, 146–51.

29. "Berks Mills Must Sign Pact," *Hosiery Worker*, September 29, 1933; Schlesinger, *The Coming of the New Deal*, 150, 151; "Workers Vote Stoppages as Manufacturers Defy NLB," *Hosiery Worker*, October 6, 1933; "First Case in Arbitration," *Hosiery Worker*, October 13, 1933.

30. "Reading Labor Shows Might," *Hosiery Worker*, July 14, 1933.

31. "Strike on Job in Reading," *Hosiery Worker*, October, 6, 1933; "Strike on Job Puts Men Back in Lansdale," *Hosiery Worker*, October 27, 1933; "Gandhi Again!," *Hosiery Worker*, November, 3, 1933.

32. Howell John Harris, *Bloodless Victories: The Rise and Fall of the Open Shop in the Philadelphia Metal Trades, 1890–1940* (Cambridge: Cambridge University Press, 2000), 22, 24; Daniel Nelson, *American Rubber Workers and Organized Labor, 1900–1941* (Princeton, N.J.: Princeton University Press, 1988), 133–38.

33. "20,000 Stage 1 Hour Anti-Dolfuss Strike," *Hosiery Worker*, February 23, 1934.

34. Rieve report, National Executive Committee, November 12, 1933, Box 1, AFHWR; Motion by William Leader, National Executive Committee, ibid.; Proceedings, Twenty-Second Annual Convention, September 1933, p. 564, Box 24, AFHWR.

35. "Report from the Convention," *Hosiery Worker*, September 15, 1933; "Labor's New Deal?," *Hosiery Worker*, April 6, 1934.

36. The most comprehensive study of the 1934 textile strike can be found in Janet Irons, *Testing the New Deal: The General Textile Strike of 1934 in the American South* (Urbana: University of Illinois Press, 2000).

37. Philip Scranton, *Figured Tapestry: Production, Markets, and Power in Philadelphia Textiles, 1885–1941* (Cambridge: Cambridge University Press, 1989); *Hosiery Worker*, August 15, 1934. For a detailed explanation of the Bedaux system, see Sidorick, *Condensed Capitalism*.

38. "Textile Strike Makes Many Martyrs," *Hosiery Worker*, September 7, 1934; Irons, *Testing the New Deal*, 2, 4.

39. Motion by O'Driscoll and Leader, National Executive Committee, August 21, 1934, Box 1, AFHWR; *Hosiery Worker*, September 4, 1934; "11,000 out in Georgia, Tenn., N.C. Hosiery Mills," *Hosiery Worker*, September 14, 1934.

40. "5,000 Attend Norwood Rites," *Hosiery Worker*, September 7, 1934.

41. Motion by O'Driscoll and Leader, National Executive Committee, September 8, 1934, Box 1, AFHWR.

42. "Report from Washington," *Hosiery Worker*, August 31, 1934; *Hosiery Worker*, September 18, 1934; Irons, *Testing the New Deal*, 5.

43. *Hosiery Worker*, August 17, 1934, September 14, 1934.

44. *Hosiery Worker*, September 14, 1934; Scranton, *Figured Tapestry*, 485; *Hosiery Worker*, October 27, 1933, August 17, 1934.

45. Report from Edward Callaghan, National Executive Committee, September 8, 1934, Box 1, AFHWR.

46. Irons, *Testing the New Deal*, 10.

47. H. Harris, *Bloodless Victories*, 374.

48. Interview with John Edelman and "Tiny" Hoffmann by Constance Williams; Zieger, *The CIO*; Proceedings, Thirty-Fourth National Convention, February 1946, p. 2, Box 16, AFHWR. For the UE, see also James J. Matles and James Higgins, *Them and Us: Struggles of a Rank-and-File Union* (Englewood Cliffs, N.J.: Prentice-Hall, 1974); Ronald Schatz, *The Electrical Workers: A History of Labor at General Electric and Westinghouse, 1923–1969* (Urbana: University of Illinois Press, 1983); Rosemary Feurer, *Radical Unionism in the Midwest, 1900–1950* (Urbana: University of Illinois Press, 2006); Ronald L. Filipelli and Mark D. McColloch, *Cold War in the Working Class: The Rise and Decline of the United Electrical Workers* (Albany: State University of New York, 1995).

49. Don Harris, interviewed by Merle Davis, August 20, 1982, Tucson, Arizona, ILHP; Howard Kreckman, interview with author, Willingboro, New Jersey, October 7, 8, 1998.

50. "General Baking Company Drivers Strike in Protest," *Kensington News*, July 5, 1935, NCF; "Kensington Homes Bombed in Bakery Strike," *Kensingtonian*, March 27, 1936, NCF; John W. Edelman, *Labor Lobbyist: The Autobiography of John W. Edelman* (Indianapolis: Bobbs-Merrill, 1974), 124, 134, 136, 147; "Mrs. Roosevelt to Speak for Congress Here," *Philadelphia Tribune*, February 3, 1938; "Folk Choir of 100 Voices to Sing at Mrs. F.D.R. Meeting," *Philadelphia Tribune*, February 10, 1938.

51. "1800 Sing and Dance as First Sitdown Strike Occurs Here," *Philadelphia Record*, January 5, 1937; "Philadelphia Unit of CIO Organized by 10 Labor Unions," *Philadelphia Record*, January 14, 1937; "War Chest of $25,000 Raised by Philadelphia CIO Branch," *Philadelphia Record*, January 21, 1937.

52. Letter from John Edelman to Tiny Hoffmann, June 8, 1936, Box 5, JEP.

53. Edelman, *Labor Lobbyist*, 121; Irving Bernstein, *The Turbulent Years: A History of the American Worker, 1933–1941* (Boston: Houghton Mifflin, 1970), 617, 618, 619.

54. Bernstein, *The Turbulent Years*, 618–20; "CIO Votes Textile Drive," *Philadelphia Record*, March 11, 1937; "Brownhill Kramer Sitdown," *Philadelphia Bulletin*, August 25, 1937; *Philadelphia Record*, April 2, 1937, June 25, 1937; Alice Kreckman, interview with author, Willingboro, New Jersey, October 7, 8, 1998.

55. "Battery Workers Join Bolt to CIO," *Philadelphia Record*, March 15, 1937; "85 CIO Delegates Walk Out on CLU at Stormy Meeting," *Philadelphia Record*, March 25, 1937.

56. "May Day Plans Are Completed," *Philadelphia Tribune*, April 9, 1936.

57. Bernstein, *The Turbulent Years*, 622.

58. For current discussions and debates about the changes in direction needed for a revived labor movement—often one that looks remarkably like Branch 1's Kensington of the 1920s and 1930s—see Bill Fletcher Jr. and Fernando Gapasin, *Solidarity Divided: The Crisis in Organized Labor and a New Path toward Social Justice* (Berkeley: University of California Press, 2008), and journals such as *Labor Notes* and *New Labor Forum*.

59. Interview with Howard Kreckman.

60. *Hosiery Worker*, October 27, 1933; Lynd, *"We Are All Leaders."*

61. H. Harris, *Bloodless Victories*, 383–86.

62. Daniel T. Rodgers, *Atlantic Crossings: Social Politics in a Progressive Age* (Cambridge, Mass.: Belknap Press of Harvard University Press, 1998), 386, 391.

63. Ibid., 402; Edelman, *Labor Lobbyist*, 98, 99.

64. Interview with William Jeanes by Nora Piori, September 24, 1936, Box 4, WIR; Gail Radford, *Modern Housing for America: Policy Struggles in the New Deal Era* (Chicago: University of Chicago Press, 1996).

65. Catherine Bauer, *Modern Housing* (New York: Houghton Mifflin, 1934); *Carl Mackley Houses* (brochure), 1934, Box 99, JEP.

66. *Carl Mackley Houses*; interview with William Jeanes by Nora Piori; Radford, *Modern Housing for America*, 132, 133; interview with Howard Kreckman; "Public Housing by and for Labor," n.d. [1940], Box 99, JEP.

67. Radford, *Modern Housing for America*, 132, 133; interview with Alice Kreckman.

68. Margaret Kohn, *Radical Space: Building the House of the People* (Ithaca, N.Y.: Cornell University Press, 2003), 109 and passim; "Mural to Immortalize Slain Striker: Community Housing Project Will Contain Tribute to Mackley," *Philadelphia Record*, April 16, 1934; Piero Santostefano, *Le Mackley Houses di Kastner e Stonorov a Philadelphia* (Rome: Officina Edizioni, 1982).

69. *Mackley Messenger*, May 1936, Box 99, JEP; interview with Howard Kreckman; Radford, *Modern Housing for America*, 137.

70. Jean Coman, associate management supervisor, Housing Division, "Report of Recreation and Welfare Activities of the Carl Mackley Houses, Project No. H-1," July 31 to August 6, 1936, pamphlet no. 245-11, HDWPA.

71. Ibid.; Santostefano, *Le Mackley Houses*; *Hosiery Worker*, October, 15, 1935; interview with Alice Kreckman; "Woman's Club," Box 1, KEP.

72. "Soviet Men Laud Housing Project, 4 Architects in Moscow Mission Visit Construction," *Philadelphia Bulletin*, November 15, 1934; "Public Housing by and for Labor."

73. Coman, "Report of Recreation and Welfare"; "Public Housing by and for Labor."

74. Interview with William Jeanes by Nora Piori; William Jeanes, *Housing of Families of the American Federation of Full-Fashioned Hosiery Workers, Local Nos. 1 and 39* (New York: Kastner and Stonorov, 1932); Edward Bellamy, *Looking Backward: 2000–1887* (Boston: Houghton Mifflin, 1926; first published 1887).

75. For the CIO and post–World War II labor feminism, see Dorothy Sue Cobble, *The Other Women's Movement: Workplace Justice and Social Rights in Modern America* (Princeton, N.J.: Princeton University Press, 2004).

76. "Union Speaks at Bryn Mawr," *Hosiery Worker*, September 15, 1929; *Hosiery Worker*, 1927–40, passim; "Freda Maurer and the WTUL," *Hosiery Worker*, November 20, 1931.

77. On Perkins, see Coman, "Report of Recreation and Welfare"; *Hosiery Worker*, August 3, 1936; Bauer, *Modern Housing* (Boston: Houghton Mifflin, 1934); Bernard J. Frieden and William W. Nash, *Shaping an Urban Future: Essays in Memory of Catherine Bauer Wurster* (Cambridge, Mass.: MIT Press, 1968). On Pinchot, see *Hosiery Worker*, April 10, 1931, May 11, 1934; "Cornelia Pinchot Accuses Police of Violating Rights of Strikers"; "Mrs. Pinchot Raps Harriman, Lauds Workers," *Hosiery Worker*, August 17, 1934; interview with Alice Kreckman; Nancy R. Miller, "Cornelia Bryce Pinchot and the Struggle for Protective Labor Legislation in Pennsylvania," *Pennsylvania Magazine of History and Biography*, 132, no. 1, (January 2008): 33–64.

78. Letter from William Rafsky to Frieda Miller, February 12, 1944, Box 8, AFHWR; letter from William Rafsky to Mary Anderson, July 26, 1945, Box 8, AFHWR. For the Women's Bureau, see also Mark Hendrickson, *American Labor and Economic Citizenship: New Capitalism from World War I to the Great Depression* (New York: Cambridge University Press, 2013), chap. 5.

79. Alice Kessler Harris, *In Pursuit of Equity: How Gender Shaped American Economic Citizenship* (New York: Oxford University Press, 2001), 79. On pay equity, see letter from William Rafsky to Frieda Miller, January 21, 1944; reply, Miller to Rafsky, February 12, 1944; letter from Mary Anderson to Anne Murkovich, July 10, 1945; letter from Anderson to Rafsky, September 5, 1945; letter from Anderson to William Smith, August 1, 1945; Rafsky to Anderson, August 6, 1945; on the ERA, see letter from William Rafsky to Mary Anderson, July 26, 1945; letter from Alexander McKeown to Senator Carl Hayden, June 8, 1953, all in Box 8, Correspondence Files, AFHWR.

80. *Hosiery Worker*, May 1, 1935; "Try New Plan in Milwaukee to Build Union," *Hosiery Worker*, December 4, 1931; "Important Meeting Branch 1," *Hosiery Worker*, October 12, 1933.

81. Union memorandum, Office of the Impartial Chairman, Full-Fashioned Hosiery Industry, "Union Appeal of a Company Policy That Unmarried Female Employees Forfeit Their Jobs upon Marrying," December 2, 1935, Box 4, WIR.

82. "Berks Mill Baron Willing Tool for Nazi Propaganda," *Hosiery Worker*, August 7, 1936.

83. "Nazi Viewpoint at Berkshire," *Reading Labor Advocate*, October 2, 1936; "21 Hurt, Autos Damaged at Launching of Strike against Berkshire Mill," *Reading Labor Advocate*, November 20, 1936; "Pickets Return to Mill Today," *New York Times*, Decem-

ber 1, 1936; "56 Pickets Gassed, Then Sent to Jail," *Chattanooga News*, November 2, 1936; "Strikers to Prostrate Selves at Gates," *Reading Times*, November 30, 1936; "Strikers Lie Down at Gates to Keep Workers Out," *Philadelphia Public Ledger*, November 17, 1936; John Edelman, press release, Box 2, AFHWR; "'Bearing the Cross' for Their Children," *Reading Times*, December 8, 1936; "Gold Star Mother—1937," *Hosiery Worker*, December 18, 1936; "Don't Buy Hosiery Made by Berkshire," broadside, n.d. [1936], Box 2, AFHWR; Proceedings, Twenty-Seventh Annual Convention, May 2–6, 1938, p. 14, Box 2, AFHWR; "In the Matter of Berkshire Knitting Mills and American Federation of Hosiery Workers, Branch #10," Case No. C-385, November 3, 1939, NLRB.

84. Letter to Emily Sims Marconier, National Consumers League, from John Edelman, November 4, 1936, Box 2, AFHWR; telegram from League of Women Shoppers to Edelman, November 16, 1936, Box 2, AFHWR; "Women Picket Woolworth Store in Anti-Berkshire Campaign," *New York Times*, November 15, 1936; letter from Margaret Davis, Proprietor, The White House, to Alfred Hoffmann, November 24, 1936, Box 2, AFHWR.

85. "Labor Riots in Philadelphia, Pa.," June 14, 1937, p. 1, Box 2845, File 10110-2663, MID.

86. Interview with Howard Kreckman; Margaret B. Tinkcom, "Depression and War, 1929–1946," in *Philadelphia: A 300 Year History*, ed. Russell Weigley (New York: W. W. Norton, 1982), 601–48.

87. Reel 27, MIR.

88. Joseph Burge, "The Philadelphia Hosiers' Hectic Years," in author's possession.

89. "5,000 Workers Overwhelm 100 Police and Seize Control of Hosiery Mill," *Philadelphia Record*, May 7, 1937; "18 Hurt as Crowd Battles Police in Seizing Apex Mill," *Philadelphia Bulletin*, May 7, 1937; Burge, "The Philadelphia Hosiers' Hectic Years."

90. Reel 27, MIR.

91. The agent claimed to have attended a "communistic" meeting at the Labor Lyceum in which about one hundred men and twenty women, presided over by one "Rose Rosebush," were taking lessons. He used the term "communistic" freely, and it was often difficult to determine the actual political affiliation of people. "Labor Riots in Philadelphia, Pa.," June 14, 1937, pp. 7, 8.

92. Ibid.

93. Proceedings, Twenty-Seventh Annual Convention, May 2–6, 1938, p. 14, Box 2, AFHWR; "Parties Map New Fight in Apex Strike," *Philadelphia Bulletin*, June 24, 1937; interview with Alice Kreckman.

94. "Labor: Hatters and Hosiers," *Time*, March 27, 1939.

95. Interview with Howard Kreckman; *New York Times*, June 21, 1941.

96. "Union Wins Closed Shop," *Philadelphia Bulletin*, February 21, 1938; interview with Howard Kreckman; *Apex Hosiery Company v. Leader et al.*, 310 U.S. 469, decided May 27, 1940.

97. International Labour Organization, Declaration concerning the Aims and Purposes of the International Labour Organization (adopted May 10, 1944, in Philadelphia), http://blue.lim.ilo.org/cariblex/pdfs/ILO_dec_philadelphia.pdf, accessed May 5, 2016.

98. Burge, "The Philadelphia Hosiers' Hectic Years."

Epilogue

1. Proceedings, Twenty-Ninth Annual Convention, AFHW, June 1940, p. 689, Box 2, AFHWR; Proceedings, Thirtieth Annual Convention, September 1941, Box 2, AFHWR; Proceedings, Thirty-First Annual Convention, June 1942, Box 2, AFHWR; Joseph Burge, "The Philadelphia Hosiers' Hectic Years," in author's possession; "Union Protest of Company's Refusal to Return Evelyn Salvo to Former Knitting Machine," Impartial Chairman Hearing, June 19, 1957, Box 2, AFHWR.

2. "Statement before the Subcommittee of the Joint Congressional Committee on Housing," January 1948, Box 2, AFHWR.

3. Proceedings, Twenty-Ninth Annual Convention, June 1940, p. 7, Box 2, AFHWR; Proceedings, Thirty-Second Annual Convention, May 1943, p. 4, Box 2, AFHWR.

4. "Textile Union to File Non-Communist Oath," *New York Times*, October 6, 1947; Proceedings, Thirty-Sixth Annual Convention, May 1948, p. 1232, Box 16, AFHWR; "CIO Textile Workers Oust Hosiery Rebels," *New York Times*, April 23, 1948; letter from Alex McKeown to Philip Murray, July 8, 1948, Box 7, folder "American Federation of Hosiery Workers," JEP; letters to James Carey supporting AFHW request, various dates, Box 7, folder "American Federation of Hosiery Workers," JEP; "Hosiery Workers in AFL Again," *Minneapolis Star*, August 10, 1951; Proceedings, Thirty-Ninth Annual Convention, May 1951, Box 16, AFHWR.

5. Memo from Aileen Lenk Newman to Fred Held, April 12, 1950, Research and Education, Box 7, AFHWR; memo from Dorothy Garfein to Eileen L. Newman, October 3, 1950, Research and Education, Box 7, AFHWR; Proceedings, Thirty-Fourth National Convention, February 1946, pp. 6, 8, Box 16, AFHWR.

6. Memo from John J. McCoy to Alexander McKeown, September 20, 1950, Folder 1, Box 17, AFHWR. *What Has Happened to the American Federation of Hosiery Workers? A Taft-Hartley Case Study*, Industrial Union Department AFL-CIO, Washington, D.C., n.d. [1957]; David Harvey, *A Brief History of Neoliberalism* (New York: Oxford University Press, 2005); Robert Brenner, *The Economics of Global Turbulence: The Advanced Capitalist Economies from Long Boom to Long Downturn, 1945–2005* (London: Verso, 2006).

7. Proceedings, Thirty-Fourth National Convention, February 1946, p. 2, Box 16, AFHWR. The speaker was Harry Block, also the president of the Philadelphia Council, CIO.

8. Proceedings, Thirty-Fifth National Convention, May 1947, p. 27, Box 2, AFHWR.

9. Howard Kreckman, interview with author, Willingboro, New Jersey, October 7, 8, 1998.

10. "Textiles: Apex Hosiery Quits," *Time*, April 19, 1954; interview with Howard Kreckman; Alice Kreckman, interview with author, Willingboro, New Jersey, October 7, 8, 1998.

11. Interview with Howard Kreckman; interview with Alice Kreckman.

12. Ronald Filipelli and Mark McColloch, *Cold War in the Working Class: The Rise and Decline of the United Electrical Workers* (Albany: State University of New York Press, 1995), 11; Ellen Schrecker, "McCarthyism and Organized Labor: Fifty Years of

Lost Opportunities," *Working USA* 3, no. 5 (January/February 2000): 93–101; interview with Howard Kreckman.

13. Dorothy Sue Cobble, *The Other Women's Movement: Workplace Justice and Social Rights in Modern America* (Princeton, N.J.: Princeton University Press, 2004); Judith Stepan-Norris and Maurice Zeitlin, *Left Out: Reds and America's Industrial Unions* (Cambridge: Cambridge University Press, 2003); Kate Weigand, *Red Feminism: American Communism and the Making of Women's Liberation* (Baltimore: Johns Hopkins University Press, 2002); interview with Alice Kreckman.

14. See David McAllister, "Realtors and Racism in Working-Class Philadelphia, 1945–1970," in *African American Urban History since World War II*, ed. Kenneth L. Kusmer and Joe W. Trotter (Chicago: University of Chicago Press, 2009), 123–41.

15. The October 4th Organization (O4O), was named after an event that occurred on that date in 1779 in which Kensington residents "liberated" hoarded food in a downtown Philadelphia warehouse and redistributed it to hungry people; see Amy Sonnie and James Tracy, *Hillbilly Nationalists, Urban Race Rebels, and Black Power: Community Organizing in Radical Times* (New York: Melville House, 2011).

16. John W. Edelman, *Labor Lobbyist: The Autobiography of John W. Edelman*, ed. Joseph Carter (Indianapolis: Bobbs-Merrill, 1974); "William L. Rafsky, Urban Planner," *Philadelphia Inquirer*, June, 13, 2001; "Emil Rieve, Unionist, Dies," *New York Times*, January 26, 1975; "McKeown, 67 and Ill, Retiring as Head of Once-Great Union He Helped Build," *Sunday Bulletin*, May 5, 1957; interview with Howard Kreckman; interview with Alice Kreckman.

17. Selina Todd, *The People: The Rise and Fall of the Working Class* (London: John Murray, 2014), 408.

Index

Aberle Hosiery Mill, 77–78, 98, 131, 147; strike at, 133, 153–58, 256 (n. 58)
Adams, Henry, 184
Addams, Jane, 126
AFFFHW. *See* American Federation of Full-Fashioned Hosiery Workers / American Federation of Hosiery Workers
AFHW. *See* American Federation of Full-Fashioned Hosiery Workers / American Federation of Hosiery Workers
African Americans: in hosiery and textile industry, 6–7, 28, 29, 60, 233 (n. 42), 239 (n. 36); and hosiery workers' union, 60, 66, 151; in Kensington and Philadelphia, 6, 14–15, 27–29, 224–25; racial riots against, 14, 43, 93; in strike battles, 184, 193; and unemployed movement, 151; and working-class unity, 200
Allegheny Theater, 26, 154
Alternative unionism, 84–85, 208
Amalgamated Clothing Workers of America (ACWA), 171, 182; and CIO, 177, 198; Philadelphia branch of, 246 (n. 60), 246 (n. 66), 251 (n. 39)
American Birth Control League, 54, 114–15, 140
American Federation of Full-Fashioned Hosiery Workers / American Federation of Hosiery Workers: centralization in, 136, 195; and CIO, 177–78, 197–98, 198–99; community-based approach of, 8, 87, 134, 137, 138, 139–40, 148–49, 153, 201, 244 (n. 48); community services offered by, 139–40; constitution of, 58, 59, 60, 191; democratic decision making in, 52, 58–59, 220; educational programs of, 89–94, 114, 119–20, 143–44, 187, 245–46 (n. 59); entertainment programs of, 144–47; feminized iconography of, 8, 127–28; as "fighting" union, 57–58, 60, 67, 134, 226; founding of, 41, 44; health care clinics of, 139–40; as independent union, 42; intergenerational relations in, 79, 88–89; Kensington as center of power of, 4–5; leaders of, 52–56; legacy of, 216–18, 225–26; library and reading rooms of, 92–93, 143; and McCarthyite witch-hunt, 220, 223–24; McKeown becomes president of, 208, 209, 219; membership of, 5, 98–99, 105, 170; name change, 182; and national labor agreement, 134, 135–36, 158–60, 254 (n. 10); and national women's organizations, 114, 115, 141, 207–9; and New Deal, 178, 181, 182, 201–7; organizing drives of, 62–68, 182–83, 184–86; postwar decline of, 219; and public housing, 202–6, 207, 220; rank-and-file involvement in, 58, 86, 178, 201; resolutions on women, 129–31, 165–66; Rieve-Geisinger rift in, 172, 182–84; rights-based language of, 8, 101, 109; social activities of, 94–96, 143; socialist ideology in, 5, 58–59; and Socialist Party, 6, 8, 39–40, 52, 53, 54, 55, 172, 173–74, 238 (n. 21); solidarity as hallmark of, 6, 8, 52, 60–61, 62, 66, 96–97, 137, 148–49, 150–51; special

American Federation of Full-Fashioned Hosiery Workers (cont.)
  women's meetings in, 117–18, 131; and struggle against racism, 6–7, 93, 184, 220; support for women's rights by, 103–4, 113–14, 131–32, 207–8, 209–11; and Taft-Hartley Act, 221–22; treasury of, 57–58, 137; and TWUA affiliation, 221, 223; and unemployed movement, 149–50, 168–69, 171; and UTWA Local 706, 50; women and executive board in, 59, 118, 129, 165–67, 210; women's role in, 113–20, 129–31, 165–66; and working-class unity, 87, 200, 244 (n. 48); and workplace control, 45–46, 81–83, 101, 150; youth militants in, 7–8, 70; youth recreation programs of, 140–41. *See also Hosiery Worker*; Organizing drives; Strikes
  —Branch 1: as center of hosiery union, 59, 69; community approach of, 8, 87, 134, 138, 139–40, 148–49, 153, 201, 244 (n. 48); educational programs of, 92–93, 143–47, 245–46 (n. 59); executive board of, 55, 59, 60, 103, 118, 129; headquarters of, 41; health care clinics of, 139–40; industrial organization of, 52; membership of, 67, 98–99, 105; radical slate in, 160; rank-and-file involvement in, 52, 86, 178, 201; reunites with UTWA Local 706, 42, 43, 50; Rieve conflict with, 191–92, 193, 195–96, 200–201, 202, 208, 220; and Socialist Party, 52, 53–54, 172, 173–74; social life of, 94–96, 143; special women's meetings of, 87–88, 117–18, 244 (n. 52); street meetings held by, 86–87; women's division in, 131; youth recreation programs of, 140–41
  —national conventions: of 1922, 62; of 1926, 65, 99, 115; of 1927, 94, 115; of 1928, 91, 128, 129–31; of 1929, 136; of 1930, 148; of 1931, 165–66; of 1932, 166–67; 172–73; of 1933, 166, 191; of 1940, 220; of 1946, 221, 222

American Federation of Iron, Steel, and Tin Workers, 198
American Federation of Labor (AFL), 28, 133, 152, 170, 174–75; and CIO, 176–77, 200; and hosiery workers' union, 42, 177–78, 221
American Federation of Musicians, 190
American Federation of Radio Workers, 188, 196–97
American Federation of Teachers, 198
Anderson, Mary, 119, 129, 209, 250 (n. 32)
Anderson, Sherwood, 161
Annesley, Clare, 119, 173
Apex Hosiery Co. v. Leader, 5, 179, 212, 216
Apex Hosiery strike (1937), 212–16, 219, 265 (n. 91)
Asch, Sholom, 146
Atlantic Crossings (Rodgers), 11
Atlantic Monthly, 69, 84

Bachman, Alberta, 163–64
Baldanzi, George, 199
Barkas, Benjamin, 143
Barney, William Pope, 203
Battery Workers Union, 198
Bauer, Catherine, 207, 209
Bauman, John, 139
Beauty contests, 121–22, 251 (n. 47)
Bellamy, Edward, 207
Bennett, Josephine and Martin, 245 (n. 56)
Benson, Susan Porter, 18–19, 111
Berkshire Mills, 192; national boycott of, 208, 212; organizing drive at, 63–64; strikes at, 188–89, 211–12
Billings, Warren, 61, 239 (n. 39)
Birth control, 114–15, 140, 250 (n. 28)
Black, Hugo, 180
Black bottom, 96, 246 (n. 71)
Block, Harry, 197
Bombings, 43–44, 125–26

Bonus March, 169, 179
Bow, Clara, 110
Branch 1. *See* American Federation of Full-Fashioned Hosiery Workers / American Federation of Hosiery Workers
Brookwood Labor College, 90–91, 117, 187, 245 (n. 56)
Brookwood Labor Players, 146
Brownhill and Kramer Hosiery, 98, 99, 122, 199
Bryn Mawr Summer School for Women, 89–90, 117, 187, 245 (n. 55)
Budget, working-class, 19–21, 231–32 (n. 22)
Burge, Joseph, 143, 204, 213, 217, 220; as Branch 1 leader, 56, 160, 195; as CIO organizer, 197–98; later history of, 223–24
Burge, Margaret, 204
Burns, Lucy, 109
Butler, Judith, 85
Butler, Smedley, 71

Callaghan, Edward, 156, 171; as strike organizer, 65, 66, 125; as union leader, 53–54
Callahan, Jeanne, 49; childhood recollections of, 20, 25, 30, 71–72, 81, 107, 140
Callahan, Joseph, 27
Cambria strike (1933), 186–88
Camden, N.J., 12
Canada, 64
Carey, James, 196
Carl Mackley Houses, 178, 202–6, 209, 220
Carnegie, Andrew, 156, 233 (n. 42)
Carpet Workers Union, 198
Carter, John F., 69
Casement, Roger, 238 (n. 26)
Central Labor Union (CLU), Philadelphia, 40, 143, 154, 171, 200, 236 (n. 73)

Chanel, Gabrielle "Coco," 110
Chicago, Ill., 124, 126, 127
Childcare, 119–20
Children in workforce, 18, 21, 140
Children's Crusade (1903), 38
Christianson, Edith, 115, 129
Churches, 24–26
Class legislation, 165, 167, 211
Cloth, Hat, Cap, and Millinery Workers, 182
Coal "bootlegging," 32, 148, 152–53
Cobble, Dorothy Sue, 224, 248 (n. 3)
Cohen, Lizabeth, 51–52
Cole, G. D. H., 153
Communists, 153, 173, 256 (n. 48); in hosiery union, 52, 55–56, 220, 238 (n. 21); and unemployed movement, 150, 171
Community: Branch 1 approach to, 8, 87, 134, 138, 139–40, 148–49, 153, 201, 244 (n. 48); culture of, 34, 80–81; networks of, 21, 30–31, 51, 142, 147–48, 152–53; support to hosiery workers from, 51
Conboy, Sara Agnes, 123
Conference for Progressive Labor Action (CPLA), 150, 255 (n. 40)
Congress of Industrial Organizations (CIO): and AFL, 176–77, 200; anticommunist purges by, 220–21, 225; and hosiery workers' union, 5, 197–98, 201, 221; message of, 200; Philadelphia branch of, 198–99, 200; and TWOC, 199–200; and UE, 196, 197, 198, 225
Connor, Jane, 25, 26, 29, 30, 75, 142
Connor, Margaret, 18
Contracts, written, 59
Control, workplace, 45–46, 81–83, 101, 150, 243 (n. 33)
Cooke, Edwin, 37
Corbin, David, 97
Cotton, William, 15, 19, 231–32 (n. 22)
Cramp Shipyard, 46, 50

Crawford, Joan, 110, 126
Cripples, 146
Crosswaith, Frank, 174
Crusade for Human Rights, 120
Culture, 106; community, 34, 80–81; fashion, 111–12; flapper, 2, 39, 110–11; labor, 70, 72, 83–84, 96–97, 101, 111; mass and popular, 72, 75–76, 110–11, 127, 145, 241 (n. 9); union programs in, 144–45; of unity, 72, 241 (n. 9); work, 31, 79–81, 111, 121–22; youth, 75–76, 77–79, 80–81, 110–11, 112

Dances, 95, 96, 121
Danton, 145
Darrow, Clarence, 126
Davis, Jeff, 88
Debs, Eugene, 40, 243 (n. 37)
De Jarnette, A. L., 188
De Schweinitz, Dorothea, 81
Detective agencies, 99, 155
De Valera, Eamon, 169
Didrikson, Babe, 109
Direct action, 149–50, 191, 200, 202, 211
Doyle, Michael Francis, 204, 238 (n. 26)
Dubinsky, David, 177
Dubofsky, Melvyn, 175
Dues check-off, 160
Dumenil, Lynn, 75
Durham, N.C., 7, 65–67, 184, 193

Earhart, Amelia, 109–10
Edelman, John, 99, 171, 172, 197, 199; biographical information, 55, 238 (n. 26); and CIO, 197, 198; as McCarthyism victim, 225; as newspaper editor, 93, 152; and public housing, 202–3, 207; in strike battles, 64, 66, 67, 125; as supporter of women's rights, 112–13; and women's organizations, 114, 128–29; on "youth militant," 100
Ederle, Gertrude, 109

Education: public, 72–73; within union, 88, 89–94, 114, 119–20, 143–44, 187, 245–46 (nn. 59–60)
Engels, Friedrich, 13, 93
Enstad, Nan, 112, 249 (n. 18)
Equal pay, 119, 209, 210
Equal Rights Amendment (ERA), 116, 210, 250–51 (n. 32)
Ethical Society, 35
Ethnic shops, 72

Faber, or The Lost Years (Wassermann), 112
Faludi, Susan, 104
Fashion and dress: flapper clothing, 4, 69, 75, 110; women's, 74–75, 110, 111–12, 116, 141–42, 249 (n. 18)
Femininity, 33–34, 74
Feminism: 1920s narrative of, 104; second-wave, 224. *See also* Labor feminism
Ferrell, John, 14
Feurer, Rosemary, 256 (n. 48)
Filipelli, Ronald, 224
Firestone, Shulamith, 104
Fitzgerald, F. Scott, 4, 229 (n. 8)
Flapper clothing and culture, 4, 39, 69, 75, 110–11
Flexner, Eleanor, 248 (n. 14)
Foster, William Z., 153
Frey, Marion, 65
Friends of Soviet Russia, 61
Full-fashioned hosiery, 15–16. *See also* Hosiery industry
Full-Fashioned Hosiery Manufacturers Association (FHMA), 44–45, 47, 49–50, 51

Gandhi, Mohandas K., 64, 93, 163, 169, 190, 211
Gandhi strikes, 190, 191, 211
Geiges, Gustave, 62, 115; on education, 90, 91, 245 (n. 54); resigns as union president, 54, 136; on strikes and

organizing drives, 57, 98; as union president, 53
Geisinger, Anna, 117, 119, 171, 172, 194; on importance of women's issues, 103–4; as key union leader, 55, 118, 165; Rieve firing of, 183–84; in strikes and organizing drives, 125, 163, 182–83, 185; on women's role in union, 129–30, 166; and Women's Trade Union League, 118, 208
Gender roles and identity, 7, 32–34, 74, 105, 109
General Textile Strike (1934), 192–93, 194–95, 196
Georgia Nigger (Spivak), 143
Germany, 40, 61; Nazis in, 141, 211
Gibran, Kahlil, "On Marriage," 132
Giovanitti, Arturo, 174
Girard Smelting and Refining Company, 190–91
Glenn, Susan, 81
Goebbels, Joseph, 211
Golden Mountain, 145
Goldman, Emma, 250 (n. 28)
Gordon, Eleanor, 33
Gordon, Linda, 250 (n. 28)
Gorky, Maxim, 145
Gotham Hosiery, 47, 53, 55, 95
Gramsci, Antonio, 80, 83, 243 (n. 36)
Great Depression, 134, 137–39, 141–42; defense of community during, 137–38, 152–53; impact on hosiery industry of, 139, 159; "no evictions" campaign during, 150–51, 152; unemployed struggle during, 148–51, 168–69, 171
Green, William, 133, 163, 170–71, 180–81, 191
Grew, Elizabeth, 115
Gunther, Robert, 27, 28, 35–36; childhood reminiscences of, 25, 29, 31–32, 33, 140

Hall, Jacquelyn Dowd, 104, 249 (n. 18)
Hall, Tobias, 89
Hanson, Alice, 141, 173
Harding, Warren, 97
Harris, Alice Kessler, 209–10
Harris, Don, 184, 197
Harris, Howell John, 190
Hays, Arthur Garfield, 92
Health care, 139–40
Hearst, William Randolph, 205
Hepburn, Katharine, 116
Hillman, Sidney, 172, 177, 183
Hinton, James, 82, 243 (n. 33)
Hoffman, Freda, 117
Hoffmann, Alfred "Tiny," 91, 186; biographical information, 55; jailing of, 163, 164, 167; organizing in South by, 65, 66
Holderman, Carl, 53, 54, 136, 197, 255 (n. 40)
Holmes, Jesse, 92
Homelessness, 138–39
Homosexuality, 116–17
Hoover, Herbert, 180
Hoovervilles, 151, 255 (n. 42)
Hosiery industry: African Americans in, 6–7, 28, 29, 60, 233 (n. 42), 239 (n. 36); contraction of in 1930s, 134–35, 139, 159; expansion of in 1920s, 4–5, 38, 56–57, 62–63, 70, 76–77; eyestrain of workers in, 77, 140; history of, 15, 16; Kensington and, 13–14, 29–30, 38–39, 69, 221–22; national labor agreement for, 134, 135–36, 158–60, 254 (n. 10); postwar decline of, 221–22; proprietary capitalists in, 13, 16–17; wages in, 18, 31, 44, 56–57, 77, 159; working conditions in, 13, 17, 44, 46, 82, 103, 184, 186. *See also* Full-fashioned hosiery
Hosiery Worker, 16, 109, 141, 174–75, 181, 209; advertisements in, 71, 76; on culture and arts, 145–46, 147; educational role of, 88, 90, 93–94; Mooney column for, 164; on need for

Hosiery Worker (cont.)
  working-class action, 85–86, 149–50, 168–70; on "no evictions" campaign, 150–51, 152; strike coverage in, 48, 57, 66, 67, 124, 126, 127, 154, 156, 161, 163, 193; on women's issues and involvement, 104, 116, 120–21, 122–23, 124, 161, 210
Housing: in Philadelphia, 150–51; public, 178, 202–6, 207, 209, 220, 226. *See also* "No evictions" campaign
Human rights, 152, 153, 256 (n. 48)

Identity: gender, 7, 32–34, 74, 105, 109; union and working-class, 34, 36, 70, 100–101, 107–8, 122, 138, 224
Independent Labor Party, 96–97, 171–73
Industrial Union Department, AFL-CIO, 221–22
Industrial unionism, 52, 101
Industrial Workers of the World, 28, 44, 52
Injunctions, 46, 63, 99–100, 125, 126, 154, 186
Insurance, 19, 61–62, 232 (n. 23)
Intergenerational relations, 79, 88–89
International Federation of Working Women, 248 (n. 3)
International Labor Organization, 199, 217
International Ladies Garment Workers Union, 62, 97, 177, 182, 198
International Pocketbook Makers Union, 182
Interracial marriage, 30
Iowa, 184–85
Irish Republicans, 36, 169
Irons, Janet, 195

Jailed for Freedom (Stevens), 108
Jeanes, William, 207
A Jew at War (Roshal), 145
Jews, 21, 142
"Jewtown," 27, 233 (n. 39)

Job security, 119, 135
Johnson, Amy, 109–10
Johnson, Lyndon B., 226
Jones, Mary Harris "Mother," 16, 38

Karl Marx Singing Society, 40
Kastner, Alfred, 203, 207
Katz, Daniel, 97
Keeney, Chuck, 2
Keeney, Frank, 173–74
Kenosha, Wis., 64, 124–27, 134
Kensington: African Americans in, 14–15, 27–29, 224–25; churches in, 24–25; cultural and neighborhood networks in, 21, 30–31, 32, 51; ethnic diversity of, 14, 21, 23–25, 26–27, 72, 73–74, 232 (n. 27), 241 (n. 13); Great Depression's impact on, 139, 141–42; homelessness in, 138–39; hosiery industry in, 13–14, 29–30, 38–39, 69, 221–22; identity of, 3–4, 31, 34–35; Knights of Labor in, 1, 16, 37–38; labor feminism in, 106–12; as labor union center, 4–5, 13, 34–35, 38; landscape of, 21; in late twentieth century, 219, 224–25; living conditions in, 17; Mackley funeral procession in, 133, 156–57, 256 (n. 58); mass transit system in, 21, 23, 72, 73; Philco plant in, 196–97; population of, 14; public education in, 72–73; riots in, 14, 37; row houses in, 23, 24; solidarity traditions in, 39, 51, 113, 150–51; stereotypes of, 2–3; stores, restaurants, and taverns in, 24, 72, 142; theaters in, 26, 76, 145, 146; traditions of resistance in, 34–38, 39; working-class family budgets in, 19–21. *See also* Philadelphia, Pa.
Kensington Labor Lyceum, 118, 146, 162–63, 215
Kensington Small Businessmen's Association, 39
Kensington Welfare Rights Organization, 225

Kitch, Carolyn, 249 (n. 18)
Knights of Labor, 1, 16, 37–38, 96; and women, 38, 106, 114, 210
Knitters, 15, 43, 47, 131
Know-Nothing riots, 2, 14
Kohn, Margaret, 204
Kornfeld, Ernest, 173
Kreckman, Alice Nelson, 72, 116–17, 138–39, 209; anticlericalism of, 25–26; on anticommunist witch hunt, 223–24; on female cultural network, 32, 70–71, 75, 77; gets job at mill, 8–9, 18, 29; in later years, 223, 226; and Mackley House, 204, 206; parents of, 30, 33, 80; union activities of, 118, 150, 171, 215; union identity of, 34, 107–8, 122, 224; and YWCA, 116, 117
Kreckman, Howard, 8–9, 43, 86, 138–39, 150, 160, 224; on capitalism and socialism, 40, 223; goes to work at mill, 11, 18, 29; later history of, 223, 226; and Mackley Houses, 204, 205; on neighborly networks, 32, 80–81, 148, 152; parents of, 30, 33, 75; and religion, 25–26, 141; and strike battles, 44, 45, 155, 156, 213, 215; on union education program, 92, 245–46 (n. 59); on union identity, 36, 70, 101, 122

Labor culture, 70, 72, 83–84, 96–97, 101, 111
Labor education, 88, 89–94, 143–44, 245–46 (nn. 59–60)
Labor feminism, 210, 224; history and development of, 38, 101–2, 105; hosiery workers' union and, 178, 207–12; in Kensington, 106–12. *See also* Women
Labor Housing Conference, 206–7
Labor Institute, 92, 93
Labor party, 96–97, 171–73, 194
Labor plays, 145–46
Labor schools, 89–91
Labor's News, 101, 158

Lanza, Mario, 254 (n. 24)
Leacock, Eleanor Burke, 122
Lead, Oil, Varnish and Paint Makers Union, 190–91
Leader, William, 144–45, 186, 192, 195; and Apex strike, 213, 215; and Philadelphia CIO, 198–99
League of Women Shoppers, 187, 212
Le Corbusier, 203
Lenglen, Suzanne, 109
Lenin, V. I., 82, 237 (n. 6)
Levine, Susan, 32, 106
Lewis, John L., 94, 176–77
Like a Family (Dowd Hall et al.), 65
Lindley, Ernest K., 180
Little, Esther Louise, 19, 231–32 (n. 22)
Looking Backward (Bellamy), 207
Looping, 15, 59
Lowell, Mass., 13
Luddites, 15, 215, 230 (n. 12)
Lundeen bill, 209–10

Mackley, Carl, 133, 153, 155–57, 158
Makin, John, 1, 16, 37, 88
Marion, N.C., 118–19
Marshall Field and Company, 82
Martyrs: from Aberle strike, 133, 153, 155–57, 158; from Cambria strike, 187–88; from Mammoth strike, 163–64; from southern textile strike, 188, 193
Marx, Karl, 93
Mass culture. *See* Popular and mass culture
The Masses, 114
Maugham, Somerset, *Rain*, 76
Maurer, Freda, 18, 81, 113, 117, 208
Maurer, James, 55, 171, 255 (n. 40); biographical information, 54; and birth control, 54, 114–15, 140; as Socialist candidate, 54, 63–64, 173; and workers' education, 54, 90, 92, 245 (n. 56)
McCall, Fred, 199

McCarthyism, 223–24, 225
McColloch, Mark, 224
McElvaine, Robert, 152–53
McGirr, Lisa, 41
McGrady, Edward, 133, 156, 174–75
McKeown, Alexander, 54, 136, 148, 221, 226; biographical information, 53; as national union president, 208, 209, 219; and Northeast Progressive League, 154, 171–72; and Rieve, 191, 195, 220; as Socialist and labor party advocate, 53, 172–73, 174, 220; and strike battles, 163, 186, 215–16, 222–23
McMahon, Thomas, 64, 177
McPherson Square, 133, 156, 157, 165, 171, 188, 205
Meyer, William, 50, 212, 213
Mickenberg, Julia, 248 (n. 3)
Milfay Company, 123
Miller, Frieda, 209
Mill Shadows (Tippett), 146
Milnor, Frank, 187–88
Montgomery, David, 36; "The Shuttle and the Cross," 2
Mooney, Tom, 61, 146, 164, 167, 239 (n. 39)
Moore, J. Hampton, 46
Morehouse, Ward, 76
Morgan, Carol, 7
Movies, 76, 110, 142, 145
Movie theaters, 26, 76, 145
Mowitz, Arno, 163
Music, 145, 146–47
Muste, A. J., 163–64, 245 (n. 46), 255 (n. 40)

National Association of Manufacturers (NAM), 42, 47
National Consumers League, 212
National Industrial Recovery Act (NIRA), 5, 178, 179, 181–82, 188
National Labor Board (NLB), 179, 188–89, 191

National Labor Relations Act (Wagner Act), 189, 198
National Recovery Administration (NRA), 181–82, 187, 189, 192, 201
National Women's Party, 108, 116, 248 (n. 14)
Nearing, Scott, 40, 236 (n. 72), 243 (n. 37)
Networks, social and cultural: community and neighborly, 21, 30–31, 51, 142, 147–48, 152–53; of women, 30, 32, 70–71, 75, 77
New Deal: hosiery workers union and, 178, 181, 201–7; legislation of, 178, 181–82, 201; Rieve support for, 181, 189, 193–94, 201
New Leader, 167–68
"No evictions" campaign, 150, 151, 152
Northeast Progressive League, 154, 171–72
Norwood, Clement, 187–88, 193
Norwood, Stephen, 247–48 (n. 2)
Nottinghamshire, England, 15, 16

Oberlaender, Gustave, 211
October 4th Organization, 225, 267 (n. 15)
O'Driscoll, Leo, 192
Oestreicher, Richard, 96
Opera, 144, 254 (n. 24)
Organizing drives, 62–68; appeals to women in, 104; imaginative techniques in, 83; in Kenosha, 64, 124; in Philadelphia, 185; in Reading, 63–64, 132, 178, 185; in South, 64–67; in southern New Jersey, 185–86; youth participation in, 98
Otto, Samuel G., 199
Outings, 95–96

Palmer, Bryan, 84
Palmer, Gladys, 36
Paterson, N.J., 121, 244 (n. 51)

Paul, Alice, 108–9
Penn, William, 12
Pennsylvania Federation of Labor, 64, 163
Pensions, 61–62
Perkins, Frances, 206, 208–9
Philadelphia, Pa.: African Americans in, 6, 14, 28–29, 224–25; Central Labor Union in, 40, 143, 154, 171, 200, 236 (n. 73); CIO in, 198–99, 200; history of, 12; housing situation in, 150–51; immigration to, 11, 13–14, 18, 21, 23–24, 73–74, 139; mass transit in, 21–22, 72; population of, 14, 224; Prohibition enforcement in, 3, 71–72; "proprietary" capitalism in, 13, 17; as "Scab City," 17; Socialist Party in, 40, 168–69, 172, 173–74, 180; strikes in, 38, 185, 186–88, 187–88, 190–91, 198–99, 201–2, 212–16; textile and hosiery industry in, 12–13, 223; theaters in, 26, 76, 145, 147; transatlantic associations of, 11–12; transformed from commercial to industrial city, 12, 40; unemployed movement in, 148–51, 168–69; unemployment in, 139; women in workforce of, 32. *See also* Kensington
Philadelphia Bulletin, 213
Philadelphia Labor College, 101, 120
Philadelphia Record, 39, 155, 157, 161, 188
Philadelphia Workers Education Project, 92
Philco radio and electrical plant, 196–97
Piedmont Organizing Council, 65–66
Pilot, Wanda, 199
Pinchot, Cornelia Bryce, 115, 119, 187, 209, 260 (n. 22)
Pinchot, Gifford, 163, 164, 171
Pinski, David, 146
Pioneer Youth Club, 140
Plush Workers' Union, 198
Police violence, 46, 48, 99, 100–101, 160–61, 162, 186

Popular and mass culture, 110–11, 127, 145, 241 (n. 9); representation of women in, 75–76; young people and, 72
Precedent, 146
Pressoff Special, 26, 27, 77–78, 131, 141, 142
Preston, Evelyn, 245 (n. 56)
Prohibition, 3, 71–72
Public education, 72–73
Public housing, 178, 202–6, 207, 209, 220, 226
Public Works Administration (PWA), 5, 178, 202

Rafsky, William, 225–26
Randolph, A. Philip, 198
Rand School, 89
Rapp, Rayna, 249 (n. 18)
Rationalism, 35
Reading, Pa., 195, 219; labor parades in, 190, 194; organizing activities in, 63–64, 178, 182, 185; strikes in, 63, 188–89, 211–12
Reading Formula, 5, 178, 179, 189, 201–2, 260 (n. 23)
Religion, 24–26, 141
"Responsible" unionism, 208
Rieve, Emil, 183, 199; biographical information, 54; Branch 1 conflict with, 191–92, 193, 195–96, 200–201, 202, 208, 220; and CIO, 199, 200; elected hosiery union president, 53, 54, 136; and expulsion of AFHW, 220–21; Geisinger tensions with, 172, 183–84; and labor party question, 172, 173; New Deal supported by, 181, 189, 193–94, 201; opposition to women's rights resolution, 166; and strike battles, 158, 187, 195
Riots: anti-railroad, 37; Know-Nothing, 2, 14; racial, 14, 43, 93
Ripka, Joseph, 13
Rizzo, Frank, 225
Rodgers, Daniel, 11, 202

Roosevelt, Eleanor, 198
Roosevelt, Franklin D., 175, 180, 193, 214–15, 220; New Deal program of, 178, 181
Roshal, Grigori, 145
Ross, Ellen, 249 (n. 18)
Rossville, Ga., 188
Russian Revolution, 82, 84

Sacco and Vanzetti, 87
Sanger, Margaret, 250 (n. 28)
Sangster, Joan, 251 (n. 47)
Schneiderman, Rose, 245 (n. 56)
Schofield, Lemuel B., 160–61, 163
Schrecken der Garnison, 145
Schrecker, Ellen, 224
Schubert's Dream of Spring, 145
Scottsboro Boys, 169, 258 (n. 88)
Scranton, Philip, 45
Seaming, 15–16, 59
Segregation, 28, 29, 226, 233 (n. 42)
Sentner, William, 197
Sexuality, 75–76, 78–79
Shaw, Arthur, 173
Sher, Fannia, 130–31
Sherman Anti-Trust Act, 5, 178, 216
Shostakovich, Dmitri, 145
Sidorick, Daniel, 233 (n. 42)
Silk stockings, 111–12
Sit-down strikes, 178, 190, 198–99; at Apex, 212–15
SKF Corporation, 201–2
Smith, William, 156, 184, 191, 220
Social Darwinism, 6, 233 (n. 42)
Socialism, 40, 173, 207–8, 221; resurgence of interest in, 2, 226; Soviet Russia and, 84, 121; union educational program on, 143–44
Socialist Party: election campaigns of, 54, 63–64, 126–27, 141, 172, 173–74, 180; hosiery workers' union and, 8, 39–40, 52, 53, 54, 55, 172, 173–74, 238 (n. 21); left wing of, 6, 39, 52, 172, 183, 238 (n. 21); and Nazi Germany, 141; program of, 173; racial discrimination opposed by, 6–7; street meetings of, 40, 86; and unemployed, 150, 168–69, 171; and women's rights, 114
Solidarity: across gender and age lines, 7, 81, 98, 99–101; black-white, 6, 66; as hosiery union hallmark, 6, 8, 52, 60–61, 62, 66, 96–97, 137, 150–51; Kensington's traditions of, 39, 47, 51, 113, 150–51; Mackley Houses' promotion of, 204; of women, 117, 118, 166
South: 1934 textile strike in, 192–93, 194–95, 196; organizing drives in, 64–67
Southern Summer School for Women, 117
Spencer, Herbert, 233 (n. 42)
Spivak, John L., 143
Sports, 31, 246 (n. 66); hosiery union and, 94–95, 142; women and, 109, 118
Stepan-Norris, Judith, 224
Stephens, Uriah S., 1, 228 (n. 1)
Stevens, Doris, 108
Stokowski, Leopold, 40, 146–47
Stonorov, Oskar, 203, 205, 207
The Street, 146
Street meetings, 86–87
Strikebreakers, 61, 99, 125, 202; in 1921 strike, 48–49, 237 (n. 15); in Aberle strike, 154, 155, 157–58
Strikes: of 1919, 44–45, 50–51; of 1921, 42, 46–51, 57, 69; of 1931, 158, 160–64; 1933 wave of, 178, 179–96; Aberle, 133, 153–58, 256 (n. 58); Apex Hosiery, 212–16, 219, 265 (n. 91); Cambria, 186–88; Durham, 65–67, 184, 193; following Wagner Act, 198; high stakes in, 217; history of Kensington, 38; injunctions against, 46, 63, 99–100, 125, 126, 154, 186; jailing of strikers during, 126, 161, 163, 186; Kenosha, 64, 124–27; in Philadelphia, 38, 185, 186–88, 190–91,

198–99, 201–2, 212–16; police violence against, 46, 48, 99, 100–101, 160–61, 162, 186; postwar wave of (1945–46), 222–23; Reading, 63, 188–89, 211–12; Rodgers Company, 98; sit-down, 178, 190–91, 198–99, 212–15; SKF, 201–2; Southern general textile strike, 192–93, 194–95, 196; in TWOC organizing drive, 199–200; women's participation in, 81, 97–98, 122, 123, 161–62, 186–87, 199–200
Strube, Harry, 213
Sugrue, Thomas, 6
Sunday, Billy, 26
Supreme Court, 5, 179, 212, 216
Sylvis, William, 37

Taft-Hartley Act, 220, 221–22, 223, 224
Taylor, George, 31, 39, 77
Ten Days that Shook the World (Eisenstein), 145
"Terrorism," 162
Textile Workers Industrial Union, 44
Textile Workers Organizing Committee (TWOC), 178, 199–200
Textile Workers Union of America (TWUA), 178; establishment of, 200; and hosiery workers' union, 5, 219, 221, 223
Theaters, 26, 76, 145, 147
Third-party politics, 171–72, 194, 226
Thomas, Norman, 40, 54, 141, 173, 174, 180, 191
Tippett, Tom, 146
Todd, Selina, 80, 226
Topping, 15, 59
Trade Union News, 161
Transport Workers Union, 220
Tribune, 200
"Two-machine system", 46–47, 135, 136

Unemployed, 138–39, 142; movement of, 148–51, 168–69, 171

Unemployed Citizens League (UCL), 6, 8, 144, 150, 151–53, 171
Unemployed Councils, 150
Union democracy, 52, 178, 220
Union Labor Record, 150, 151–52
United Cannery, Agricultural, Packing, and Allied Workers of America, 225
United Electrical and Radio Workers (UE), 5, 178, 222, 256 (n. 48); and CIO, 196, 197, 198, 225; formation of, 195
United Hatters of North America, 182
United States Housing Act (Wagner-Steagall Act), 207
United Textile Workers of America (UTWA), 65, 152, 171, 195–96; and CIO, 177, 199; Local 706 of, 42, 44–45, 47–49, 50; and Southern textile strike, 193–94, 196
Universalism, 35
Upholstery Weavers' Union, 198

Vare, William S., 174
Veblen, Thorstein, 249 (n. 18)
Volstead Act, 3

Wages, 18, 44, 77, 159; "just wage" concept, 31; three-tier system of, 56–57
Wagner Act. *See* National Labor Relations Act
Walker, Columbus P., 188
Wallace, Henry, 220
Wanamaker, John, 26
Webb, Sidney and Beatrice, 16
West, Mae, 76, 110, 116
White, Walter, 93
Wills, Helen, 109
Wilson, Elizabeth, 249 (n. 18)
Wilson, S. Davis, 213
Wishart Theater, 173
Women: and childcare, 119; and correcting past wrongs, 166–67; cultural networks of, 30, 32, 70–71, 75, 77; dress and fashion for, 39, 69, 74–75,

Women (cont.)
110–11, 141–42, 249 (n. 18); dress and hairstyles of, 75, 116; and equal pay issue, 119, 209, 210; and Equal Rights Amendment, 116, 210, 250–51 (n. 32); and family economy, 20; fight for economic independence of, 131–32, 209–10; gender roles and identity of, 7, 32–34, 74, 105, 109; "heroic," 109–10, 120; history of resistance by, 104–5, 108, 248 (n. 3); hosiery union resolutions on, 129–31, 165–66; *Hosiery Worker* on, 120–21, 131–32; and Knights of Labor, 38, 106, 114, 210; and leadership, 55, 130; in Mackley House, 206; married, 18, 75, 79, 103, 105, 210–11; in movies, 76, 110; partnership with men, 81; rights-oriented discourse of, 105, 113–14, 165–67, 210–11; role in union of, 55, 60, 101–2, 117, 129–32, 210; and sexuality, 75–76; special union meetings for, 117–18, 131; and sports, 109, 118; in strike battles, 81, 97–98, 122, 123, 161–62, 186–87, 199–200; union efforts to organize, 64, 113–20, 131; and union executive board, 59, 60, 129, 165–67, 210; work conditions of, 15–16, 113–14, 210; within workforce, 18, 32–33, 36, 74, 79, 103–4, 178. *See also* Labor feminism

Women's Bureau, 187
Women's Equal Pay Act, 210
Women's suffrage, 108–9
Women's Trade Union League (WTUL), 115, 118, 119, 187, 208
Women's Union Label League, 122, 129
Work culture, 31, 79–80, 111, 121–22
Workers' Education Bureau, 90, 115–16
World War I, 43, 69, 85, 240 (n. 2)

Young Men's Christian Association (YMCA), 26, 27, 140–41
Young Men's Hebrew Association (YMHA), 140–41
Young Women's Christian Association (YWCA), 129, 140–41, 187, 212; hosiery union ties to, 115, 116, 117, 141, 208
Youth: and public education, 72–73; recreation programs for, 140–41; and unions, 81, 83, 84–85, 97–98; in U.S. population, 71; "youth militant" term, 7–8, 100, 126
Youth culture, 70–81, 112; and community culture, 80–81; and flapper culture, 110–11; and sexuality, 75–76, 78–79

Zieger, Robert H., 177

www.ingramcontent.com/pod-product-compliance
Lightning Source LLC
Chambersburg PA
CBHW030528230426
43665CB00010B/802